The only OFFICIAL Guide to

CAMPING AND CARAVAN PARKS

Sea View International,
Mevagissey

Where to Stay
in Britain 2004
England • Scotland • Wales

VisitBritain

VisitBritain is a new organisation created on 1 April 2003 to market Britain to the rest of the world and England to the British. Formed by the merger of the British Tourist Authority and the English Tourism Council, its mission is to build the value of tourism by creating world class destination brands and marketing campaigns. It will also build partnerships with – and provide insights to – other organisations which have a stake in British and English tourism.

- This guide contains the widest choice of quality assured accommodation to suit all budgets and tastes.

- It includes an EXCLUSIVE listing of Caravan and Camping Parks in VisitBritain's quality standard.

- This guide also includes information about Hostel Accommodation, Holiday Villages and Boat Accommodation.

Looking for accommodation in a particular area?

- The guide's divided by country and the listings for England are divided into the English Regional Tourist Board areas. Accommodation is listed alphabetically by place name.

- Find on the maps the location of all accommodation featured in the full colour entry pages.

- Look in the town index at the back of the guide. It also includes tourism areas such as the New Forest or Cotswolds.

- A handy reference to counties is also at the back.

The **only** official guide to quality accommodation in England

More information as well as places to stay

Each section is packed with information:

Visitor Attractions

A selection of places to visit highlighting those receiving our quality assurance marque.

Tourist Information Centres

Phone numbers are shown in the blue bands next to place names in accommodation entries.

Guides and maps

As well as contact details, we list tourist board free and saleable tourism publications.

Travel details

Directions for travel by road and rail.

Town descriptions

At the end of each section is a brief description of the main places where accommodation is listed.

This page L-R
Penhalt Farm Holiday Park, Bude
Brixham holiday Park, Brixham

Contents

Key to Symbols:

A key to symbols can be found on the inside back
cover. Keep it open for easy reference.

Touring
Britain

Britain is a country of beautiful landscapes and historic interest where the traveller can enjoy a great variety of scenery within short distances.

Camping or caravanning is a good way to see Britain. You can go as you please without sticking to a set programme, enjoy the country air and have a lot of fun. Wherever you stay, you can use your park as a base for sightseeing and touring the surrounding area.

Le tourisme en Grande-Bretagne (Voir page 6)

Unterwegs in Großbritannien (Lesen Sie Seite 7)

Rondtrekken in Groot-Brittannië (Zie pag 9)

Alla scoperta della Gran Bretagna (Vedi 11)

As the birthplace of camping, Britain has a large number of places to stay of every kind – from small, quiet spots to big lively parks offering a wide range of facilities and entertainment. Many have a restaurant, bar, nightclub, regular barbeques and evening entertainment (eg dinner dance, cabaret).

An increasing number of parks now make ideal centres for an activity holiday. Fishing, sailing and golfing are just three of the more popular activities offered by more and more parks. Many also have indoor swimming pools, tennis courts, games room and provide a wide range of facilities and activities to keep the children amused.

Most parks admit tents, touring and motor caravans and provide a wide range of central facilities for the tourer. Many have caravan holiday homes for hire. These are often very spacious, luxurious and well equipped with two to three good sized bedrooms, a lounge with comfortable furnishings and a separate dining area.

Many have modern conveniences such as colour televisions, fridges, hot showers, en-suite bathrooms and microwaves. In addition to caravan holiday homes, many parks also have chalets and lodges for hire, designed and equipped to the same standard as the caravans. All are truly a home from home, giving you the facilities and freedom you need to enjoy your holiday.

To help you select the type of park to suit you, with the facilities and standards you require, the British Graded Holiday Parks Rating Scheme will be of great assistance. Each park involved in this scheme has been visited by an independent assessor and given a rating based on cleanliness, environment and the quality of facilities and services provided.

Many parks are open all year and can be an excellent way to have a short break in the spring, autumn and even in the winter months. Prices will be cheaper than during the main season and many facilities will still be available (although it might be wise to check).

If you intend to stay in a popular holiday area during the main season (June to September), you are advised to book in advance. It is essential either to send written confirmation of any reservations made or to arrive very early at your chosen park.

Le tourisme en
Grande-Bretagne

La Grande-Bretagne est un pays qui abonde en panoramas superbes et en sites d'intérêt historique, où les touristes n'ont pas besoin de parcourir des kilomètres pour pouvoir admirer des paysages très variés. Le camping et le caravaning sont d'excellents moyens d'explorer la Grande-Bretagne. On peut aller où on le désire sans adhérer à un plan fixe, profiter du bon air de la campagne et se divertir. Quelle que soit la région où se trouve le terrain dans lequel on séjourne, on peut s'en servir comme point de chute pour faire du tourisme et rayonner dans la région.

C'est en Grande-Bretagne qu'est né le camping, on y trouve donc un grand nombre de terrains de toutes sortes, allant de petits terrains tranquilles à de grands parcs pleins d'animation proposant une vaste gamme d'équipements et de distractions. Un grand nombre de terrains possèdent des restaurants, bars, night-clubs, et organisent régulièrement des barbecues et des distractions nocturnes (par ex. dîners dansants, spectacles de cabaret).

Les terrains de camping sont des endroits merveilleux pour passer des vacances à thème, et un nombre de plus en plus important de terrains proposent cette formule. La pêche, la navigation de plaisance et le golf, entre autres, font partie des activités les plus populaires qu'on peut pratiquer dans des terrains de plus en plus nombreux. Un grand nombre de terrains mettent également à la disposition des vacanciers des piscines couvertes chauffées, des courts de tennis, des salles de jeux, et proposent une large gamme d'installations et d'activités destinées aux enfants.

La plupart de terrains acceptent les tentes, les caravanes de tourisme et les camping-cars, et mettent un vaste éventail d'équipements à la disposition des vacanciers. Un grand nombre de terrains louent des caravanes fixes, qui sont souvent très spacieuses, luxueuses et bien aménagées, comportant deux ou trois belles chambres à coucher, un salon confortable et un coin salle à manger séparé.

Un grand nombre de ces logements de vacances ont tout le confort moderne: télévision couleur, réfrigérateur, douche avec eau chaude, salle de bains et four à micro-ondes. En plus des caravanes de vacances, de nombreux terrains louent également des chalets et des pavillons, conçus et équipés avec le même soin et dotés du même confort. Vous vous sentirez comme chez vous dans tous ces terrains et vous y trouverez les aménagements et la liberté dont vous avez besoin pour profiter au mieux de vos vacances.

Pour sélectionner le meilleur terrain/centre offrant les services et normes dont vous avez besoin, le British Graded Holiday Parks Rating Scheme (système d'évaluation des centres de vacances/terrains de camping britanniques) vous sera très utile. Des inspecteurs indépendants ont visité chaque terrain participant à ce projet et les ont classés selon la propreté, l'environnement et la qualité de leurs services.

De nombreux terrains sont ouverts toute l'année, et permettent ainsi de prendre quelques jours de vacances agréables au printemps, en automne et même en hiver. Les tarifs sont moins élevés que pendant la haute saison, et de nombreux équipements sont encore à la disposition des vacanciers (il est toutefois prudent de vérifier).

Si vous avez l'intention de séjourner, en haute saison (de juin à septembre), dans une région de villégiature très fréquentée, nous vous conseillons de réserver à l'avance. Il est indispensable soit de confirmer toute réservation par écrit, soit d'arriver très tôt au terrain de votre choix.

Unterwegs in
Großbritannien

Großbritannien ist reich an schönen Landschaften und historischen Stätten und die Natur zeigt sich dem Besucher innerhalb weniger Kilometer von ihrer abwechslungsreichsten Seite. Die Übernachtung auf dem Campingplatz oder im Wohnwagen eignet sich gut, um Großbritannien kennen zu lernen. Sie können nach Lust und Laune ins Blaue fahren, die würzige Landluft genießen und viel Interessantes erleben. Wo Sie sich auch aufhalten mögen, Ihr Platz ist stets ein idealer Ausgangsort für Besichtigungstouren und Ausflüge in die Umgebung.

Großbritannien ist der Geburtsort des Zeltens und bietet eine große Anzahl an Plätzen jeder Art - von kleinen, ruhigen bis zu großen, lebhaften Plätzen mit einer großen Auswahl an Einrichtungen und einem reichen Unterhaltungsprogramm. Zahlreiche Plätze verfügen über ein Restaurant, eine Bar, einen Nachtklub und veranstalten regelmäßige Grillpartys und Abendunterhaltung (z.B. Abendessen mit Tanz, Kabarett).

Immer mehr Plätze sind ideale Ferienorte für Aktivferien. Angeln, Segeln und Golf, nur drei der beliebtesten Aktivitäten, werden von einer wachsenden Zahl von Plätzen angeboten. Viele verfügen auch über ein Hallenbad, Tennisplätze, Spielzimmer und bieten eine große Auswahl an Einrichtungen und Aktivitäten für Kinder.

Die meisten Plätze sind für Zelte, Wohnwagen und Wohnmobile eingerichtet und bieten dem Besucher eine Reihe von Einrichtungen. Zahlreiche Plätze vermieten Wohnwagen. Diese sind oft äußerst geräumig, luxuriös und gut ausgestattet und verfügen über zwei oder drei Schlafzimmer, ein Wohnzimmer mit komfortablen Möbeln und einen getrennten Essbereich. Viele bieten auch Farbfernseher, Kühlschrank, Dusche mit warmem Wasser, Bad und Mikrowellenherd. Zusätzlich zu den Wohnwagen gibt es auf zahlreichen Plätzen auch Chalets und Hütten mit demselben Komfort. Alle sind in der Tat ein zweites Zuhause und bieten die Einrichtungen und die Unabhängigkeit, die für erfolgreiche Ferien unerlässlich sind.

Um Ihnen bei der Auswahl des Parktyps zu helfen, dessen Standards und Leistungsumfang Ihren Anforderungen und Wünschen am besten entspricht, wird Ihnen das British Graded Holiday Parks Rating Scheme (Beurteilungssystem für britische Ferienparks) von großem Nutzen sein. Alle an diesem System beteiligten Parks sind von unabhängigen Gutachtern besucht und im Hinblick auf Sauberkeit, Umwelt und Qualität von Angebot und Service beurteilt worden.

Zahlreiche Plätze sind ganzjährig geöffnet und ideal für Kurzurlaube im Frühling, Herbst oder auch Winter. Die Preise sind während der Nebensaison billiger als während der Hochsaison und zahlreiche Einrichtungen sind immer in Betrieb (es ist jedoch ratsam, sich zuerst zu erkundigen).

Falls Sie während der Hochsaison (Juni bis September) eine beliebte Feriendestination wählen, ist es ratsam, im Voraus zu buchen. Sie müssen die Buchung entweder schriftlich bestätigen oder sehr früh auf dem Platz Ihrer Wahl eintreffen.

WIN a holiday
with the Caravan Club!

The Caravan Club is pleased to offer you the opportunity to win a wonderful seven-day family holiday for up to 2 adults and 2 children on one of its 5* graded sites.

There will be two lucky winners of this competition, first prize will be a 7 night stay and second prize will be a 3 night stay at Bognor Regis.

The Caravan Club spends around £10 million a year on redeveloping its site network and in 2003 Bognor Regis underwent extensive refurbishment. This club site now offers a little more than the already high standards found on over 200 Caravan Club Sites in the UK.

The town of Bognor Regis is a traditional seaside resort only half a mile away from the site with a shingle and sand beach and plenty of entertainment to ensure that there is something to do for everyone in the family.

For a chance to win, just answer the following question:

Q: What type of beach can you find at Bognor Regis ?

Two winners will be selected at random from correct entries received by the closing date.

Please send the answers on a postcard, including your full name and address to:
VisitBritain Competition, Sites Marketing,
The Caravan Club
East Grinstead House, East Grinstead
West Sussex, RH19 1UA

Closing date for the competition will be 31 August 2004

COMPETITION RULES
All entrants should be tourer caravanners, motorcaravanners or trailer tenters.Only ONE entry per household. No correspondence or communications will be entered into. Prizes are valid 01/10/04 to 30/09/05, subject to availability at time of booking. Prizes are not transferable and no cash or alternative prizes are available. Entry into the competition implies acceptance of the rules. Employees of the Caravan Club and its associated companies are ineligible to enter. The winners will be notified in writing after 31 August 2004.

Rondtrekken in
Groot-Brittannie

In Groot-Brittannië vindt u prachtige landschappen en een interessante geschiedenis. De reiziger treft op korte afstand van elkaar allerlei verschillende gebieden aan, en kamperen met de tent of de caravan is de ideale manier om echt van Groot-Brittannië te genieten. Ga en sta waar u wilt, zonder aan een programma vast te zitten, geniet van de frisse lucht en maak plezier! Waar u ook bent, u kunt uw kampeerplaats uw basis maken en in het omliggende gebied rondtrekken.

Groot-Brittannië is het geboorteland van het kamperen, en wij hebben dan ook een groot aantal terreinen in allerlei soorten en maten: vanaf kleine rustige terreintjes tot en met grote gezellige parken met allerlei faciliteiten en amusement. Vele hebben een restaurant, bar, nachtclub, en organiseren regelmatig barbecues en amusement 's avonds (zoals diner dansant, cabaret).

Steeds meer parken vormen tegenwoordig een ideaal centrum voor een actieve vakantie. Vissen, zeilen en golfen zijn slechts drie mogelijkheden die de steeds meer terreinen organiseren. Vaak vindt u ook overdekte zwembaden, tennisbanen, spellenkamers en allerlei faciliteiten en activiteiten om de kinderen bezig te houden.

Op de meeste terreinen worden tenten, trekcaravans en kampeerauto's toegelaten en vindt u een groot aantal centrale faciliteiten voor de trekker. Ook zijn er vaak stacaravans te huur: deze zijn vaak zeer ruim, luxueus en goed uitgerust, met twee of drie ruime slaapkamers, een zitkamer met gerieflijk meubilair en een aparte eetkamer. Vaak vindt u er ook moderne gemakken zoals kleuren t.v., ijskast, warme douches, en-suite badkamers en magnetronovens.

Vele parken bieden niet alleen stacaravans maar ook huisjes te huur, die al net zo goed zijn ingericht en uitgerust. Geniet van de faciliteiten en de vrijheid om echt vakantie te vieren.

Om u te helpen met het selecteren van een bepaald type park metvoorzieningen en op het niveau dat u zoekt, zal het British Graded Holiday Parks Rating Scheme u zeker van pas komen. Elk park dat aan dit systeem meedoet is bezocht door een onafhankelijke controleur en heeft een classificatie gekregen op basis van hygiëne, omgeving en de kwaliteit van de voorzieningen en diensten die er aanwezig zijn.

Vele parken zijn het hele jaar open en bieden de ideale manier om er even tussenuit te gaan in de lente, herfst of zelfs in winter. De prijzen zijn dan lager dan in het hoogseizoen, terwijl toch vele faciliteiten beschikbaar zijn (het is wel raadzaam dit van te voren na te gaan).

Als u in een populair vakantiegebied denkt te verblijven in het hoogseizoen (juni tot september), raden wij u aan van te voren te reserveren. Bevestig de reservering schriftelijk of kom zeer vroeg aan op het terrein.

South Coast
and New Forest

RALLIES WELCOME AT ALL SITES

CHOICE OF FOREST OR COASTAL LOCATIONS

With three high quality destinations to choose from, Shorefield Holidays offers you the best of both worlds in touring locations.

All three of our touring parks are set in peaceful, unspoilt parkland in the beautiful New Forest or South Coast area. There are comprehensive facilities including entertainment and Free Leisure Club membership. For full details ask for our brochure or browse on-line.

For further details telephone:

01590 648331

SHOREFIELD
HOLIDAYS LIMITED

Lytton Lawn Touring Park
Lymore Lane, Milford on Sea, Hants SO41 0TX

Oakdene Forest Park
St. Leonards, Ringwood, Hants BH24 2RZ

Forest Edge Touring Park
St. Leonards, Ringwood, Hants BH24 2SD

e-mail: holidays@shorefield.co.uk   www.shorefield.co.uk   Ref. WTST

10

Alla scoperta della
Gran Bretagna

La Gran Bretagna è uno stupendo paese di grande interesse storico che offre un'ampia varietà di paesaggi. Il campeggio in tenda o roulotte è uno dei modi più efficaci di visitare la Gran Bretagna, dato che consente di viaggiare quando e dove si vuole, senza dover rispettare un itinerario prestabilito, divertendosi e respirando l'aria fresca della campagna. Ovunque si decida di andare, il campeggio può servire da base dalla quale il turista può visitare la zona circostante.

Il campeggio è un'invenzione britannica, ne consegue che in Gran Bretagna vi sono numerosissimi campeggi di tutti i tipi: da quelli piccoli e tranquilli a quelli grandi e animatissimi che offrono un'ampia gamma di strutture e intrattenimenti. Molti campeggi offrono anche ristoranti, bar, locali notturni, banchetti all'aperto con barbecue e spettacoli serali (p.es. serate di ballo, cabaret).

Molti campeggi sono ideali per trascorrere periodi di vacanza di tipo più dinamico, dato che un numero sempre maggiore di essi offre la possibilità, ad esempio, di pescare, praticare la vela o giocare al golf.

Molti dispongono di piscine, campi da tennis e palestre al coperto e di numerose strutture e attività per il divertimento dei bambini.

La maggior parte dei campeggi accetta tende, campers e roulottes e offre un'ampia gamma di strutture centralizzate per il campeggiatore. Molti offrono anche roulottes a noleggio Queste roulottes sono spesso spaziosissime, lussuose e ben attrezzate con due o tre camere doppie, un salotto comodamente ammobiliato e una sala da pranzo separata. Molte offrono anche altre moderne comodità come televisioni a colori, frigoriferi, docce calde, camere con bagno e forni a microonde. Oltre alle roulottes a noleggio, molti campeggi offrono anche chalet e casette a noleggio progettate e attrezzate con gli stessi criteri. Sono tutte abitazioni dove ci si sente come a casa propria, e che offrono libertà e tutte le attrezzature necessarie a godersi la propria vacanza.

Per aiutare a scegliere il tipo di parco più adatto, che offra i requisiti e gli standard richiesti, sarà molto utile il British Graded Holiday Parks Rating Scheme (progetto di assegnazione di punteggio ai parchi vacanze del Regno Unito). Ogni parco iscritto viene ispezionato da ispettori indipendenti, con assegnazione di punteggio sulla base dei criteri di pulizia, qualità dell'ambiente e delle risorse e dei servizi offerti.

Molti dei campeggi sono aperti tutto l'anno e sono dunque ideali per trascorrere una breve vacanza anche in primavera, in autunno o in inverno, stagioni in cui i prezzi sono più bassi che durante i mesi di alta stagione, anche se restano disponibili molte delle strutture (consigliamo comunque di controllare prima dell'arrivo).

Si consiglia a chi intenda trascorrere una vacanza in una delle località turistiche più frequentate durante i mesi di alta stagione (da giugno a settembre) di prenotare in anticipo. È essenziale confermare la prenotazione per iscritto o arrivare molto presto al campeggio prescelto.

With facilities this good...

You Should Call for our FREE SITES GUIDE

Visit one of the Camping and Caravanning Club's sites and chances are, you'll never want to stay on a non-Club site again. Our 93 UK Club sites are well equipped, with excellent facilities and a legendary reputation for cleanliness.

With excellent gradings from Tourist Boards and reduced site charges for members, you can be sure of quality as well as great value-for-money. Whether your ideal holiday includes sight seeing, walking, cycling, fishing, boating or simply relaxing, we have sites that are the perfect place for you to stay.

Call for your FREE Sites Guide today, then come along and see our sites for yourself - you will not be disappointed. Non-members are welcome on most of our sites and all of our guests receive free vouchers with fabulous discounts off local attractions.

FOR YOUR

FREE GUIDE*
TO OVER 90 GREAT SITES
OF BRITAIN CALL:
024 7685 6797
PLEASE QUOTE REF 9884

REDUCED SITE CHARGES IF YOU ARE 55 OR OVER | **...and Special Deals** *for Families and Backpackers*

FOR FURTHER INFORMATION VISIT OUR WEBSITE:
www.campingandcaravanningclub.co.uk

GREAT SITES AND GREAT
SERVICES FOR OVER 100 YEARS

*We will use details you provide for servicing your enquiry and informing you of member services. We will disclose your information to our service providers only for these purposes and will not keep it beyond a reasonable period of time.

The Camping and Caravanning Club
The friendly Club

£5 OFF

YOUR SITE FEE ON PRESENTATION OF THIS VOUCHER

Simply present this Voucher when you arrive on any Camping and Caravanning Club Site to receive £5 off your site fees.
Ref: 9884

The Camping and Caravanning Club
The friendly Club

MAP 1

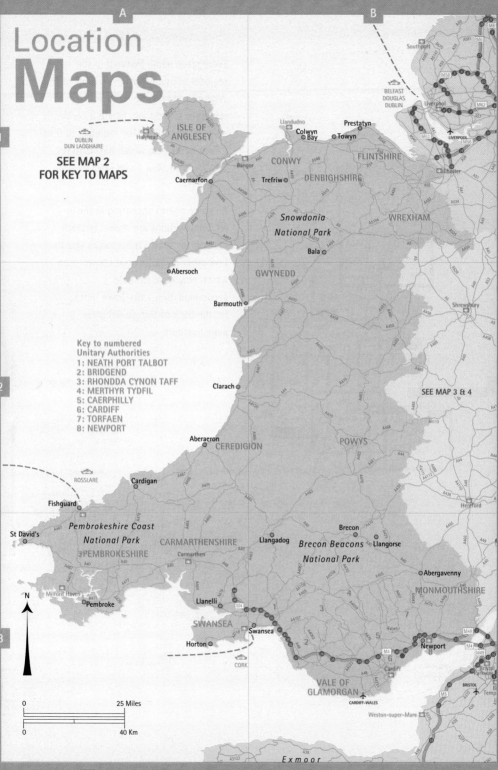

Location
Maps

**SEE MAP 2
FOR KEY TO MAPS**

Key to numbered
Unitary Authorities
1: NEATH PORT TALBOT
2: BRIDGEND
3: RHONDDA CYNON TAFF
4: MERTHYR TYDFIL
5: CAERPHILLY
6: CARDIFF
7: TORFAEN
8: NEWPORT

SEE MAP 3 & 4

ISLE OF ANGLESEY
CONWY
FLINTSHIRE
DENBIGHSHIRE
WREXHAM
Snowdonia National Park
GWYNEDD
POWYS
CEREDIGION
Pembrokeshire Coast National Park
PEMBROKESHIRE
CARMARTHENSHIRE
MONMOUTHSHIRE
Brecon Beacons National Park
SWANSEA
VALE OF GLAMORGAN

DUBLIN
DUN LAOGHAIRE
Holyhead
Caernarfon
Llandudno
Colwyn Bay
Prestatyn
Towyn
Bangor
Trefriw
Bala
Abersoch
Barmouth
Clarach
Aberaeron
ROSSLARE
Cardigan
Fishguard
St David's
Milford Haven
Pembroke
Llanelli
Carmarthen
Horton
Swansea
Llangadog
Brecon
Llangorse
Abergavenny
Cardiff
Newport
CORK
CARDIFF–WALES
Weston-super-Mare
Exmoor

BELFAST
DOUGLAS
DUBLIN
Southport
Liverpool
LIVERPOOL
Chester
Shrewsbury
Hereford
BRISTOL
Bristol Parkway
Temp

N

0   25 Miles
0   40 Km

Key to regions: ☐ Wales   *All place names in black offer parks in this guide.*

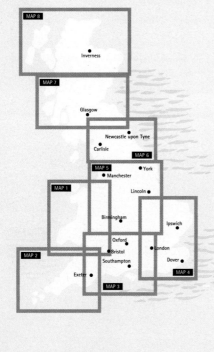

MAP 2

Every place name featured in the regional accommodation sections of this Where to Stay guide has a map reference to help you locate it on the maps which follow. For example, to find Colchester, Essex, which has 'Map ref 3B2', turn to Map 3 and refer to grid square B2.

All place names appearing in the regional sections are shown in black type on the maps. This enables you to find other places in your chosen area which may have suitable accommodation - the Town Index (at the back of this guide) gives page numbers.

ISLES OF SCILLY

Key to regions: ▮ South West

MAP 2

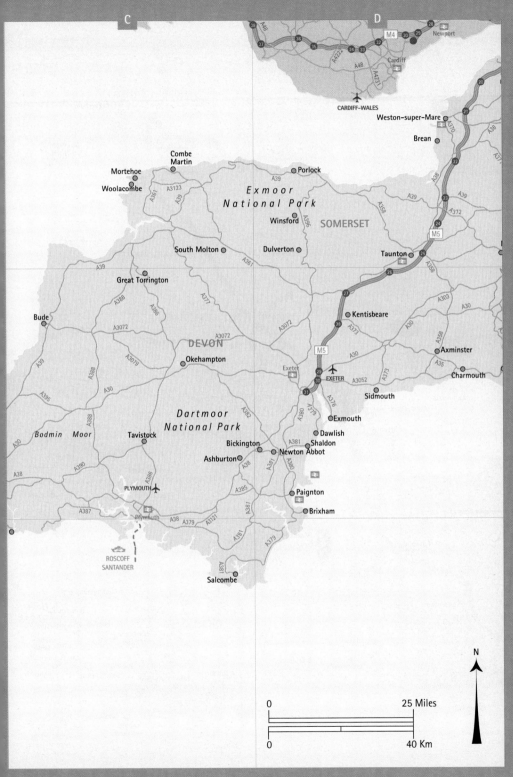

C D

Newport
M4
Cardiff
CARDIFF–WALES
Weston-super-Mare
Brean

Combe Martin
Porlock
Mortehoe
Woolacombe

Exmoor National Park

Winsford
SOMERSET

South Molton
Dulverton
Taunton
M5

Great Torrington
Kentisbeare

Bude
DEVON
Axminster
M5
Okehampton
Charmouth
Exeter
EXETER
Sidmouth
Dartmoor National Park
Exmouth
Bodmin Moor
Tavistock
Dawlish
Bickington
Shaldon
Ashburton
Newton Abbot
PLYMOUTH
Paignton
Plymouth
Brixham

ROSCOFF SANTANDER

Salcombe

N

0   25 Miles
0   40 Km

All place names in black offer parks in this guide.

MAP 3

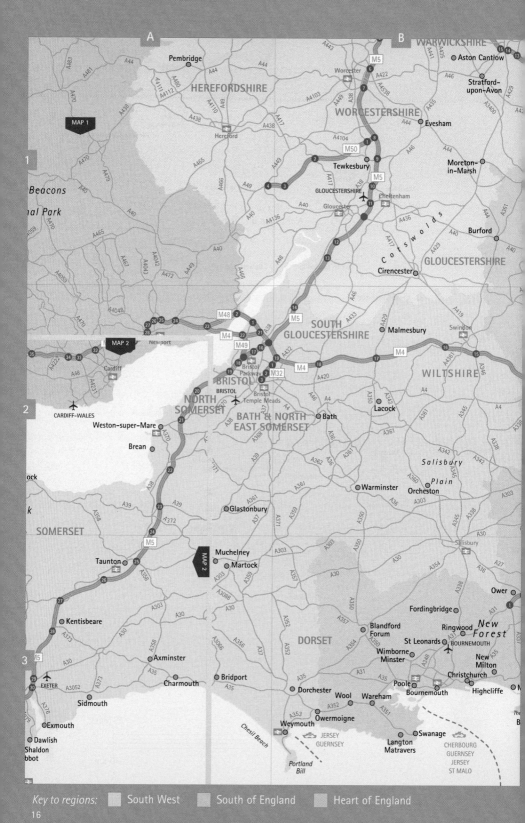

MAP 3

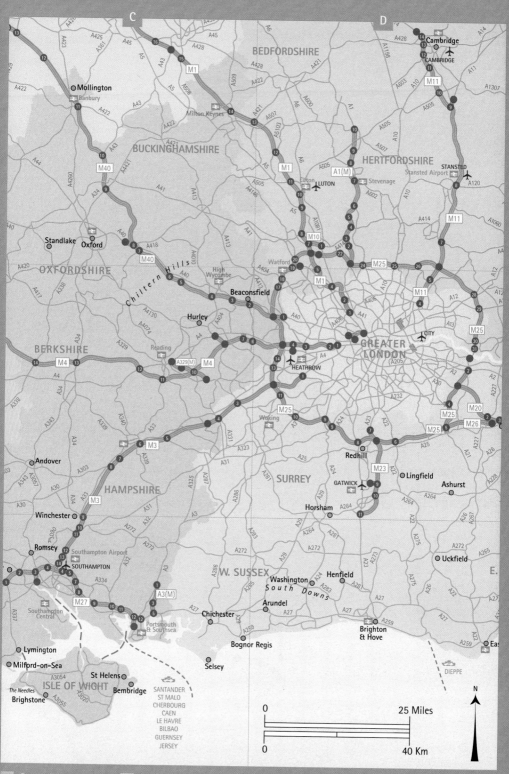

South East England East of England

All place names in black offer parks in this guide.

MAP 4

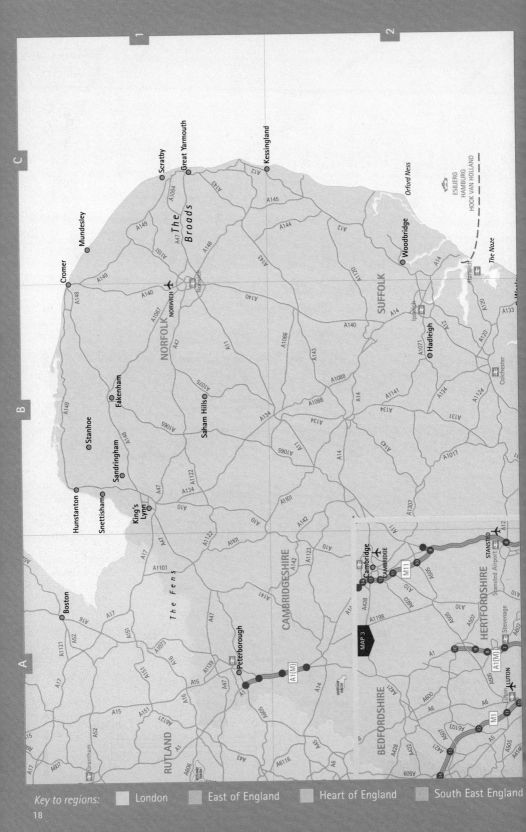

Key to regions: London   East of England   Heart of England   South East England

MAP 4

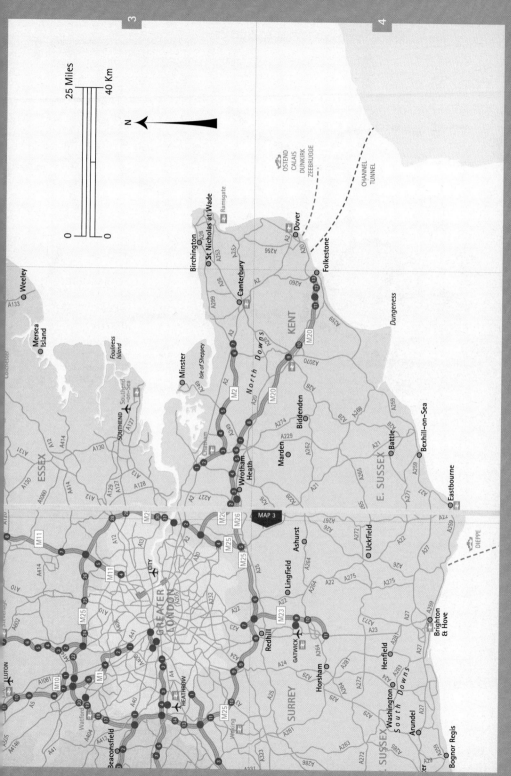

All place names in black offer parks in this guide.

MAP 5

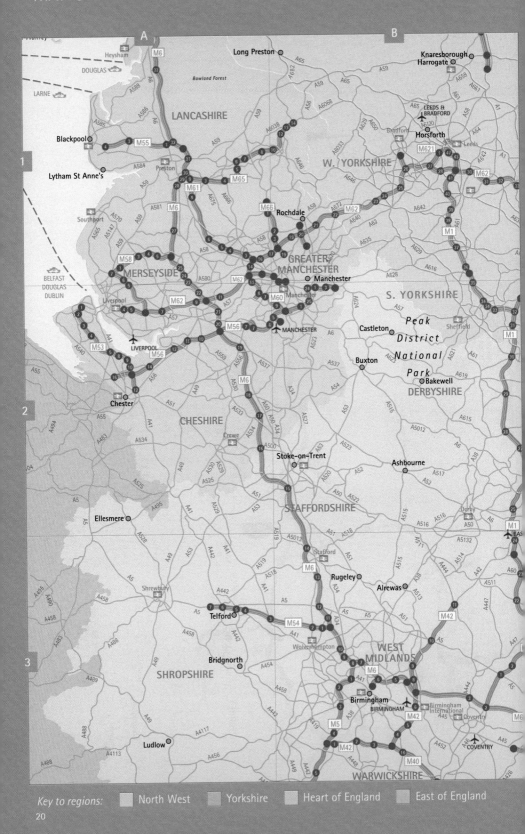

Key to regions: North West   Yorkshire   Heart of England   East of England

MAP 5

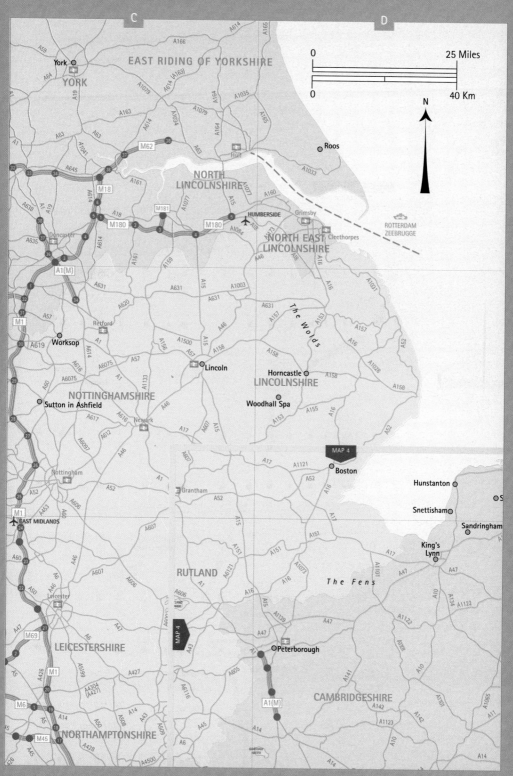

All place names in black offer parks in this guide.

MAP 6

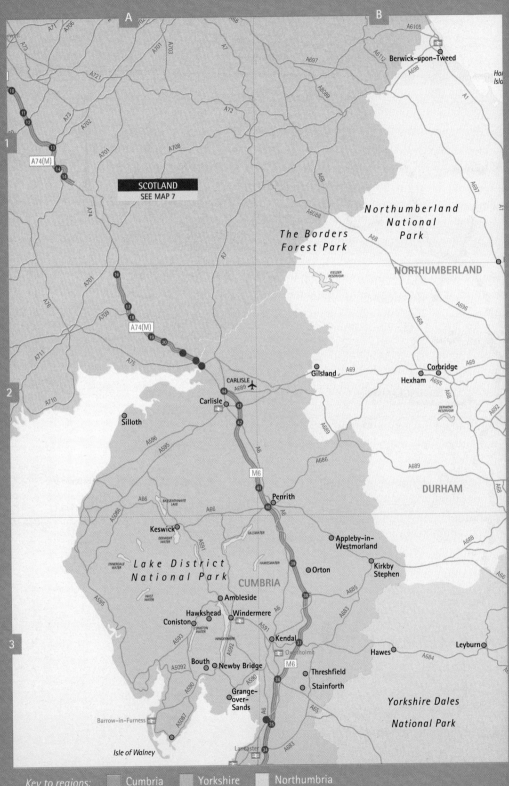

MAP 6

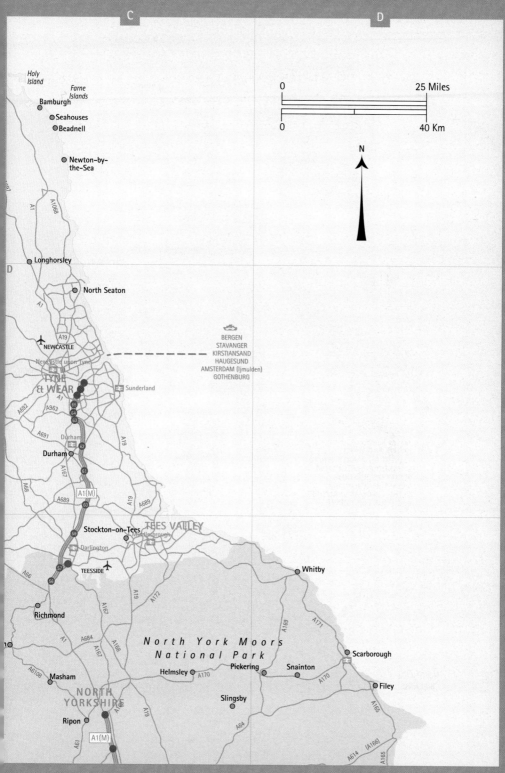

C   D

Holy Island

Farne Islands

Bamburgh
Seahouses
Beadnell

Newton-by-the-Sea

0   25 Miles

0   40 Km

N

A1068
A1

D

Longhorsley

North Seaton

A1

A19
NEWCASTLE
Newcastle upon Tyne
TYNE & WEAR
A1
Sunderland

BERGEN
STAVANGER
KIRSTIANSAND
HAUGESUND
AMSTERDAM (Ijmulden)
GOTHENBURG

A692
A963
65
64
63
A691
Durham
A19
Durham
62
A167
61
A68
A689
A1(M)
60
A19
A689

59
Stockton-on-Tees
TEES VALLEY
Middlesbrough
Darlington
57
A66
56
TEESSIDE

Whitby

Richmond

A19
A172

A167

A169
A171

A1
A684
A167
A168

North York Moors
National Park

Scarborough

A6108
Masham

Helmsley
A170
Pickering
Snainton
A170

Filey

NORTH
YORKSHIRE

Slingsby

A165

Ripon
A1(M)
A61
A64
A614 (A166)
A165

All place names in black offer parks in this guide.

MAP 7

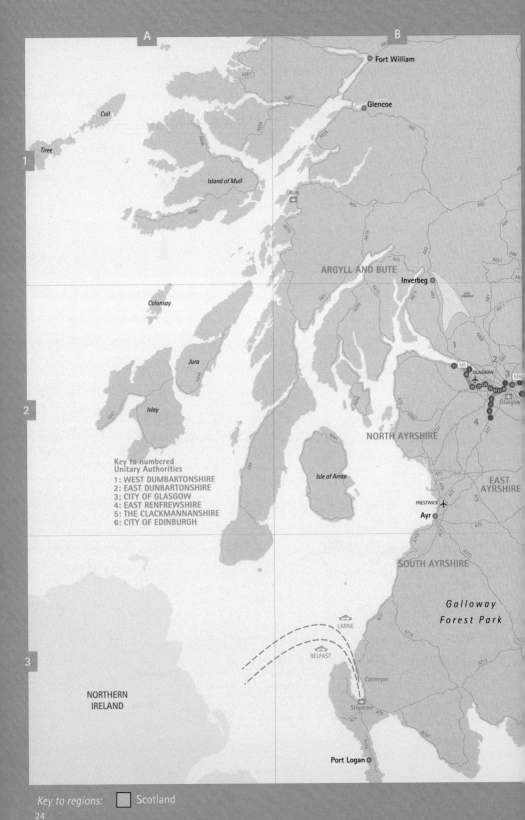

A   B

● Fort William

● Glencoe

Coll

Tiree

1

Island of Mull

Oban

ARGYLL AND BUTE

Inverbeg ○

Colonsay

1

GLASGOW
M8
2
3
Glasgow
4

Jura

Islay

2

NORTH AYRSHIRE

EAST
AYRSHIRE

Key to numbered
Unitary Authorities
1: WEST DUMBARTONSHIRE
2: EAST DUNBARTONSHIRE
3: CITY OF GLASGOW
4: EAST RENFREWSHIRE
5: THE CLACKMANNANSHIRE
6: CITY OF EDINBURGH

Isle of Arran

PRESTWICK ✈

Ayr ○

SOUTH AYRSHIRE

Galloway
Forest Park

⛴ LARNE

⛴ BELFAST

Cairnryan

3

NORTHERN
IRELAND

Stranraer

Port Logan ○

Key to regions: ▢ Scotland

24

MAP 7

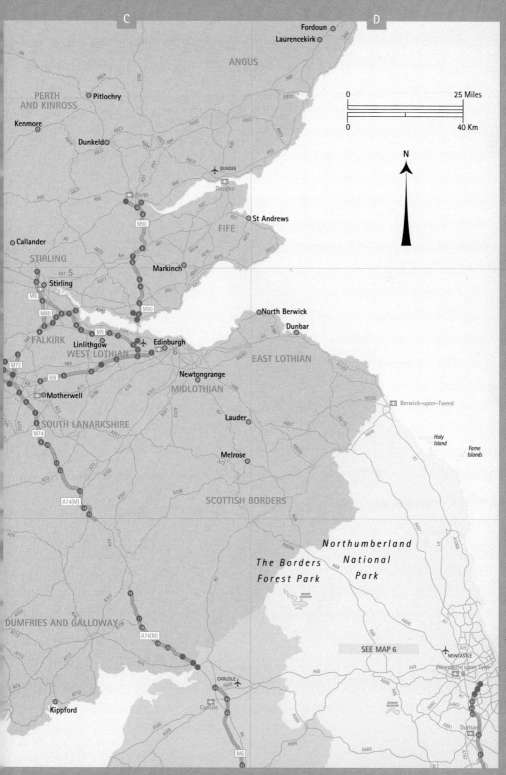

All place names in black offer parks in this guide.

MAP 8

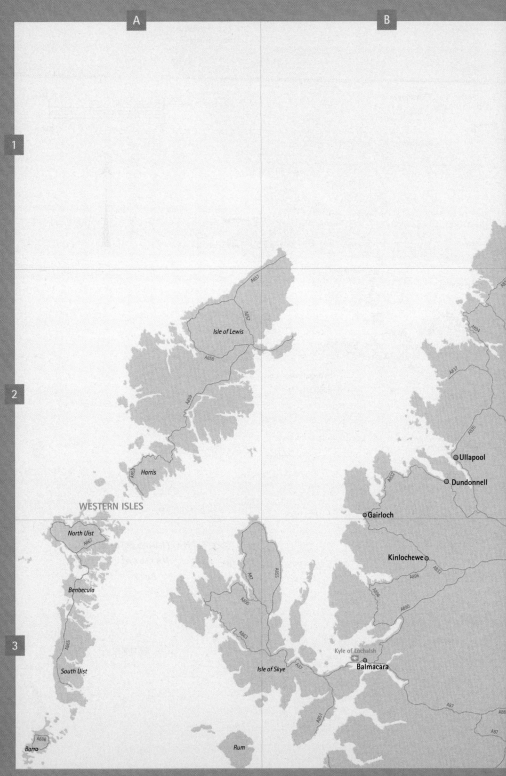

A

B

1

2

3

Isle of Lewis

A857

A857

A858

A859

A858

Harris

A857

WESTERN ISLES

North Uist

A867

Benbecula

South Uist

A865

Barra

A888

A856

A857

A855

A87

A850

A863

Isle of Skye

A87

A851

Rum

A835

A832

A837

● **Ullapool**

● **Dundonnell**

● **Gairloch**

Kinlochewe ●

A832

A896

A896

A890

A890

Kyle of Lochalsh

● **Balmacara**

A87

A87

A887

A87

MAP 8

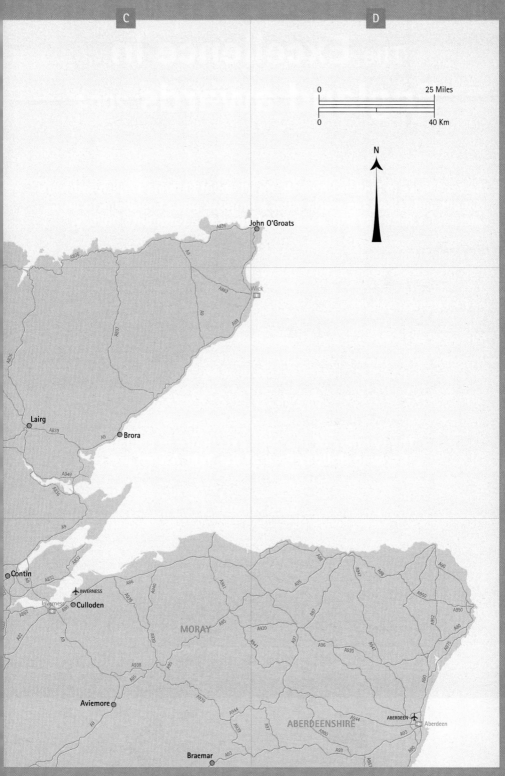

0   25 Miles

0   40 Km

N

John O'Groats

Wick

Lairg

Brora

Contin

INVERNESS

Inverness

Culloden

MORAY

Aviemore

ABERDEENSHIRE

ABERDEEN

Aberdeen

Braemar

All place names in black offer parks in this guide.

The **Excellence in England awards** 2004

The Excellence in England Awards are all about blowing English tourism's trumpet and telling the world what a fantastic place England is to visit, whether it's for a day trip, a weekend break or a fortnight's holiday.

The Awards, now in their 15th year, are run by VisitBritain in association with England's regional tourist boards. This year there are 12 categories including B&B of the Year, Hotel of the Year and Visitor Attraction of the Year and an award for the best tourism website.

Winners of the 2004 awards will receive their trophies at an event to be held on Thursday 22nd April 2004 followed by a media event to be held on St George's Day (23 April) in London. The day will celebrate excellence in tourism in England.

The winners of the 2003 Excellence in England Caravan Holiday Park of the Year Award are:

Gold winner
Oakdown Touring and Holiday Home Park, Weston, Sidmouth, Devon

Silver winners:
Merley Court Touring Park, Merley, Wimborne, Dorset
Oxon Hall Touring Park, Shrewsbury, Shropshire

For more information about the Excellence in England Awards visit
www.visitengland.com

EXCELLENCE
IN ENGLAND
Awards for Tourism

Marketing **English** Tourism

VISIT BRITAIN

How to use this guide

Camping and Caravan Parks listed in this guide have accommodation for touring caravans or tents or both and most welcome motor caravans. Many parks also have caravan holiday homes to let.

THE QUALITY ASSURANCE STANDARD

When you're looking for a place to stay, you need a rating system you can trust. The British Graded Holiday Parks Scheme, relaunched in 2000, gives you a clear guide of what you can expect, in an easy-to-understand form. The scheme has quality at its heart and reflects consumer expectation.

VisitBritain uses Stars to show the quality rating of parks participating in the scheme. Parks are visited annually by trained, impartial assessors who award a rating from One to Five Stars. These are based on cleanliness, environment and the quality of facilities and services provided.

Parks are also given a 'designator' so you can identify the type of site at-a-glance - a Holiday Park, a Touring Park or a Camping Park, for example. (If no rating or designator is shown, the park was awaiting assessment at the time of going to press.)

The British Graded Holiday Parks Scheme was devised jointly by the national tourist boards for England, Northern Ireland, Scotland and Wales in association with the British Holiday & Home Parks Association (see page 43) and the National Caravan Council (see page 47).

FACILITIES

Facilities are indicated by means of the at-a-glance symbols explained on the fold-out back cover flap.

PRICES

Prices given for touring pitches are based on the minimum and maximum charges for one night for two persons, car and either caravan or tent. It is more usual in Britain to charge simply for the use of the pitch, but a number of parks charge separately for car, caravan or tent, and for each person. Some parks may charge extra for caravan awnings. Minimum and maximum prices for caravan holiday homes are given per week. Prices quoted are those supplied to us by the park operators concerned, and are intended to give an indication of the prices which will be charged during the currency of this publication. Prices are shown in pounds (£) and pence (p). VAT (Value Added Tax) at 17.50% is included in the prices shown. In order to avoid misunderstandings, it is particularly advisable to check prices with the park concerned when making reservations.

MAKING A BOOKING

When enquiring about accommodation, as well as checking prices and other details, you will need to state your requirements clearly and precisely - for example:

- arrival and departure dates with acceptable alternatives if appropriate.
- the accommodation you need.
- tell the management about any particular requirements.

Misunderstandings can occur very easily over the telephone so we recommend that all bookings be confirmed in writing if time permits. Remember to include your name and address and please enclose a stamped addressed envelope or an international reply coupon (if writing from outside Britain) for each reply.

Deposits and Advance Payments

In the case of caravan, camping and chalet parks and holiday centres the full charge often has to be paid in advance. This may be in two instalments - a deposit at the time of booking and the balance by, say, two weeks before the start of the booked period.

Cancellations

When you accept offered accommodation, in writing or on the telephone, you are entering into a legally binding contract with the proprietor of the establishment. This means that if you cancel a reservation, fail to take up the accommodation or leave prematurely (regardless of the reasons) the proprietor may be entitled to compensation if it cannot be relet for all or a good part of the booked period. If a deposit has been paid it is likely to be forfeited and an additional payment may be demanded.

It is therefore in your interest to advise the management immediately if you have to change your travel plans, cancel a booking or leave prematurely.

Electric hook-up points

Most parks now have electric hook-up points for caravans and tents. Voltage is generally 240v AC, 50 cycles, although variations between 200v and 250v may still be found. An adaptor for use with hook-ups may be necessary. Parks will usually charge extra for this facility, and it is advisable to check rates when making a booking.

Finding your park

Parks in this guide are listed in England by region followed by Scotland and Wales. They are listed alphabetically under the name of the town in or near which they are situated.

The Town Index on page 249 and colour location maps at the front of the guide show all cities, towns and villages with park listings in this guide.

Use these as a quick and easy way to find suitable accommodation. If you know which park you wish to stay at, check under the Index to Parks on page 246.

If the place you wish to stay is included in the Town Index, turn to the page number given to find the parks available there. The town names appear in black on the maps at the front of the guide as indicated by the map reference in the entry. Also check on the colour maps to find other places nearby which also have parks listed in this guide.

If the place you want is not in the town index - or you only have a general idea of the area in which you wish to stay - use the colour location maps.

The maps show all place names under which a park is listed in this guide. For a precise location read the directions in each entry. If you have any difficulties finding a particular park, we suggest that you ask for final directions within the neighbourhood.

 The International Direction Signs shown here are in use in Britain and are designed to help visitors find their park. They have not yet been erected for all parks and do not display the name of any particular one. They do show, however, whether the park is for tents or caravans or both.

The International Camping Carnet is rarely recognised in Britain except at parks organised by the major clubs.

London sites
London is a great attraction to many visitors, so the camping and caravan parks in the Greater London area tend to become full very quickly, and early booking is required. Parks are also available at most ports of entry to the country and many of these are listed in this guide and marked on the maps at the front.

Park finding services
Tourist Information Centres throughout Britain (see end pages) are able to give campers and caravanners information about parks in their areas.

Some Tourist Information Centres have camping and caravanning advisory services which provide details of park availability and often assist with park booking.

AVOIDING PEAK SEASON
In the summer months of June to September, parks in popular areas such as North Wales, Cumbria, the West Country or the New Forest in Hampshire may become full. Campers should aim to arrive at parks early in the day or, where possible, should book in advance. Some parks have overnight holding areas for visitors who arrive late. This helps to prevent disturbing other campers and caravanners late at night and means that fewer visitors are turned away. Caravans or tents are directed to a pitch the following morning.

OTHER CARAVAN AND CAMPING PLACES
If you enjoy making your own route through Britain's countryside, it may interest you to know that the Forestry Commission operates forest camp parks in Britain's seven Forest Parks as well as in the New Forest. Some offer reduced charges for youth organisations on organised camping trips, and all enquiries about them should be made, well in advance of your intended stay, to the Forestry Commission.

Hostel Accommodation
Although most accommodation in this guide is suitable for people looking for relatively low-cost places to stay, some make a special point of providing safe, budget-priced accommodation for young people, for families or for larger groups. Hostel accommodation includes independently owned hostels, Youth Hostels, bunkhouses and camping barns.

Bunkhouses
Offer a similar style of accommodation to Hostels but usually with more limited services and facilities, usually on a self-catering basis.

Camping Barns
Provide very simple self-catering accommodation, often referred to as 'stone tents', they have the advantage of being roomy and dry. These are usually redundant farm buildings which have been converted to provide simple accommodation, for up to 15 visitors, at a reasonable cost. Facilities are basic with somewhere to sleep, eat and prepare food, a supply of cold running water and flush toilet.

The Youth Hostels Association has a network of camping barns stretching from the Forest of Bowland in Lancashire, through Durham and into North Yorkshire. Further information and bookings details can be obtained from the
YHA, Trevelyan House,
Dimple Road, Matlock, Derbyshire DE4 3YH
Tel: (017687) 72645
(for camping barns in Lake District)
Tel: 0870 7706113
(for barns in all areas except Lake District)
Internet: www.yha.org.uk

PETS
Many places accept guests with dogs, but we do advise that you check this when you book, and ask if there are any extra charges or rules about exactly where your pet is allowed. The acceptance of dogs is not always extended to cats and it is strongly advised that cat owners contact the establishment well in advance. Some establishments do not accept pets at all. Pets are welcome where you see this symbol 🐕.

Bringing Pets to Britain
The quarantine laws have changed in England and a Pet Travel Scheme (PETS) is currently in operation. Under this scheme pet dogs and cats are able to come into Britain from over 50 countries via certain sea, air and rail routes into England.

Dogs and cats that have been resident in these countries for more than 6 months may enter the UK under the Scheme, providing they are accompanied by the appropriate documentation. Pet dogs and cats from other countries will still have to undergo 6 months quarantine.

For dogs and cats to be able to enter the UK without quarantine under the PETS Scheme they will have to meet certain conditions and travel with the following documents: the Official PETS Certificate, a certificate of treatment against tapeworm and ticks and a declaration of residence. A European Regulation on the movement of pet animals will apply from 3 July 2004. Broadly, the rules of PETS will continue to apply to dogs and cats entering the UK but certain other pet animals will also be included.

For details of participating countries, routes, operators and further information about the PETS Scheme and the new EU Regulations please contact the PETS Helpline, DEFRA (Department for Environment, Food and Rural Affairs), 1a Page Street, London SW1P 4PQ

Tel: +44 (0) 870 241 1710 Fax: +44 (0) 20 7904 6834 Email: pets.helpline@defra.gsi.gov.uk, or visit their web site at www.defra.gov.uk/animalh/quarantine

DRUGS WARNINGS FOR INCOMING TOURISTS
The United Kingdom has severe penalties against drug smuggling. Drug traffickers may try to trick travellers. If you are travelling to the United Kingdom avoid any involvement with drugs. Never carry luggage or parcels through customs for someone else.

LEGAL POINTS
The best source of legal advice for motorists in Britain will be your motoring organisation. What the caravanner or camper needs to know in addition is relatively simple.

If you are towing a caravan or camping trailer you must not exceed 96 kph (60 mph) on dual carriageways and motorways, 80 kph (50 mph) on single carriageways, and on a motorway with three lanes each side you must not enter the third (fastest) lane. Do not light cooking stoves in motorway service areas.

In most towns parking is restricted both by regulations and practical difficulties. Cars with trailers may not use meter-controlled parking spaces, and many town car parks are designed with spaces for single vehicles only. However, a number can accommodate long vehicles as well as cars.

At night a trailer or a car attached to a trailer, if parked on the roadway, must show two front and two rear lights even where a car by itself would be exempt.

The brakes, lights, weight etc. of foreign vehicles do not have to comply with British technical requirements. However, a trailer must not exceed the British size limits - 7 metres (23 feet) long and 2.3 metres (7 feet 6 inches) wide. They must carry your national identification plates. Do not stop overnight on roadside grass verges or lay-bys, because these are considered by law to be part of the road.

Finally, it is important to find out the time you are expected to vacate your pitch on your departure day. You should then leave in good time in the morning, or you may be asked to pay an extra day's charge.

ADVICE FOR VISITORS
VisitBritain welcomes your comments on any aspects of your stay in Britain, whether favourable or otherwise. We hope that you will have no cause to complain, but if you do, the best advice is to take up the complaint immediately with the management of the enterprise concerned: for example the park, shop or transport company. If you cannot obtain satisfaction in this way, please let us know and we ourselves may investigate the matter or suggest what action you might take.

You may bring currency in any denomination and up to any amount into Britain and there is no restriction on the number of travellers' cheques you can change. If you need to change money when the banks are closed you can do so at some large hotels, travel agents and stores or at independent bureaux de change. Be sure to check in advance the rate of exchange and the commission charges. All large shops, department stores and most hotels and restaurants will accept the usual internationally recognised credit cards. If you go shopping in local street markets, patronise only the large, recognised ones, and examine goods carefully.

Always ask the price of goods and services before committing yourself. Beware of pick-pockets in crowded places.

If your possessions are stolen or if you are involved in an accident or fire, telephone 999 (no charge will be made) and ask for the police, the ambulance service or the fire brigade.

Every effort has been made by VisitBritain to ensure accuracy in this publication at the time of going to press. The information is given in good faith on the basis of information submitted to VisitBritain by the promoters of the caravan parks listed. However, VisitBritain cannot guarantee the accuracy of this information and accepts no responsibility for any error or misrepresentation. All liability for loss, disappointment, negligence or other damage caused by reliance on the information contained in this guide or in the event of the bankruptcy or liquidation of any company, individual or firm mentioned, or in the event of any company, individual or firm ceasing to trade, is hereby excluded. It is advisable to confirm the information given with the establishments concerned at the time of booking.

All parks in this guide conform to VisitBritain Standards. A list of these Standards for Camping and Caravan Parks may be found on page 227.

All the establishments included in the full colour section of this guide have paid for inclusion.

Mode d'emploi du guide

La plupart des terrains répertoirés ici possèdent des emplacements pour les caravanes de tourisme ou les tentes, ou les deux, et la plupart accueillent volontiers les camping-cars De nombreux terrains ont aussi des caravanes fixes à louer.

LA NORME D'ASSURANCE-QUALITÉ

Lorsque vous cherchez un endroit où faire étape, vous voulez un système d'évaluation de confiance. Le British Holiday Parks Scheme, relancé en l'an 2000, vous indique clairement et en toute simplicité à quoi vous attendre. La qualité reste la préoccupation principale de ce système, en réponse aux exigences des consommateurs.

VisitBritain utilise des Etoiles pour indiquer la qualité des terrains et centres de vacances participant à ce système. Des inspecteurs agréés et impartiaux visitent ces terrains chaque année et les récompensent de une à cinq Etoiles. Celles-ci indiquent la propreté, l'environnement et la qualité des services fournis.

Les terrains reçoivent également un symbole pour vous permettre d'identifier le type de terrain en un clin d'œil - centre de vacances familial, terrain de camping ou de caravanes, par exemple (si aucun symbole/aucune étoile n'est indiqué pour un terrain/centre particulier, celui-ci n'a pas encore reçu son évaluation à l'heure de mise sous presse).

Le British Graded Holiday Parks Scheme (système d'évaluation des centres de vacances/terrains de camping britanniques) a été conçu par les agences de tourisme d'Angleterre, d'Irlande du Nord, d'Ecosse et du Pays de Galles en collaboration avec The British Holiday & Home Parks Association (l'Association britannique des centres familiaux de vacances et de terrains de camping) (voir page 43) et le National Caravan Council (le bureau national des caravaniers) (voir page 47).

EQUIPEMENTS

Les installations sont indiquées au moyen de symboles illustratifs, dont la légende est donnée ici.

TARIFS

Les tarifs indiqués pour les emplacements sont établis sur la base du tarif minimum et du tarif maximum pour une nuitée et pour 2 personnes accompagnées d'une voiture et d'une tente ou d'une caravane La pratique générale veut qu'en Grande-Bretagne on ne fasse payer que l'emplacement, mais certains terrains de camping pratiquent des tarifs séparés pour la voiture, la tente ou la caravane ainsi que pour chaque personne. Certains terrains appliquent parfois des suppléments pour les auvents des caravanes.

SIGNES CONVENTIONNELS

BH& British Holiday &
HPA Home Parks Association (voir page 43)
NCC National Caravan Council (voir page 47)
🚐 Caravanes admises (suivi du nombre d'emplacements et des tarifs)
🚍 Camping-cars admis (suivi du nombre d'emplacements et des tarifs). Dans certains cas, les emplacements pour camping-cars sont compris dans le total des emplacements pour caravanes
▲ Tentes admises (suivi du nombre d'emplacements et des tarifs)
🚐 Nombre de caravanes disponibles pour la location (voir la rubrique 'emplacements' ci-dessous)
🏠 Location de bungalows et logements similaires
🛏 Aire de séjour d'une nuit
🔌 Branchements électriques pour caravanes (voir la rubrique 'alimentation électrique pour caravanes' ci-dessous)
🚿 Douches

♨ Décharge pour WC chimiques
⟳ Service de remplacement des bouteilles de gaz butane ou propane
🅦 Décharge pour véhicules automobiles
🛒 Magasin d'alimentation fixe/itinérant
✕ Café/restaurant
🍸 Bar
📺 Salle de télévision couleur
📞 Cabine(s) teléphonique(s)
🔲 Laverie
✂ Dispositifs de séchage du linge
🎯 Salle de jeux
🚲 Location de vélos
🏊 Piscine couverte chauffée sur le terrain
🏊 Piscine de plein air sur le terrain
∪ Equitation/randonnée à dos de poney depuis le terrain
🎾 Tennis sur le terrain
🎣 Pêche sur le terrain
🏌 Golf sur le terrain ou à proximité
🐕 Les chiens sont acceptés
🎵 Distractions nocturnes

Les tarifs minimum et maximum de location des caravanes sont donnés par semaine. Les prix indiqués nous ont été fournis par les responsables des terrains concernés, et ont pour but de donner une idée des prix en vigueur au moment de la publication de ce guide. Les prix sont libellés en livres (£) et pence (p). La T.V.A. (Taxe à la Valeur Ajoutée) de 17,5% est comprise dans les tarifs indiqués Afin d'éviter tout malentendu, il est fortement conseillé de vérifier les prix auprès du terrain de camping concerné au moment d'effectuer les réservations.

MODALITÉS DE RÉSERVATION

Lorsque vous vous renseignerez sur l'hebergement offert ainsi que sur les tarifs et autres détails, vous devrez énoncer avec clarté et précision quels sont vos besoins, notamment;

- dates d'arrivée et de départ, avec dates de remplacement acceptables le cas échéant.
- type d'hebergement requis.
- autres besoins particuliers à signaler à la direction.

Les malentendus sont très courants par téléphone, aussi vous est-il recommandé de confirmer par écrit toutes vos réservations si le délais vous le permettent. N'oubliez pas de mentionner votre nom et votre adresse et prenez soin de joindre une enveloppe timbrée à votre adresse ou un coupon-réponse international (si vous écrivez depuis l'étranger) pour la réponse.

Arrhes et paiements anticipés

Les terrains de camping, de caravaning, ou avec bungalows, ainsi que les centres de vacances exigent souvent le versement intégral du paiement à l'avance. Celui-ci peut s'effectuer en deux fois: vous devez payer des arrhes lors de la réservation et vous acquitter du solde deux semaines avant le début de la période de location, par exemple.

Annulations

Lorsque vous acceptez l'hébergement qui vous est offert par écrit ou par téléphone, bous êtes lié par contrat avec le propriétaire de l'établissement. Cela signifie que si vous annulez une réservation, si vous ne venez pas prendre possession du logement ou si vous partez plus tôt que prévu (quelle qu'en soit la raison), le propriétaire est en droit d'exiger un dédommagement s'il ne peut pas relouer pour la durée totale ou une grande partie de la location. Si vous avez versé des arrhes, vous ne serez probablement pas remboursé, et l'on peut vous demander de payer une somme supplémentaire.

Vous avez donc intérêt à aviser immédiatement la direction si vous devez changer vos projets de voyage, annuler une réservation ou partir plus tôt que prévu.

Point de branchement électrique:

La plupart des terrains ont à présent des points de branchement électrique pour les caravanes et les tentes. Le voltage est en général de 240v 50Hz en courant alternatif, bien qu'on puisse encore trouver des courants variant entre 200v et 250v. Il se peut qu'un adaptateur soit nécessaire pour le branchement. En général, les terrains font payer un

supplément pour ce service, et il est conseillé de se renseigner sur les tarifs en vigueur au moment de la réservation.

COMMENT CHOISIR UN TERRAIN

Les terrains sont répertoriés dans ce guide en plusieurs sections : Angleterre (par région), Écosse et Pays de Galles. Dans chaque section, ils sont répertoriés par ordre alphabétique selon le nom de la ville la plus proche. L'Index des Villes en page 249 ainsi que les cartes en couleur au début du guide vous indiquent toutes les villes et villages pour lesquels un terrain apparaît dans ce guide. Utilisez-les pour trouver un terrain rapidement et très facilement. Si vous savez quel est le terrain où vous voulez séjourner, vous le trouverez immédiatement en consultant l'index des terrains en page 246.

Si le lieu où vous désirez séjourner figure dans l'index des villes, reportez-vous au numéro de page indiqué pour voir quels terrains y sont disponibles. Le nom de la ville est indiqué en noir sur les cartes au début du guide à l'endroit indiqué par la référence carte donnée dans chaque entrée. Consultez également les cartes en couleur pour trouver des lieux proches pour lesquels des terrains sont également répertoriés dans ce guide.

Si le lieu où vous désirez séjourner ne figure pas dans l'index des villes (ou bien si vous avez seulement une idée générale du lieu dans lequel vous désirez séjourner), utilisez les cartes en couleur. Certaines régions apparaissent sur plus d'une carte mais les noms de villes (imprimés en noir sur les cartes) sont indiqués une fois seulement.

Toutes les localités dans lesquelles un terrain est répertorié dans le guide figurent sur la carte. Pour avoir la position précise du terrain, veuillez consultez la rubrique qui lui est consacrée. Si vous avez des difficultés pour trouver un terrain donné, nous vous suggérons de demander votre chemin dans le voisinage.

 Pour aider les visiteurs à trouver leur terrain de camping, la Grande-Bretagne emploie les panneaux de signalisation internationaux ci-contre. Tous les terrains ne sont pas encore signalés de cette manière et les panneaux n'affichent pas le nom de terrains particuliers. Ces panneaux indiquent en revanche si le terrain peut accueillir des tentes, des caravanes ou les deux. L'International Camping Carnet est rarement reconnu en Grande-Bretagne sauf dans les terrains gérés par les grands clubs.

Sites à Londres

Londres attire de nombreux visiteurs, aussi les terrains de Camping-caravaning du Grand Londres ont-ils tendance à se remplir tres rapidement. Des terrains sont également disponibles dans la plupart des ports d'entrée du pays: bon nombre d'entre eux sont répertoriés dans ce guide et indiqués sur les cartes au début du guide.

Services-conseils disponibles

Les Centres d'Information Touristique de toute la Grande-Bretagne (voir dernières pages) sont en mesure de donner aux campeurs et au caravaniers des renseignements sur les terrains de leur région.

Certains Centres d'Information Touristique possèdent des services-conseils pour le camping-caravaning qui vous donneront des détails sur les terrains disponibles et pourront souvent vous aider à effectuer votre réservation.

PRÉCAUTIONS À PRENDRE EN HAUTE SAISON

Lors des mois d'été, de juin à septembre, les terrains situés dans des régions très fréquentées comme le Nord Gallois, le Cumbria, le Sud-Ouest de l'Angleterre ou la New Forest, dans le Hampshire, risquent d'être complets. Les campeurs doivent s'efforcer d'arriver sur les terrains de bonne heure dans la journée ou, si c'est possible, de réserver à l'avance. Certains terrains ont des aires de séjour temporaire où les visiteurs arrivant tard le soir peuvent passer la nuit. Cela permet de ne pas déranger les autres campeurs et caravaniers pendant la nuit et d'accepter un plus grand nombre de vacanciers. Les caravanes et les tentes se voient attribuer un emplacement le lendemain matin.

AUTRES TERRAINS DE CAMPING-CARAVANING

Si vous souhaitez suivre votre propre itinéraire dans la campagne britannique, il peut vous être utile de savoir que la Forestry Commission gère des terrains de camping en forêt dans les sept Parcs forestiers de Grande-Bretagne ainsi que dans la New Forest. Certains terrains offrent des tarifs réduits pour les organisations de jeunesse effectuant des séjours de groupes: il vous est conseillé de vous renseigner à ce sujet auprès de la Forestry Commission très à l'avance.

FOYERS ET REFUGES

La plupart des établissements qui figurent dans ce guide proposent un hébergement à prix raisonnable, mais certains se veulent particulièrement économiques et sont destinés aux jeunes, aux familles ou aux groupes qui recherchent un hébergement sûr à petit prix. Il s'agit de foyers privés (hostels), d'auberges de jeunesse (youth hostels), de refuges (bunkhouses) et de granges aménagées (camping barns). Les bunkhouses offrent un hébergement similaire aux foyers, mais avec des services et installations plus limités. On peut généralement faire sa cuisine. Les camping barns offrent un hébergement très simple, souvent appelé 'tentes en pierre'. Leur avantage est d'être grandes et sèches, et l'on peut y faire sa cuisine. Il s'agit généralement d'anciens bâtiments agricoles de bâtiments de ferme aujourd'hui superflus qui ont été aménagés pour permettre d'héberger - en toute simplicité - jusqu'à 15 personnes,à un prix raisonnable. Les installations sont ce qu'il y a de plus simple: un endroit pour dormir, manger et préparer les repas, l'eau froide et les WC avec chasse d'eau. La Youth Hostels Association exploite un réseau de granges aménagées pour le camping qui va de la région de Forest Bowland dans le Lancashire au North Yorkshire, en passant par Durham. Pour obtenir de plus amples renseignements et des détails sur la façon de réserver, veuillez vous adresser à:
YHA, Trevelyan House,
Dimple Road, Matlock, Derbyshire DE4 2YH
Tel: (017687) 72645 (pour les granges aménagées dans le Pays des Lacs)
Tel: (01200) 420102 (pour les granges aménagées dans toute les régions sauf le Pays des Lacs)
www.yha.org.uk

LES ANIMAUX

De nombreux terrains acceptent les chiens, mais nous vous conseillons de vérifier si c'est bien le cas lorsque vous réservez. Demandez également s'il y a des frais supplémentaires et si votre chien sera exclu de certaines zones. Lorsque les chiens sont acceptés, les chats ne le sont pas automatiquement et nous conseillons vivement aux propriétaires de chats de contacter l'établissement longtemps à l'avance. Certains terrains n'acceptent aucun animal familier. Les chiens sont acceptés lorsque vous voyez ce symbole 🐕 .

Amener votre animal en Grande-Bretagne

Les lois sur la quarantaine ont changé en Angleterre. Un système, appelé Pet Travel Scheme (PETS) est actuellement à l'essai. Ce système autorise les chiens et les chats venus de 50 autres pays d'entrer en Angleterre à certains points (par avion, bateau et train).

Les chiens et chats qui résident dans ces pays depuis plus de 6 mois peuvent entrer au Royaume-Uni grâce au système PETS, pourvu qu'ils possèdent la documentation nécessaire. Les chiens et chats qui viennent d'autres pays doivent cependant passer six mois en quarantaine.

Pour que les chiens et chats puissent entrer au Royaume-Uni sans quarantaine grâce au système PETS, ils doivent répondre à certaines conditions et avoir les documents suivants: certificat officiel PETS, certificat de traitement contre le ténia et les tiques et déclaration de résidence.

Une nouvelle réglementation européenne concernant le transport des animaux domestiques entrera en vigueur le 3 juillet 2004. En gros, la loi concernant les animaux domestiques continuera de s'appliquer aux chiens et aux chats pénétrant en Grande-Bretagne mais inclura désormais certains autres animaux domestiques.

Pour avoir la liste des pays participant à ce programme, ainsi que la liste des points d'entrée et des opérateurs, ou pour tout complément d'information sur le projet pilote PETS et la nouvelle réglementation européenne veuillez contacter le téléphone rouge PETS, DEFRA (Department for Environment, Food and Rural Affairs), 1a Page Street, London SW1P 4PQ
Tel: +44 (0) 870 241 1710
Fax: +44 (0) 20 7904 6834
Email: pets.helpline@defra.gsi.gov.uk, ou consultez le site web www.defra.gov.uk/animalh/quarantine

RÉGLEMENTATION CONTRE LA DROGUE

Le Royaume-Uni applique des sanctions sévères contre la contrebande de la drogue. Les trafiquants de drogue peuvent essayer de duper les voyageurs. Si vous voyagez à destination du Royaume-Uni, ne soyez pas mêlé au trafic de drogue. Ne passez jamais de bagages ou de colis pour autrui par les douanes.

ASPECTS JURIDIQUES

La meilleure source de renseignements juridiques pour les automobilistes voyageant en Grande-Bretagne reste l'association des automobilistes de leur pays d'origine. Les détails supplémentaires que doivent connaître le campeur ou le caravanier sont relativement simples.

Si vous tractez une caravane ou une remorque de camping, vous ne devez pas dépasser 96 km/h sur les voies express ou sur les autoroutes, 80 km/h sur les routes à deux voies; en outre, sur les autoroutes ayant trois voies dans chaque direction, vous ne devez pas rouler sur la troisième voie (la plus rapide). N'allumez pas de réchauds à gaz sur les aires de service des autoroutes.

Dans la plupart des villes, le stationnement est limité à la fois par la réglementation et par le manque de place. Les voitures dotées de remorques ne peuvent pas occuper les espaces de stationnement limité à parcmètres et de nombreux parcs de stationnement de ville ne sont conçus que pour accueillir des véhicules indépendants. Toutefois, certains parcs peuvent accueillir des véhicules plus longs en plus des voitures.

La nuit, les remorques ou les voitures dotées de remorques, lorsqu'elles sont en stationnement au bord de la route, doivent avoir les deux feux avant et les deux feux arrière allumés même dans le cas où cela n'est pas jugé nécessaire pour une voiture seule.

Les freins, l'éclairage, le poids, etc. des véhicules étrangers n'ont pas à respecter les prescriptions techniques britanniques. Toutefois, une remorque ne doit pas dépasser les limites dimensionnelles britanniques: 7m de long et 2,3m de large. Elle doit être munie de votre plaque d'immatriculation nationale. Vous ne devez pas vous arrêter pour la nuit vos accotements ou sur les petites aires de stationnement des bas-côtés car la loi stipule que ces emplacements font partie de la route.

Enfin, il est important de vous renseigner sur l'heure à laquelle il vous est demandé de libérer votre emplacement le jour du départ. Vous devrez prévoir de partir assez tôt, sans quoi vous risquez d'avoir à payer une journée de location supplémentaire.

CONSEILS AUX VISITEURS

VisitBritain vous invite à formuler vos observations sur tout aspect de votre séjour en Grande-Bretagne, qu'elles soient favorables ou non. Nous espérons que vous n'aurez pas lieu de vous plaindre, mais dans l'affirmative, il vous est conseillé de faire part de votre mécontentement immédiatement auprès de la direction de l'établissement concerné comme par exemple:

camping, magasin ou société de transport. Si vous ne pouvez pas obtenir satisfaction de cette manière, veuillez nous le faire savoir et nous examinerons la question nous-mêmes ou nous vous suggèrerons une procédure éventuelle à suivre.

Vous pouvez emporter en Grande-Bretagne les devises de votre choix en quantité illimitée et aucune restriction ne s'applique a la quantité de chèques de voyage changés. Si vous avez besoin de devises britanniques pendant les heures de fermeture des banques, vous pouvez vous les procurer dans certains grands hôtels, agences de voyages, grands magasins ou dans les bureaux de change indépendants. Ne manquez pas de vérifier à l'avance le taux de change et la commission appliqués.

Tous les grands magasins et boutiques et la plupart des hôtels et restaurants accepteront les cartes de crédit usuelles reconnues dans le monde entier. Si vous aimez faire vos achats au marché, limitez-vous aux grands marchés de rue officiels et examinez toujours les articles soigneusement.

Demandez toujours le prix des marchandises avant de vous engager. Prenez garde aux pickpockets en cas d'affluence. Si l'on vous vole des objets personnels ou si vous vous trouvez sur le lieu d'un incendie ou d'un accident, composez le 999 (numéro gratuit) et demandez la police, les services d'ambulance ou les pompiers.

VisitBritain a pris toutes les dispositions nécessaires pour assurer l'exactitude des Informations contenues dans la présente publication au moment de mettre sous presse. Ces Informations sont fournies en toute bonne foi sur la base des renseignements donnés à VisitBritain par les exploitants des terrains de camping répertoriés. Toutefois, VisitBritain ne peut garantir l'exactitude de ces renseignements et décline toute responsablilité en cas d'erreur ou de déformation des faits. Toute responsabilité est également déclinée pour toutes pertes, déceptions, négligences ou autres dommages que pourrait subir quiconque se fie aux renseignements contenus dans le présent guide, pour les cas de faillite ou de liquidation de toute personne morale ou physique mentionnée, et pour les cas de cessation d'activités de toute personne morale ou physique. Il est conseillé de se faire confirmer les renseignements fournis par les établissements concernés lors de la réservation.

Tous les terrains inclus dans ce guide respectent les normes VisitBritain. On trouvera à la page 227 une liste de ces normes relatives aux terrains de camping-caravaning.

Tous les établissements répertoriés dans la section eu couleurs figurent dans le présent guide à titre payant.

Unterwegs in Großbritannien

Die meisten der hier aufgeführten Parks verfügen über Stellplätze für Wohnwagen bzw. Zelte oder beides und die meisten nehmen auch Wohnmobile auf. Des Weiteren vermieten viele Parks auch Ferienwohnwagen.

QUALITÄTSGEWÄHRLEISTUNGSSTANDARD

Bei der Suche nach einer geeigneten Unterkunft braucht man ein verlässliches Einstufungssystem. Das 'British Graded Holiday Parks Scheme' (britisches Beurteilungssystem für Ferienparks), das im Jahr 2000 neu lanciert wurde, vermittelt Ihnen in leicht verständlicher Form einen klaren Eindruck von dem, was Sie erwarten können. Das System spiegelt die Kundenerwartungen und beurteilt in erster Linie die Qualität.

VisitBritain kennzeichnet die Qualitätsstufe der an diesem Programm teilnehmenden Parks durch die Vergabe von Sternen. Die betreffenden Parks werden jährlich von sachlich geschulten, unparteiischen Prüfern inspiziert und dann mittels einer Skala von einem bis fünf Sterne eingestuft. Die Anzahl der vergebenen Sterne hängt von der Sauberkeit, dem Ambiente sowie der Qualität der vorhandenen Einrichtungen und gebotenen Dienstleistungen ab.

Außerdem werden die einzelnen Parks nach Typ gekennzeichnet, so dass man auf einen Blick erkennt, um was für eine Art von Gelände es sich handelt - z.B. Ferienpark, Touringpark oder Campingpark. (Weist der Park keine Einstufung oder Kennzeichnung auf, so

bedeutet das, dass die Beurteilung zum Zeitpunkt der Drucklegung noch nicht stattgefunden hat.)

Das 'British Graded Holiday Parks Scheme' entstand in partnerschaftlicher Zusammenarbeit der nationalen Fremdenverkehrsstellen für England, Nordirland, Schottland und Wales, in Verbindung mit der British Holiday & Home Parks Association (siehe Seite 43) und dem National Caravan Council (siehe Seite 47).

EINRICHTUNGEN

Die jeweiligen Einrichtungen sind durch Symbole bezeichnet, deren Bedeutung Sie der Zeichenerklärung auf einen Blick entnehmen können.

PREISE

Die angegebenen Preise für Stellplätze beruhen auf den Mindest- bzw. Höchstgebühren pro Nacht für zwei Personen, ein Auto und einen Wohnwagen bzw. ein Zelt. In Großbritannien ist es im Allgemeinen üblich, einfach eine Gebühr für die Nutzung des Stellplatzes zu berechnen, allerdings erheben einige Parks separate Gebühren für das Auto, den Wohnwagen bzw. das Zelt und pro Person. Manche Parks verlangen unter Umständen eine Zusatzgebühr für am Wohnwagen angebrachte Sonnenzelte. Die Mindest- und Höchstpreise für Ferienwohnwagen sind pro Woche angegeben. Die Preise wurden jeweils von der betreffenden Parkleitung zur Verfügung gestellt und bilden lediglich eine Richtschnur für die tatsächlich berechneten Preise während der Gültigkeit der vorliegenden Veröffentlichung. Die Preise sind in Pfund Sterling (£)

ZEICHENERKLÄRUNG

BH& British Holiday &
HPA Home Parks Association (siehe Seite 43)
NCC National Caravan Council (siehe Seite 47)

🚐 Wohnwagen zugelassen (mit Anzahl der Stellplätze und Preisen)

🚍 Wohnmobile zugelassen (mit Anzahl der Stellplätze und Preisen)

🛆 Zelte zugelassen (mit Anzahl der Stellplätze und Preisen)

🏠 Anzahl der vermietbaren Ferienwohnwagen (mit Anzahl und Preisen)

🏠 Bungalows, Chalets, Wohnkabinen zum Vermieten

🏠 Auffangstelle für spät im Park eintreffende Gäste

🔌 Stromanschluß für Wohnwagen und Zelte

🚿 Duschen

🚽 Chemische Toiletten

🚾 Sanitäre Entsorgungsstelle

♻ Umtauschstelle für Butan- /oder Propangaszylinder

🛒 Lebensmittelgeschäft/Wagen für Lebensmittelverkauf

✕ Restaurant

🍸 Bar

📺 Aufenthaltsraum mit Farbfernseher

📞 Öffentliche Fernsprecher

🗄 Wäscherei

✄ Wäschetrockner

🎯 Hallenspiele

🚲 Fahrradverleih

🏊 Hallenbad

🏊 Freibad

U Reiten/Ponyreiten in der Nähe

🎾 Tennis

🎣 Angeln

▸ Golf im Park oder in der Nähe

🐾 Haustiere willkommen

🎵 Abendunterhaltung

und Pence (p) angegeben. Die Mehrwertsteuer (VAT) zum Satz von 17,5% ist im Preis enthalten. Um etwaigen Missverständnissen vorzubeugen, ist es ratsam, sich bei der Reservierung nach den genauen Preisen zu erkundigen.

RESERVIERUNGEN

Bei Anfragen über mögliche Unterkünfte, Preise und weitere Angaben sollten Sie Ihre Wünsche klar und genau angeben - zum Beispiel:

- Ankunfts- und Abreisetermin, falls möglich mit akzeptablen Ausweichterminen

- gewünschte Unterkunft

- Teilen Sie der Parkleitung mit, falls Sie besondere Anforderungen haben.

Bei Telefongesprächen kommt es leicht zu Missverständnissen. Deshalb empfehlen wir Ihnen, Ihre Reservierung schriftlich zu bestätigen, falls dies zeitlich möglich ist. Denken Sie bitte daran, Ihren Namen und Ihre Anschrift anzugeben und einen adressierten Freiumschlag, bei Anfragen aus dem Ausland einen internationalen Antwortschein, beizulegen

Anzahlungen und Vorauszahlungen

Bei Wohnwagen-, Camping-, Chaletparks und Ferienzentren ist der gesamte Betrag häufig im Voraus zu entrichten. Die Zahlung kann in zwei Raten erfolgen: bei der Reservierung wird eine Anzahlung fällig und der Restbetrag ist zwei Wochen vor Beginn des Aufenthalts zu leisten.

Stornierungen

Wenn Sie ein Unterkunftsangebot schriftlich oder telefonisch akzeptieren, gehen Sie mit dem Besitzer der betreffenden Unterkunft einen rechtlich bindenden Vertrag ein. Das hat zur Folge, dass der Besitzer, wenn Sie eine Reservierung stornieren, nicht wahrnehmen oder die Unterkunft (gleichgültig aus welchen Gründen) vorzeitig räumen, unter Umständen berechtigt ist, Schadensersatz zu verlangen, sofern er nicht in der Lage ist, die Unterkunft für den ganzen bzw. einen Teil des gebuchten Zeitraums weiterzuvermieten. Falls eine Anzahlung geleistet wurde, wird sie wahrscheinlich hierfür angerechnet und unter Umständen erfolgt eine weitere Zahlungsforderung.

Es ist daher in Ihrem Interesse, die Geschäftsleitung umgehend zu benachrichtigen, wenn Sie Ihre Reisepläne ändern, eine Reservierung stornieren oder die Unterkunft vorzeitig verlassen möchten.

Anschluss ans Stromnetz

Die meisten Parks verfügen inzwischen über Stromanschlussstellen für Wohnwagen und Zelte. Es handelt sich dabei im Allgemeinen um Wechselstrom mit einer Spannung von 240 Volt, 50 Schwingungen, allerdings können Spannungsschwankungen zwischen 200 V und 250 V auftreten. Unter Umständen benötigen Sie einen Adapter. Die Parks erheben normalerweise eine Zusatzgebühr für diesen Service und es ist ratsam, sich bei der Reservierung nach deren Höhe zu erkundigen.

SO FINDEN SIE IHREN PARK

In der vorliegenden Broschüre sind die Parks in England nach Region, danach die Parks in Schottland und Wales aufgeführt. Sie sind in alphabetischer Reihenfolge unter dem Namen der Ortschaft, in der oder in deren Nähe sie liegen, verzeichnet. Im Ortsverzeichnis auf Seite 249 und auf den farbigen Lagekarten am Anfang dieser Veröffentlichung sind alle Städte, Ortschaften und Dörfer aufgeführt, die in dieser Broschüre mit einem Park vertreten sind. Anhand des Verzeichnisses und der Karten finden Sie schnell und mühelos eine geeignete Unterkunft. Wenn Sie bereits wissen, in welchem Park Sie übernachten möchten, schlagen Sie im Verzeichnis der Parks auf Seite 246 nach.

Wenn die Ortschaft, in der Sie übernachten möchten, im Ortsverzeichnis aufgeführt ist, schlagen Sie auf der angegebenen Seite nach, wo die dort vorhandenen Parks verzeichnet sind. Die Namen der Ortschaften sind gemäß des beim betreffenden Eintrag genannten Planquadrats auf den Karten am Anfang dieses Reiseführers schwarz gedruckt. Sehen Sie auch auf den farbigen Karten nach, um Ortschaften in der Nähe zu finden, wo sich ebenfalls Parks befinden, die in dieser Veröffentlichung aufgeführt sind.

Falls die Ortschaft, in der Sie übernachten möchten, nicht im Ortsverzeichnis aufgeführt ist oder Sie nur eine ungefähre Vorstellung von der Gegend haben, in der Sie übernachten möchten, so benutzen Sie die farbigen Lagekarten.

Auf den Karten sind alle Orte verzeichnet, die in der vorliegenden Veröffentlichung mit einem Park vertreten sind. Die genaue Lage ist jeweils in den betreffenden Einträgen beschrieben. Sollten Sie Schwierigkeiten haben, einen bestimmten Park zu finden, so schlagen wir vor, dass Sie sich vor Ort eine genaue Wegbeschreibung geben lassen.

 Die hier abgebildeten internationalen Hinweisschilder, die in Großbritannien vielfach zu finden sind, erleichtern Ihnen das Auffinden eines Parks. Allerdings sind sie noch nicht für alle Camping-, Wohnwagen- bzw. Ferienparks vorhanden und geben nicht den Namen des Parks an, doch zeigen sie, ob es sich um einen Park für Wohnwagen, Zelte oder beides handelt. Der internationale Campingausweis ist in Großbritannien nur in Parks gültig, die von größeren Klubs verwaltet werden.

Plätze in London

Da London ein großer Anziehungspunkt für Besucher ist, sind die Camping- und Wohnwagenparks im Umkreis der britischen Hauptstadt schnell ausgebucht, daher ist eine frühzeitige Reservierung ratsam. Auch in den meisten Einreisehäfen gibt es entsprechende Parks, von denen viele in dieser Veröffentlichung aufgeführt und auf den Karten am Anfang verzeichnet sind.

Die Touristeninformationszentren in allen Teilen Großbritanniens (auf den letzten Seiten aufgeführt) geben Ihnen gerne Auskunft über die Camping- und Wohnwagenparks in ihrem Gebiet.

Einige Touristeninformationszentren haben einen Wohnwagen- und Camping-Beratungsdienst, der über freie Plätze Auskunft geben und häufig auch Reservierungen vornehmen kann.

VERMEIDEN VON PROBLEMEN IN DER HOCHSAISON

In den Sommermonaten Juni bis September sind die Camping- und Wohnwagenparks in den beliebten Urlaubsgebieten wie etwa Nordwales, Cumbria, im West Country oder im New Forest in Hampshire schnell ausgebucht. Treffen Sie daher frühzeitig am Tag am Park ein oder buchen Sie nach Möglichkeit im Voraus. Manche Parks verfügen über Auffangstellen für spät eintreffende Gäste. Auf diese Weise werden die anderen Gäste zu fortgeschrittener Stunde nicht gestört und es werden weniger Besucher abgewiesen. Es wird dann am nächsten Morgen ein Stellplatz zugewiesen.

SONSTIGE WOHNWAGEN- UND CAMPINGPLÄTZE

Wenn Sie Ihre Reiseroute durch die britische Landschaft lieber auf eigene Faust planen, dürften Sie an den Campingplätzen in Waldgebieten interessiert sein, die von der Forestry Commission verwaltet werden. Hierzu gehören sieben Forest Parks und der New Forest. In einigen erhalten Jugendorganisationen beim Campingurlaub Preisermäßigungen. Alle diesbezüglichen Anfragen sind frühzeitig im Voraus an die Forest Commission zu richten.

UNTERKUNFT IN HOSTELS (HERBERGEN)

Zwar eignet sich der Großteil der in der vorliegenden Broschüre aufgeführten Unterkünfte durchaus für Leute, die nach einer relativ preiswerten Übernachtungsmöglichkeit suchen, doch bieten manche Häuser eigens sichere Unterkünfte für junge Leute, Familien bzw. größere Gruppen zum kleinen Preis an. Zu diesen sogenannten Hostels gehören Herbergen in privater Hand, Jugendherbergen, Bunkhouses (einfache Unterkünfte mit Etagenbetten) und Campingscheunen.

Bunkhouses fallen in eine ähnliche Unterkunftskategorie wie Hostels, nur ist das Dienstleistungsangebot dort begrenzter und die Ausstattung einfacher. Bunkhouses sind in der Regel für Selbstversorger gedacht.Campingscheunen sind ganz schlichte Unterkünfte für Selbstversorger und werden häufig auch als „Steinzelte" bezeichnet. Gegenüber herkömmlichen Zelten haben sie allerdings den Vorteil, geräumig und trocken zu sein. Bei Campingscheunen handelt es sich im Allgemeinen um ausgediente Farmgebäude, die zu einfachen, günstigen Unterkünften für bis zu 15 Personen umgebaut wurden. Die Einrichtungen sind anspruchslos. Es gibt eine Schlaf-, Koch- und Essstelle, kaltes Wasser und ein WC.

Die Youth Hostels Association (der Jugendherbergsverband) verfügt über ein Netz von Campingscheunen, das sich vom Forest of Bowland in Lancashire über Durham bis nach North Yorkshire erstreckt. Für weitere Informationen und Reservierungen wenden Sie sich bitte an die YHA, Trevelyan House, Dimple Road, Matlock,Derbyshire DE4 2YH Tel: (017687) 72645 (für Campingscheunen im Lake District) Tel: (01200) 420102 (für Scheunen in allen Gebieten, außer im Lake District) www.yha.org.uk

HAUSTIERE

In vielen Unterkünften werden Gäste mit Hunden aufgenommen, allerdings raten wir Ihnen, sich bei der Reservierung danach zu erkundigen. Außerdem sollten Sie fragen, ob für den Hund eine zusätzliche Gebühr berechnet wird, und ob es Regeln gibt, wo genau Ihr Haustier sich aufhalten darf. Der Umstand, dass Hunde aufgenommen werden, bedeutet nicht unbedingt, dass das Gleiche auch für Katzen gilt und wir raten Katzenbesitzern dringend, sich diesbezüglich frühzeitig mit der betreffenden Unterkunft zu verständigen. Manche Unterkünfte lassen überhaupt keine Haustiere zu. Wo Sie das Zeichen 🐾 sehen, sind Haustiere willkommen.

Das Mitbringen von Haustieren nach Großbritannien
In England wurden die Quarantänevorschriften novelliert und momentan läuft das 'Pet Travel Scheme (PETS)'. Im Rahmen dieser Aktion können als Haustier gehaltene Hunde und Katzen auf bestimmten Schiffs-, Flug- und Bahnstrecken aus über 50 Ländern nach England mitgebracht werden.

Hunde und Katzen, die länger als 6 Monate in den betreffenden Ländern gehalten wurden, können im Rahmen der Aktion nach Großbritannien eingeführt werden, vorausgesetzt, dass die entsprechenden Dokumente vorhanden sind. Hunde und Katzen aus anderen Ländern müssen nach wie vor 6 Monate lang in Quarantäne gegeben werden.

Um im Rahmen der Aktion PETS ohne Quarantäne nach Großbritannien einreisen zu können, müssen Hunde und Katzen bestimmte Kriterien erfüllen und es müssen folgende Unterlagen vorgelegt werden: das offizielle PETS-Zertifikat, eine Behandlungsbescheinigung gegen Bandwurm, Zecken sowie eine Bestätigung des Haltungsorts. Am 3. Juli 2004 tritt eine europäische Direktive über den Transport von Haustieren in Kraft. Im Großen und Ganzen gelten auch danach die Regeln für PETS für das Mitbringen von Hunden und Katzen nach Großbritannien, allerdings werden die genannten Bestimmungen auch auf bestimmte andere Haustiere ausgedehnt.

Für weitere Auskünfte über die an dieser Aktion teilnehmenden Länder, die Strecken, Reiseunternehmer sowie ausführlichere Informationen über die Aktion PETS und die neuen EU-Bestimmungen wenden Sie sich bitte an die PETS Helpline, DEFRA (Department for Environment, Food and Rural Affairs), 1a Page Street, London SW1P 4PQ,

Tel: +44 (0) 870 241 1710, Fax: +44 (0) 20 7904 6834, E-Mail: pets.helpline@defra.gsi.gov.uk oder schauen Sie auf der Website vorbei: www.defra.gov.uk/aimalh/quarantine

DROGENWARNUNG FÜR EINREISENDE TOURISTEN

Großbritannien geht gegen Rauschgiftschmuggel sehr scharf vor. Drogenhändler versuchen häufig, unschuldige Reisende in ihre Geschäfte zu verwickeln. Seien Sie daher bei der Reise nach Großbritannien sehr auf der Hut und tragen Sie niemals Gepäckstücke für andere Personen durch die Zollkontrolle.

RECHTLICHES

Wenden Sie sich vor dem Antritt Ihrer Reise am besten an Ihren Automobilverband, der Ihnen gerne Auskunft über alle rechtlichen Fragen in Bezug auf Reisen in Großbritannien gibt. Wenn Sie mit dem Wohnwagen oder Zelt unterwegs sind, sollten Sie zusätzlich ein paar einfache Regeln beachten.

Wenn Sie mit einem Wohnwagen oder einem Camping-Anhänger unterwegs sind, dürfen Sie auf vierspurigen Fernstraßen und Autobahnen höchstens 96 km/h fahren. Auf zweispurigen Fernstraßen gilt das Tempolimit 80 km/h. Auf sechsspurigen Autobahnen dürfen Sie niemals - auch nicht zum Überholen - in der dritten (schnellsten) Spur fahren. Auf den Raststätten an der Autobahn dürfen keine Kochöfen angezündet werden.

In den meisten Städten ist das Parken durch gesetzliche Bestimmungen oder praktische Probleme stark eingeschränkt. Autos mit Anhängern dürfen nicht an Parkuhren parken. Ferner nehmen die meisten Parkplätze nur Wagen ohne Anhänger auf. Allerdings sind einige Parkplätze vorhanden, die überlange Fahrzeuge und Fahrzeuge mit Anhängern zulassen.

Nachts müssen auf der Straße geparkte Anhänger bzw. Autos mit Anhänger vorn und hinten jeweils zwei Lampen aufweisen. Dies gilt auch an Stellen, wo ein Auto ohne Anhänger davon ausgenommen wäre.

Die britischen Vorschriften über Bremsen, Beleuchtung, zulässiges Gewicht und sonstige technische Punkte gelten nicht für ausländische Fahrzeuge. Ein Anhänger muss jedoch die britischen Vorschriften erfüllen und darf nicht länger als 7 m und nicht breiter als 2,30 m sein. Anhänger müssen mit den amtlichen Zulassungsschildern Ihres Heimatlandes versehen sein. Übernachten Sie nicht auf dem Grasrand einer Straße oder in einer Ausweichbucht, weil diese Stellen als zur Straße gehörig angesehen werden.

Abschließend sei betont, wie wichtig es ist, dass Sie sich erkundigen, wann Sie den Stellplatz in einem Camping- oder Wohnwagenpark am Abreisetag räumen müssen. Reisen Sie morgens rechtzeitig ab, sonst müssen Sie vielleicht die Gebühr für einen weiteren Tag bezahlen.

RATSCHLÄGE FÜR BESUCHER

VisitBritain würde sich über Ihren Kommentar hinsichtlich aller Gesichtspunkte Ihres Aufenthalts in Großbritannien freuen, ganz gleich, ob er positiv oder negativ ausfällt. Wir hoffen, dass Sie keinen Grund zur Beanstandung haben, falls Sie aber doch Anlass zu Beschwerden haben sollten, ist es am besten, sich sofort an die Leitung des entsprechenden Unternehmens zu wenden, z. B. des Parks, des Geschäfts oder der Verkehrsgesellschaft. Wenn Sie mit der Behandlung, die Sie dort erfahren, nicht zufrieden sind, so geben Sie uns bitte Bescheid. Wir werden dann der Angelegenheit entweder selbst nachgehen oder Sie darüber beraten, welche Maßnahmen Sie ergreifen können.

Sie können Währungen jeder Art in beliebiger Höhe nach Großbritannien mitbringen. Reiseschecks werden in beliebiger Anzahl eingelöst. Wenn Ihnen das Bargeld ausgeht, wenn die Banken geschlossen sind, so können Sie Geld in einigen großen Hotels, Reisebüros, Kaufhäusern und in unabhängigen Wechselstuben umtauschen. Prüfen Sie vor dem Geldumtausch, welcher Wechselkurs Anwendung findet und wie hoch die Bearbeitungsgebühr ist. Alle größeren Geschäfte, Kaufhäuser und die meisten Hotels und Restaurants akzeptieren international gängige Kreditkarten als Zahlungsmittel. Wenn Sie auf örtlichen Straßenmärkten einkaufen, so halten Sie sich an die großen, bekannten Märkte und prüfen Sie die Waren sorgfältig.

Erkundigen Sie sich vor dem Kauf stets nach dem Preis der Waren oder Dienstleistungen. Nehmen Sie sich in Menschenmengen vor Taschendieben in Acht.

Wenn Sie Opfer eines Diebstahls oder Zeuge eines Unfalls oder Brands werden, wählen Sie den Notruf unter der Nummer 999 (der Anruf ist kostenlos) und verlangen Sie die Polizei (police), einen Krankenwagen (ambulance) oder die Feuerwehr (fire brigade).

VisitBritain hat sich alle erdenkliche Mühe gegeben, die Richtigkeit der in der vorliegenden Veröffentlichung gemachten Angaben zum Zeitpunkt der Drucklegung zu gewährleisten. Die Informationen werden in gutem Glauben erteilt und beruhen auf den Angaben, die VisitBritain von den aufgeführten Wohnwagenparks erteilt wurden. VisitBritain gibt jedoch keine Garantie für die Genauigkeit der Angaben und übernehmen keinerlei Verantwortung für Fehler oder fälschliche Darstellungen. Hiermit ausgeschlossen wird die Haftung für Verluste, nicht erfüllte Erwartungen, Fahrlässigkeit oder andere Schäden, die sich daraus ergeben, dass sich Leser auf die Informationen in der vorliegenden Veröffentlichung verlassen, oder die sich daraus ergeben, dass in der Veröffentlichung genannte Unternehmen, Firmen oder Einzelpersonen Konkurs anmelden, in Liquidation gehen oder ihre Geschäftstätigkeit einstellen. Es wird empfohlen, sich die in der vorliegenden Veröffentlichung gemachten Angaben bei der Reservierung von den betreffenden Stellen bestätigen zu lassen. Alle in diesem Reiseführer genannten Parks entsprechen den Standards von VisitBritain. Eine Liste der Standardbedingungen für Camping- und Wohnwagenparks befindet sich auf Seite 227.

Sämtliche im farbigen Teil dieser Veröffentlichung genannten Stellen haben für die Aufnahme eine Gebühr entrichtet.

Hoe u deze gids moet gebruiken

Op de meeste vermelde terreinen zijn trekcaravans, tenten of kampeerauto's of alledrie welkom. Bij de meeste zijn vakantiecaravans te huur.

DE KWALITEITS GARANTIE STANDAARD

Als u een verblijfsplaats zoekt, dan heeft u een classificatiesysteem nodig dat u kunt vertrouwen. De British Graded Holiday Parks Scheme, in 2000 opnieuw gepubliceerd, geeft u een duidelijk overzicht van wat u kunt verwachten in een gemakkelijk te begrijpen vorm. Het systeem houdt kwaliteit hoog in het vaandel en weerspiegelt de verwachtingen van de consument.

VisitBritain gebruikt sterren om de kwaliteitsclassificatie van de deelnemende parken weer te geven. De parken worden jaarlijks door getrainde, onafhankelijke controleurs bezocht, die 1 tot 5 sterren toekennen. Deze zijn gebaseerd op hygiëne,omgeving en kwaliteit van de voorzieningen en diensten, die er aanwezig zijn.

De parken hebben ook een 'aanwijzer' zodat u het type standplaats in één oogopslag kunt herkennen b.v. een vakantie park, een tourcaravan park en een camping. (Als er geen gradatie of aanwijzer is gegeven dan is men in afwachting van een classifcatie ten tijde van het drukken van deze brochure.)

The British Graded Holiday Parks Scheme is gezamenlijk ontworpen door de nationale toeristencentra van Engeland, Noord-Ierland, Schotland en Wales en de British Holiday & Home Parks Association (zie pagina 43) en de National Caravan Council (zie pagina 47).

FACILITEITEN

De faciliteiten worden aangeduid d.m.v. de hieronder in het kort verklaarde tekens.

PRIJZEN

De vermelde tarieven zijn de minimale en maximale prijzen voor een overnachting voor 2 personen, auto plus caravan of tent. Over het algemeen berekent men in Groot-Brittannië voor de staanplaats, maar een aantal terreinen belast u apart voor de auto, caravan of tent, en elke persoon. Bij sommige parken moet u eventueel extra betalen voor een tent of voortent die aan een caravan vastgebouwd is. Minimale en maximale tarieven voor vakantiecaravans zijn per week. Vermelde prijzen werden verstrekt door de terreinbeheerders en dienen als richtlijn voor de prijzen die tijdens de geldendheid van dit boekje gerekend zullen worden. Vermelde prijzen zijn in ponden (£) en pence (p). VAT (BTW) à 17,5% is bij de prijzen inbegrepen. Om misverstanden te vermijden, raden wij u dringend aan de prijzen te controleren als u een reservering maakt.

VERKLARING VAN DE TEKENS

BH& British Holiday &
HPA Home Parks Association (zie blz 43)
NCC National Caravan Council (zie blz 47)
- caravans toegestaan (met aantal staanplaatsen en tarieven)
- kampeerauto's toegestaan (met aantal staanplaatsen en tarieven) In sommige gevallen is het aantal plekjes voor kampeerauto's opgenomen in het totaal voor toercaravans
- Å tenten toegestaan (met aantal plekjes en tarieven)
- aantal vakantiecaravans te huur (Zie 'Vakantiecaravans')
- bungalows/chalets/huisjes te huur
- terrein voor late aankomers op het park
- elektrische aansluiting voor caravans (zie 'Elektriciteit. Elektrische aansluiting voor caravans)
- douches

- lozing van chemische toiletten mogelijk
- Lozing chemische toiletten van motorvoertuigen
- omwisseling van butaan- en propaangasflessen
- levensmiddelenwinkel/rijdende winkel
- ✗ café/restaurant
- Bar
- Zitkamer met kleurentelevisie
- openbare telefoons
- wasserette op terrein aanwezig
- drogen van wasgoed mogelijk
- recreatiekamer
- fietsenverhuur
- verwarmd binnenbad op park
- openluchtbad op park
- U manège (paard/pony) op terrein
- tennis op terrein
- vissen op terrein
- ► golf op of bij park
- huisdieren welkom
- ♫ amusement 's avonds

40

RESERVEREN

Bij het maken van een reservering, of het inwinnen van inlichtingen, moet u vooral duidelijk en precies aangeven wat u wilt - bij voorbeeld:

- aankomst- en vertrekdata met mogelijke alternatieven.
- gewenste accommodatie.
- vertel de beheerder vooral wat voor speciale wensen of eisen u heeft.

Misverstanden kunnen heel gemakkelijk voorkomen over de telefoon en wij raden u daarom aan alle reserveringen, als de tijd dat toelaat, schriftelijk te bevestigen. Vergeet vooral niet uw naam en adres te vermelden en een aan uzelf geadresseerde envelop met postzegel of internationale antwoordcoupon (als u uit het buitenland schrijft) in te sluiten voor elk antwoord.

Aan- en vooruitbetalingen

Campings, caravanterreinen, bungalow- en vakantieparken moeten meestal van tevoren geheel betaald worden. Dit kan gedaan worden in tweeën - een aanbetaling bij de reservering en betaling van het saldo bijvoorbeeld twee weken voor de aanvang van de geboekte periode.

Annuleren

De aanvaarding van geboden accommodatie, hetzij schriftelijk of telefonisch, wordt over het algemeen beschouwd als een wettelijk bindend contract. Dit betekent dat als u annuleert, niet verschijnt op het park, of vroegtijdig het park verlaat (het geeft niet om welke reden), de eigenaar compensatie van u kan verlangen als de staanplaats voor het overgrote deel van de geboekte periode niet opnieuw verhuurd kan worden. Als u een aanbetaling gedaan heeft, kan deze vervallen worden verklaard en een aanvullend bedrag van u verlangd worden.

Het is daarom in uw eigen belang de bedrijfsleiding onmiddelijk in kennis te stellen, als u uw reisplannen moet wijzigen, een boeking moet annuleren, of voortijdig moet vertrekken.

Elektrische aansluiting:

De meeste parken hebben elektrische aansluitpunten voor caravans en tenten. De voltage is meestal 240v AC, 50Hz, hoewel nog steeds voltages tussen 200v en 250v worden aangetroffen. Het kan zijn dat u een adaptor nodig heeft voor de aansluiting. Meestal moet u extra betalen voor deze faciliteit. Het is raadzaam de tarieven na te vragen voor u reserveert.

HET VINDEN VAN EEN PARK OF TERREIN

De parken in dit gidsje zijn ingedeeld in Engeland per regio, gevolgd door Schotland en Wales. Zij staan in alfabetische volgorde onder de naam van de meest nabijgelegen plaats. De index van plaatsen op blz 249 en de gekleurde lokatiekaarten voorin de gids vertonen alle steden, plaatsen en dorpen met parken die in deze gids voorkomen. Zo kunt u snel en gemakkelijk ergens een park vinden. Als u al weet op welk park u wilt staan, kunt u de index van parken raadplegen op blz 246.

Als uw bestemming in de index van plaatsen voorkomt, raadpleeg dan de gegeven bladzij, waar de aldaar gevestigde parken worden vermeld. De plaatsnamen staan in zwart op de kaarten voorin het gidsje, aangeduid met coördinaten bij de vermelding. Ook kunt u de kleurenkaarten raadplegen om nabijgelegen plaatsen te vinden die ook in de gids voorkomende parken hebben.

Als uw bestemming niet in de index van plaatsen voorkomt, of als u alleen een vaag idee heeft van het gebied dat u wilt bezoeken, kunt u eveneens de kleurenkaarten raadplegen. De kaarten bevatten alle plaatsnamen waaronder een park in het gidsje wordt vermeld. Voor de precieze locatie dient u de routebeschrijvingen bij iedere vermelding te raadplegen. Heeft u moeite met het vinden van een bepaald park, dan raden wij u aan in de buurt om verdere aanwijzingen te vragen.

 De hiernaast vertoonde internationale verkeersborden worden in Groot-Brittannië gebruikt en zijn speciaal ontworpen voor het gebruik van de parkbezoekers en kampeerders. Ze zijn nog niet bij alle parken opgesteld en vermelden niet de naam van een park of camping. Ze duiden echter wel aan of het park geschikt is voor caravans, tenten of beide.

Het Internationale Kampeerkarnet wordt maar weinig in Groot-Brittannië erkend, behalve op terreinen die beheerd worden door de grote clubs.

Campings bij Londen

Londen is een grote trekpleister voor toeristen en daarom raken de campings en caravanterreinen in de streek van Greater London erg snel vol en boeking ver van tevoren is daarom noodzakelijk. Bij de meeste aankomsthavens zijn ook campings te vinden en de meeste worden vermeld in deze gids en aangeduid op de kaarten voorin.

Hulp bij het vinden van een park

De Toeristische Informatiecentra over heel Groot-Brittannië (zie aan het einde van deze gids) kunnen kampeerders en caravaneigenaars informatie verschaffen over lokale parken en terreinen. Een aantal Toeristische Informatiecentra biedt ook een adviesdienst, die inlichtingen kan geven over mogelijke plaats op campings en vaak kan helpen met het maken van een reservering.

VERMIJDING VAN PROBLEMEN IN HET HOOGSEIZOEN

In de zomermaanden juni t/m september kunnen parken in populaire gebieden, zoals Noord-Wales, Cumbria, de West Country en het New Forest in Hampshire bijzonder vol raken. Bezoekers moeten proberen zo vroeg mogelijk op de dag bij het park aan te komen, of nog beter, van tevoren boeken. Een aantal parken heeft een speciaal terrein voor bezoekers die laat in de avond arriveren. Dit is om te voorkomen dat andere bezoekers in hun slaap gestoord worden en minder kampeerders weggestuurd worden. De volgende morgen worden de caravans en tenten dan een juiste plek gegeven.

ANDERE MOGELIJKHEDEN VOOR CARAVANS EN TENTEN

Als u ervan houdt om door landelijke streken in Groot-Brittanië te trekken, vindt u het misschien interessant te weten, dat de Forestry Commission (staatsbosbeheer) bos-kampeerterreinen in zeven van Groot-Brittanië's Forest Parks en het New Forest beheert. Sommige bieden gereduceerde tarieven voor jeugdorganisaties op georganiseerde kampeertochten, en alle inlichtingen hierover moeten ver van tevoren ingewonnen worden bij de Forestry Commission.

JEUGDHERBERGEN EN ANDERE BUDGETACCOMMODATIE

Hoewel de meeste accommodatie in deze gids geschikt is voor mensen die een relatief goedkope overnachtingsgelegenheid zoeken, zijn er een aantal die zich speciaal toeleggen op het bieden van veilige, goedkope accommodatie voor jongeren, gezinnen of grotere groepen. Hieronder vallen onafhankelijke herbergen, Jeugdherbergen, zgn. bunkhouses en kampeerschuren.

'Bunkhouses' bieden dezelfde soort accommodatie als een jeugdherberg, maar meestal met minder diensten en faciliteiten, en meestal moet men zelf koken.

Kampeerschuren bieden zeer eenvoudige accommodatie met zelf koken. Ze worden vaak 'stenen tenten' genoemd, en zijn ruim en droog. Dit zijn meestal niet meer in gebruik zijnde dit zijn meestal niet meer in gebruik zijnde boerengebouwen die zijn verbouwd tot simpele logies voor een groep tot 15 personen, tegen redelijke prijs. De faciliteiten zijn eenvoudig: u kunt er slapen, eten, en eten bereiden, er is koud stromend water en een doortrek w.c. De Jeugherberg Vereniging heeft een heel netwerk van kampeerschuren, van de Forest of Bowland in Lancashire tot en met Durham en Noord-Yorkshire. Meer informatie bij de
YHA, Trevelyan House,
Dimple Road, Matlock, Derbyshire DE4 2YH
Tel: (017687) 72645
(voor kampeerschuren in het Lake District)
Tel: (01200) 420102
(voor kampeerschuren in alle andere regio's)
www.yha.org.uk

HUISDIEREN

Op veel parken zijn honden toegestaan, maar we raden u aan voor het reserveren na te vragen of dit het geval is, of er een extra tarief wordt geheven, en waar uw hond precies is toegestaan. Als er honden worden toegelaten, wil dit niet altijd zeggen dat ook katten toegestaan zijn, en we raden u ten sterkste aan van te voren contact op te nemen met het etablissement als u uw kat mee wilt nemen. Op sommige parken zijn huisdieren in het geheel niet toegestaan. Honden zijn toegestaan als u dit symbool ziet 🐾.

Uw huisdier meenemen op vakantie in Groot-Brittannië

De quarantainewetten zijn gewijzigd in Engeland, en er is op dit moment een zgn. Pet Travel Scheme van toepassing. Onder dit systeem kunnen honden en katten uit meer dan 50 landen Engeland binnen via bepaalde zee-, lucht- en treinroutes.

Honden en katten die langer dan zes maanden in die landen hebben vertoefd mogen Groot-Brittannië binnen mits de eigenaar de juiste documentatie bij zich heeft voor de dieren. Voor honden en katten uit andere landen blijft de oude regeling geldig: zij moeten 6 maanden in quarantaine.

Als u zonder quarantaine een hond of kat mee wilt nemen naar Groot-Brittannië, onder het PETS-systeem, dan moet het dier aan bepaalde voorwaarden voldoen en u over de volgende documentatie beschikken: het officiële PETS-certificaat, een certificaat van behandeling tegen lintworm en teken, en een verklaring van verblijf.

Op 3 juli 2004 treedt een nieuwe Europese Richtlijn over het transport van huisdieren in werking. Het komt erop neer dat de voorschriften wat betreft huisdieren nog steeds van toepassing zijn op honden en katten die GB betreden, maar nu ook uitgebreid zullen worden naar bepaalde andere huisdieren.

Neem voor meer informatie over deelnemende landen, toegestane routes, reisoperators andere details van het PETS-systeem en de nieuwe EU-voorschriften contact op met de PETS-lijn, DEFRA (Department for Environment, Food and Rural Affairs), 1a Page Street, Londen, SW1P 4PQ, Engeland. Tel: +44 (0) 870 241 1710, fax: +44 (0) 20 7904 6834. E-mail: pets.helpline@defra.gsi.gov.uk, of bezoek hun website op www.defra.gov.uk/animalh/quarantine

DRUGSWAARSCHUWING VOOR INKOMENDE TOERISTEN

In het Vereningd Koninkrijk staan er zware straffen op het illegaal invoeren van drugs. Drugshandelaars proberen onschuldige reizigers te misleiden en wij raden u daarom aan alle betrokkenheid met drugs te vermijden. Draag nooit pakjes of bagage door de douane die niet van uzelf zijn.

WETTELIJKE BEPALINGEN

De allerbeste bron van wettelijk advies voor automobilisten is een Club voor Automobilisten (b.v. ANWB). Wat de kampeerder of caravaneigenaar nog meer moet weten is betrekkelijk eenvoudig. Als u een caravan of kampeerwagentje achter de auto heeft, mag u niet meer dan 96 km (60 mijl) per uur rijden op tweebaanswegen of snelwegen, 80 km (50 mijl) per uur op eenbaanswegen, en op snelweg met drie banen aan elke kant mag u niet in de derde (snelste) baan. Kooktoestellen mogen niet bij een wegrestaurant met benzinestation aangestoken worden.

In de meeste steden is parkeren beperkt, zowel door wettelijke bepalingen als uit praktische overwegingen. Auto's met aanhangende caravans mogen niet parkeren bij een parkeermeter en vele stadsparkeerterreinen zijn alleen geschikt voor auto's zonder aanhangende caravans of kampeerwagentjes.

's Nachts moet een kampeerwagen, of een auto verbonden met een aanhangwagen, die aan de weg geparkeerd staat, zowel z'n twee voorlichten als z'n achterlichten aanhebben, terwijl een auto alleen dit niet hoeft.

De remmen, lampen, het gewicht, etc. van buitenlandse voertuigen hoeven niet te voldoen aan de Britse technische voorschriten. Hoe dan ook, een aanhangwagen mag de Britse wettelijke afmetingsbepalingen - 7m lang en 2,3m breed - niet overschrijden. Ze moeten het internationale kenteken (NL of B) voeren en niet overnachten in de berm of op de parkeerhavens, daar deze wettelijk onderdeel uitmaken van de weg.

Tenslotte is het ook heel belangrijk van tevoren uit te vinden hoe laat u op de dag van vertrek moet opbreken. U moet zich daar aan houden, anders kan men u een extra dag in rekening brengen.

ADVIES AAN BEZOEKERS

VisitBritain stelt er prijs op uw op- of aanmerkingen op uw verblijf in Groot-Brittannië te vernemen. wij hopen dat u geen reden tot klagen heeft, maar mocht dit toch het geval zijn, raden wij u dringend aan om uw klacht onmiddellijk kenbaar te maken aan de leiding van het desbetreffende park, de winkel of vervoersmaatschappij. Indien u hieruit geen genoegdoening verkrijgt, laat u ons dit dan weten, zodat wij zelf een onderzoek kunnen instellen, of u kunnen adviseren over eventuele verder te nemen stappen.

U mag het geeft niet hoeveel geld, en in welke munteenheid dan ook, meenemen en er bestaan geen beperkingen op het aantal inwisselbare reischeques. Als u geld wilt wisselen als de banken gesloten zijn, kunt u dit doen bij de grotere hotels, reisbureaus en warenhuizen of bij onafhankelijke wisselkantoren. Controleer vooral van tevoren de berekende wisselkoers en commissietarieven.

Alle grote winkels, warenhuizen, en de meeste hotels en restaurants accepteren de gebruikelijke, internationaal erkende credit cards. Als u ook graag op markten winkelt, koop dan alleen op grote, erkende markten, en bekijk de artikelen eerst zorgvuldig.

Vraag altijd wat de prijs is voor u tot de aankoop overgaat. Pas op voor zakkenrollers in drukke menigten.

Indien u bestolen bent, of betrokken bent bij een ongeval of brand, bel dan 999 (waarvoor geen geld nodig is) en vraag om de 'police' (politie), 'ambulance service' (ambulance) of de 'fire brigade' (brandweer).

VisitBritain heeft alle pogingen in het werk gesteld om deze publicatie bij het ter perse gaan van nauwkeurigheid te verzekeren. De informatie werd in goed vertrouwen verstrekt, gebaseerd op inlichtingen gegeven aan VisitBritain door de organisatoren van de vermelde caravanparken en campings. VisitBritain kan echter niet garanderen dat deze informatie correct is en kan geen verantwoording aanvaarden voor foute of onjuiste voorstellingen. VisitBritain kan beslist niet verantwoordelijk worden gesteld voor verlies, teleurstelling, nalatigheid of enige andere schade die voortvloeit uit het vertrouwen in de informatie in deze gids, of problemen voortkomend uit het faillisement of liquidatie van enige vermelde maatschappij, individu of bedrijf, of indien een maatschappij, individu of bedrijf ophoudt handel te drijven. Het is daarom raadzaam de gegeven informatie bij het maken van een reservering goed te controleren.

Alle parken in deze gids houden zich aan de richtlijnen van VisitBritain. Een lijst van de aan de campings en caravanparken gestelde eisen kunt u vinden op pagina 227.

All genoemde instellingen in het gedeelte in kleur hebben betaald voor hun vermelding in deze gids.

BRITISH HOLIDAY AND HOME PARKS ASSOCIATION

The Association represents commercial operators of all kinds throughout Britain. Its aim is to ensure a high standard of excellence in members' parks for the satisfaction of the visitor.

Parks listed in this Guide all conform to the standards set by the British Tourist Authority but BH&HPA Members' Parks, which are identified in the Guide by (BH&HPA), must also abide by the BH&HPA Code of Conduct. This gives the visitor an assurance of a high standard of facilities and reliability.

The BH&HPA works with the British Tourist Authority, English Tourism Council, and the national and regional tourist boards to safeguard tourist interests. It also works with Government and local government authorities to ensure that all aspects of legislation and control are applied and that proper safety measures are carried out for the comfort and protection of the visitor.

The BH&HPA will investigate problems encountered by visitors and can provide details of self-catering holidays and residential parks.

Contact:
British Holiday and Home Parks Association Ltd, Chichester House, 6 Pullman Court, Great Western Road, Gloucester GL1 3ND
Telephone: (01452) 526911
Fax: (01452) 508508

Come usare questa Guida

I campeggi elencati in questa guida sono per la maggior parte aperti sia alle roulottes che alle tende e molti di essi accolgono anche i camper e le motorhome. Molti campeggi dispongono anche di roulottes a noleggio.

STANDARD DI GARANZIA DI QUALITÀ

Per chi va in cerca di un posto dove soggiornare, è necessario un sistema di classificazione affidabile. Il programma britannico di classificazione dei parchi vacanze (British Graded Holiday Parks Scheme) del 2000 offre una guida chiara e comprensibile su ciò che ci si può aspettare. Il programma è sempre imperniato sulla qualità e rispecchia le aspettative del cliente.

VisitBritain utilizza ora delle stelle per illustrare le categorie dei parchi partecipanti al programma. I parchi vengono ispezionati annualmente da funzionari competenti e imparziali, che assegnano una classificazione da una a cinque stelle, basandosi sulla pulizia, sull'ambiente e sulla qualità delle strutture e dei servizi offerti.

Inoltre, i parchi vengono ora contrassegnati da un simbolo, in modo che se ne possa identificare immediatamente il tipo - ad esempio Parco Vacanze, Parco Turistico o Campeggio. (L'assenza di classifica o contrassegno significa che il parco in oggetto non è stato ancora valutato al momento di andare in stampa).

Il programma di classificazione è stato ideato congiuntamente dagli enti nazionali per il turismo dell'Inghilterra, dell'Irlanda del Nord, della Scozia e del Galles in collaborazione con l'associazione britannica dei parchi per roulotte e vacanze (British Holiday & Home Parks Association) (vedere a pagina 43) e con l'organo nazionale per le roulotte (National Caravan Council) (vedere a pagina 47).

STRUTTURE

Le strutture vengono indicate per mezzo di simboli, comprensibili a prima vista, spiegati qui di seguito.

PREZZI

I prezzi indicati per i posteggi sono il prezzo minimo e il prezzo massimo di un pernottamento per 2 persone, un'automobile e una tenda o una roulotte. I campeggi britannici preferiscono in genere includere tutto in un solo prezzo, benché in alcuni vi siano prezzi separati per automobili, roulottes o tende e per ogni persona. In alcuni campeggi possono essere richiesti supplementi per i tendoni delle roulottes. I prezzi minimi e massimi delle roulottes a noleggio sono i prezzi per settimana. I prezzi indicati sono quelli forniti dagli esercenti dei campeggi in questione e sono un'indicazione dei prezzi che verranno praticati per il periodo di validità di questa pubblicazione. I prezzi indicati sono in sterline (£) e pence (p). L'IVA (Imposta sul Valore Aggiunto) al 17,5% è compresa nei prezzi indicati. Per evitare qualsiasi equivoco, si consiglia vivamente di controllare i prezzi al momento di effettuare la prenotazione.

SPIEGAZIONE DEI SIMBOLI

BH& British Holiday &
HPA Home Parks Association (v. pagina 43)
NCC National Caravan Council (v. pagina 47)
- Roulottes ammesse (con numero di posteggi e prezzi)
- Camper/motorhome ammessi (con numero di posteggi e prezzi) In alcuni casi il numero di posteggi per camper/motorhome è compreso nel numero di posteggi per roulottes
- **Å** Tende ammesse
- Numero di roulottes a noleggio (v. posteggi per roulottes a noleggio a seguito)
- Bungalow/chalet/casette a noleggio
- Zona di pernottamento temporaneo
- Allacciamento elettrico per roulottes (v. Alimentazione elettrica: prese di allacciamento per roulottes)
- Docce
- WC a trattamento chimico
- Allacciamento alla fognatura per camper/motorhome
- Cambio di bombole di gas butano o propano
- Negozio/negozio ambulante di alimentari
- **✕** Bar/ristorante
- **♀** Bar
- **TV** Salone con televisione a colori
- Telefono pubblico
- Lavanderia sul posto
- Attrezzature per asciugare la biancheria
- Sala giochi
- Locazione biciclette
- Piscina riscaldata al coperto sul posto
- Piscina all'aperto sul posto
- **U** Equitazione/escursioni a dorso di pony partendo dal campeggio
- Tennis sul posto
- Pesca sul posto o nelle vicinanze
- Golf sul posto o nelle vicinanze
- Si accettano animali domestici
- **♫** Spettacoli/intrattenimenti serali

PRENOTAZIONE

Nel richiedere informazioni sulle possibilità di sistemazione, è necessario, oltre a controllare il prezzo, illustrare chiaramente le proprie esigenze, per esempio:

- date di arrivo e partenza, e se possibile date alternative;
- tipo di sistemazione richiesto;
- qualsiasi particolare esigenza.

Quando si prenota per telefono c'è sempre il rischio di errori. Tempo permettendo, si consiglia dunque di confermare sempre le prenotazioni per iscritto. Ricordarsi di indicare il proprio nome e indirizzo e di accludere, per ogni risposta, una busta preindirizzata e preaffrancata o un buono internazionale per riposta pagata.

Anticipi

Per la prenotazione di posti nei campeggi per tende, roulottes e chalets, il prezzo intero va normalmente versato in anticipo. Il versamento può normalmente essere effettuato in due rate: un anticipo al momento della prenotazione e il saldo circa due settimane prima dell'inizio del periodo prenotato.

Annullamenti

Nel Regno Unito, l'accettazione di un alloggio offerto, sia per iscritto che per telefono, equivale per legge alla firma di un contratto vincolante tra l'inquilino e il proprietario dell'alloggio. Ciò significa che se l'inquilino annulla la propria prenotazione, non prende domicilio o parte prima del previsto (per qualsiasi ragione), il proprietario potrebbe avere diritto a un risarcimento qualora non riuscisse a riaffittare l'alloggio per tutto o parte del periodo prenotato. Se è stato versato un anticipo, è probabile che venga ritenuto dal proprietario, il quale potrebbe anche esigere un ulteriore addebito.

È consigliabile dunque avvisare immediatamente il proprietario sia di qualsiasi cambiamento di itinerario, sia dell'intenzione di annullare una prenotazione o di partire prima del previsto.

Prese di allacciamento elettrico:

I campeggi dispongono per la maggior parte di prese di allacciamento alla rete di distribuzione dell'energia elettrica adoperabili sia per la roulottes che per le tende. La tensione è di 240V circa e 50Hz, benché in alcuni casi possa ancora variare tra 200V e 250V. In alcuni campeggi potrebbe essere necessario un adattatore per l'allacciamento. La fornitura di energia elettrica è normalmente soggetta ad un addebito supplementare e si consiglia di controllare le tariffe al momento della prenotazione.

COME TROVARE IL CAMPEGGIO PRESCELTO

I campeggi in questa guida sono raggruppati per regione in Inghilterra, seguiti dalle liste relative a Scozia e Galles, e sono stati elencati in ordine alfabetico sotto il nome della città in cui si trovano, o vicino a cui si trovano. L'Indice delle Città a pagina 249 e le Mappe a colori all'inizio della guida riportano tutte le città, i centri e i villaggi che hanno

un campeggio elencato in questa guida. Usate questi riferimenti per trovare in un modo facile e veloce un alloggio adatto. Se sapete in quale campeggio volete stare, controllate l'Indice dei Campeggi a pagina 246.

Se il luogo dove volete stare è compreso nell'indice delle città, andate alla pagina indicata per trovarvi i campeggi disponibili. I nomi delle città appaiono in nero sulla mappa all'inizio della guida nel modo in cui sono stati indicati dal riferimento alla mappa nella voce relativa. Controllate anche le mappe a colori per trovarvi altri luoghi vicini che hanno anche dei campeggi elencati in questa guida.

Se il luogo dove volete stare non si trova nell'indice delle città – o avete solo un'idea generale della zona in cui volete stare – usate le cartine a colori.

Le cartine illustrano tutti i nomi delle località in cui viene elencato un campeggio nella guida. Per trovare la località precisa leggete le indicazioni di ogni voce. In caso di difficoltà è consigliabile chiedere indicazioni a qualcuno nelle vicinanze del campeggio.

 I segnali internazionali indicati qui vengono usati in Gran Bretagna per aiutare i visitatori a trovare i campeggi. Non sono ancora stati installati per tutti i campeggi e non indicano il nome di nessun campeggio. Indicano però se il campeggio è per tende, roulottes o ambedue.

Il carnet internazionale del campeggiatore è raramente riconosciuto in Gran Bretagna, salvo nei campeggi organizzati dai principali club.

Campeggi di Londra

Londra rappresenta una grande attrazione per molti visitatori, per cui i campeggi per tende e roulotte nell'area della Greater London tendono a riempirsi molto rapidamente, e bisogna prenotare molto in anticipo.

Sono anche disponibili campeggi presso la maggior parte dei porti d'entrata nel paese, e molti di questi sono elencati in questa guida e indicati sulla mappa all'inizio.

Servizi di ricerca campeggi

I Tourist Information Centre di tutta la Gran Bretagna (v. pagine finali) possono fornire ai campeggiatori informazioni sui campeggi nelle loro zone di responsabilità. Alcuni Tourist Information Centre offrono servizi di ricerca campeggi che forniscono informazioni sulla disponibilità di posteggi e spesso aiutano a effettuare le prenotazioni.

COME EVITARE I PROBLEMI DELL'ALTA STAGIONE

Nei mesi estivi, da giugno a settembre, i campeggi nelle zone più frequentate del paese: Galles settentrionale, Cumbria, Inghilterra sud-occidentale e la New Forest nel Hampshire, registrano molto presto il tutto esaurito.

Si consiglia ai campeggiatori di arrivare presto o, se possibile, di prenotare in anticipo. Alcuni campeggi dispongono di zone di pernottamento temporaneo per i campeggiatori che arrivano tardi. Queste zone di pernottamento consentono di non disturbare gli altri campeggiatori durante la notte e di accogliere un maggior numero di nuovi arrivati, i quali vengono condotti a uno dei posti liberi la mattina seguente.

ALTRI LUOGHI DI CAMPEGGIO

A chi preferisce seguire il proprio itinerario attraverso la campagna britannica potrebbe interessare sapere che la Forestry Commission gestisce dei campeggi forestali nei sette parchi forestali del paese e nella New Forest. Alcuni offrono tariffe ridotte a gruppi organizzati di giovani in campeggio. Tutte le richieste d'informazioni vanno indirizzate direttamente alla Forestry Commission con qualche mese di anticipo sulla data di arrivo.

ALLOGGIO IN ALBERGO

Anche se la maggior parte degli alloggi in questa guida è adatta a persone che cercano posti dove stare relativamente economici, alcuni ci tengono molto a fornire un alloggio sicuro ed economico ai giovani, alle famiglie o ai gruppi più numerosi. Gli alloggi in ostello comprendono ostelli di proprietà indipendente, Ostelli della Gioventù, dormitori e granai per campeggiatori.

I dormitori (bunkhouses) offrono un tipo di alloggio simile agli Ostelli, ma di solito con servizi e strutture più limitate, di solito su una base di alloggio indipendente.

I granai da campeggio (camping barns) forniscono un alloggio indipendente molto semplice, e vengono spesso chiamati "tende di pietra", ma, rispetto alle tende, hanno il vantaggio di essere spaziosi e asciutti.

Sono spesso degli edifici agricoli inutilizzati e trasformati in semplici alloggi per un massimo di 15 visitatori a prezzi ragionevoli. Le strutture sono le minime indispensabili: un posto per dormire, mangiare e cucinare, acqua corrente fredda e WC.

La Youth Hostel Association dispone di una rete di granai da campeggio che copre la zona tra Forest Bowland nel Lancashire, Durham e lo Yorkshire settentrionale. Per ulteriori informazioni, anche sulle modalità di prenotazione, rivolgersi a:
YHA, Trevelyan House,
Dimple Road, Matlock, Derbyshire DE4 2YH
Tel: (017687) 72645 (granai del Lake District)
Tel: (01200) 420102 (granai di utte le altre zone).

ANIMALI DOMESTICI

Molti campeggi accettano ospiti con cani, ma si consiglia di controllare al momento della prenotazione e di chiedere se è necessario versare un supplemento o se esistono delle regole particolari per l'ammissione degli animali domestici. Spesso anche se sono ammessi i cani, non è consentito portare gatti; è consigliabile per i proprietari di gatti contattare l'esercizio in anticipo. Gli esercizi che accettano animali domestici sono contrassegnati dal simbolo ⊓.

Ingresso degli animali domestici in Gran Bretagna

In Inghilterra la normativa sulla quarantena è stata modificata; attualmente è in vigore PETS, un programma per l'ingresso degli animali domestici, che consente l'ingresso in Gran Bretagna dei cani e dei gatti provenienti da oltre 50 paesi diversi attraverso determinati itinerari in nave, aereo e treno.

L'ingresso nel Regno Unito dei cani e dei gatti residenti da oltre 6 mesi in questi paesi è consentito ai sensi del Programma, a condizione che gli animali siano accompagnati dalla relativa documentazione. I cani e i gatti provenienti da altri paesi continueranno a essere soggetti a una quarantena di 6 mesi.

Per entrare nel Regno Unito senza quarantena ai sensi del programma PETS, i cani e i gatti devono rispondere a determinate condizioni e viaggiare con i seguenti documenti: Certificato ufficiale PETS, un certificato di cura contro tenia e zecche e dichiarazione di residenza.

Il 3 luglio 2004 entrerà in vigore un nuovo regolamento comunitario sullo spostamento degli animali domestici. Essenzialmente le regole PETS rimarranno in vigore per i cani e i gatti portati nel Regno Unito ma saranno compresi anche vari altri tipi di animali domestici.

Per particolari sui paesi partecipanti, gli itinerari, gli operatori e altre informazioni sul programma PETS e sulle nuove norme comunitarie, rivolgersi a:
PETS Helpline, DEFRA (Department for Environment, Food and Rural Affaris),
1a Page Street, London SW1P 4PQ
Tel: +44 (0) 870 241 1710
Fax: +44 (0) 20 7904 6834
Email: pets.helpline@defra.gsi.gov.uk
www.defra.gov.uk./animalh/quarantine

AVVERTIMENTO SUGLI STUPEFACENTI PER I TURISTI IN ARRIVO

Le leggi britanniche sul contrabbando di stupefacenti prevedono delle sanzioni estremamente severe per i trasgressori. I trafficanti di droga tentano a volte di ingannare i viaggiatori. Si consiglia a chiunque abbia deciso di visitare il Regno Unito di evitare qualsiasi coinvolgimento con lo spaccio di stupefacenti e di non attraversare mai la dogana portando le valige o i pacchi di altri viaggiatori.

ASPETTI GIURIDICI

La migliore fonte d'informazioni per gli automobilisti che intendono visitare la Gran Bretagna è l'organizzazione automobilistica del paese di origine. Le regole che deve conoscere l'automobilista campeggiatore sono relativamente semplici.

Le automobili con roulotte o rimorchi al traino non devono superare i 96 chilometri orari (60 miglia all'ora) sulle strade a doppia carreggiata e sulle autostrade, e gli 80 chilometri orari (50 miglia all'ora) sulle strade normali. Sulle autostrade a tre carreggiate in ogni direzione, le roulotte ed i rimorchi non sono ammessi nella terza carreggiata (la più veloce). È vietato accendere fornellini nelle aree di servizio autostradali.

Nella maggior parte delle città, parcheggiare è reso difficile sia dai regolamenti che da difficoltà pratiche. Alle automobili con rimorchio è vietato l'uso di spazi con parchimetri e i posteggi di molti parcheggi cittadini sono intesi per automobili senza rimorchio, sebbene in alcuni di essi vi siano spazi anche per veicoli più lunghi.

Se parcheggiati sulla strada di notte, i rimorchi, o le automobili attaccate ai rimorchi, devono avere due luci anteriori e due luci posteriori accese, anche dove l'automobile senza il rimorchio sarebbe esonerata da quest'obbligo.

I freni, le luci, il peso ecc. dei veicoli provenienti dall'estero devono soddisfare i criteri tecnici delle norme britanniche. I rimorchi tuttavia non devono superare i limiti britannici, che sono: 7 metri di lunghezza e 2,3 metri di larghezza. I rimorchi devono recare il numero di targa del paese di provenienza. È vietato sostare di notte sui lati erbosi o nelle piazzole di sosta delle strade, dato che queste zone sono per legge considerate parti della strada.

Per concludere, è importante sapere l'ora entro la quale si è obbligati a liberare il posteggio nel giorno previsto per la partenza. Si consiglia di partire presto la mattina per evitare di dover pagare il prezzo di una giornata in più.

CONSIGLI PER I VISITATORI

VisitBritain è sempre lieta di ricevere i commenti e le osservazioni dei turisti su qualsiasi aspetto del loro soggiorno in Gran Bretagna, che siano o meno favorevoli. Ci auguriamo che chiunque visiti il nostro paese non abbia mai occasione di lamentarsi. Se vi fosse ragione di lamentarsi, il consiglio è di rivolgersi in primo luogo alla gestione del campeggio, negozio o società di trasporti. Qualora la risposta non sia soddisfacente, consigliamo ai turisti di rivolgersi a VisitBritain che prenderà in esame la questione o suggerirà le misure da prendere.

Si possono portare in Gran Bretagna valute di qualsiasi denominazione senza limiti di quantità. Si può cambiare anche qualsiasi numero di traveller's cheque. Per cambiare le valute straniere durante le ore di chiusura delle banche ci si può rivolgere alle ricezioni di alcuni grandi alberghi, alle agenzie di viaggio, alle agenzie di cambiavalute indipendenti. Raccomandiamo di controllare il tasso e la commissione di cambio prima di cambiare i soldi.

Tutti i grandi negozi, i grandi magazzini la maggior parte degli alberghi e dei ristoranti accettano le carte di credito normalmente riconosciute nel mondo. A chi decida di fare spese nei mercati consigliamo di comprare solo in quelli grandi e riconosciuti e di esaminare accuratamente gli articoli prima di acquistarli.Consigliamo di chiedere sempre il prezzo dei beni e dei servizi prima di impegnarsi all'acquisto e di fare attenzione ai borsaioli nei luoghi affollati.

Chiunque sia vittima di un furto, o coinvolto in un incidente o un incendio può telefonare al 999 (chiamata gratuita) e chiedere la polizia, il servizio ambulanze o i vigili del fuoco.

VisitBritain ha fatto del tutto per garantire l'esattezza delle informazioni contenute in questa pubblicazione al momento di andare in stampa. Le informazioni vengono date in buona fede in base ai dati forniti a VisitBritain dai promotori del campeggi elencati. VisitBritain tuttavia non può né garantire l'esattezza delle informazioni né assumersi la responsabilltà di qualsiasi errore o falsità. È esclusa tutta la responsabilità di perdite, delusioni, negligenza o di altri danni che risultino dall'aver fatto affidamento sulle informazioni contenute in questa guida o dal fallimento o dalla liquidazione di qualsiasi società, individuo o ditta, o dalla cessazione delle attività di qualsiasi società, individuo o ditta. Si consiglia di verificare l'esattezza delle informazioni al momento di effettuare la prenotazione.

Tutti i parchi elencati in questa guida sono conformi agli Standard di VisitBritain. A pagina 227 riportiamo un elenco di queste norme applicabili ai campeggi per tende e roulottes.

Tutti i campeggi elencati nella seqione a colori hanno pagato per la loro inserzione nella guida.

THE NATIONAL CARAVAN COUNCIL

The National Caravan Council is the trade body for the British caravan industry - touring caravans, motorhomes and caravan holiday homes.

The Council operates an approval system for caravans, certifying that they are manufactured in accordance with the relevant European Standard. All Dealer and Park Operator members, which are identified in the Guide by (NCC), agree to comply with Conditions of Membership which require them to provide their customers with a high standard of service.

The Council works closely with the VisitBritain, national and regional tourist organisations to promote tourism and particularly to promote the important role which all kinds of caravans play in providing tourists with modern facilities to enjoy the outdoors.

Full information on its members and its activities together with assistance on any difficulties encountered can be obtained from:

The National Caravan Council,
Catherine House, Victoria Road, Aldershot,
Hampshire GU11 1SS.
Telephone: (01252) 318251
Fax: (01252) 322596
E-mail: info@nationalcaravan.co.uk
Internet: www.thecaravan.net

Caravan Holiday Home Award Scheme

Rose Award,
VisitBritain,
Thames Tower, Black's Road,
Hammersmith, London W6 9EL

Thistle Award,
VisitScotland,
Thistle House, Beechwood Park
North, Inverness IV2 3ED

Dragon & Daffodil Awards,
Wales Tourist Board,
Brunel House, 2 Fitzalan Road,
Cardiff CF24 0UY

VisitBritain and the national tourist boards for Scotland and Wales run similar Award schemes for holiday caravan homes on highly graded caravan parks. They recognise high standards of caravan accommodation and enable you to step into a comfortable, fully furnished holiday home set amongst landscaped surroundings with all the amenities you could wish for.

All the caravan parks included in the Award scheme have been inspected and meet the criteria demanded by the scheme. In addition to complying with joint tourist board standards for 'Holiday Caravan Parks and Caravan Holiday Homes' all Award caravans must have a shower or bath, toilet, mains electricity and water heating (at no extra charge) and a refrigerator (many also have a colour television).

A complete list of the parks in each country, plus further information about them, can be obtained free from the national tourist boards (see page 238). Look out for these plaques displayed by all Award winning parks, and by each caravan which meets the required standards. Many parks listed in this guide are participating in these schemes and are indicated accordingly.

VisitBritain's Where to Stay Camping and Caravan Parks in Britain 2004

Published by: VisitBritain, Thames Tower, Black's Road, Hammersmith, London W6 9EL

Publishing Manager: Michael Dewing

Production Manager: Iris Buckley

Compilation, Design & Production: Jackson Lowe Marketing, www.jacksonlowe.com

Typesetting: Tradespools Ltd, Somerset and Jackson Lowe Marketing, Lewes

Maps: © Maps in Minutes™ (1999)

Printing and Binding: Mozzon Giuntina S.p.A, Florence and Officine Grafiche De Agostini S.p.A, Novara

Advertisement Sales: Jackson Lowe Marketing, 173 High Street, Lewes, East Sussex BN7 1YE.

(01273) 487487

©**VisitBritain** (except where stated)

ISBN 0 7095 7756 7 Distribution Code: C4CACEN

London

A dynamic mix of history and heritage, cool and contemporary. Great museums, stunning art collections, royal palaces, hip nightlife and stylish shopping, from ritzy Bond Street to cutting-edge Hoxton.

Classic sights
St Paul's Cathedral – Wren's famous church
Tower of London – 900 years of British history
London Eye – spectacular views from the world's highest 'big wheel'

Arts for all
National Gallery – Botticelli, Rembrandt, Turner and more
Tate Modern – 20thC art in a former power station
Victoria & Albert Museum – decorative arts

City lights
Theatre: Musicals – West End;
drama – Royal Court and National Theatre;
Music: Classical – Wigmore Hall and Royal Festival Hall;
jazz – Ronnie Scott's;
Ballet & Opera – Royal Opera House

Insider London
Dennis Severs's House, E1 – candlelit tours of this authentically 18thC house

Greater London, comprising the 32 London Boroughs

For more information contact:
Visit London
1 Warwick Row,
London SW1E 5ER

www.visitlondon.com

Telephone enquiries -
see London Line on page 54

1. Piccadilly Circus
2. Millennium Bridge across River Thames and St Paul's

Places to **Visit**

You will find hundreds of interesting places to visit during your stay, just some of which are listed in these pages. Contact any Tourist Information Centre in and around London for more ideas on days out.

Awarded VisitBritain's 'Quality Assured Visitor Attraction' marque.

British Airways London Eye
Jubilee Gardens, South Bank, SE1 7PB
Tel: 0870 5000600 www.ba-londoneye.com
The British Airways London eye is the world's largest observation wheel. Take in over 55 of London's most famous landmarks in just 30 minutes!

British Museum
Great Russell Street, WC1B 3DG
Tel: (020) 7323 8000
www.thebritishmuseum.ac.uk
One of the great museums of the world, showing the works of man from prehistoric to modern times with collections drawn from the whole world.

Cabinet War Rooms
Clive Steps, King Charles Street, SW1A 2AQ
Tel: (020) 7930 6961 www.iwm.org.uk
The underground headquarters used by Winston Churchill and the British Government during World War II. Includes Cabinet Room, Transatlantic Telephone Room and Map Room.

Chessington World of Adventures
Leatherhead Road, Chessington, KT9 2NE
Tel: (01372) 729560 www.chessington.com
Fun family adventures include the 'fang-tastic' New Vampire ride, Tomb Blaster, an action packed adventure ride, and a mischievous new attraction in Beanoland.

Design Museum
28 Shad Thames, SE1 2YD
Tel: (020) 7403 6933 www.designmuseum.org
The world's leading museum of industrial design, fashion and architecture. Its exhibition programme captures the excitement and ingenuity of design's evolution.

Hampton Court Palace
Hampton Court, East Molesey, KT8 9AU
Tel: (020) 8781 9500 www.hrp.org.uk
The oldest Tudor palace in England with many attractions including the Tudor kitchens, tennis courts, maze and State Apartments and King's Apartments.

HMS Belfast
Morgan's Lane, Tooley Street, SE1 2JH
Tel: (020) 7940 6300 www.iwm.org.uk
World War II cruiser weighing 11,500 tonnes, now a floating naval museum, with 9 decks to explore, from the Captain's Bridge to the Boiler and Engine rooms.

Imperial War Museum
Lambeth Road, SE1 6HZ
Tel: (020) 7416 5320 www.iwm.org.uk
Museum tells the story of 20thC war from Flanders to Bosnia. Special features include the Blitz Experience, the Trench Experience and the world of Espionage.

Kensington Palace State Apartments
Kensington Gardens, W8 4PX
Tel: 0870 7515180 www.hrp.org.uk
Furniture and ceiling paintings from Stuart-Hanoverian periods, rooms from Victorian era and works of art from the Royal Collection. Also Royal Ceremonial Dress Collection.

Kew Gardens (Royal Botanic Gardens)
Richmond, TW9 3AB
Tel: (020) 8332 5655 www.kew.org
300 acres (120ha) containing living collections of over 40,000 varieties of plants. Seven spectacular glasshouses, 2 art galleries, Japanese and rock garden.

London Aquarium
County Hall, Riverside Building, SE1 7PB
Tel: (020) 7967 8000
www.londonaquarium.co.uk
Dive down deep beneath the Thames and submerge yourself in one of Europe's largest displays of aquatic life from sharks and piranhas to seahorses and starfish.

London Planetarium
Marylebone Road, NW1 5LR
Tel: 0870 4003000
www.london-planetarium.com
Visitors can experience a virtual reality trip through space and find out about Black Holes and extra terrestrials in the interactive Space Zones before the show.

London Transport Museum
Covent Garden Piazza, WC2E 7BB
Tel: (020) 7379 6344 www.ltmuseum.co.uk
The history of transport for everyone, from spectacular vehicles, special exhibitions, actors and guided tours to film shows, gallery talks and children's craft workshops.

London Zoo
Regent's Park, NW1 4RY
Tel: (020) 7722 3333 www.londonzoo.co.uk
Escape the stress of city life and visit the amazing animals at the world famous London Zoo. See Asian lions, Sloth bears and the incredible 'Animals in Action'.

Museum of London
150 London Wall, EC2Y 5HN
Tel: (020) 7600 3699
www.museumoflondon.org.uk
Discover over 2000 years of the capital's history, from prehistoric to modern times. Regular temporary exhibitions and lunchtime lecture programmes.

National Gallery
Trafalgar Square, WC2N 5DN
Tel: (020) 7747 2885
www.nationalgallery.org.uk
Gallery displaying Western European painting from about 1250-1900. Includes work by Botticelli, Leonardo da Vinci, Rembrandt, Gainsborough, Turner, Renoir, Cezanne.

National Maritime Museum
Romney Road, SE10 9NF
Tel: (020) 8858 4422 www.nmm.ac.uk
This national museum explains Britain's worldwide influence through its explorers, traders, migrants and naval power. Features on ship models, costume, and ecology of the sea.

National Portrait Gallery
St Martin's Place, WC2H 0HE
Tel: (020) 7306 0055 www.npg.org.uk
Permanent collection of portraits of famous men and women from the Middle Ages to the present day. Free, but charge for some exhibitions.

Natural History Museum
Cromwell Road, SW7 5BD
Tel: (020) 7942 5000 www.nhm.ac.uk
Home of the wonders of the natural world with hundreds of exciting, interactive exhibits. Don't miss 'Dinosaurs', 'Creepy-Crawlies' and the new Darwin Centre.

Royal Mews
Buckingham Palace, SW1A 1AA
Tel: (020) 7321 2233 www.royal.gov.uk
One of the finest working stables in existence, the Royal Mews is responsible for all road travel arrangements for the Queen and Royal Family.

1. The London Eye
2. Buckingham Palace
3. Notting Hill Carnival

Royal Observatory Greenwich
Greenwich Park, SE10 9NF
Tel: (020) 8858 4422 www.nmm.ac.uk
Museum of time and space and site of the
Greenwich Meridian. Working telescopes and
planetarium, timeball, Wren's Octagon Room and
intricate clocks and computer simulations.

St Paul's Cathedral
St Paul's Churchyard, EC4M 8AD
Tel: (020) 7236 4128 www.stpauls.co.uk
Wren's famous cathedral church of the diocese
of London incorporating the Crypt, Ambulatory
and Whispering Gallery.

Science Museum
Exhibition Road, SW7 2DD
Tel: 0870 8704868
www.sciencemuseum.org.uk
See, touch and experience the major scientific
advances of the last 300 years at the largest
Museum of its kind in the world.

Shakespeare's Globe Exhibition and Tour
Bankside, SE1 9DT
Tel: (020) 7902 1500
www.shakespeares-globe.org
Against the historical background of Elizabethan
Bankside, the City of London's playground in
Shakespeare's time, the exhibition focuses on
actors, architecture and audiences.

Tate Britain
Millbank, SW1P 4RG
Tel: (020) 7887 8008 www.tate.org.uk
The world's greatest collection of British art
including work by Constable, Gainsborough,
Hockney, Rossetti and Turner, presented in a
dynamic series of new displays and exhibitions.

Tate Modern
Bankside, SE1 9TG
Tel: (020) 7887 8008 www.tate.org.uk
Houses the Tate Collection of international
modern art from 1900 to the present day,
including major works by Matisse and Picasso
plus contemporary work by Sarah Lucas and
Rachel Whiteread.

Theatre Museum
Russell Street, WC2E 7PA
Tel: (020) 7943 4700 www.theatremuseum.org
Exhibitions, events based on the world's most
exciting performing arts collections, and galleries
brought to life by tour guides, all celebrate
performance in Britain.

Tower Bridge Experience
Tower Bridge, SE1 2UP
Tel: (020) 7403 3761
www.towerbridge.org.uk
Exhibition explaining the history of the bridge and
how it operates. Enjoy the panoramic views from
the Walkway 150ft (45m) above the Thames and
visit the original Engines.

Tower of London
Tower Hill, EC3N 4AB
Tel: 0870 7567070
www.hrp.org.uk

Home of the 'Beefeaters' and
ravens, the building spans 900
years of British history. On
display are the nation's Crown
Jewels, regalia and armoury
robes.

Victoria and Albert Museum
Cromwell Road, SW7 2RL
Tel: (020) 7942 2000 www.vam.ac.uk
Large and varied collections of decorative arts
from 3000BC to the present day. The new British
Galleries explore British art and design from
Tudor times to the Victorian era.

Vinopolis - London's Wine Tasting Visitor Attraction
1 Bank End, SE1 9BU
Tel: 0870 2414040 www.vinopolis.co.uk
Vinopolis is London's Wine Tasting Visitor
Attraction. For anyone who enjoys a glass of
wine it is one of the few attractions where
guests grow merrier as they walk through!

Westminster Abbey
Parliament Square, SW1P 3PA
Tel: (020) 7222 5152
www.westminster-abbey.org
One of Britain's finest Gothic buildings. Scene of
the coronation, marriage and burial of British
monarchs. Nave and cloisters, Royal Chapels and
Undercroft Museum.

Visit London
1 Warwick Row, London SW1E 5ER
www.visitlondon.com

1. Tower Bridge
2. Houses of Paliament
3. Queens Guard

Tourist Information Centres

INNER LONDON

- **Britain and London Visitor Centre,**
  1 Regent Street, Piccadilly Circus, SW1Y 4XT.
  Open: Mon 0930-1830,Tue-Fri 0900-1830, Sat &
  Sun 1000-1600; Jun-Oct, Sat 0900-1700.

- **Greenwich TIC,** Pepys House, 2 Cutty Sark
  Gardens, Greenwich SE10 9LW.
  Tel: 0870 608 2000; Fax: 020 8853 4607.
  Open: Daily 1000-1700.

- **Lewisham TIC,** Lewisham Library,
  199-201 Lewisham High Street, SE13 6LG.
  Tel: 020 8297 8317; Fax: 020 8297 9241.
  Open: Mon 1000-1700, Tue-Fri 0900-1700,
  Sat 1000-1600.

- **London Visitors Centre,** Arrivals Hall,
  Waterloo International Terminal, SE1 7LT.
  Open: Daily 0830-2230.

OUTER LONDON

- **Bexley Hall Place TIC,** Bourne Road,
  Bexley, Kent, DA5 1PQ.
  Tel: 01322 558676; Fax 01322 522921.
  Open: Mon-Sat 1000-1630, Sun 1400-1730.

- **Croydon TIC, Katharine Street,**
  Croydon, CR9 1ET.
  Tel: 020 8253 1009; Fax: 020 8253 1008.
  Open: Mon-Wed & Fri 0900-1800, Thu 0930-
  1800, Sat 0900-1700, Sun 1400-1700.

- **Harrow TIC,** Civic Centre, Station Road,
  Harrow, HA1 2XF.
  Tel: 020 8424 1103; Fax: 020 8424 1134.
  Open: Mon-Fri 0900-1700.

- **Hillingdon TIC,** Central Library,
  14-15 High Street, Uxbridge, UB8 1HD.
  Tel: 01895 250706; Fax: 01895 239794.
  Open: Mon, Tue & Thu 0930-2000,
  Wed 0930-1730, Fri 1000-1730, Sat 0930-1600.

- **Hounslow TIC,** The Treaty Centre, High Street,
  Hounslow, TW3 1ES.
  Tel: 0845 4562929; Fax: 0845 4562904
  Open: Mon, Tues & Thurs 0930-2000;
  Wed, Fri & Sat 0930-1730; Sun 1130-1600.

- **Kingston TIC,** Market House, Market Place,
  Kingston upon Thames, KT1 1JS.
  Tel: 020 8547 5592; Fax: 020 8547 5594.
  Open: Mon-Sat 1000-1700.

- **Richmond TIC,** Old Town Hall,
  Whittaker Avenue; Richmond, TW9 1TP.
  Tel: 020 8940 6899; Fax: 020 8940 6899.
  Open: Mon-Sat 1000-1700;
  May-Sep, Sun 1030-1330.

- **Swanley TIC,** London Road, BR8 7AE.
  Tel: 01322 614660; Fax: 01322 666154.
  Open: Mon-Thu 0930-1730, Fri 0930-1800,
  Sat 0900-1600.

- **Twickenham TIC,** The Atrium, Civic Centre,
  York Street, Twickenham, Middlesex, TW1 3BZ.
  Tel: 020 8891 7272; Fax: 020 8891 7738.
  Open: Mon-Thu 0900-1715, Fri 0900-1700.

INFORMATION PACK
For a London information pack call 0870 240 4326. Calls are charged at national rate.

LONDON LINE
Visit London's recorded telephone information service provides information on museums, galleries, attractions, riverboat trips, sightseeing tours, accommodation, theatre, what's on, changing the Guard, children's London, shopping, eating out and gay and lesbian London.

Available 24 hours a day. Calls cost 60p per minute as at July 2003. Call 09068 663344.

ARTSLINE
London's information and advice service for disabled people on arts and entertainment. Call (020) 7388 2227.

HOTEL ACCOMMODATION SERVICE
Accommodation reservations can be made throughout London. Call Visit London's Telephone Accommodation Service on (020) 7932 2020 with your requirements and MasterCard/Visa/Switch details or email your request on book@visitlondon.com

WHICH PART OF LONDON
The majority of tourist accommodation is situated in the central parts of London and is therefore very convenient for most of the city's attractions and nightlife.

However, there are many hotels in outer London which provide other advantages, such as easier parking. In the 'Where to Stay' pages which follow, you will find accommodation listed under INNER LONDON (covering the E1 to W14 London Postal Area) and OUTER LONDON (covering the remainder of Greater London). Colour maps 6 and 7 at the front of the guide show place names and London Postal Area codes and will help you to locate accommodation in your chosen area of London.

Getting to London

BY ROAD: Major trunk roads into London include: A1, M1, A5, A10, A11, M11, A13, A2, M2, A23, A3, M3, A4, M4, A40, M40, A41, M25 (London orbital). London Transport is responsible for running London's bus services and the underground rail network. (020) 7222 1234 (24 hour telephone service; calls answered in rotation).

BY RAIL: Main rail termini: Victoria/Waterloo/Charing Cross - serving the South/South East; King's Cross - serving the North East; Euston - serving the North West/Midlands; Liverpool Street - serving the East; Paddington - serving the Thames Valley/West.

1. London Underground Station
2. The Mall

Where to stay in London

Parks in London are listed in alphabetical order of place name, and then in alphabetical order of park.

Map references refer to the colour location maps at the front of this guide. The first number indicates the map to use; the letter and number which follow refer to the grid reference on the map.

At-a-glance symbols can be found inside the back cover flap. Keep this open for easy reference.

LONDON E4

★★★★

**TOURING &
CAMPING PARK**

See Ad p56

LEE VALLEY CAMPSITE
Sewardstone Road, Chingford, London
E4 7RA
T: (020) 8529 5689
F: (020) 8559 4070
E: scs@leevalleypark.org.uk
I: www.leevalleypark.org.uk

CC: Amex, Delta, JCB,
Mastercard, Solo, Switch, Visa

200	£11.50
200	
200	£11.50
200 touring pitches	

Take junction 26 off the M25, then follow signs to Chingford. Turn left at the roundabout and the campsite is 2 miles on the right.

LONDON SE2

Rating
Applied For

See Ad on inside front cover

ABBEY WOOD CARAVAN CLUB SITE

Federation Road, Abbey Wood, London SE2 0LS
T: (020) 8311 7708
F: (020) 8311 1465
I: www.caravanclub.co.uk

A green, gently sloping site with mature trees. Good rail connections (35 minutes) into central London are within walking distance, and nearby Greenwich has plenty to offer. Non-members welcome.

OPEN All Year.
CC: Delta, Mastercard, Solo, Switch, Visa

On M2 turn off at A221. Then turn right into McLeod Road, right into Knee Hill and the site is the 2nd turning on the right.

220	£12.00–£21.50
220	£12.00–£21.50
130	
220 total touring pitches	

CREDIT CARD BOOKINGS If you book by telephone and are asked for your credit card number it is advisable to check the proprietor's policy should you cancel your reservation.

QUALITY ASSURANCE SCHEME

For an explanation of the quality and facilities represented by the Stars please refer to the front of this guide.

Cumbria

Cumbria's dynamic and breathtaking landscapes, from the famous Lakes to the rugged mountains and fells, have inspired poets and artists for hundreds of years.

Classic sights
Hadrian's Wall – a reminder of Roman occupation
Lake Windermere – largest lake in England

Coast & country
Scafell Pike – England's highest mountain
Whitehaven – historic port

Literary links
William Wordsworth – the poet's homes: Wordsworth House, Dove Cottage and Rydal Mount
Beatrix Potter – her home, Hill Top; The Beatrix Potter Gallery; The World of Beatrix Potter attraction.

Distinctively different
The Gondola – sail Coniston Water aboard the opulent 1859 steam yacht Gondola
Cars of the Stars Museum – cars from TV and Film, including Chitty Chitty Bang Bang and the Batmobile.

The County of Cumbria

For more information contact:
Cumbria Tourist Board
Ashleigh, Holly Road,
Windermere, Cumbria
LA23 2AQ

E: info@golakes.co.uk
www.golakes.co.uk
www.lakedistrictoutdoors.co.uk
www.lastminutelakedistrict.co.uk

Telephone enquiries -
T: (015394) 44444
F: (015394) 44041

1. Jetty on Derwent Water
2. Snowboarder, near Alston
3. Bluebells at Brantwood

Places to Visit

You will find hundreds of interesting places to visit during your stay, just some of which are listed in these pages. Contact any Tourist Information Centre in the region for more ideas on days out.

Awarded VisitBritain's 'Quality Assured Visitor Attraction' marque.

The Beacon
West Strand, Whitehaven
Tel: (01946) 592302
www.copelandbc.gov.uk
Award-winning attraction and museum superbly situated overlooking the Georgian harbour of Whitehaven, one of England's 'gem towns'.

Brantwood, Home of John Ruskin
Standish Street, Coniston
Tel: (015394) 41396 www.brantwood.org.uk
The most beautifully situated house in the Lake District, home of John Ruskin from 1872 until 1900. Discover the wealth of things to do at Brantwood.

Cars of the Stars Motor Museum
Keswick
Tel: (017687) 73757 www.carsofthestars.com
Features TV and film vehicles including the Batmobile, Chitty Chitty Bang Bang, the James Bond Aston Martin, Herbie, FAB 1 plus many other famous cars and motorcycles.

The Dock Museum
North Road, Barrow-in-Furness
Tel: (01229) 894444 www.dockmuseum.org.uk
Spectacular modern museum built over an original Victorian graving dock. Galleries include multi-media interactives, and impressive ship models.

Dove Cottage and Wordsworth Museum
Town End, Grasmere, Ambleside
Tel: (015394) 35544 www.wordsworth.org.uk
Wordsworth's home 1799-1808. Museum with manuscripts, farmhouse reconstruction, paintings and drawings. Special events throughout the year.

Furness Abbey (English Heritage)
Barrow-in-Furness
Tel: (01229) 823420
www.english heritage.org.uk
Ruins of 12thC Cistercian abbey, the 2nd wealthiest in England. Extensive remains include transepts, choir and west tower of church, canopied seats, arches, church.

Gleaston Water Mill
Gleaston, Ulverston
Tel: (01229) 869244 www.watermill.co.uk
A truly rural experience abounding with all things country - a water cornmill, artefacts, traditions, folklore and cooking and of course the acclaimed Pig's Whisper Store.

Heron Glass Ltd
The Lakes Glass Centre, Ulverston
Tel: (01229) 581121
www.herongiftware.com
Heron Glass Ltd and Cumbria Crystal, displays of making handblown glass giftware and lead crystal. Lighthouse cafe and restaurant. A Gateway to Furness Exhibition.

Hill Top (National Trust)
Near Sawrey, Ambleside
Tel: (015394) 36269 www.nationaltrust.org.uk
Beatrix Potter wrote many of her popular Peter Rabbit stories and other books in this charming little house which still contains her own china and furniture.

Holker Hall and Gardens
Cark in Cartmel, Grange-over-Sands
Tel: (015395) 58328
www.holker-hall.co.uk
Including Victorian new wing, formal and woodland garden, deer park, motor museum, adventure playground, cafe and gift shop.

Jennings Brothers plc
The Castle Brewery, Cockermouth
Tel: 0845 1297185
www.jenningsbrewery.co.uk
Guided tours of Jennings traditional brewery and sampling of the ales in the Old Cooperage Bar.

K Village Outlet Centre
Lound Road, Kendal,
Tel: (01539) 732363 www.kvillage.co.uk
Famous named brands such as K-shoes, Van Heusen, Denby, National Trust Shop, Tog24 and Ponden Mill all at discounts. Open 7 days per week with full disabled access.

The Lake District Coast Aquarium Maryport
South Quay, Maryport,
Tel: (01900) 817760
www.lakedistrict-coastaquarium.co.uk
Purpose-built independent aquarium with over 35 displays. Largest collection of native marine species in Cumbria. Cafe and gift shop.

The Lake District Visitor Centre Brockhole
Windermere
Tel: (015394) 46601
www.lake-district.gov.uk
Brockhole is an Edwardian house on the shores of Windermere with extensive landscaped gardens, superb views, lake cruises, adventure playground, walks, events & activities.

Lakeland Sheep and Wool Centre
Egremont Road, Cockermouth
Tel: (01900) 822673
www.sheep-woolcentre.co.uk
Live farm show including cows, sheep, dogs and ducks, all displaying their working qualities. Large gift shop and licensed cafe/restaurant. All weather attraction.

Levens Hall
Levens, Kendal
Tel: (015395) 60321
www.levenshall.co.uk
Elizabethan home of the Bagot family incorporating 13thC pele tower, world-famous topiary gardens, Bellingham Buttery, Potting Shed gift shop, plant centre and play area.

Muncaster Castle, Gardens, Owl Centre and Meadow Vole Maze
Ravenglass
Tel: (01229) 717614 www.muncaster.co.uk
Muncaster Castle with the most beautifully situated Owl Centre in the world. See the birds fly, picnic in the gardens, visit the Pennington family home.

Ravenglass and Eskdale Railway
Ravenglass
Tel: (01229) 717171
www.ravenglass-railway.co.uk
England's oldest narrow-gauge railway runs for 7 miles (12km) through glorious scenery to the foot of England's highest hills. Most trains are steam hauled.

Rheged - The Village in the Hill
Redhills, Penrith
Tel: (01768) 868000 www.rheged.com
Award-winning Rheged is home to giant cinema screen showing 3 movies daily, the National Mountaineering Exhibition, speciality shops, indoor play area and restaurant.

The Rum Story
27 Lowther Street, Whitehaven
Tel: (01946) 592933 www.rumstory.co.uk
'The Rum Story' - the world's first exhibition depicting the unique story of the UK rum trade in the original Jefferson's wine merchant premises.

1. Lake Windermere
2. Esk River, Eskdale
3. Thirlmere Valley

Rydal Mount and Gardens
Rydal, Ambleside
Tel: (015394) 33002
www.wordsworthlakes.co.uk
Nestling between the majestic fells, Lake Windermere and Rydal Water, lies the 'most beloved' home of William Wordsworth from 1813-1850.

Senhouse Roman Museum
The Battery, Sea Brows, Maryport
Tel: (01900) 816168
www.senhousemuseum.co.uk
Once the headquarters of Hadrian's Coastal Defence system. UK's largest group of Roman altar stones and inscriptions on one site.

Sizergh Castle (National Trust)
Kendal
Tel: (015395) 60070 www.nationaltrust.org.uk
Strickland family home for 750 years, now National Trust owned, with 14thC pele tower, 15thC great hall, 16thC wings and Stuart connections. Rock garden, rose garden, daffodils.

South Lakes Wild Animal Park Ltd
Crossgates, Dalton-in-Furness
Tel: (01229) 466086
www.wildanimalpark.co.uk
Wild zoo park in over 17 acres (7ha) of grounds. Giraffe, rhino, tiger, lions, toilets, car/coach park. Miniature railway. Over 120 species of animals from all around the world.

South Tynedale Railway
Railway Station, Alston
Tel: (01434) 381696 www.strps.org.uk
Narrow gauge railway along part of the route of the former Alston to Haltwhistle branch line through South Tynedale with preserved steam and diesel engines.

Steam Yacht Gondola (National Trust)
Pier Cottage, Coniston
Tel: (015394) 41288
www.nationaltrust.org.uk/gondola
Victorian steam-powered vessel now National Trust owned and completely renovated with an opulently-upholstered saloon. Superb way to appreciate the beauty of Coniston Water.

Theatre by the Lake
Lakeside, Keswick
Tel: (017687) 74411
www.theatrebythelake.com
Offering a summer season of plays, a Christmas show and an Easter production. The theatre also hosts visiting drams, music, dance, talks and comedy.

Tullie House Museum and Art Gallery

Castle Street, Carlisle
Tel: (01228) 534781
www.tulliehouse.co.uk
Visit our Georgian Mansion housing our magnificent pre-Raphaelite collection, Victorian childhood gallery, 1689 fireplace and Jacobean oak staircase.

Ullswater 'Steamers'
The Pier House, Glenridding
Tel: (017684) 82229
www.ullswater-steamers.co.uk
Relax and enjoy a beautiful Ullswater cruise with walks and picnic areas. Boat services operating all year round.

Windermere Lake Cruises
Ambleside, Bowness-on-Windermere
Tel: (015395) 31188
www.windermere-lakecruises.co.uk
Steamers and launches sail daily throughout the year between Ambleside, Lakeside and Bowness. Seasonal sailings to Brockhole, L&H Steam Railway and Aquarium of the Lakes.

Windermere Steamboats & Museum
Rayrigg Road, Bowness-on-Windermere
Tel: (015394) 45565
www.steamboat.co.uk
A wealth of interest and information about life on bygone Windermere. Regular steam launch trips, vintage vessels and classic motorboats. Model boat pond, lakeside picnic area.

The World Famous Old Blacksmith's Shop Centre
Gretna Green
Tel: (01461) 338441 www.gretnagreen.com
The original Blacksmith's Shop museum and a shopping centre selling, cashmere and woollen knitwear, crystal and china. Taste local produce in the Old Smithy Restaurant.

Cumbria Tourist Board

Ashleigh, Holly Road, Windermere,
Cumbria L23 2AQ
T: (015394) 44444 F: (015394) 44041
E: info@golakes.co.uk
www.golakes.co.uk
www.lakedistrictoutdoors.co.uk
www.lastminutelakedistrict.co.uk

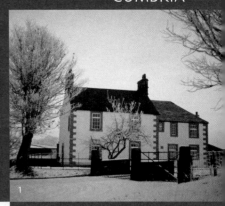

**THE FOLLOWING PUBLICATIONS ARE
AVAILABLE FROM THE CUMBRIA
TOURIST BOARD**

Cumbria – the Lake District Holidays &
Breaks Guide (free) T: 08705 133059

The Flora and Fauna of Cumbria -
the Lake District (free)

The Caravan and Camping Guide of Cumbria –
the Lake District (free)

The Taste District (free) Food & drink guide
Events Listing (free)

Getting to Cumbria

BY ROAD: The M1/M6/M25/
M40 provide a link with London
and the South East and the
M5/M6 provide access from the
South West. The M6 links the
Midlands and North West and the
M62/M6 links the East of England
and Yorkshire. Approximate
journey time from London is 5
hours, from Manchester 1 hour
30 minutes.

BY RAIL: From London (Euston)
to Oxenholme (Kendal) takes
approximately 3 hours 30
minutes. From Oxenholme
(connecting station for all main
line trains) to Windermere takes
approximately 20 minutes. From
Carlisle to Barrow-in-Furness via
the coastal route, with stops at
many of the towns in between,
takes approximately 2 hours.
Trains from Edinburgh to Carlisle
take approximately 2 hours 15
minutes. The historic Settle-
Carlisle line also runs through the
county bringing passengers from
Yorkshire via the Eden Valley.

www.golakes.co.uk/transport.html

1. The village of Kikoswald,
   Eden Valley
2. Wordsworth House,
   Cockermouth

Where to stay in **Cumbria**

Parks in this region are listed in alphabetical order of place name, and then in alphabetical order of park.

Map references refer to the colour location maps at the front of this guide. The first number indicates the map to use; the letter and number which follow refer to the grid reference on the map.

At-a-glance symbols can be found inside the back cover flap. Keep this open for easy reference.

AMBLESIDE, Cumbria Map ref 6A3 *Tourist Information Centre Tel: (015394) 32582*

★★★★
HOLIDAY PARK

BH&HPA

GREENHOWE CARAVAN PARK
Great Langdale, Ambleside LA22 9JU
T: (015394) 37231
F: (015394) 37464
I: www.greenhowe.com

46   £150.00–£425.00

Leave M6 jct 36 and follow signs for Kendal, Windermere and Ambleside. From Ambleside take the A593 then the B5343. The site is on the right-hand side.

APPLEBY-IN-WESTMORLAND, Cumbria Map ref 6B3 *Tourist Information Centre Tel: (017683) 51177*

★★★★★
HOLIDAY, TOURING
& CAMPING PARK

BH&HPA

WILD ROSE PARK
Ormside, Appleby-in-Westmorland
CA16 6EJ
T: (017683) 51077
F: (017683) 52551
E: hs@wildrose.co.uk
I: www.wildrose.co.uk

CC: Delta, JCB, Mastercard,
Solo, Switch, Visa

240   £10.40–£17.20
80   £10.40–£17.20
20   £10.40–£17.20
240 touring pitches

Leave M6 jct 37 and take B6260 in the direction of Appleby. Turn off the B6260 (Appleby to Tebay) at Burrells. Follow the signposts to Ormside. After approximately 2 miles the park is on right-hand side.

BOUTH, Cumbria Map ref 6A3

★★★★★
HOLIDAY &
TOURING PARK

BLACK BECK CARAVAN PARK
Bouth, Ulverston LA12 8JN
T: (01229) 861274
F: (01229) 861041
E: reception@blackbeck.net

CC: Delta, Mastercard, Switch,
Visa

48   £12.60–£19.95
4   £11.55–£14.70
3   £170.00–£430.00
73 touring pitches

Leave M6 at jct 36. Take A590 west. In Newby Bridge go right for Bouth. Pass Rusland Pool hotel take next left turn, at T-junction turn left. Our entrance along road on right-hand side.

CARLISLE, Cumbria Map ref 6A2 *Tourist Information Centre Tel: (01228) 625600*

★★★★
TOURING &
CAMPING PARK

BH&HPA

DANDY DINMONT CARAVAN AND CAMPING SITE
Blackford, Carlisle CA6 4EA
T: (01228) 674611
F: (01228) 674611
E: dandydinmont@btopenworld.com
I: www.caravan-camping-carlisle.itgo.com

27   £8.50–£8.75
27   £8.50–£8.75
20   £7.25–£7.75
74 touring pitches

Exit the M6 at jct 44. Take A7 north, 1.5 miles. After Blackford sign follow the road directional signs to site. Site is on the right-hand side of the A7.

CONISTON, Cumbria Map ref 6A3

★★★★★
HOLIDAY PARK

ROSE AWARD

BH&HPA

CRAKE VALLEY HOLIDAY PARK
Water Yeat, Blawith, Ulverston LA12 8DL
T: (01229) 885203
F: (01229) 885203
E: crakevalley@coniston1.fslife.co.uk
I: www.crakevalley.co.uk

15   £185.00–£500.00

Leave M6 at jct 30 and take A590 towards Barrow. Turn right off the A590, Barrow road at Greenodd. Go onto the A5092, within 2 miles fork right onto the A5084 for Coniston. The park is 3 miles along on your left-hand side.

★★★★★
TOURING PARK

See Ad on inside front cover

PARK COPPICE CARAVAN CLUB SITE
Coniston LA21 8LA
T: (015394) 41555
I: www.caravanclub.co.uk

Landscaped site set in 63 acres of NT woodland; many pitches in secluded glades. Lake for water sports, on-site play areas, orienteering courses and Red Squirrel Nature Trail. Non-members welcome.

CC: Delta, Mastercard, Solo, Switch, Visa

Follow A593, 1.5 miles south of Coniston village. Final approach from the north or south is narrow in places.

280	£9.50–£19.50
280	£9.50–£19.50
20	
280 total touring pitches	

GRANGE-OVER-SANDS, Cumbria Map ref 6A3 *Tourist Information Centre Tel: (015395) 34026*

★★★★
**HOLIDAY &
TOURING PARK**

BH&HPA

GREAVES FARM CARAVAN PARK
Field Broughton, Grange-over-Sands
LA11 6HR
T: (015395) 36329

3	£8.00–£11.00
3	£8.00–£11.00
5	£8.00–£10.00
2	£190.00–£250.00
8 touring pitches	

Leave M6 at jct 36 and take A590. Leave the A590 1 mile south of Newby Bridge, signed Cartmel 4. Proceed 2 miles to 3 bungalows on the left. Approximately 200yds before Field Broughton church.

★★★★★
TOURING PARK

See Ad on inside front cover

MEATHOP FELL CARAVAN CLUB SITE
Grange-over-Sands LA11 6RB
T: (015395) 32912
F: (015395) 32243
I: www.caravanclub.co.uk

Peaceful site, ideal for exploring the Southern Lake District. Kendal, famous for its mint cake, is within easy reach; Grange-over-Sands and Ulverston are close by. Non-members welcome.

OPEN All Year.
CC: Delta, Mastercard, Solo, Switch, Visa

Exit the M6 at jct 36 and follow the A590 to Barrow. After about 3.25 miles take the slip road and follow the A590 to Barrow. At the 1st roundabout follow the International Camping signs to Meathop Fell Caravan Club. Steep approach.

130	£14.50–£19.50
130	£14.50–£19.50
130 total touring pitches	

NB **IMPORTANT NOTE** Information on accommodation listed in this guide has been supplied by the proprietors. As changes may occur you are advised to check details at the time of booking.

HAWKSHEAD, Cumbria Map ref 6A3

★★★★

HOLIDAY, TOURING & CAMPING PARK

THE CROFT CARAVAN AND CAMP SITE
North Lonsdale Road, Hawkshead,
Ambleside LA22 0NX
T: (015394) 36374
F: (015394) 36544
E: enquiries@hawkshead-croft.com
I: www.hawkshead-croft.com

CC: Delta, Mastercard, Solo, Switch, Visa

25	£15.00–£18.00
	£12.00–£14.25
75	£12.00–£14.25
20	£200.00–£420.00

From Ambleside follow B5286, 5 miles to Hawkshead.

KENDAL, Cumbria Map ref 6B3 *Tourist Information Centre Tel: (01539) 725758*

★★★★

TOURING PARK

See Ad on inside front cover

LOW PARK WOOD CARAVAN CLUB SITE

Sedgwick, Kendal LA8 0JZ
T: (015395) 60186
I: www.caravanclub.co.uk

This peaceful country site is a haven for birdwatchers, freshwater fishermen and wild-flower enthusiasts. A dog-friendly site with extensive woodland to walk them in. Non-members welcome.

CC: Delta, Mastercard, Solo, Switch, Visa

Leave the M6 at jct 36 and go onto the A590 signed South Lakes. After approximately 3.25 miles leave via the slip road (signed Milnthorpe, Barrow) at the roundabout and follow caravan signs.

161	£9.50–£19.50
161	£9.50–£19.50
161 total touring pitches	

★★★★

HOLIDAY, TOURING & CAMPING PARK

BH&HPA

WATERS EDGE CARAVAN PARK
Crooklands, Kendal LA7 7NN
T: (015395) 67708
F: (015395) 67610
I: www.watersedgecaravanpark.co.uk

CC: Mastercard, Visa

30	£11.00–£16.00
30	£11.00–£16.00
5	£5.00–£16.00
65 touring pitches	

Leave M6 at jct 36. Take A65 to Crooklands. Site about 0.75 miles on the right.

KESWICK, Cumbria Map ref 6A3 *Tourist Information Centre Tel: (017687) 72645*

★★★★

TOURING & CAMPING PARK

CASTLERIGG FARM CAMPING & CARAVAN SITE
Keswick CA12 4TE
T: (017687) 72479
F: (017687) 74718
E: info@castleriggfarm.com
I: www.castleriggfarm.com

3	£10.00–£14.00
	£8.50–£14.00
30	£8.20–£8.80
33 touring pitches	

From M6 jct 40 take A66 to Keswick. Take A591 out of Keswick to Windermere for 1.5 miles. Turn right near top of the hill at camping and caravanning sign. Castlerigg Farm is 0.5 miles on the left.

SPECIAL BREAKS

Many establishments offer special promotions and themed breaks. These are highlighted in red. (All such offers are subject to availability.)

KESWICK continued

CASTLERIGG HALL CARAVAN AND CAMPING PARK

★★★★
HOLIDAY, TOURING
& CAMPING PARK

BH&HPA

Castlerigg Hall, Keswick CA12 4TE
T: (017687) 74499
F: (017687) 74499
E: info@castlerigg.co.uk
I: www.castlerigg.co.uk

CC: JCB, Mastercard, Solo, Switch, Visa

45		£13.50–£15.50
45		£11.50–£14.00
120		£9.80–£11.50
7		£180.00–£390.00
210 touring pitches		

Leave M6 at jct 40 and follow signs for Keswick. About 1.5 miles south east of Keswick off A591, turn right 100yds on the right.

LAKESIDE HOLIDAY PARK

★★★★
HOLIDAY &
TOURING PARK

Norman Garner Ltd, Crow Park Road, Keswick CA12 5EW
T: (017687) 72878
F: (017687) 72017
E: welcome@lakesideholidaypark.co.uk
I: www.lakesideholidaypark.co.uk

CC: Delta, JCB, Mastercard, Solo, Switch, Visa

10		£110.00–£480.00

Leave the M6 at jct 40. Exit A66 at roundabout near Keswick, 16 miles. Follow signs for town centre. Follow camping and caravan signs.

KIRKBY STEPHEN, Cumbria Map ref 6B3 *Tourist Information Centre Tel: (017683) 71199*

PENNINE VIEW CARAVAN PARK

★★★★★
TOURING &
CAMPING PARK

BH&HPA

Station Road, Kirkby Stephen CA17 4SZ
T: (017683) 71717

CC: Delta, JCB, Mastercard, Solo, Switch, Visa

43		£12.25–£13.35
43		£12.25–£13.35
15		£10.00–£11.60
58 touring pitches		

Just off A685.

NEWBY BRIDGE, Cumbria Map ref 6A3

NEWBY BRIDGE CARAVAN PARK

★★★★★
HOLIDAY PARK

ROSE AWARD

BH&HPA

Canny Hill, Newby Bridge, Ulverston LA12 8NF
T: (015395) 31030
F: (015395) 30105
E: info@cumbriancaravans.co.uk
I: www.cumbriancaravans.co.uk

CC: Delta, Mastercard, Switch, Visa

5		
5		
7		£185.00–£445.00
5 touring pitches		

Leave M6 at jct 36 and follow A590 in the direction of Barrow. Just before entering Newby Bridge about 2.25 miles beyond High Newton turn left off the A590 signposted Canny Hill. Park entrance 200yds on the right-hand side.

ORTON, Cumbria Map ref 6B3

TEBAY CARAVAN SITE

★★★★
HOLIDAY &
TOURING PARK

BH&HPA

Orton, Penrith CA10 3SB
T: (015396) 24511
F: (015396) 24511
E: julie@rheged.com

70		£10.00–£15.00
70		£10.00–£15.00
70 touring pitches		

One mile north of M6, jct 38. At Tebay accessed via Westmorland Service area.

TOWN INDEX

This can be found at the back of the guide. If you know where you want to stay, the index will give you the page number listing all accommodation in your chosen town, city or village.

★★★★★
TOURING PARK

See Ad on inside front cover

THE CARAVAN CLUB

TROUTBECK HEAD CARAVAN CLUB SITE

Troutbeck, Penrith CA11 0SS
T: (017684) 83521
F: (017684) 83839
I: www.caravanclub.co.uk

Classic Lakeland country. Attractive site sitting in a valley alongside a babbling brook with spectacular views of Blencathra. Numerous attractions and activities within 10-mile radius. Non-members welcome.

CC: Delta, Mastercard, Solo, Switch, Visa

From north or south on the M6, leave at jct 40 onto the A66 signposted Keswick. In about 7.25 miles turn left onto A5091, signposted Dockray/ Ullswater, site on right after 1.5 miles.

119	🚐	£17.00–£20.50
119	🚐	£17.00–£20.50
119 total touring pitches		

★★
HOLIDAY, TOURING & CAMPING PARK

NCC

See Ad on this page

THE SOLWAY HOLIDAY VILLAGE
Skinburness Drive, Silloth, Wigton CA7 4QQ
T: (016973) 31236
F: (016973) 32553
E: finlinson8@aol.com
I: www.hagansleisure.co.uk

CC: Delta, Mastercard, Switch, Visa

60	🚐	£9.00–£15.00
60	🚐	£9.00–£15.00
60	▲	£9.00–£15.00
76	🏠	£130.00–£440.00

Leave the M6 at jct 41 and make your way to Wigton. Then follow signs to Silloth on the B5302. When you get into Silloth turn right at Raffa Club and follow road for 0.5 miles, holiday park on the right.

★★★★★
HOLIDAY, TOURING & CAMPING PARK

ROSE AWARD

BH&HPA
NCC

STANWIX PARK HOLIDAY CENTRE

Greenrow, West Silloth, Silloth, Wigton CA7 4HH
T: (016973) 32666
F: (016973) 32555
E: enquiries@stanwix.com
I: www.stanwix.com

Situated on the Solway coast, popular touring site with leisure and entertainment facilities for all ages. All pitches have hook-ups. Base to explore the Lake District. Check our website for special deals during certain periods. You could save up to 25% off your next holiday.

CC: Delta, Mastercard, Solo, Switch, Visa

Leave M6 at jct 44, follow signs to Carlisle, Wigton and Silloth. From south leave M6 at jct 41, follow signs to Wigton and Silloth.

121	🚐	£14.50–£17.70
121	🚐	£14.50–£17.70
121	▲	£14.50–£17.70
77	🏠	£170.00–£525.00
121 touring pitches		

MAP REFERENCES The map references refer to the colour maps at the front of the guide. The first figure is the map number; the letter and figure which follow indicate the grid reference on the map.

WINDERMERE, Cumbria Map ref 6A3 *Tourist Information Centre Tel: (015394) 46499*

★★★★★
**HOLIDAY &
TOURING PARK**

PARK CLIFFE CARAVAN AND CAMPING ESTATE

Birks Road, Windermere LA23 3PG
T: (015395) 31344
F: (015395) 31971
E: info@parkcliffe.co.uk
I: www.parkcliffe.co.uk

A tranquil family park, 600 metres from Lake Windermere. Mountain-view tourers, lake-view tents. Own pub, heated shower block, with private bathrooms for hire.

CC: Delta, Mastercard, Solo, Switch, Visa

Exit the M6 at jct 36, A590 towards Barrow. At Newby Bridge turn right onto the A592 towards Windermere. After 4 miles turn right into Birks Road, 0.3 miles on the right.

70	⚐	£13.00–£16.00
70	⚑	£13.00–£16.00
180	▲	£10.00–£14.00
250	touring pitches	

AT-A-GLANCE SYMBOLS

Symbols at the end of each accommodation entry give useful information about services and facilities. A key to symbols can be found inside the back cover flap. Keep this open for easy reference.

A brief guide to the main Towns and Villages offering accommodation in **Cumbria**

A AMBLESIDE, CUMBRIA - Market town situated at the head of Lake Windermere and surrounded by fells. The historic town centre is now a conservation area and the country around Ambleside is rich in historic and literary associations. Good centre for touring, walking and climbing.

APPLEBY-IN-WESTMORLAND, CUMBRIA - Former county town of Westmorland, at the foot of the Pennines in the Eden Valley. The castle was rebuilt in the 17th C, except for its Norman keep, ditches and ramparts. It now houses a Rare Breeds Survival Trust Centre. Good centre for exploring the Eden Valley.

C CARLISLE, CUMBRIA - Cumbria's only city is rich in history. Attractions include the small red sandstone cathedral and 900-year-old castle with magnificent view from the keep. The award-winning Tullie House Museum and Art Gallery brings 2,000 years of Border history dramatically to life. Excellent centre for shopping.

CONISTON, CUMBRIA - The 803m fell Coniston Old Man dominates the skyline to the east of this village at the northern end of Coniston Water. Arthur Ransome set his "Swallows and Amazons" stories here. Coniston's most famous resident was John Ruskin, whose home, Brantwood, is open to the public. Good centre for walking.

G GRANGE-OVER-SANDS, CUMBRIA - Set on the beautiful Cartmel Peninsula, this tranquil resort, known as Lakeland's Riviera, overlooks Morecambe Bay. Pleasant seafront walks and beautiful gardens. The bay attracts many species of wading birds.

H HAWKSHEAD, CUMBRIA - Lying near Esthwaite Water, this village has great charm and character. Its small squares are linked by flagged or cobbled alleys, and the main square is dominated by the market house, or Shambles, where the butchers had their stalls in days gone by.

K KENDAL, CUMBRIA - The "Auld Grey Town" lies in the valley of the River Kent with a backdrop of limestone fells. Situated just outside the Lake District National Park, it is a good centre for touring the Lakes and surrounding country. Ruined castle, reputed birthplace of Catherine Parr.

KESWICK, CUMBRIA - Beautifully positioned town beside Derwentwater and below the mountains of Skiddaw and Blencathra. Excellent base for walking, climbing, watersports and touring. Motor-launches operate on Derwentwater, and motor boats, rowing boats and canoes can be hired.

KIRKBY STEPHEN, CUMBRIA - Old market town close to the River Eden, with many fine Georgian buildings and an attractive market square. St Stephen's Church is known as the "Cathedral of the Dales". Good base for exploring the Eden Valley and the Dales.

N NEWBY BRIDGE, CUMBRIA - At the southern end of Windermere on the River Leven, this village has an unusual stone bridge with arches of unequal size. The Lakeside and Haverthwaite Railway has a stop here, and steamer cruises on Lake Windermere leave from nearby Lakeside.

P PENRITH, CUMBRIA - Ancient and historic market town, the northern gateway to the Lake District. Penrith Castle was built as a defence against the Scots. Its ruins, open to the public, stand in the public park. High above the town is the Penrith Beacon, made famous by William Wordsworth.

S SILLOTH, CUMBRIA - Small port and coastal resort on the Solway Firth with wide cobbled roads and an attractive green leading to the promenade and seashore, known for its magnificent sunsets.

W WINDERMERE, CUMBRIA - Once a tiny hamlet before the introduction of the railway in 1847, it now adjoins Bowness which is on the lakeside. Centre for sailing and boating. A good way to see the lake is a trip on a passenger steamer. Steamboat Museum has a fine collection of old boats.

 IMPORTANT NOTE Information on accommodation listed in this guide has been supplied by the proprietors. As changes may occur you are advised to check details at the time of booking.

Northumbria

Romans, sailors and industrial pioneers have all left their mark here. Northunbria's exciting cities, castle-studded countyside and white-sanded coastline make it an undiscovered gem.

Classic sights
Lindisfarne Castle – on Holy Island
Housesteads Roman Fort – the most impressive Roman fort on Hadrian's Wall
Durham Cathedral & Hadrian's Wall – 2 World Heritage Sites

Coast & country
Kielder Water and Forest Park – perfect for walking, cycling and watersports
Saltburn – beach of broad sands
Seahouses – picturesque fishing village

Maritime history
HMS Trincomalee – magnificent 1817 British warship
Captain Cook – birthplace museum and replica of his ship, *Endeavour*
Grace Darling – museum commemorating her rescue of shipwreck survivors in 1838

Arts for all
Angel of the North – awe-inspiring sculpture by Antony Gormley
BALTIC – The Centre for Contemporary Art in Gateshead

Distinctively different
St Mary's Lighthouse – great views from the top

The Counties of Durham, Northumberland, Tees Valley and Tyne & Wear

For more information contact:
Northumbria Tourist Board
Aykley Heads,
Durham DH1 5UX

www.visitnorthumbria.com

Telephone enquiries -
T: (0191) 375 3049
F: (0191) 386 0899

1. The Angel of the North, Gateshead
2. Town Crier, Alnwick Fair
3. Walkers on the Northumbrian Coast

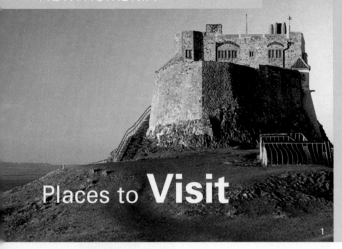

You will find hundreds of interesting places to visit during your stay, just some of which are listed in these pages. Contact any Tourist Information Centre in the region for more ideas on days out.

Places to Visit

Awarded VisitBritain's 'Quality Assured Visitor Attraction' marque.

Alnwick Castle
Alnwick
Tel: (01665) 510777 www.alnwickcastle.com
Home of the Percy's, Dukes of Northumberland, since 1309, this imposing medieval fortress has magnificent 19thC interiors in the Italian Renaissance style.

Alnwick Garden
Alnwick
Tel: (01665) 511350 www.alnwickgarden.com
New 12-acre (5ha) garden with fabulous water feature, rose garden, ornamental garden, woodland walk and viewpoint.

BALTIC The Centre for Contemporary Art
Quayside, Gateshead
Tel: (0191) 478 1810 www.balticmill.com
A major international centre for contemporary art in a converted warehouse, with a constantly changing programme of exhibitions and events.

Bamburgh Castle
Bamburgh
Tel: (01668) 214515
www.bamburghcastle.com
Magnificent coastal castle completely restored in 1900. Collections of china, porcelain, furniture, paintings, arms and armour.

Beamish The North of England Open Air Museum
Beamish
Tel: (0191) 370 4000
www.beamish.org.uk
Visit the town, colliery village, working farm, Pockerley Manor and 1825 railway, recreating life in the North East in the early 1800s and 1900s.

Bede's World
Church Bank, Jarrow
Tel: (0191) 489 2106
www.bedesworld.co.uk
Discover the exciting world of the Venerable Bede, early medieval Europe's greatest scholar. Church, monastic site, museum with exhibitions and recreated Anglo-Saxon farm.

Belsay Hall, Castle and Gardens (English Heritage)
Belsay, Newcastle upon Tyne
Tel: (01661) 881636
www.english-heritage.org.uk
Home of the Middleton family for 600 years. 14thC castle, ruined 17thC manor house and neo-classical hall, set in 30 acres (12ha) of landscaped gardens and winter garden.

Blue Reef Aquarium
Grand Parade, Tynemouth
Tel: (0191) 258 1031
www.bluereefaquarium.co.uk
More than 30 living displays exploring the drama of the North Sea and the dazzling beauty of a spectacular coral reef with its own underwater tunnel.

Bowes Museum
Barnard Castle
Tel: (01833) 690606
www.bowesmuseum.org.uk
French-style chateau, housing art collections of national importance and archaeology of south west Durham.

Captain Cook Birthplace Museum
Stewart Park, Middlesborough
Tel: (01642) 311211
Early life and voyages of Captain Cook and the
countries he visited. Temporary exhibitions. One
person free with every group of 10 visiting.

Centre For Life
Times Square, Newcastle upon Tyne
Tel: (0191) 243 8210 www.centre-for-life.co.uk
Meet your 4 billion year old family, explore what
makes us all different, test your brain power and
enjoy the thrill of the crazy motion ride.

Cherryburn: Thomas Bewick Birthplace Museum (National Trust)
Station Bank, Stocksfield
Tel: (01661) 843276 www.nationaltrust.org.uk
Birthplace cottage (1700) and farmyard. Printing
house using original printing blocks. Introductory
exhibition of the life, work and countryside.

Chesters Roman Fort (Cilurnum), Hadrian's Wall
Chollerford, Humshaugh, Hexham
Tel: (01434) 681379
Fort built for 500 cavalrymen. Remains include 5
gateways, barrack blocks, commandant's house
and headquarters. Finest military bath house
in Britain.

Chillingham Castle
Chillingham, Wooler
Tel: (01668) 215359
www.chillingham-castle.com
Medieval fortress with Tudor additions, torture
chamber, shop, dungeon, tearoom, woodland
walks, furnished rooms and topiary garden.

Cragside House, Gardens and Estate (National Trust)
Rothbury, Morpeth
Tel: (01669) 620333 www.nationaltrust.org.uk
Built in 1864-84 for Tyneside industrialist Lord
Armstrong, Cragside was the first house to be lit
by electricity generated by water power.

Discovery Museum
Blandford Square, Newcastle upon Tyne .
Tel: (0191) 232 6789 www.twmuseums.org.uk
Discovery Museum offers a wide variety of
experiences for all the family to enjoy. Explore
the Newcastle Story, Live Wires, Science Maze
and Fashion Works.

Dunstanburgh Castle (English Heritage)
Craster, Alnwick
Tel: (01665) 576231
www.english-heritage.org.uk
Romantic ruins of extensive 14thC castle in
dramatic coastal situation on 100ft (30.5km)
cliffs. Built by Thomas, Earl of Lancaster.
Remains include gatehouse and curtain wall.

Durham Castle
Palace Green, Durham
Tel: (0191) 374 3863 www.durhamcastle.com
Castle founded in 1072, Norman chapel dating
from 1080. Kitchens and great hall dated 1499
and 1284 respectively. Fine example of motte-
and-bailey castle.

Durham Cathedral
The College, Durham
Tel: (0191) 386 4266
www.durhamcathedral.co.uk
Durham Cathedral is thought by many to be the
finest example of Norman church architecture in
England. Contains the tombs of St Cuthbert and
The Venerable Bede.

1. Lindisfarne Castle, Holy Island
2. Hadrian's Wall
3. Bridges over the Tyne, Newcastle

71

Hall Hill Farm
Lanchester, Durham
Tel: (01388) 730300 www.hallhillfarm.co.uk
Family fun set in attractive countryside with an opportunity to see and touch the animals at close quarters. Farm trailer ride, riverside walk, teashop and play area.

Hartlepool Historic Quay
Maritime Avenue, Hartlepool
Tel: (01429) 860006
www.destinationhartlepool.com

Hartlepool Historic Quay is an exciting reconstruction of a seaport of the 1800s with buildings and lively quayside, authentically reconstructed.

Housesteads Roman Fort (Vercovicium), Hadrian's Wall (National Trust)
Haydon Bridge, Hexham
Tel: (01434) 344363 www.nationaltrust.org.uk
Best preserved and most impressive of the Roman forts. Vercovicium was a 5-acre (2ha) fort for an extensive 800 civil settlement. Only example of a Roman hospital.

Killhope, The North of England Lead Mining Museum
Cowshill, Bishop Auckland
Tel: (01388) 537505
www.durham.gov.uk/killhope
Most complete lead mining site in Great Britain. Mine tours available, 34-ft- (10m-) diameter waterwheel, reconstruction of Victorian machinery, miners lodging and woodland walks.

Lindisfarne Castle (National Trust)
Holy Island, Berwick-upon-Tweed
Tel: (01289) 389244 www.nationaltrust.org.uk
The castle was built in 1550 and restored and converted into a private home for Edward Hudson by the architect Sir Edwin Lutyens in 1903.

National Glass Centre
Liberty Way, Sunderland
Tel: (0191) 515 5555
www.nationalglasscentre.com
A unique visitor attraction presenting the best in contemporary glass. Master craftspeople will demonstrate glass-making techniques. Classes and workshops available.

Nature's World at the Botanic Centre
Ladgate Lane, Middlesborough
Tel: (01642) 594895 www.naturesworld.org.uk
Demonstration gardens, wildlife pond, white garden, environmental exhibition hall, shop, tearoom and River Tees model. Hydroponicum and Eco centre now open.

Otter Trust's North Pennines Reserve
Bowes, Barnard Castle
Tel: (01833) 628339
A branch of the famous Otter Trust. Visitors can see Asian and British otters, red and fallow deer and several rare breeds of farm animals in this 230-acre (93ha) wildlife reserve.

Raby Castle
Staindrop, Darlington
Tel: (01833) 660202 www.rabycastle.com
The medieval castle, home of Lord Barnard's family since 1626, includes a 200-acre (80ha) deer park, walled gardens, carriage collection, adventure playground, shop and tearoom.

St Nicholas Cathedral
St Nicholas Street, Newcastle upon Tyne
Tel: (0191) 232 1939
www.newcastle-ang-cathedralstnicholas.org.uk
13thC and 14thC church, added to in 18thC-20thC. Famous lantern tower, pre-reformation font and font cover, 15thC stained glass roundel in the side chapel.

Wallington House, Walled Garden and Grounds (National Trust)
Wallington, Morpeth
Tel: (01670) 773600 www.nationaltrust.org.uk
Escape to the beautiful walled garden and its conservatory or enjoy a walk in the woods or along by the river. Bring the family to one of the many events at Wallington.

Washington Old Hall (National Trust)
The Avenue, Washington
Tel: (0191) 416 6879 www.nationaltrust.org.uk
From 1183 to 1399 the home of George Washington's direct ancestors, remaining in the family until 1613. The manor, from which the family took its name, was restored in 1936.

Wildfowl and Wetlands Trust Washington
District 15, Washington

Tel: (0191) 416 5454 www.wwt.org.uk
Collection of 1,000 wildfowl of 85 varieties. Viewing gallery, picnic areas, hides and winter wild bird-feeding station, flamingos and wild grey heron. Waterside cafe.

Northumbria Tourist Board

Aykley Heads, Durham DH1 5UX.
Tel: (0191) 375 3049 Fax: (0191) 386 0899
www.visitnorthumbria.com

1

THE FOLLOWING PUBLICATIONS ARE
AVAILABLE FROM NORTHUMBRIA TOURIST
BOARD UNLESS OTHERWISE STATED:

Northumbria 2004 –
information on the region, including hotels, bed
and breakfast and self-catering accommodation,
caravan and camping parks, attractions,
shopping, eating and drinking

Group Travel & Education Directory –
guide contains information on group
accommodation providers, places to visit,
suggested itineraries, coaching information and
events. Also provides information to help plan
educational visits within the region. Uncover a
wide variety of places to visit with unique
learning opportunities

Discover Northumbria on two wheels –
information on cycling in the region including an
order form allowing the reader to order
maps/leaflets from a central ordering point

Discover Northumbria on two feet –
information on walking in the region including an
order form allowing the reader to order
maps/leaflets from a central ordering point

Getting to Northumbria

BY ROAD: The north/south routes
on the A1 and A19 thread the
region as does the A68. East/
west routes like the A66 and A69
easily link with the western side of
the country. Within Northumbria
you will find fast, modern
interconnecting roads between all
the main centres, a vast network
of scenic, traffic-free country roads
to make motoring a pleasure and
frequent local bus services
operating to all towns and villages.

BY RAIL: London to Edinburgh
InterCity service stops at
Darlington, Durham, Newcastle
and Berwick upon Tweed. 26
trains daily make the journey
between London and Newcastle in
just under 3 hours. The London to
Middlesbrough journey (changing
at Darlington) takes 3 hours.
Birmingham to Darlington 3 hours
15 minutes. Bristol to Durham 5
hours and Sheffield to Newcastle
just over 2 hours. Direct services
operate to Newcastle from
Liverpool, Manchester, Glasgow,
Stranraer and Carlisle. Regional
services to areas of scenic beauty
operate frequently, allowing the
traveller easy access. The Tyne &
Wear Metro makes it possible to
travel to many destinations within
the Tyneside area, such as
Gateshead, South Shields, Whitley
Bay and Newcastle International
Airport, in minutes.

1. Dunstanburgh Castle

Where to stay in Northumbria

Parks in this region are listed in alphabetical order of place name, and then in alphabetical order of park.

Map references refer to the colour location maps at the front of this guide. The first number indicates the map to use; the letter and number which follow refer to the grid reference on the map.

At-a-glance symbols can be found inside the back cover flap. Keep this open for easy reference.

BAMBURGH, Northumberland Map ref 6C1

★★★
HOLIDAY, TOURING & CAMPING PARK

GLORORUM CARAVAN PARK
Glororum, Bamburgh NE69 7AW
T: (01668) 214457
F: (01668) 214622
E: info@glororum-caravanpark.co.uk
I: www.glororum-caravanpark.co.uk

10	🚐	£13.00–£15.00
80	🚛	£13.00–£15.00
10	▲	£13.00–£15.00

From the A1 take the B1341 at Adderstone Garage, signposted.

★★★★
HOLIDAY, TOURING & CAMPING PARK

MEADOWHEAD'S WAREN CARAVAN AND CAMPING PARK
Waren Mill, Bamburgh NE70 7EE
T: (01668) 214366
F: (01668) 214224
E: waren@meadowhead.co.uk
I: www.meadowhead.co.uk

CC: Delta, Mastercard, Switch, Visa

130	🚐	£8.75–£14.45
	🚛	£8.75–£14.45
50	▲	£6.00–£10.00
27	🏠	£215.00–£410.00
180 touring pitches		

Follow B1342 from A1 to Waren Mill towards Bamburgh. By Budle Bay turn right, follow Meadowhead's Waren Caravan and Camping Park signs.

BEADNELL, Northumberland Map ref 6C1

★★★★
HOLIDAY, TOURING & CAMPING PARK

BH&HPA

BEADNELL LINKS CARAVAN PARK
Beadnell Harbour, Beadnell, Chathill
NE67 5BN
T: (01665) 720526
F: (01665) 720526
E: b.links@talk21.com
I: www.caravanningnorthumberland.com

CC: Switch, Visa

17	🚐	£10.00–£16.50
17	🚛	£10.00–£16.50
17 touring pitches		

Follow roads B6347 or B1342 from A1. Signed thereafter.

COUNTRY CODE Always follow the Country Code 🐾 Enjoy the countryside and respect its life and work 🐾 Guard against all risk of fire 🐾 Fasten all gates 🐾 Keep your dogs under close control 🐾 Keep to public paths across farmland 🐾 Use gates and stiles to cross fences, hedges and walls 🐾 Leave livestock, crops and machinery alone 🐾 Take your litter home 🐾 Help to keep all water clean 🐾 Protect wildlife, plants and trees 🐾 Take special care on country roads 🐾 Make no unnecessary noise

BERWICK-UPON-TWEED, Northumberland Map ref 6B1 *Tourist Information Centre Tel: (01289) 330733*

★★★★
**TOURING &
CAMPING PARK**

See Ad on inside front cover

SEAVIEW CARAVAN CLUB SITE
Billendean Road, Spittal, Berwick-upon-Tweed TD15 1QU
T: (01289) 305198
I: www.caravanclub.co.uk

100	🚐	£9.50–£19.50
100	🚐	£9.50–£19.50
100 total touring pitches		

Spectacular scenery of Northumberland, wonderful views of Holy Island, miles of safe, unspoilt beaches, small castles, pele towers and romantic ruins. Edinburgh within easy reach. Non-members welcome.

CC: Delta, Mastercard, Solo, Switch, Visa

From A1(M) from north, avoiding the town centre, stay on the A1 Berwick bypass for about 4.5 miles. Turn left onto the A1167 signposted Tweedmouth, Spittal. In about 1.5 miles at the roundabout into Billendean Terrace, site on the right.

CORBRIDGE, Northumberland Map ref 6B2

★★★
**TOURING &
CAMPING PARK**

WELL HOUSE FARM—CORBRIDGE
Newton, Corbridge, Stocksfield NE43 7UY
T: (01661) 842193

15	🚐	£8.00
15	🚐	£8.00
15	⛺	£8.00
45 touring pitches		

Turn off the A69 (north) at Stocksfield/Mowden Hall crossroads onto B6309. Straight over crossroads after about 0.5 miles. The site is down bank on left, signposted.

DURHAM, Durham Map ref 6C2 *Tourist Information Centre Tel: (0191) 384 3720*

★★★
**HOLIDAY, TOURING
& CAMPING PARK**

BH&HPA

STRAWBERRY HILL FARM CAMPING & CARAVANNING PARK
Running Waters, Old Cassop, Durham
DH6 4QA
T: (0191) 372 3457
F: (0191) 372 2512
E: howarddunkerley@strawberryhillfarm.
freeserve.co.uk

CC: Delta, Mastercard, Solo,
Switch, Visa

10	🚐	£10.00–£13.50
10	🚐	£10.00–£13.50
10	⛺	£8.50–£11.50
1		£155.00–£299.00
30 touring pitches		

Exit A1(M) at jct 61, on roundabout take exit signed A177 Peterlee. Turn right at the A19, Peterlee to join A181. Park is approximately 2.5 miles on the left.

HEXHAM, Northumberland Map ref 6B2 *Tourist Information Centre Tel: (01434) 652220*

★★★
**HOLIDAY, TOURING
& CAMPING PARK**

BH&HPA

CAUSEY HILL CARAVAN PARK
Causey Hill, Hexham NE46 2JN
T: (01434) 602834
F: (01434) 602834
E: causeyhillcp@aol.com

35	🚐	£10.00
35	🚐	£10.00
20	⛺	£7.00
35 touring pitches		

From Hexham take the B6306 south to Blanchland. First right, after 1.5 miles turn right at crossroads, right again and down hill for 150yds on the left.

RATING All accommodation in this guide has been rated, or is awaiting a rating, by a trained Tourist Board assessor.

LONGHORSLEY, Northumberland Map ref 6C1

★★★★
**HOLIDAY, TOURING
& CAMPING PARK**

BH&HPA

FORGET–ME–NOT CARAVAN PARK
Croftside, Longhorsley, Morpeth NE65 8QY
T: (01670) 788364
F: (01670) 788715
E: info@forget-me-notcaravanpark.co.uk
I: www.forget-me-notcaravanpark.co.uk

CC: Delta, JCB, Mastercard,
Switch, Visa

26		£12.00–£15.00
		£12.00–£15.00
30	▲	£10.00–£14.00
56 touring pitches		

Approximately 1 mile west of the A697 from Longhorsley village, which is about 5 miles north of the A1/A697 jct.

NEWTON–BY–THE–SEA, Northumberland Map ref 6C1

★★★★
**HOLIDAY, TOURING
& CAMPING PARK**

BH&HPA

NEWTON HALL CARAVAN PARK
Newton Hall, Newton-by-the-Sea, Alnwick
NE66 3DZ
T: (01665) 576239
F: (01665) 576900
E: ianpatterson@newtonholidays.co.uk
I: www.newtonholidays.co.uk

CC: Delta, JCB, Mastercard,
Solo, Switch, Visa

15		£9.00–£15.00
15		£9.00–£15.00
51		£220.00–£525.00
16 touring pitches		

Turn off A1 trunk road, take the B1430, and then the unclassified road to Newton-by-the-Sea.

NORTH SEATON, Northumberland Map ref 6C2

★★★
**HOLIDAY &
TOURING PARK**

BH&HPA
NCC

SANDY BAY HOLIDAY PARK
North Seaton, Ashington NE63 9YD
T: (01670) 815055
F: (01670) 812705
E: Sandybay@gbholidayparks.co.uk
I: www.gbholidayparks.co.uk

CC: Delta, Mastercard, Solo,
Switch, Visa

50		
50		£13.00–£15.00
38		£180.00–£480.00
50 total touring pitches		

Follow the signposts for Ashington on the A189 then to Newbiggin (B1334).

SEAHOUSES, Northumberland Map ref 6C1

★★★★★
**HOLIDAY &
TOURING PARK**

BH&HPA

SEAFIELD CARAVAN PARK
Seafield Road, Seahouses NE68 7SP
T: (01665) 720628
F: (01665) 720088
E: info@seafieldpark.co.uk
I: www.seafieldpark.co.uk

Luxurious holiday homes for hire on Northumberland's premier park. Fully appointed caravans offering the very best of self-catering accommodation. Superior touring facilities including fully serviced pitches. Seasonal discounts available on 3-, 4- and 7-day breaks.

CC. Delta, JCB, Mastercard, Solo, Switch, Visa

Take the B1340 from Alnwick for 14 miles. East to coast.

10		£13.00–£21.00
20		£13.00–£21.00
25		£180.00–£500.00
30 touring pitches		

CHECK THE MAPS
The colour maps at the front of this guide show all the cities, towns and villages for which you will find park entries. Refer to the town index to find the page on which it is listed.

★★★★★
**TOURING &
CAMPING PARK**

See Ad on inside front cover

WHITE WATER CARAVAN CLUB PARK

Tees Barrage, Stockton-on-Tees TS18 2QW
T: (01642) 634880
I: www.caravanclub.co.uk

Pleasantly landscaped site, part of the largest white-water canoeing and rafting course built to an international standard in Britain. Nearby Teesside Park for shopping, restaurants etc. Non-members welcome.

OPEN All Year
CC: Delta, Mastercard, Solo, Switch, Visa

Come off the A66 signposted Teesside Retail Park. Follow Teesdale sign, go over Tees Barrage Bridge, turn right. Site 200yds on the left.

117	🚐	£7.00–£15.50
117	🚍	£7.00–£15.50
117 total touring pitches		

QUALITY ASSURANCE SCHEME

For an explanation of the quality and facilities represented by the Stars please refer to the front of this guide.

A brief guide to the main Towns and Villages
offering accommodation in **Northumbria**

BAMBURGH, NORTHUMBERLAND
- Village with a spectacular red
sandstone castle standing 150 ft
above the sea. On the village green
the magnificent Norman church
stands opposite a museum
containing mementoes of the
heroine Grace Darling.

BEADNELL, NORTHUMBERLAND -
Charming fishing village on Beadnell
Bay. Seashore lime kilns (National
Trust), dating from the 18th C, recall
busier days as a coal and lime port
and a pub is built on to a medieval
pele tower which survives from
days of the border wars.

**BERWICK-UPON-TWEED,
NORTHUMBERLAND -** Guarding the
mouth of the Tweed, England's
northernmost town with the best
16th C city walls in Europe. The
handsome Guildhall and barracks
date from the 18th C. Three bridges
cross to Tweedmouth, the oldest
having been built in 1634.

CORBRIDGE, NORTHUMBERLAND
- Small town on the River Tyne.
Close by are extensive remains of
the Roman military town
Corstopitum, with a museum
housing important discoveries from
excavations. The town itself is
attractive with shady trees, a 17th C
bridge and interesting old buildings,
notably a 14th C vicarage.

DURHAM, DURHAM - Ancient city
with its Norman castle and
cathedral, now a World Heritage
site, set on a bluff high over the
Wear. A market and university town
and regional centre, spreading
beyond the market place on both
banks of the river.

HEXHAM, NORTHUMBERLAND -
Old coaching and market town near
Hadrian's Wall. Since pre-Norman
times a weekly market has been
held in the centre with its market
place and abbey park. The richly
furnished 12th C abbey church has a
superb Anglo-Saxon crypt.

**NEWTON-BY-THE-SEA,
NORTHUMBERLAND -** Attractive
hamlet at the south end of Beadnell
Bay with a sandy beach and
splendid view of Dunstanburgh
Castle. In a designated Area of
Outstanding Natural Beauty, Low
Newton, part of the village, is now
owned by the National Trust.

SEAHOUSES, NORTHUMBERLAND
- Small, modern resort developed
around a 19th C herring port. Just
offshore, and reached by boat from
here, are the rocky Farne Islands
(National Trust) where there is an
important bird reserve. The bird
observatory occupies a medieval
pele tower.

QUALITY ASSURANCE SCHEME
For an explanation of the quality and facilities
represented by the Stars please refer to the front
of this guide.

North West

Home of pop stars, world-famous football teams, Blackpool Tower and Coronation Street, the great North West has vibrant cities, idyllic countryside and world-class art collections too.

Classic sights
Blackpool Tower & Pleasure Beach – unashamed razzamatazz
Football – museums and tours at Manchester United and Liverpool football clubs
The Beatles – The Beatles Story, Magical Mystery Tour Bus and Macca's former home

Coast & country
The Ribble Valley – unchanged rolling landscapes
Formby – a glorious beach of sand dunes and pine woods
Wildfowl & Wetlands Trust, near Ormskirk – 120 types of birds including flamingos

Arts for all
The Tate Liverpool – modern art
The Lowry – the world's largest collection of LS Lowry paintings

The Counties of Chesire, Greater Manchester, Lancashire, Merseyside and the High Peak District of Derbyshire

For more information contact:
North West Tourist Board
Swan House,
Swan Meadow Road,
Wigan Pier, Wigan WN3 5BB

www.visitnorthwest.com

Telephone enquiries -
T: (01942) 821222
F: (01942) 820002

1. Blackpool Tower
2. Walkers on Kinder Scout, Derbyshire

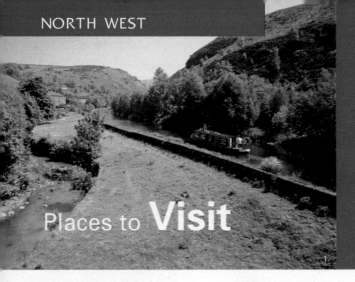

Places to **Visit**

You will find hundreds of interesting places to visit during your stay, just some of which are listed in these pages. Contact any Tourist Information Centre in the region for more ideas on days out.

Awarded VisitBritain's 'Quality Assured Visitor Attraction' marque.

Arley Hall and Gardens
Arley, Northwich
Tel: (01565) 777353
www.arleyestate.zuunet.co.uk

Early Victorian building set in 12 acres (5ha) of magnificent gardens, with a 15thC tithe barn. Plant nursery, gift shop and restaurant. A plantsman's paradise!

Astley Hall Museum and Art Gallery
Astley Park, Chorley
Tel: (01257) 515555 www.astleyhall.co.uk
Astley Hall dates from 1580 with subsequent additions. Unique collections of furniture including a fine Elizabethan bed and the famous Shovel Board Table.

The Beatles Story
Albert Dock, Liverpool
Tel: (0151) 709 1963 www.beatlesstory.com
Liverpool's award-winning visitor attraction with a replica of the original Cavern Club. Available for private parties.

Blackpool Pleasure Beach
Ocean Boulevard, Blackpool
Tel: 0870 4445566
www.blackpoolpleasurebeach.co.uk
Europe's greatest show and amusement park. Blackpool Pleasure Beach offers over 145 rides and attractions, plus spectacular shows.

Blackpool Tower and Circus
The Promenade, Blackpool
Tel: (01253) 292029
www.theblackpooltower.co.uk
Inside Blackpool Tower you will find the UK's best circus, world famous Tower Ballroom, children's entertainment plus Jungle Jim's Playground, Tower Top Ride and Undersea World.

Boat Museum
South Pier Road, Ellesmere Port
Tel: (0151) 355 5017
www.boatmuseum.org.uk
Home to the UK's largest collection of inland waterway craft. Working forge, Power Hall, Pump House, 7 exhibitions of industrial heritage. Gift shop and cafeteria.

Botany Bay Villages and Puddletown Pirates
Canal Mill, Chorley
Tel: (01257) 261220 www.botanybay.co.uk
A shopping, leisure and heritage experience including Puddletown Pirates, the North West's largest indoor adventure play centre.

Bridgemere Garden World
Bridgemere, Nantwich
Tel: (01270) 520381 www.bridgemere.co.uk
Bridgemere Garden World, 25 fascinating acres (10ha) of plants, gardens, greenhouses and shop. Coffee shop, restaurant and over 20 different display gardens in the Garden Kingdom.

Camelot Theme Park
Charnock Richard, Chorley
Tel: (01257) 453044
www.camelotthemepark.co.uk
The Magical Kingdom of Camelot voted Lancashire's Family Attraction of the Year 2002 is a world of thrilling rides, fantastic entertainment and family fun.

CATALYST: Science Discovery Centre
Mersey Road, Widnes
Tel: (0151) 420 1121 www.catalyst.org.uk
Catalyst is the award-winning family day out where science and technology fuse with fun.

Chester Zoo

Upton-by-Chester, Chester
Tel: (01244) 380280
www.chesterzoo.org.uk
Chester Zoo is one of Europe's leading conservation zoos, with over 7,000 animals in spacious and natural enclosures. Now featuring the 'Tsavo' African Black Rhino Experience.

Croxteth Hall and Country Park

Croxteth Hall Lane, Liverpool
Tel: (0151) 228 5311
www.croxteth.co.uk
An Edwardian stately home set in 500 acres (200ha) of countryside (woodlands and pasture), featuring a Victorian walled garden and animal collection.

Dunham Massey Hall Park and Garden (National Trust)
Altrincham
Tel: (0161) 941 1025
www.thenationaltrust.org.uk
An 18thC mansion in a 250-acre (100-ha) wooded deer park with furniture, paintings and silver. A 25-acre (10-ha) informal garden with mature trees and waterside plantings.

East Lancashire Railway
Bolton Street, Bury
Tel: (0161) 764 7790
www.east-lancs-rly.co.uk
Eight miles of preserved railway, operated principally by steam. Traction Transport Museum close by.

Jodrell Bank Science Centre, Planetarium and Arboretum
Lower Withington, Macclesfield
Tel: (01477) 571339 www.jb.man.ac.uk/scicen
Exhibition and interactive exhibits on astronomy, space, energy and the environment. Planetarium, 3D theatre and the world-famous Lovell telescope, plus a 35-acre (14-ha) arboretum.

Knowsley Safari Park
Prescot
Tel: (0151) 430 9009
www.knowsley.com
A 5-mile safari through 500 acres (200ha) of rolling countryside and the world's wildest animals roaming free - that's the wonderful world of freedom you'll find at the park.

Lady Lever Art Gallery

Port Sunlight Village, Wirral
Tel: (0151) 478 4136
www.ladyleverartgallery.org.uk
The 1st Lord Leverhulme's magnificent collection of British paintings dated 1750-1900, British furniture, Wedgewood pottery and oriental porcelain.

Lancaster Castle
Castle Parade, Lancaster
Tel: (01524) 64998 www.lancastercastle.com
Shire Hall has a collection of coats of arms, a crown court, a grand jury room, a 'drop room' and dungeons. Also external tour of castle.

Lyme Park (National Trust)
Disley, Stockport
Tel: (01663) 762023 www.nationaltrust.org.uk
Lyme Park is a National Trust country estate set in 1,377 acres (557ha) of moorland, woodland and park. This magnificent house has 17 acres (7ha) of historic gardens.

1. Rochdale Canal
2. Imperial War Museum North, Salford Quays, Manchester
3. Blackpool Pleasure Beach

Macclesfield Silk Museum
Roe Street, Macclesfield
Tel: (01625) 613210 www.silk-macclesfield.org
A silk museum is situated in the Heritage
Centre, a Grade II Listed former Sunday school.

Merseyside Maritime Museum

Albert Dock, Liverpool
Tel: (0151) 478 4499
www.merseysidemaritimemuseum.org.uk
Liverpool's seafaring heritage brought to life in
the historic Albert Dock.

The Museum of Science & Industry in Manchester
Castlefield, Manchester
Tel: (0161) 832 2244 www.msim.org.uk
Based in the world's oldest passenger railway
station, this museum has galleries that amaze,
amuse and entertain, full of working exhibits
including industrial machines and historic planes.

The National Football Museum
Deepdale Stadium, Preston
Tel: (01772) 908442
www.nationalfootballmuseum.com
The National Football Museum exists to explain
how and why football has become the
people's game.

Norton Priory Museum and Gardens
Manor Park, Runcorn
Tel: (01928) 569895
www.nortonpriory.org
Medieval priory remains, purpose-built museum,
St Christopher's statue, sculpture trail and
award-winning walled garden, all set in 38 acres
(15ha) of beautiful gardens.

Pleasureland Theme Park
Marine Drive, Southport
Tel: 0870 2200204 www.pleasureland.uk.com
Over 100 rides and attractions, including the
TRAUMAtizer and the Lucozade Space Shot.

Rufford Old Hall (National Trust)
Rufford, Ormskirk
Tel: (01704) 821254 www.nationaltrust.org.uk
One of the finest 16thC buildings in Lancashire,
with a magnificent hall, particularly noted for its
immense moveable screen.

Sandcastle Tropical Waterworld

South Promenade, Blackpool
Tel: (01253) 343602
www.blackpool-sandcastle.co.uk
Wave pool, fun pools, giant water flumes, sauna,
white-knuckle water slides, kiddies safe harbour,
play area, catering, bar shops and amusements.

Southport Zoo and Conservation Trust
Princes Park, Southport
Tel: (01704) 538102 www.southportzoo.co.uk
Zoological gardens and conservation trust.
Southport Zoo has been run by the Petrie family
since 1964. Talks on natural history are held in
the schoolroom.

Tate Liverpool
Albert Dock, Liverpool
Tel: (0151) 702 7400
www.tate.org.uk/liverpool/
The Tate Liverpool in historic Albert Dock has 4
floors of art and houses the National Collection
of Modern Art.

Tatton Park (National Trust)

Knutsford
Tel: (01625) 534400
www.tattonpark.org.uk
Historic mansion with a 50-acre (20-ha) garden,
traditional working farm, Tudor manor-house and
a 1,000-acre (400-ha) deer park and children's
adventure playground.

Wigan Pier
Trencherfield Mill, Wigan
Tel: (01942) 323666
www.wiganmbc.gov.uk
Wigan Pier combines interaction with displays
and reconstructions and the Wigan Pier Theatre
Company. Facilities include shops and a cafe.

Wildfowl and Wetland Trust Martin Mere
Burscough, Ormskirk
Tel: (01704) 895181 www.wwt.org.uk
Martin Mere Wildfowl and Wetland Centre is
home to over 1,600 ducks, geese and swans.

North West Tourist Board

Swan House, Swan Meadow Road,
Wigan Pier, Wigan WN3 5BB
T: (01942) 821222 F: (01942) 820002
www.visitnorthwest.com

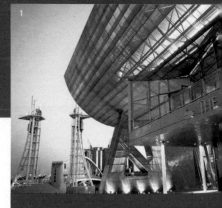

**THE FOLLOWING PUBLICATIONS ARE
AVAILABLE FROM NORTH WEST
TOURIST BOARD:**

Discover England's North West –
a guide to information on the region

Great Days Out in England's North West –
a non-accommodation guide, A1 (folded to A4)
map including list of visitor attractions, what to
see and where to go

Freedom –
forming part of a family of publications about
camping and caravan parks in the north of
England

Stay on a Farm –
a guide to farm accommodation in the north
of England

Group Travel Planner –
a guide to choosing the right accommodation,
attraction or venue for group organisers

Getting to the North West

BY ROAD: Motorways intersect
within the region which has the
best road network in the
country. Travelling north or south
use the M6, and east or west
the M62.

BY RAIL: Most North West
coastal resorts are connected to
InterCity routes with trains from
many parts of the country, and
there are through trains to major
cities and towns.

1. The Lowry,
   Salford Quays,
   Manchester

2. Chester Clock

Where to stay in the

North West

Parks in this region are listed in alphabetical order of place name, and then in alphabetical order of park.

Map references refer to the colour location maps at the front of this guide. The first number indicates the map to use; the letter and number which follow refer to the grid reference on the map.

At-a-glance symbols can be found inside the back cover flap. Keep this open for easy reference.

BLACKPOOL, Lancashire Map ref 5A1 *Tourist Information Centre Tel: (01253) 478222*

★★★★
HOLIDAY, TOURING & CAMPING PARK

PIPERS HEIGHT CARAVAN & CAMPING PARK
Peel Road, Peel, Blackpool FY4 5JT
T: (01253) 763767

100	🚐	£10.00–£15.00
100	🚎	£10.00–£15.00
100	⛺	£10.00–£15.00
100 touring pitches		

Leave the M55 at jct 4. Turn left straight at roundabout A583 to lights turn right. Right and sharp left, park is 30m on right.

★★★
HOLIDAY, TOURING & CAMPING PARK

WINDY HARBOUR HOLIDAY CENTRE
Little Singleton, Blackpool FY6 8NB
T: (01253) 883064
E: info@windyharbour.net
I: www.windyharbour.net

CC: Delta, JCB, Mastercard, Switch, Visa

240	🚐	£12.00–£19.00
240	🚎	£12.00–£19.00
110	⛺	£10.50–£14.50
100	🏠	£135.00–£450.00
240 touring pitches		

Leave the M55 at Fleetwood exit and take the A585. The Park is located at T-junction, A586.

CHESTER, Cheshire Map ref 5A2 *Tourist Information Centre Tel: (01244) 402111*

★★★★★
TOURING PARK

See Ad on inside front cover

CHESTER FAIROAKS CARAVAN CLUB SITE

Rake Lane, Little Stanney, Chester CH2 4HS
T: (0151) 355 1600
I: www.caravanclub.co.uk

A tranquil site only six miles from the walled city of Chester with its famous zoo, historic sites, top-class entertainment and excellent shopping. Non-members welcome.

OPEN All Year
CC: Delta, Mastercard, Solo, Switch, Visa

99	🚐	£12.00–£20.50
99	🚎	£12.00–£20.50
5	⛺	
99 total touring pitches		

From the M53 take jct 10 and join the A5117. Travel towards Queensferry, follow the brown signs. Turn left in Little Stanney at signpost for Chorlton. Site on left in 0.25 miles.

THE CARAVAN CLUB

PRICES Please check prices and other details at the time of booking

LYTHAM ST ANNES, Lancashire Map ref 5A1 *Tourist Information Centre Tel: (01253) 725610*

★★

**HOLIDAY &
TOURING PARK**

BH&HPA

EASTHAM HALL CARAVAN PARK
Saltcotes Road, Lytham St Annes FY8 4LS
T: (01253) 737907

CC: Amex, JCB, Mastercard,
Solo, Switch, Visa

140   Min £12.50
20   Min £12.50
140 touring pitches

Left off M55 jct 3 onto A585, at 3rd roundabout straight ahead onto B5259. Through village of Wrea Green and over level crossing in Moss Side. Park 1 mile on the left.

ROCHDALE, Greater Manchester Map ref 5B1 *Tourist Information Centre Tel: (01706) 864928*

★★★

**TOURING &
CAMPING PARK**

BH&HPA

HOLLINGWORTH LAKE CARAVAN PARK
Rakewood, Littleborough OL15 0AT
T: (01706) 378661

40   £10.00–£12.00
10   £8.00–£12.00
   £6.00–£12.00
50 touring pitches

From M62 jct 21 follow Hollingworth Lake Country Park signs. Go past the Fisherman's Inn, and 2nd on the right is Rakewood Road.

AT-A-GLANCE SYMBOLS

Symbols at the end of each accommodation entry give useful information about services and facilities. A key to symbols can be found inside the back cover flap. Keep this open for easy reference.

A brief guide to the main Towns and Villages offering accommodation in the **North West**

C **CHESTER, CHESHIRE -** Roman and medieval walled city rich in treasures. Black and white buildings are a hallmark, including 'The Rows' - 2-tier shopping galleries. 900-year-old cathedral and the famous Chester Zoo.

L **LIVERPOOL, MERSEYSIDE -** Vibrant city which became prominent in the 18th C as a result of its sugar, spice and tobacco trade with the Americas. Today the historic waterfront is a major attraction. Home to the Beatles, the Grand National, 2 20th C cathedrals and many museums and galleries.

LYTHAM ST ANNES, LANCASHIRE - Pleasant resort famous for its championship golf-courses, notably the Royal Lytham and St Annes. Fine sands and attractive gardens. Some half-timbered buildings and an old restored windmill.

M **MANCHESTER, GREATER MANCHESTER -** The Gateway to the North, offering one of Britain's largest selections of arts venues and theatre productions, a wide range of chain stores and specialist shops, a legendary, lively nightlife, spectacular architecture and a plethora of eating and drinking places.

B **BLACKPOOL, LANCASHIRE -** Britain's largest fun resort, with Blackpool Pleasure Beach, 3 piers and the famous Tower. Host to the spectacular autumn illuminations.

DAVID BELLAMY CONSERVATION AWARDS

If you are looking for a site that's environmentally friendly look for those that have achieved the David Bellamy conservation Award. Launched in conjunction with the British Holiday & Home Parks Association, this award is given to sites which are committed to protecting and enhancing the environment – from care of the hedgerows and wildlife to recycling waste – and are members of the Association. More information about award scheme can be found at back of the guide.

Yorkshire

Yorkshire combines wild and brooding moors with historic cities, elegant spa towns and a varied coastline of traditional resorts and working fishing ports.

Classic sights
Fountains Abbey & Studley Royal – 12thC Cistercian abbey and Georgian water garden
Nostell Priory – 18thC house with outstanding art collection
York Minster – largest medieval Gothic cathedral north of the Alps

Coast & country
The Pennines – dramatic moors and rocks
Whitby – unspoilt fishing port, famous for jet (black stone)

Literary links
Bronte parsonage, Haworth – home of the Bronte sisters; inspiration for 'Wuthering Heights' and 'Jane Eyre'

Arts for all
National Museum of Photography, Film and Television, Bradford – hi-tech and hands-on

Distinctively different
The Original Ghost Walk of York – spooky tours every night

The Counties of North, South, East and West Yorkshire, and Northern Lincolnshire

For more information contact:
Yorkshire Tourist Board
312 Tadcaster Road,
York YO24 1GS

E: info@ytb.org.uk
www.yorkshirevisitor.com

Telephone enquiries -
T: (01904) 707070
(24-hr Brochure Line)
F: (01904) 701414

1. Yorkshire Dales
2. Castle Howard, North Yorkshire
3. Flamborough, East Riding of Yorkshire

Places to Visit

You will find hundreds of interesting places to visit during your stay, just some of which are listed in these pages. Contact any Tourist Information Centre in the region for more ideas on days out.

Awarded VisitBritain's 'Quality Assured Visitor Attraction' marque.

Beningbrough Hall & Gardens (National Trust)
Beningborough, York
Tel: (01904) 470666 www.nationaltrust.org.uk
Handsome Baroque house, built in 1716. With 100 pictures from the National Portrait Gallery, Victorian laundry, potting shed and restored walled garden.

Bolton Abbey Estate
Skipton
Tel: (01756) 718009 www.boltonabbey.com
Ruins of 12thC priory in a parkland setting by the River Wharfe. Tearooms, catering, nature trails, fishing, fell-walking and picturesque countryside.

Cusworth Hall Museum of South Yorkshire Life
Cusworth Lane, Doncaster
Tel: (01302) 782342
www.museum@doncaster.gov.uk
Georgian mansion in landscaped park containing Museum of South Yorkshire Life, with displays of costumes, childhood and transport. Special educational facilities.

The Deep
Hull
Tel: (01482) 381000 www.thedeep.co.uk
Find out all about the world's oceans in entertaining and informative displays. The Deep also has a learning centre and research facility.

Eden Camp Modern History Theme Museum
Malton
Tel: (01653) 697777 www.edencamp.co.uk
This museum transports you back to wartime Britain in a series of expertly-recreated scenes covering all aspects of World War II.

Eureka! The Museum for Children
Discovery Road, Halifax
Tel: (01422) 330069 www.eureka.org.uk
Eureka! is the first museum of its kind designed especially for children up to the age of 12 with over 400 hands-on exhibits.

Fountains Abbey and Studley Royal (National Trust)
Studley Park, Ripon
Tel: (01765) 608888
www.fountainsabbey.org.uk
Largest monastic ruin in Britain, founded by Cistercian monks in 1132. Landscaped garden laid between 1720-40 with lake, formal water garden, temples and deer park.

Freeport Hornsea Outlet Village
Rolston Road, Hornsea
Tel: (01964) 534211 www.freeportplc.com
Set in 25 acres (10ha) of landscaped gardens with over 40 quality high-street names all selling stock with discounts of up to 50%, licensed restaurant. Leisure attractions.

Helmsley Castle (English Heritage)
Helmsley, York
Tel: (01439) 770442
www.english-heritage.org.uk
Great ruined keep dominates the town. Other remains include a 16thC domestic range with original panelling and plasterwork. Spectacular earthwork defences.

JORVIK – The Viking City
Coppergate, York
Tel: (01904) 543403
www.vikingjorvik.com

Journey back to York in AD975 and experience the sights, sounds and even smells of the Viking Age. Special exhibitions complete the experience.

Last of the Summer Wine Exhibition (Compo's House)
30 Huddersfield Road, Holmfirth
Tel: (01484) 681408
Collection of photographs and memorabilia connected with the television series 'Last of the Summer Wine'.

Leeds City Art Gallery
The Headrow, Leeds
Tel: (0113) 247 8248
www.leeds.gov.uk/tourinfo/attract/museums/artgall.html
Interesting collections of British paintings, sculptures, prints and drawings of the 19th/20thC. Henry Moore gallery with permanent collection of 20thC sculpture.

Lightwater Valley Theme Park and Country Shopping Village
North Stainley, Ripon
Tel: 0870 4580060 www.lightwatervalley.net
Set in 175 acres (70ha) of parkland, Lightwater Valley features a number of white-knuckle rides and attractions for all the family, shopping, a restaurant and picnic areas.

Magna
Sheffield Road, Rotherham
Tel: (01709) 720002
www.magnatrust.org.uk

Magna is the UK's 1st Science Adventure Centre set in the vast Templeborough steelworks in Rotherham. Fun is unavoidable here with giant interactive displays.

National Centre for Early Music
St Margarets Church, York
Tel: (01904) 645738 www.yorkearlymusic.org
The National Centre for Early Music is a unique combination of music, heritage and new technology and offers a perfect venue for musicmaking, drama, recordings and conferences.

National Fishing Heritage Centre
Alexandra Dock, Grimsby
Tel: (01472) 323345
www.welcome.to/NFHCentre/
A journey of discovery, experience the reality of life on a deep-sea trawler. Interactive games and displays. Children's area.

National Museum of Photography, Film & Television
Bradford
Tel: (01274) 202030 www.nmpft.org.uk
Experience the past, present and future of photography, film and television with amazing interactive displays and spectacular 3D IMAX cinema. Museum admission is free.

National Railway Museum
Leeman Road, York
Tel: (01904) 621261 www.nrm.org.uk
Discover the story of the train in a great day out for all the family. The National Railway Museum mixes fascination and education with hours of fun. And best of all, it's free.

Newby Hall & Gardens
Ripon
Tel: (01423) 322583
www.newbyhall.com
Late 17thC house with additions, interior by Robert Adam, classical sculpture, Gobelins tapestries, 25 acres (10ha) of gardens, miniature railway, children's adventure garden.

1. Worsbrough Mill Museum, South Yorkshire
2. Staithes, North Yorkshire
3. North Yorkshire Moors, Railway Steam Train

North Yorkshire Moors Railway
Pickering Station, Pickering
Tel: (01751) 472508
www.nymr.demon.co.uk

Britain's most popular heritage railway travelling through the beautiful North York Moors National Park.

Nunnington Hall (National Trust)
Nunnington, York
Tel: (01439) 748283 www.nationaltrust.org.uk
Large 17thC manor-house situated on banks of River Rye. With hall, bedrooms, nursery, maid's room (haunted), Carlisle collection of miniature rooms. National Trust shop.

Pleasure Island Family Theme Park
Kings Road, Cleethorpes
Tel: (01472) 211511 www.pleasure-island.co.uk
The East Coast's biggest fun day out, with over 50 rides and attractions. Whatever the weather, fun is guaranteed with lots of undercover attractions. Shows from around the world.

Ripley Castle
Ripley, Harrogate
Tel: (01423) 770152
www.ripleycastle.co.uk
Ripley Castle, home to the Ingilby family for over 26 generations is set in the heart of a delightful estate with Victorian walled gardens, deer park and pleasure grounds.

Royal Armouries Museum
Armouries Drive, Leeds
Tel: (0113) 220 1916 www.armouries.org.uk
Experience more than 3,000 years of history covered by over 8,000 spectacular exhibits and stunning surroundings. Arms and armour.

Ryedale Folk Museum
Hutton-le-Hole, York
Tel: (01751) 417367
www.ryedalefolkmuseum.co.uk
Reconstructed local buildings including cruck-framed long-houses Elizabethan manor-house, furnished cottages, craftsmen's tools, household/agricultural implements.

Sea Life and Marine Sanctuary
Scalby Mills, Scarborough
Tel: (01723) 376125 www.sealife.co.uk
At the Sea Life Centre you have the opportunity to meet creatures that live in and around the oceans of the British Isles, ranging from starfish and crabs to rays and seals.

Sheffield Botanical Gardens
Clarkehouse Road, Sheffield
Tel: (0114) 267 6496 www.sbg.org.uk
Extensive gardens with over 5,500 species of plants, Grade II Listed garden pavilion (now closed).

Skipton Castle
Skipton
Tel: (01756) 792442
www.skiptoncastle.co.uk

Fully-roofed Skipton Castle is in excellent condition. One of the most complete and well-preserved medieval castles in England.

Wensleydale Cheese Visitor Centre
Gayle Lane, Hawes
Tel: (01969) 667664 www.wensleydale.co.uk
Viewing gallery, see real Wensleydale cheese being made by hand. Interpretation area, including rolling video, display and photographic boards. Museum, shop and cafe.

Wigfield Farm
Worsbrough Bridge, Barnsley
Tel: (01226) 733702
http://sites.barnsley.ac.uk/wigfield
Open working farm with rare and commercial breeds of farm animals including pigs, cattle, sheep, goats, donkeys, ponies and small pet animals.

York Castle Museum
The Eye of York, York
Tel: (01904) 653611 www.york.gov.uk
England's most popular museum of everyday life including reconstructed streets and period rooms.

York Minster
Deangate, York
Tel: (01904) 557200 www.yorkminster.org
York Minster is the largest medieval Gothic cathedral north of the alps. Museum of Roman/Norman remains. Chapter house.

Yorkshire Tourist Board

312 Tadcaster Road, York YO24 1GS.
T: (01904) 707070 (24-hour brochure line)
F: (01904) 701414
E: info@ytb.org.uk
www.yorkshirevisitor.com

THE FOLLOWING PUBLICATIONS ARE AVAILABLE FROM YORKSHIRE TOURIST BOARD:

Yorkshire Visitor Guide 2004 –
information on Yorkshire and Northern
Lincolnshire, including hotels, self-catering,
camping and caravan parks. Also attractions,
shops, restaurants and major events

Walk Yorkshire –
a walking pack tailored to meet the individual's
needs according to the area they are interested in

Hidden Yorkshire –
a guide to Yorkshire's less well known haunts

Yorkshire on Screen –
a guide to Yorkshire's TV, Movie, and
Literary heritage

Eating out Guide –
information on eateries in Yorkshire

Getting to Yorkshire

BY ROAD: Motorways: M1, M62,
M606, M621, M18, M180, M181,
A1(M). Trunk roads: A1, A19, A57,
A58, A59, A61, A62, A63, A64,
A65, A66.

BY RAIL: InterCity services to
Bradford, Doncaster, Harrogate,
Kingston upon Hull, Leeds,
Sheffield, Wakefield and York.
Frequent regional railway services
city centre to city centre including
Manchester Airport service to
Scarborough, York and Leeds.

1. The Humber Bridge
2. Whitby, North Yorkshire

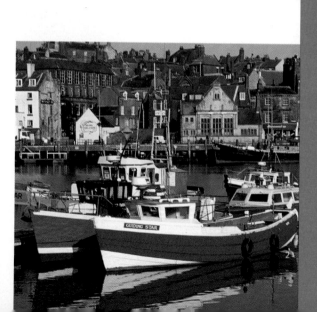

Where to stay in Yorkshire

Parks in this region are listed in alphabetical order of place name, and then in alphabetical order of park.

Map references refer to the colour location maps at the front of this guide. The first number indicates the map to use; the letter and number which follow refer to the grid reference on the map.

At-a-glance symbols can be found inside the back cover flap. Keep this open for easy reference.

FILEY, North Yorkshire Map ref 6D3

★★★★★
HOLIDAY &
TOURING PARK

BH&HPA

ORCHARD FARM HOLIDAY VILLAGE
Stonegate, Hunmanby, Filey YO14 0PU
T: (01723) 891582
F: (01723) 891582

40	🚐	£9.00–£15.00
20	🚙	£9.00–£15.00
25	⛺	£9.00–£15.00
85 touring pitches		

At Staxton roundabout take Filey Road, pick up signs for Hunmanby and then follow brown tourist signs for caravan park.

HARROGATE, North Yorkshire Map ref 5B1 *Tourist Information Centre Tel: (01423) 537300*

★★★★★
HOLIDAY, TOURING
& CAMPING PARK

BH&HPA

RUDDING HOLIDAY PARK

Rudding Park, Follifoot, Harrogate HG3 1JH
T: (01423) 870439
F: (01423) 870859
E: holiday-park@ruddingpark.com
I: www.ruddingpark.com

Award-winning campsite. Three miles south of Harrogate, in peaceful setting, offering Deer House Pub, swimming pool, golf course, driving range and shop. Peak season: 7 nights for the price of 6. Off-peak season: 4 nights for the price of 3.

CC: Delta, Mastercard, Solo, Switch, Visa

Three miles south of Harrogate, to the north of the A658 between its jct with the A61 to Leeds and the A661 to Wetherby.

141	🚐	£11.50–£26.00
141	🚙	£11.50–£26.00
141	⛺	£11.50–£26.00
	🏠	£250.00–£835.00
141 touring pitches		

HAWES, North Yorkshire Map ref 6B3 *Tourist Information Centre Tel: (01969) 667450*

★★
HOLIDAY &
CAMPING PARK

BAINBRIDGE INGS CARAVAN AND CAMPING SITE
Hawes DL8 3NU
T: (01969) 667354
E: janet@bainbridge-ings.co.uk
I: www.bainbridge-ings.co.uk

25	🚐	£9.00
5	🚙	£8.50
40	⛺	£8.50
2	🏠	£140.00–£190.00
70 touring pitches		

Approaching Hawes from the east on the A684 turn left at signpost marked Gayle.

CONFIRM YOUR BOOKING
You are advised to confirm your booking in writing.

HELMSLEY, North Yorkshire Map ref 6C3

★★★★★
**TOURING &
CAMPING PARK**

BH&HPA

FOXHOLME TOURING CARAVAN PARK
Harome, York YO62 5JG
T: (01439) 770416
F: (01439) 771744

60	🚐	£8.50–£9.50
60	🚏	£8.50–£9.50
60	⛺	£8.50–£9.50
60 touring pitches		

Leave Helmsley on the A170 in the direction of Scarborough. After 0.5 miles turn right for Harome. Turn left at the church, through the village and then follow the caravan signs.

🔲🔲🔲🔲🔲🔲🔲🔲🔲🔲

★★★★★
**TOURING &
CAMPING PARK**

BH&HPA

GOLDEN SQUARE CARAVAN AND CAMPING PARK
Oswaldkirk, Helmsley, York YO62 5YQ
T: (01439) 788269
F: (01439) 788236
E: barbara@goldensquarecaravanpark.com
I: www.goldensquarecaravanpark.com

100	🚐	£8.50–£12.50
100	🚏	£8.50–£12.50
29	⛺	£8.50–£12.50
129 touring pitches		

From Helmsley A170 to Thirsk take the 1st left onto the B1257 to York. Take the 1st right to Ampleforth and the turning is after 0.5 miles on the right. From Thirsk 'caravan route' on A19 to York. Turn left for Coxwold. Turn left for Byland Abbey, Wass, Ampleforth.

🔲🔲🔲🔲🔲🔲🔲🔲🔲🔲🔲🔲🔲🔲🔲🔲

HORSFORTH, West Yorkshire Map ref 5B1

★★★★
**HOLIDAY, TOURING
& CAMPING PARK**

BH&HPA

ST HELENA'S CARAVAN SITE
Wardens Bungalow, Otley Old Road,
Horsforth, Leeds LS18 5HZ
T: (0113) 284 1142

40	🚐	£6.00–£9.00
10	🚏	£6.00–£9.00
10	⛺	£5.00–£7.00
60 touring pitches		

Follow the A65 to the A658 past the airport to Carlton crossroads, then turn right at sign for Cookridge and Horsforth down Otley Old Road for 0.75 miles.

🔲🔲🔲🔲🔲🔲🔲

KNARESBOROUGH, North Yorkshire Map ref 5B1

★★★★★
**TOURING &
CAMPING PARK**

See Ad on inside front cover

KNARESBOROUGH CARAVAN CLUB SITE

New Road, Scotton, Knaresborough HG5 9HH
T: (01423) 860196
I: www.caravanclub.co.uk

Popular family destination located in Lower Nidderdale, gateway to the Yorkshire Dales. The historic market town of Knaresborough and the city of Harrogate are within easy reach. Non-members welcome.

CC: Delta, Mastercard, Solo, Switch, Visa

Turn right off the A59 onto the B6165. After approximately 1.5 miles turn right immediately after the petrol station into New Road. The site is on the right hand side after 50 yds.

62	🚐	£11.00–£20.00
62	🚏	£11.00–£20.00
5	⛺	
62 total touring pitches		

THE CARAVAN CLUB

🔲🔲🔲🔲🔲🔲

LONG PRESTON, North Yorkshire Map ref 5B1

★★★★
**HOLIDAY &
TOURING PARK**

GALLABER PARK
Long Preston, Skipton BD23 4QF
T: (01729) 851397
E: info@gallaberpark.com
I: www.gallaberpark.com

CC: Amex, Delta, Diners,
Mastercard, Switch, Visa

63	🚐	£12.00–£15.00
63	🚐	£12.00–£15.00

Gallaber Park is located off the A682 between Long Preston and Gisburn.

MASHAM, North Yorkshire Map ref 6C3

★★★
TOURING PARK

BH&HPA

BLACK SWAN CARAVAN & CAMPSITE

Rear Black Swan Hotel, Fearby, Ripon HG4 4NF
T: (01765) 689477
F: (01765) 689477
E: info@blackswanholiday.co.uk
I: www.blackswanholiday.co.uk

*The holiday park is in an Area of Outstanding Natural Beauty designated by
the Countryside Commission. Pub and restaurant on park. Ideal for walking.
Special offers on web page.*

CC: Amex, Delta, Diners, JCB, Mastercard, Solo, Switch, Visa

*Over Masham bridge keep on A6108 past the garage on the right, take 2nd
turning on the left to Fearby. Park is 2.25 miles on left, at the rear of Black
Swan Hotel.*

50	🚐	£10.00–£10.00
5	🚐	£10.00–£10.00
20	⛺	£10.00–£10.00
3	🏠	£100.00–£250.00
75 touring pitches		

PICKERING, North Yorkshire Map ref 6D3 *Tourist Information Centre Tel: (01751) 473791*

★★★★★
**HOLIDAY, TOURING
& CAMPING PARK**

BH&HPA

UPPER CARR CHALET AND TOURING PARK
Upper Carr Lane, Malton Road, Black Bull,
Pickering YO18 7JP
T: (01751) 473115
F: (01751) 473115
E: harker@uppercarr.demon.co.uk
I: www.upercarr.demon.co.uk

CC: Delta, JCB, Mastercard,
Solo, Switch, Visa

80	🚐	£10.50–£12.50
80	🚐	£10.50–£12.50
80	⛺	£8.50–£10.50
	🏠	£190.00–£380.00
80 touring pitches		

*From Pickering take the A169 Malton road. After 1.5 miles turn left opposite the Black Bull Inn. From Malton
take the A169 Malton road to Pickering. After 5.5 miles turn right, opposite the Black Bull Inn.*

RICHMOND, North Yorkshire Map ref 6C3 *Tourist Information Centre Tel: (01748) 850252*

★★★★★
**HOLIDAY, TOURING
& CAMPING PARK**

BH&HPA

BROMPTON CARAVAN PARK

Brompton-on-Swale, Richmond DL10 7EZ
T: (01748) 824629
F: (01748) 826383
E: brompton.caravanpark@btinternet.com
I: www.bromptoncaravanpark.co.uk

*Relax and enjoy our family-run park in a lovely natural setting on the banks
of the River Swale. Fishing, scenic walks, site shop, heated showers.*

CC: Delta, Mastercard, Solo, Switch, Visa

*On the B6271 halfway between Brompton-on-Swale and Richmond on the
left-hand side.*

177	🚐	£10.00–£17.50
177	🚐	£10.00–£17.50
40	⛺	£5.00–£15.50
177 touring pitches		

IMPORTANT NOTE Information on accommodation listed
in this guide has been supplied by the proprietors. As changes may occur
you are advised to check details at the time of booking.

RIPON, North Yorkshire Map ref 6C3 *Tourist Information Centre Tel: (01765) 604625*

★★★★

HOLIDAY, TOURING
& CAMPING PARK

BH&HPA

WOODHOUSE FARM CARAVAN & CAMPING PARK
Winksley, Ripon HG4 3PG
T: (01765) 658309
E: woodhouse.farm@talk21.com
I: www.woodhousewinksley.com

CC: Delta, Mastercard, Solo,
Switch, Visa

100	£8.50–£13.50
15	£8.50–£13.50
44	£8.00–£10.50
150 touring pitches	

From Ripon take the B6265 Pateley Bridge. After Fountains Abbey take 2nd right and follow site signs.

ROOS, East Riding of Yorkshire Map ref 5D1

★★★★

HOLIDAY, TOURING
& CAMPING PARK

SAND-LE-MERE CARAVAN & LEISURE PARK

Seaside Lane, Tunstall, Roos, Hull HU12 0JQ
T: (01964) 670403
F: (01964) 671099
E: info@sand-le-mere.co.uk
I: www.sand-le-mere.co.uk

A great place to stay, with its natural park and mere leading to a gentle slope to the beach. No cliffs to climb.

CC: Delta, Mastercard, Solo, Switch, Visa

From Hull to Hedon take the B1362 at Withernsea, B1242 to Roos. Look for brown signs marked SLM.

	£10.00–£14.00
	£10.00–£14.00
30	£115.00–£360.00
25 touring pitches	

SCARBOROUGH, North Yorkshire Map ref 6D3 *Tourist Information Centre Tel: (01723) 373333*

★★★★★

HOLIDAY &
TOURING PARK

BH&HPA

BROWNS CARAVAN PARK

Mill Lane, Cayton Bay, Scarborough YO11 3NN
T: (01723) 582303
F: (01723) 584083
E: info@brownscaravan.co.uk
I: www.brownscaravan.co.uk

Beautifully maintained park ideally situated midway between Scarborough and Filey. Only a short stroll to the beach. Facilities include bar, children's play area and games room.

CC: Delta, JCB, Mastercard, Solo, Switch, Visa

Three miles south of Scarborough off A165. Right at lights in Cayton Bay, 100yds on right.

35	£12.00–£12.00
12	£12.00–£12.00

★★★★★

TOURING &
CAMPING PARK

BH&HPA

CAYTON VILLAGE CARAVAN PARK

Mill Lane, Cayton Bay, Scarborough YO11 3NN
T: (01723) 583171
E: info@caytontouring.co.uk
I: www.caytontouring.co.uk

Adjoining church, 0.5 miles from beach. Two inns, bus services. Scarborough three miles, Filey four miles. Free shower, dishwashing facilities, family bathroom. 4-acre dog walk. Low season offers – any 4 nights Sun-Thu inclusive £5 discount, 1 week £7 discount, 1 week (Senior Citizen) £10 discount.

CC: Delta, JCB, Mastercard, Solo, Switch, Visa

A165, south of Scarborough, turn inland at Cayton Bay, traffic lights, 0.5 miles on the right. A64, take B1261 at McDonalds roundabout. In Cayton turn 2nd left after Blacksmiths. Signposted.

125	£9.50–£15.00
125	£9.50–£15.00
75	£8.00–£14.00

SCARBOROUGH continued

★★★★★

HOLIDAY, TOURING & CAMPING PARK

CROWS NEST CARAVAN PARK
Gristhorpe, Filey YO14 9PS
T: (01723) 582206
F: (01723) 582206
E: enquiries@crowsnestcaravanpark.com
I: www.crowsnestcaravanpark.com

50		£10.00–£20.00
50		£10.00–£20.00
100		£10.00–£15.00
40		£110.00–£450.00
150 touring pitches		

On the A165, 5 miles south of Scarborough, 2 miles north of Filey.

★★★★

HOLIDAY, TOURING & CAMPING PARK

NCC

FLOWER OF MAY HOLIDAY PARK

Dept C, Flower of May Holiday Park, Lebberston Cliff,
Scarborough YO11 3NU
T: (01723) 584311
F: (01723) 581361
E: info@flowerofmay.com
I: www.flowerofmay.com

Excellent facilities on family-run, 5-star park. Luxury indoor pool and golf course. Ideal touring centre for Yorkshire's beautiful coast and country. Early booking discount: £25 off full week's hire. 10% discount off full week's pitch fees booked by post in advance.

250		£12.00–£16.50
20		£12.00–£16.50
30		£9.50–£16.50
40		£180.00–£450.00

From A64 take the A165 Scarborough/Filey coast road. Well signposted at Lebberston.

★★★★★

TOURING PARK

BH&HPA

See Ad on this page

LEBBERSTON TOURING PARK
Home Farm, Filey Road, Lebberston,
Scarborough YO11 3PE
T: (01723) 585723
E: lebberstontouring@hotmail.com
I: lebberstontouring.co.uk

CC: Delta, Mastercard, Solo,
Switch, Visa

125		£9.50–£14.00
50		£9.50–£14.00

From the A64 or the A165 take the B1261 to Lebberston and follow the signs for Lebberston Touring Park.

SLINGSBY, North Yorkshire Map ref 6C3

★★★★

HOLIDAY, TOURING & CAMPING PARK

ROBIN HOOD CARAVAN & CAMPING PARK
Green Dyke Lane, Slingsby, York YO62 4AP
T: (01653) 628391
F: (01653) 628391
E: info@robinhoodcaravanpark.co.uk
I: www.robinhoodcaravanpark.co.uk

32		£10.00–£18.00
32		£10.00–£18.00
32		£10.00
23		£125.00–£425.00
32 touring pitches		

The caravan park is situated on the edge of the village of Slingsby with access off the B1257 Malton to Helmsley road.

SPECIAL BREAKS

Many establishments offer special promotions and themed breaks. These are highlighted in red. (All such offers are subject to availability.)

SNAINTON, North Yorkshire Map ref 6D3

★★★★★
HOLIDAY, TOURING & CAMPING PARK

BH&HPA

JASMINE PARK

Cross Lane, Snainton, Scarborough YO13 9BE
T: (01723) 859240
F: (01723) 859240
E: info@jasminepark.co.uk
I: www.jasminepark.co.uk

Picturesque and peaceful park between Pickering and Scarborough. Winner of Yorkshire Caravan Park of the Year and Yorkshire in Bloom. David Bellamy Gold Award for Conservation.

CC: JCB, Mastercard, Solo, Switch, Visa

Turn south off the A170 in Snainton opposite the junior school, signposted.

74	⬡	£10.50–£15.00
74	⬡	£10.50–£15.00
20	⬡	£8.50–£15.00
1	⬡	£160.00–£300.00

STAINFORTH, North Yorkshire Map ref 6B3

★★★★
TOURING & CAMPING PARK

BH&HPA

See Ad on this page

KNIGHT STAINFORTH HALL CAMPING & CARAVAN PARK
Stainforth, Settle BD24 0DP
T: (01729) 822200
F: (01729) 823387
E: info@knightstainforth.co.uk
I: www.knightstainforth.co.uk

CC: Delta, Mastercard, Solo, Switch, Visa

50	⬡	£10.00–£12.00
50	⬡	£10.00–£12.00
50	⬡	£10.00–£12.00

Take the A65 Skipton to Kendal road and turn right opposite Settle High School, along Stackhouse Lane for 2 miles.

THRESHFIELD, North Yorkshire Map ref 6B3

★★★★
HOLIDAY, TOURING & CAMPING PARK

BH&HPA

WOOD NOOK CARAVAN PARK

Skirethorns, Threshfield, Skipton BD23 5NU
T: (01756) 752412
F: (01756) 752946
E: enquiries@woodnook.net
I: www.woodnook.net

Family-run park in the beautiful Yorkshire Dales. An ideal base for walking and touring with a complimentary coffee and cake on arrival. Discounts for Senior Citizens. Also 4 nights for 3, 7 nights for 5. Ring for details.

CC: Delta, JCB, Mastercard, Solo, Switch, Visa

From Skipton take the B6265 to Threshfield. In Threshfield take B6160 for 50m. Turn left into Skirethorns Lane. Follow signs.

48	⬡	£12.00
48	⬡	£12.00
20	⬡	£11.00
11	⬡	£250.00–£295.00
48 touring pitches		

TOWN INDEX

This can be found at the back of the guide. If you know where you want to stay, the index will give you the page number listing all accommodation in your chosen town, city or village.

YORKSHIRE

WHITBY, North Yorkshire Map ref 6D3 *Tourist Information Centre Tel: (01947) 602674*

★★★★
HOLIDAY PARK
BH&HPA

FLASK HOLIDAY HOME PARK
Robin Hoods Bay, Fylingdales, Whitby YO22 4QH
T: (01947) 880592
F: (01947) 880592
E: flaskinn@aol.com
I: www.flaskinn.com

Small, family-run site between Whitby and Scarborough, in the North York Moors. All super-luxury caravans have central heating and double glazing. Rose Award.

CC: Mastercard, Switch, Visa

Situated on the A171, 7 miles to Whitby and 12 miles to Scarborough.

10	🏠	£170.00–£320.00

★★★★★
TOURING &
CAMPING PARK
BH&HPA

LADYCROSS PLANTATION CARAVAN PARK
Egton, Whitby YO21 1UA
T: (01947) 895502
E: enquiries@ladycrossplantation.co.uk
I: www.ladycrossplantation.co.uk

CC: Delta, Mastercard, Switch, Visa

110	🚐	£11.00–£14.90
6	🚐	£11.00–£14.90
4	▲	£9.00–£12.50
120 touring pitches		

From Whitby to Guisborough (A171) take turning signed Egton/North York Moors Railway/Grosmont/Glaisdale. The caravan site is 200yds on the right. Avoid minor roads from A169.

YORK, North Yorkshire Map ref 5C1 *Tourist Information Centre Tel: (01904) 621756*

★★★★★
TOURING &
CAMPING PARK

ALDERS CARAVAN PARK
Home Farm, Alne, York YO61 1RY
T: (01347) 838722
F: (01347) 838722
E: jdwhiteley@tesco.net
I: www.alderscaravanpark.co.uk

40	🚐	£8.50–£10.25
16	🚐	£8.50–£10.25
40 touring pitches		

Situated 2 miles west of the A19 and 9 miles north of York. In the centre of the village.

★★★★★
HOLIDAY, TOURING
& CAMPING PARK
BH&HPA

ALLERTON PARK CARAVAN PARK
Allerton Park, Knaresborough HG5 0SE
T: (01423) 330569
F: (01759) 371377
E: enquiries@yorkshireholidayparks.co.uk
I: www.yorkshireholidayparks.co.uk

30	🚐	£10.00–£12.00
30	🚐	£10.00–£12.00
30	▲	£10.00–£12.00
5	🏠	£175.00–£405.00
30 touring pitches		

Site is 0.25 miles east of the A1(M) leading from the A59 York to Harrogate road.

★★★★★
TOURING PARK
See Ad on inside front cover

BEECHWOOD GRANGE CARAVAN CLUB SITE
Malton Road, York YO3 9TH
T: (01904) 424637
I: www.caravanclub.co.uk

Situated just outside York in countryside. Plenty of space for children to play. Ideal for families as there is so much to see and do in the area. Non-members welcome.

CC: Delta, Mastercard, Solo, Switch, Visa

111	🚐	£11.00–£20.00
111	🚐	£11.00–£20.00
111 total touring pitches		

From A64 on the jct of the A1237 York ring road and the A1036 leading to the A64, north of York. At 3rd roundabout turn right into road signed local traffic only. Site at end of drive.

98

YORK continued

CAWOOD HOLIDAY PARK

★★★★★

HOLIDAY, TOURING
& CAMPING PARK

BH&HPA

Ryther Road, Cawood, Selby YO8 3TT
T: (01757) 268450
F: (01757) 268537
E: william.archer13@btopenworld.com
I: www.cawoodholidaypark.co.uk

CC: Amex, Delta, Diners, JCB,
Mastercard, Solo, Switch, Visa

57	£13.00–£17.00
57	£13.00–£17.00
57	£11.00–£15.00
10	£220.00–£550.00

57 touring pitches

Take the B1222 from the A1 or York and turn at Cawood traffic lights onto the B1223, signposted Tadcaster. Site is 1 mile further on.

WEIR CARAVAN PARK

★★★★

HOLIDAY, TOURING
& CAMPING PARK

BH&HPA

Stamford Bridge, York YO41 1AN
T: (01759) 371377
F: (01759) 371377
E: enquiries@yorkshireholidayparks.co.uk
I: www.yorkshireholidayparks.co.uk

20	£10.00–£12.00
10	£10.00–£12.00
8	£185.00–£410.00

25 touring pitches

From York on the A166 turn left before bridge.

COUNTRY CODE Always follow the Country Code
Enjoy the countryside and respect its life and work Guard
against all risk of fire Fasten all gates Keep your dogs
under close control Keep to public paths across farmland
 Use gates and stiles to cross fences, hedges and walls
Leave livestock, crops and machinery alone Take your litter
home Help to keep all water clean Protect wildlife,
plants and trees Take special care on country roads
Make no unnecessary noise

A brief guide to the main Towns and Villages offering accommodation in **Yorkshire**

FILEY, NORTH YORKSHIRE - Resort with elegant Regency buildings along the front and 6 miles of sandy beaches bounded by natural breakwater, Filey Brigg. Starting point of the Cleveland Way. St Oswald's church, overlooking a ravine, belonged to Augustinian canons until the Dissolution.

HARROGATE, NORTH YORKSHIRE - Major conference, exhibition and shopping centre, renowned for its spa heritage and award-winning floral displays, spacious parks and gardens. Famous for antiques, toffee, fine shopping and excellent tea shops; also its Royal Pump Rooms and Baths. Annual Great Yorkshire Show in July.

HAWES, NORTH YORKSHIRE - The capital of Upper Wensleydale on the famous Pennine Way, Yorkshire's highest market town, renowned for great cheeses. Popular with walkers. Dales National Park Information Centre and Folk Museum. Nearby is spectacular Hardraw Force waterfall.

HELMSLEY, NORTH YORKSHIRE - Delightful small market town with red roofs, warm stone buildings and cobbled market square, on the River Rye at the entrance to Ryedale and the North York Moors. Remains of 12th C castle, several inns and All Saints' Church.

LEYBURN, NORTH YORKSHIRE - Attractive Dales market town where Mary Queen of Scots was reputedly captured after her escape from Bolton Castle. Fine views over Wensleydale from nearby.

LONG PRESTON, NORTH YORKSHIRE - Village surrounded by limestone country and overlooking Ribblesdale, with site of Roman fort to south east.

PICKERING, NORTH YORKSHIRE - Market town and tourist centre on the edge of the North York Moors. The parish church has a complete set of 15th C wall paintings depicting the lives of saints. Part of a 12th C castle still stands. Beck Isle Museum. The North York Moors Railway begins here.

RICHMOND, NORTH YORKSHIRE - Market town on the edge of Swaledale with 11th C castle and Georgian and Victorian buildings surrounding the cobbled market place. Green Howards' Museum is in the former Holy Trinity Church. Attractions include the Georgian Theatre, restored Theatre Royal, Richmondshire Museum, Easby Abbey.

RIPON, NORTH YORKSHIRE - Ancient city with impressive cathedral containing Saxon crypt which houses church treasures from all over Yorkshire. Charter granted in 886 by Alfred the Great. "Setting the Watch" tradition kept nightly by horn-blower in Market Square. Fountains Abbey is nearby.

SCARBOROUGH, NORTH YORKSHIRE - Large, popular, East Coast seaside resort, formerly a spa town. Beautiful gardens and 2 splendid sandy beaches. Castle ruins date from 1100; fine Georgian and Victorian houses. Scarborough Millennium depicts 1,000 years of the town's history. Sea Life Centre.

SLINGSBY, NORTH YORKSHIRE - Large, attractive village with ruined castle and village green, on Castle Howard estate.

WHITBY, NORTH YORKSHIRE - Holiday town with narrow streets and steep alleys at the mouth of the River Esk. Captain James Cook, the famous navigator, lived in Grape Lane. 199 steps lead to St Mary's Church and St Hilda's Abbey overlooking harbour. Dracula connections. Gothic weekend every April.

YORK, NORTH YORKSHIRE - Ancient walled city nearly 2,000 years old, containing many well-preserved medieval buildings. Its minster has over 100 stained glass windows and is the largest Gothic cathedral in England. Attractions include Castle Museum, National Railway Museum, Jorvik Viking Centre and York Dungeon.

MAP REFERENCES The map references refer to the colour maps at the front of the guide. The first figure is the map number; the letter and figure which follow indicate the grid reference on the map.

Heart of England

A multi-cultural region with a diverse mix of vibrant cities, picturesque villages and dramatic countryside, the Heart of England has much to enjoy, from its industrial heritage to the famous 'balti' curry.

Classic sights
Chatsworth House – one of the great treasure houses of England
Ironbridge – birthplace of the industrial revolution
Pottery and porcelain – world-famous Royal Crown Derby, Wedgewood and Spode potteries

Coast and country
Herefordshire – peaceful countryside with black and white timber-framed villages
Skegness – seaside fun
Peak District – stunning landscapes in England's first National Park

City lights
Birmingham – world class visual and performing arts, designer labels, jewellery and the famous Balti Quarter
Nottingham, Leicester, Derby – lively, contemporary cities with bags of culture and style

Distinctively different
Ludlow – acclaimed Michelin-starred restaurants
National Space Centre – look into the future
Alton Towers – thrills, spills and white-knuckle rides galore

The Counties of Derbyshire, Gloucestershire, Herefordshire, Leicestershire, Lincolnshire, Northamptonshire, Nottinghamshire, Rutland, Shropshire, Staffordshire, Warrickshire, Worcestershire and West Midlands.

For more information contact:
Visit Heart of England –
The Regional Tourist Board
Larkhill Road, Worcester
WR5 2EZ

www.visitheartofengland.com

Telephone enquiries -
T: (01905) 761100
F: (01905) 763450

1. Chipping Campden
2. Burghley House, Lincolnshire
3. Rutland Water

You will find hundreds of interesting places to visit during your stay, just some of which are listed in these pages. Contact any Tourist Information Centre in the region for more ideas on days out.

Awarded VisitBritain's 'Quality Assured Visitor Attraction' marque.

Places to Visit

Acton Scott Historic Working Farm
Wenlock Lodge, Church Stretton
Tel: (01694) 781306
www.actonscotmuseum.co.uk
This historic working farm demonstrates farming and rural life in south Shropshire at the close of the 19th century.

Alton Towers Theme Park
Alton, Stoke-on-Trent
Tel: 0870 5204060 www.altontowers.com
Theme park with over 125 rides and attractions such as Air, Oblivion, Nemesis, Congo River Rapids, Log Flume and many children's attractions including 'Blobmaster' live show.

The American Adventure
Ilkeston
Tel: 0845 3302929
www.americanadventure.co.uk
Action and entertainment for all ages, with The Missile white-knuckle rollercoaster, Europe's tallest skycoaster and the world's wettest log flume.

Belton House, Park and Gardens (National Trust)
Belton, Grantham
Tel: (01476) 566116
www.nationaltrust.org.uk
The crowning achievement of restoration country house architecture, built in 1685-88 for Sir John Brownlow with alterations by James Wyatt in 1777.

Belvoir Castle
Belvoir, Grantham
Tel: (01476) 871002 www.belvoircastle.com
The present castle is the 4th to be built on this site and dates from 1816. Art treasures include works by Poussin, Rubens, Holbein and Reynolds. Queens Royal Lancers display.

Birmingham Botanical Gardens and Glasshouses

Westbourne Road, Edgbaston
Tel: (0121) 454 1860
www.birminghambotanicalgardens.org.uk
15 acres (6ha) of ornamental gardens and glasshouses. Widest range of plants in the Midlands from tropical rainforest to arid desert. Aviaries with exotic birds, child's play area.

Black Country Living Museum
Tipton Road, Dudley
Tel: (0121) 557 9643 www.bclm.co.uk
A warm welcome awaits you at Britain's friendliest open-air museum. Wander around original shops and houses, or ride on fair attractions and take a look down the mine.

Museum of British Road Transport
Hales Street, Coventry
Tel: (024) 7683 2425 www.mbrt.co.uk
Two hundred cars and commercial vehicles from 1896 to date, 200 cycles from 1818 to date, 90 motorcycles from 1920 to date and 'Thrust 2' and 'Thrust SSC' land speed record cars.

Butlins
Roman Bank, Skegness
Tel: (01754) 762311
www.butlinsonline.co.uk
Butlins has a Skyline Pavilion, Toyland, Sub Tropical Waterworld, tenpin bowling and entertainment centre with live shows.

Cadbury World
Bournville, Birmingham
Tel: (0121) 451 4180 www.cadburyworld.co.uk
The story of Cadbury's chocolate includes chocolate-making demonstration and attractions for all ages, with free samples, free parking, shop and restaurant.

Chatsworth House, Garden, Farmyard & Adventure Playground
Chatsworth, Bakewell
Tel: (01246) 582204 www.chatsworth.org
Visitors to Chatsworth see more than 30 richly decorated rooms; the garden with fountains, a cascade and maze and the Farmyard and Adventure Playground.

Cotswold Farm Park
Guiting Power, Cheltenham
Tel: (01451) 850307
www.cotswoldfarmpark.co.uk
Collection of rare breeds of British farm animals. Pet's corner, adventure playground, Tractor School, picnic area, gift shop and cafe and seasonal farming displays.

Crich Tramway Village
Crich, Matlock
Tel: (01773) 852565 www.tramway.co.uk
A collection of over 70 trams from Britain and overseas from 1873-1969 with tram rides on a 1-mile (1.5-km) route, a period street scene, depots, a power station, workshops and exhibitions.

Drayton Manor Family Theme Park
Tamworth
Tel: (01827) 287979 www.draytonmanor.co.uk
A major theme park with over 100 rides and attractions, plus children's rides, Zoo, farm, museums and the new live 'Popeye Show'.

The Elgar Birthplace Museum
Lower Broadheath, Worcester
Tel: (01905) 333224 www.elgar.org
Country cottage birthplace of Sir Edward Elgar and the new Elgar Centre, giving a fascinating insight into his life, music, family, friends and inspirations.

The Galleries of Justice
Shire Hall, Nottingham
Tel: (0115) 952 0555
www.galleriesofjustice.org.uk
An atmospheric experience of justice over the ages located in and around an original 19thC courthouse and county gaol, brought to life by live actors.

The Heights of Abraham Cable Cars, Caverns and Hilltop Park
Matlock Bath, Matlock
Tel: (01629) 582365
www.heights-of-abraham.co.uk
A spectacular cable car ride takes you to the summit where, within the grounds, there are a wide variety of attractions for young and old alike. Gift shop and coffee shop.

Ikon Gallery
1 Oozells Square, Birmingham
Tel: (0121) 248 0708 www.ikon-gallery.co.uk
One of Europe's foremost galleries, presenting the work of national and international artists within an innovative educational framework.

Ironbridge Gorge Museum
Coalbrookdale, Telford
Tel: (01952) 433522
www.ironbridge.org.uk
World's first cast-iron bridge, Museum of the Gorge, Tar Tunnel, Jackfield Tile Museum, Coalport China Museum, Rosehill House, Blists Hill and Iron and Enginuity Museum.

Lincoln Castle
Castle Hill, Lincoln
Tel: (01522) 511068
www.lincolnshire.gov.uk/lccconnect/culturalse rvices/heritage/LincolnCastle
A medieval castle including towers and ramparts with a Magna Carta exhibition, a prison chapel experience, reconstructed Westgate and popular events throughout the summer.

1. Quayside Wharf, Birmingham
2. Rolling Hills and rural landscapes in the Heart of England
3. Robin Hood Statue, Nottingham

Midland Railway Centre
Butterley Station, Derby
Tel: (01773) 747674
www.midlandrailwaycentre.co.uk
Over 50 locomotives and over 100 items of
historic rolling stock of Midland and LMS origin
with a steam-hauled passenger service, a
museum site, country and farm park.

National Sea Life Centre
The Water's Edge, Birmingham
Tel: (0121) 633 4700 www.sealife.co.uk
Over 55 fascinating displays. The opportunity to
come face-to-face with literally 100's of
fascinating sea creatures from sharks to
shrimps. Now also includes otters.

Nottingham Industrial Museum
Courtyard Buildings, Nottingham
Tel: (0115) 915 3910
www.nottinghamcity.gov.uk
An 18thC stables presenting the history of
Nottingham's industries: printing, pharmacy,
hosiery and lace. There is also a Victorian beam
engine, a horse gin and transport.

Peak District Mining Museum
The Pavilion, Matlock Bath
Tel: (01629) 583834 www.peakmines.co.uk
A large exhibition on 3500 years of lead mining
with displays on geology, mines and miners,
tools and engines. The climbing shafts make it
suitable for children as well.

Rockingham Castle
Rockingham, Market Harborough
Tel: (01536) 770240
www.rockinghamcastle.com
An Elizabethan house within the walls of a
Norman castle with fine pictures, extensive
views and gardens with roses and an ancient
yew hedge.

Rugby School Museum
10 Little Church Street, Rugby
Tel: (01788) 556109
www.rugbyschool.net/bt/museum_intro.htm
Rugby School Museum tells the story of the
school, scene of 'Tom Brown's Schoolday's', and
contains the earlier memorabilia of the game
invented on the school close.

Severn Valley Railway
The Railway Station, Bewdley
Tel: (01299) 403816 www.svr.co.uk
Preserved standard gauge steam railway
running 16 miles (27km) between Kidderminster,
Bewdley and Bridgnorth. Collection of
locomotives and passenger coaches.

Shakespeare's Birthplace
Henley Street, Stratford-upon-Avon
Tel: (01789) 201822 www.shakespeare.org.uk
The world famous house where William
Shakespeare was born in 1564 and where he
grew up. See the highly acclaimed Shakespeare
Exhibition.

Shugborough Estate (National Trust)
Milford, Stafford
Tel: (01889) 881388
www.staffordshire.gov.uk/shugborough
18thC mansion house with fine collection of
furniture. Gardens and park contain beautiful
neo-classical monuments.

Skegness Natureland Seal Sanctuary

The Promenade, Skegness
Tel: (01754) 764345
www.skegnessnatureland.co.uk
Collection of performing seals, baby seals,
penguins, aquarium, crocodiles, snakes,
terrapins, scorpions, tropical birds, butterflies
(April-October) and pets.

Snibston Discovery Park
Coalville, Leicester
Tel: (01530) 278444
www.leics.gov.uk/museums
Award-winning science and industrial heritage
museum. Over 90 indoor and outdoor hands-on
displays, plus exhibits from Leicestershire's
industrial past.

Spode Visitor Centre
Church Street, Stoke-on-Trent
Tel: (01782) 744011 www.spode.co.uk
Visitors are shown the various processes in the
making of bone china. Visitors can 'have a go'
themselves in the craft demonstration area.

The Tales of Robin Hood
30-38 Maid Marian Way, Nottingham
Tel: (0115) 948 3284 www.robinhood.uk.com
Join the world's greatest medieval adventure.
Ride through the magical green wood and play
the Silver Arrow game, in the search for
Robin Hood.

Twycross Zoo

Twycross, Atherstone
Tel: (01827) 880250
www.twycrosszoo.com
A zoo with gorillas, orang-utans, chimpanzees,
a modern gibbon complex, elephants, lions,
giraffes, a reptile house, pets' corner and rides.

Walsall Arboretum
Lichfield Street, Walsall
Tel: (01922) 653148
www.walsallarboretum.co.uk
Picturesque Victorian park with over 170 acres
(70ha) of gardens, lakes and parkland. Home to
the famous Walsall Illuminations each Autumn.

Warwick Castle
Warwick
Tel: 0870 4422000 www.warwick-castle.co.uk
Set in 60 acres (24ha) of grounds with state
rooms, armoury, dungeon, torture chamber,
'A Royal Weekend Party 1898', 'Kingmaker' and
the new Mill and Engine House attraction.

The Wedgwood Story Visitor Centre

Barlaston, Stoke-on-Trent
Tel: (01782) 204218
www.thewedgwoodstory.com
This £4.5 million visitor centre exhibits centuries
of craftmanship on a plate. Audio-guided tour
includes exhibition and demonstration areas.
Shop and restaurants.

The Wildfowl and Wetlands Trust Slimbridge
Slimbridge, Gloucester
Tel: (01453) 890333 www.wwt.org.uk
Tropical house, hides, heated observatory,
exhibits, shop, restaurant and children's
playground, pond zone.

Worcester Cathedral
10A College Green, Worcester
Tel: (01905) 611002 www.cofe-
worcester.org.uk
Worcester Cathedral is England's loveliest
cathedral. We welcome families, groups and
individuals with refreshments, gift shop and
disabled access to all facilities and gardens.

1. Food and drink in the
   Heart of England
2. Stratford

Visit Heart of England – The Regional Tourist Board

Larkhill Road, Worcester WR5 2EZ.
T: (01905) 761100
F: (01905) 763450
www.visitheartofengland.com

THE FOLLOWING PUBLICATIONS ARE AVAILABLE FROM VISIT HEART OF ENGLAND:

Bed & Breakfast Touring Map including Camping and Caravan Parks 2004

Escape to the Heart 2004/5

Great Places to Visit in the Heart of England 2004

Getting to the Heart of England

BY ROAD: Britain's main motorways (M1/M6/M5) meet in the Heart of England; the M40 links with the M42 south of Birmingham while the M4 provides fast access from London to the south of the region. These road links ensure that the Heart of England is more accessible by road than any other region in the UK.

BY RAIL: The Heart of England lies at the centre of the country's rail network.
There are direct trains from London and other major cities to many towns and cities within the region.

1. Shrewsbury Castle
2. Stokesay Castle, Shropshire

Where to stay in the Heart of England

Parks in this region are listed in alphabetical order of place name, and then by park. As West Oxfordshire and Cherwell are promoted in both Heart of England and The South East, places in these areas with parks are listed in this section. See The South East for full West Oxfordshire and Cherwell entries if applicable.

Map references refer to the colour location maps at the front of this guide. The first number indicates the map to use; the letter and number which follow refer to the grid reference on the map.

At-a-glance symbols can be found inside the back cover flap. Keep this open for easy reference.

ALREWAS, Staffordshire Map ref 5B3

★★★★
HOLIDAY, TOURING & CAMPING PARK

BH&HPA

KINGFISHER HOLIDAY PARK

Fradley Junction, Alrewas, Burton upon Trent DE13 7DN
T: (01283) 790407
F: 08712 423495
E: mail@kingfisherholidaypark.com
I: www.kingfisherholidaypark.com

Picturesque old England setting, at busy junction of two canals, narrowboats galore, canalside pub, play area, games room, free fishing. Four theme parks within easy reach. Short breaks available any time of season.

CC: Delta, JCB, Mastercard, Solo, Switch, Visa

From the A38 dual carriageway. Take the A513 signposted for Kings Bromley. After 2 miles turn left for Fradley jct. At canal bridge turn right along canal bank which is tarmac road. We are just past the pub.

5	🚐	£8.00–£12.50
5	🏕	£8.00–£12.50
6	🏠	£160.00–£425.00
15 touring pitches		

ASHBOURNE, Derbyshire Map ref 5B2 *Tourist Information Centre Tel: (01335) 343666*

★★★★
TOURING PARK

See Ad on inside front cover

BLACKWALL PLANTATION CARAVAN CLUB SITE

Kirk Ireton, Ashbourne DE6 3JL
T: (01335) 370903
I: www.caravanclub.co.uk

Beautifully landscaped, within walking distance of Carsington Reservoir. Good walking and cycling area, conveniently located for exploring the Peak District National Park. Alton Towers 15 miles. Non-members welcome.

CC: Delta, Mastercard, Solo, Switch, Visa

Take the A517 from Ashbourne. In 4.5 miles, turn left at the signpost to Carsington Water/Atlow/Hognaston. In 0.75 miles at the crossroads, turn right signposted to Carsington Water. The site is on the right in 1 mile.

134	🚐	£17.50–£19.50
134	🏕	£17.50–£19.50
134 total touring pitches		

MAP REFERENCES The map references refer to the colour maps at the front of the guide. The first figure is the map number; the letter and figure which follow indicate the grid reference on the map.

★★★

HOLIDAY, TOURING & CAMPING PARK

BH&HPA

ISLAND MEADOW CARAVAN PARK
The Mill House, Aston Cantlow B95 6JP
T: (01789) 488273
F: (01789) 488273
E: holiday@islandmeadowcaravanpark.co.uk
I: www.islandmeadowcaravanpark.co.uk

24		£15.00–£15.00
24		£15.00–£15.00
10		Min £12.00
5		£250.00–£360.00
34 touring pitches		

From the A3400 between Stratford and Henley-in-Arden or from the A46 between Stratford and Alcester follow the signs for Aston Cantlow. The park is 0.25 miles west of the village.

★★★★★

TOURING PARK

See Ad on inside front cover

CHATSWORTH PARK CARAVAN CLUB SITE

Chatsworth, Bakewell DE45 1PN
T: (01246) 582226
I: www.caravanclub.co.uk

Set in the old walled garden on the Estate-a truly breathtaking setting. Farmyard and adventure playground for children. The Peak District National Park's towns are nearby. Non-members welcome.

CC: Delta, Mastercard, Solo, Switch, Visa

From Bakewell on A619. In 3.75 miles on the outskirts of Baslow turn right at roundabout (signposted Sheffield). Site entrance on right in 150 yds.

120		£12.00–£20.50
120		£12.00–£20.50
120 total touring pitches		

★★★★★

TOURING PARK

See Ad on inside front cover

CHAPEL LANE CARAVAN CLUB SITE

Wythall, Birmingham B47 6JX
T: (01564) 826483
I: www.caravanclub.co.uk

Wythall is a quiet, rural area yet convenient for Birmingham (nine miles) and the NEC (13 miles). Visit Cadbury's World or explore the surrounding countryside and local canals. Non-members welcome.

OPEN All Year
CC: Delta, Mastercard, Solo, Switch, Visa

From M1 jct 23a, jct 3 off M42 then A435 to Birmingham. After 1 mile at roundabout take 1st exit, Middle Lane. Turn right at church then immediately right into site.

106		£11.00–£20.00
106		£11.00–£20.00
106 total touring pitches		

See under Birmingham

★★★

HOLIDAY & TOURING PARK

BH&HPA

ORCHARD CARAVAN PARK
Frampton Lane, Hubberts Bridge, Boston PE20 3QU
T: (01205) 290328
F: (01205) 290247
I: www.orchardpark.co.uk

CC: Amex, Delta, Mastercard, Visa

60		£12.00–£12.00
60		£12.00–£12.00
60		£6.00–£12.00
3		£160.00–£190.00
60 touring pitches		

From A17 take the A1121 towards Boston and at the jct with the B1192 take the Hubberts Bridge turn. Frampton Lane is 1st on the left and the park is 0.25 miles down the lane.

VISITOR ATTRACTIONS For ideas on places to visit refer to the introduction at the beginning of this section. Look out too for the ETC's Quality Assured Visitor Attraction signs.

BRIDGNORTH, Shropshire Map ref 5A3 *Tourist Information Centre Tel: (01746) 763257*

★★★★
HOLIDAY PARK

BH&HPA

PARK GRANGE HOLIDAYS
Morville, Bridgnorth WV16 4RN
T: (01746) 714285
F: (01746) 714145
E: info@parkgrangeholidays.co.uk
I: www.parkgrangeholidays.co.uk

		£4.00–£6.00
		£4.00–£6.00
4		£126.00–£301.00

On the A458 Bridgnorth to Shrewsbury road, 1.5 miles beyond Morville towards Shrewsbury, look for the signs to Park Grange Holiday Luxury Caravans.

BUXTON, Derbyshire Map ref 5B2 *Tourist Information Centre Tel: (01298) 25106*

★★★
**TOURING &
CAMPING PARK**

BH&HPA

COTTAGE FARM CARAVAN PARK
Blackwell in the Peak, Blackwell, Buxton
SK17 9TQ
T: (01298) 85330
E: mail@cottagefarmsite.co.uk
I: www.cottagefarmsite.co.uk

30		Min £7.00
30		Min £7.00
30		Min £7.00
30 touring pitches		

Off A6 midway between Buxton and Bakewell. Site signposted.

★★★★★
**TOURING &
CAMPING PARK**

See Ad on inside front cover

GRIN LOW CARAVAN CLUB SITE
Grin Low Road, Ladmanlow, Buxton SK17 6UJ
T: (01298) 77735
I: www.caravanclub.co.uk

Attractively landscaped site ideally situated for Buxton, which lies at the centre of the Peak District National Park, and for visiting stately homes including Chatsworth and Haddon Hall. Non-members welcome.

CC: Delta, Mastercard, Solo, Switch, Visa

From Buxton turn left off the A53 Buxton to Leek road. Within 1.5 miles at Grin Low signpost, in 300 yds turn left into the site approach road; the site entrance is 0.25 miles away.

117		£9.50–£19.50
117		£9.50–£19.50
6		
117 total touring pitches		

★★★
**HOLIDAY, TOURING
& CAMPING PARK**

BH&HPA

NEWHAVEN CARAVAN AND CAMPING PARK
Newhaven, Buxton SK17 0DT   CC: Delta, JCB, Mastercard,
T: (01298) 84300   Switch, Visa
F: (01332) 726027

95		£7.50–£9.00
95		£7.50–£9.00
30		£7.50–£9.00
125 touring pitches		

Halfway between Ashbourne and Buxton on A515 at the jct with the A5012.

CASTLETON, Derbyshire Map ref 5B2

★★★★★
**TOURING &
CAMPING PARK**

See Ad on inside front cover

LOSEHILL CARAVAN CLUB SITE
Castleton, Hope Valley S33 8WB
T: (01433) 620636
I: www.caravanclub.co.uk

This popular site, set in the north of the Peak District National Park, is an excellent base for outdoor activities-rock-climbing, potholing, biking and horse-riding. Non-members welcome.

OPEN All Year
CC: Delta, Mastercard, Solo, Switch, Visa

From Hathersage on the B6001 in about 2.5 miles, turn left onto the A6187 (signposted Castleton), site on right in 5m.

78		£11.00–£20.00
78		£11.00–£20.00
20		
78 total touring pitches		

CHERWELL

See South East region for entries

CIRENCESTER, Gloucestershire Map ref 3B1 *Tourist Information Centre Tel: (01285) 654180*

★★★★
TOURING PARK
BH&HPA

MAYFIELD TOURING PARK
Cheltenham Road, Perrotts Brook, Cirencester GL7 7BH
T: (01285) 831301
F: (01285) 831301
E: mayfield-park@cirencester.fsbusiness.co.uk
I: www.mayfieldpark.co.uk

CC: Amex, Delta, Mastercard, Solo, Switch, Visa

36 £8.00–£11.00
25
36
97 touring pitches

On the A435 2 miles north of Cirencester, 13 miles south of Cheltenham. Exit A419 at Burford road jct.

COTSWOLDS

See under Cirencester

See also Cotswolds in South East region

ELLESMERE, Shropshire Map ref 5A2

★★★★
HOLIDAY & TOURING PARK
BH&HPA
NCC

FERNWOOD CARAVAN PARK
Lyneal, Ellesmere SY12 0QF
T: (01948) 710221
F: (01948) 710324
E: fernwood@caravanpark37.fsnet.co.uk
I: www.ranch.co.uk

CC: Delta, Mastercard, Switch, Visa

60 £12.00–£17.00
60 £12.00–£17.00
1 £220.00–£400.00
60 touring pitches

Ellesmere A495 road at Welshampton B5063, after canal follow signs.

EVESHAM, Worcestershire Map ref 3B1 *Tourist Information Centre Tel: (01386) 446944*

★★★★★
HOLIDAY & TOURING PARK
BH&HPA
NCC

THE RANCH CARAVAN PARK
Station Road, Honeybourne, Evesham WR11 7PR
T: (01386) 830744
F: (01386) 833503
E: enquiries@ranch.co.uk
I: www.ranch.co.uk

CC: Delta, Mastercard, Switch, Visa

120 £12.00–£19.50
120
4 £245.00–£380.00
120 touring pitches

From Evesham take B4035 to Badsey and Bretforton. Left to Honeybourne.

HORNCASTLE, Lincolnshire Map ref 5D2

★★★★
HOLIDAY, TOURING & CAMPING PARK
BH&HPA

ASHBY PARK
West Ashby, Horncastle LN9 5PP
T: (01507) 527966
F: (01507) 524539
E: ashbyparklakes@aol.com
I: www.ukparks.co.uk/ashby

We offer a friendly and informal atmosphere, peace and tranquillity, good walks, a diversity of wildlife. Set in seventy acres of unspoilt countryside.

CC: Amex, Mastercard, Switch, Visa

1.5 miles north of Horncastle between the A153 an the A158.

60 £9.00–£17.00
60 £9.00–£17.00
20 £9.00–£11.50
60 touring pitches

LINCOLN, Lincolnshire Map ref 5C2

★★★
TOURING PARK

HARTSHOLME COUNTRY PARK
Skellingthorpe Road, Lincoln LN6 0EY
T: (01522) 873578
F: (01522) 873577

50 £11.00–£18.00
50 £11.00–£18.00
18 £5.50–£11.00
50 touring pitches

Signposted from A46 Lincoln bypass, brown signs. Entrance on B1378

LUDLOW, Shropshire Map ref 5A3 *Tourist Information Centre Tel: (01584) 875053*

★★★★★
**HOLIDAY &
TOURING PARK**

BH&HPA

ORLETON RISE HOLIDAY HOME PARK
Green Lane, Orleton, Ludlow SY8 4JE
T: (01584) 831617
F: (01584) 831617

16	£7.00–£12.00
16	£7.00–£12.00
16 touring pitches	

A49 Ludlow/Leominster turn at Wooferton B4362. Turn left at T-junction towards Leominster. Turn at Maidenhead Inn and the park is 0.75 miles along Green Lane.

MORETON-IN-MARSH, Gloucestershire Map ref 3B1

★★★★★
**TOURING &
CAMPING PARK**

See Ad on inside front cover

MORETON-IN-MARSH CARAVAN CLUB SITE
Bourton Road, Moreton-in-Marsh GL56 0BT
T: (01608) 650519
I: www.caravanclub.co.uk

An attractive, well-wooded site within easy walking distance of market town of Moreton-in-Marsh. On-site facilities include crazy golf, volleyball and boules. Large dog-walking area. Non-members welcome.

182	£11.00–£20.00
182	£11.00–£20.00
182 total touring pitches	

OPEN All Year
CC: Delta, Mastercard, Solo, Switch, Visa

From Moreton-in-Marsh on A44 the site entrance is on the right 250 yds past the end of the speed limit sign.

PEAK DISTRICT

See under Ashbourne, Bakewell, Buxton, Castleton

PEMBRIDGE, Herefordshire Map ref 3A1

★★★★★
**TOURING &
CAMPING PARK**

TOWNSEND TOURING PARK
Townsend Farm, Pembridge, Leominster HR6 9HB
T: (01544) 388527
F: (01544) 388527
E: info@townsend-farm.co.uk
I: www.townsend-farm.co.uk

Spacious 60-pitch touring park set on the outskirts of Pembridge. Luxurious facilities block, fully serviced pitches, hardstandings, landscaped amenity area, lake, reception, farm shop and butchery.

60	£7.00–£14.00
60	£7.00–£14.00
60	£7.00–£14.00
60 touring pitches	

Follow the A44 into village of Pembridge, Townsend Touring Park is situated on the Leominster side of the village 50m within the village boundary.

CREDIT CARD BOOKINGS If you book by telephone and are asked for your credit card number it is advisable to check the proprietor's policy should you cancel your reservation.

RUGELEY, Staffordshire Map ref 5B3

★★★★
HOLIDAY PARK

ROSE AWARD

BH&HPA

SILVER TREES CARAVAN PARK
Stafford Brook Road, Penkridge Bank,
Rugeley WS15 2TX
T: (01889) 582185
F: (01889) 582373
E: enquiries@silvertreescaravanpark.co.uk
I: www.silvertreescaravanpark.co.uk

CC: Delta, Mastercard, Switch,
Visa

🚐		£12.00–£14.00
🚙		£12.00–£14.00
🛖	8	£239.00–£425.00

From Rugeley Western Springs Road turn west at traffic lights for Penkridge, after 2 miles turn right into Stafford Brook Road (unclassified). Signposted.

SHERWOOD FOREST

See under Worksop

STOKE-ON-TRENT, Staffordshire Map ref 5B2 *Tourist Information Centre Tel: (01782) 236000*

★★★★
HOLIDAY, TOURING
& CAMPING PARK

BH&HPA

THE STAR CARAVAN AND CAMPING PARK

Star Road, Cotton, Oakamoor, Stoke-on-Trent ST10 3OW
T: (01538) 702219
F: (01538) 703704
I: www.starcaravanpark.co.uk

The closest touring park to Alton Towers, strict 11pm-all-quiet rule on site. No single-sex groups allowed. Families and mixed couples always welcomed. Early-season discounts on caravan holiday homes. Stay 7 days on touring pitches for price of 6.

🚐	60	£10.00–£10.00
🚙	30	£10.00–£10.00
⛺	30	£10.00–£10.00
🛖	9	£270.00–£270.00
120 touring pitches		

From M6 jct 16 or M1 jct 23A follow all signs for Alton Towers. With Alton Towers on your right hand side, go past and follow the road (Beelow Lane) for 0.75 miles to crossroads. Turn right and proceed up hill. Site on right after 400 m.

STRATFORD-UPON-AVON, Warwickshire Map ref 3B1 *Tourist Information Centre Tel: (01789) 293127*

★★★
TOURING &
CAMPING PARK

BH&HPA

See Ad on this page

DODWELL PARK
Evesham Rd, (B439), Stratford-upon-Avon
CV37 9SR
T: (01789) 204957
F: (01926) 620199
E: enquiries@dodwellpark.co.uk
I: www.dodwellpark.co.uk

CC: Delta, Mastercard, Switch,
Visa

🚙	50	£10.00–£11.00
🚐	20	£10.00–£11.00
⛺	50	£7.00–£11.00
50 touring pitches		

On the B439 2 miles south west of Stratford-upon-Avon.

SUTTON IN ASHFIELD, Nottinghamshire Map ref 5C2

★★★★★
TOURING &
CAMPING PARK

BH&HPA

SHARDAROBA CARAVAN PARK
Silverhill Lane, Teversal, Sutton in Ashfield
NG17 3JJ
T: (01623) 551838
F: (01623) 552174
E: stay@shardaroba.co.uk
I: www.shardaroba.co.uk

CC: Delta, Mastercard, Switch,
Visa

🚐	100	£10.00–£14.00
🚙	60	£10.00–£14.00
⛺	40	£10.00–£10.00
100 touring pitches		

Turn off M1 at junction 28, take the A38 towards Mansfield. First set of traffic lights left onto B6027, over 2 mini-roundabouts, at top of hill straight over crossroads. At next crossroads turn left, at t-junction turn right onto B6014, at Carnarvon Arms turn left onto Silverhill Lane.

TELFORD, Shropshire Map ref 5A3 *Tourist Information Centre Tel: (01952) 238008*

★★★★★
**TOURING &
CAMPING PARK**

BH&HPA

SEVERN GORGE PARK
Bridgnorth Road, Tweedale, Telford TF7 4JB
T: (01952) 684789
E: info@severngorgepark.co.uk
I: www.severngorgepark.co.uk

CC: Delta, JCB, Mastercard,
Solo, Switch, Visa

50	£13.75–£15.35
50	£13.75–£15.35
20	£9.60–£11.45
70 touring pitches	

From M54 jct 4 or 5 take the A442 south signposted Kidderminster (approximately 3 miles). Follow signs for Madeley then Tweedale.

TEWKESBURY, Gloucestershire Map ref 3B1 *Tourist Information Centre Tel: (01684) 295027*

★★★★
**TOURING &
CAMPING PARK**

See Ad on inside front cover

TEWKESBURY ABBEY CARAVAN CLUB SITE
Gander Lane, Tewkesbury GL20 5PG
T: (01684) 294035
I: www.caravanclub.co.uk

Impressive location next to Tewkesbury Abbey. Only a short walk into the old town of Tewkesbury where there is much to explore. Many Costwold villages within easy driving distance. Non-members welcome.

CC: Delta, Mastercard, Solo, Switch, Visa

From M5 leave by exit 9 onto A438. In about 3 miles in town centre, at cross-junction turn right. After 200 yds turn left into Gander Lane. From M50 leave by exit 1 onto A38.

170	£9.50–£19.50
170	£9.50–£19.50
170 total touring pitches	

WEST OXFORDSHIRE

See South East region for entries

WOODHALL SPA, Lincolnshire Map ref 5D2

★★★★★
**HOLIDAY &
TOURING PARK**

BH&HPA

BAINLAND COUNTRY PARK LTD
Horncastle Road, Woodhall Spa LN10 6UX
T: (01526) 352903
F: (01526) 353730
E: bookings@bainland.com
I: www.bainland.com

CC: Delta, Mastercard, Solo,
Switch, Visa

150	£10.00–£30.00
150	£10.00–£30.00
100	£8.00–£23.00
10	£200.00–£475.00
150 touring pitches	

One-and-a-half miles from the centre of Woodhall Spa, going towards Horncastle, on the right just before the petrol station, on the B1191.

WORKSOP, Nottinghamshire Map ref 5C2 *Tourist Information Centre Tel: (01909) 501148*

★★★★★
TOURING PARK

See Ad on inside front cover

CLUMBER PARK CARAVAN CLUB SITE
Lime Tree Avenue, Clumber Park, Worksop S80 3AE
T: (01909) 484758
I: www.caravanclub.co.uk

Set in the heart of Sherwood Forest and redeveloped to a high standard in 2002. Visit Nottingham Castle and the watersports centre at Holme Pierrepont. Non-members welcome.

CC: Delta, Mastercard, Solo, Switch, Visa

From the junction of the A1 and A57, take the A614 signposted to Nottingham for 0.5 miles. Turn right into Clumber Park site. The club is signposted thereafter.

183	£12.00–£20.50
183	£12.00–£20.50
183 total touring pitches	

WHERE TO STAY
Please mention this guide when making your booking.

A brief guide to the main Towns and Villages offering accommodation in the **Heart of England**

A ALREWAS, STAFFORDSHIRE - Delightful village of black and white cottages, past which the willow-fringed Trent runs. The Trent and Mersey Canal enhances the scene and Fradley Junction, a mile away, is one of the most charming inland waterway locations in the country.

ASHBOURNE, DERBYSHIRE - Market town on the edge of the Peak District National Park and an excellent centre for walking. Its impressive church with 212-ft spire stands in an unspoilt old street. Ashbourne is well known for gingerbread and its Shrovetide football match.

ASTON CANTLOW, WARWICKSHIRE - Attractive village on the River Alne, with a black and white timbered guild house and a fine old inn.

B BAKEWELL, DERBYSHIRE - Pleasant market town, famous for its pudding. It is set in beautiful countryside on the River Wye and is an excellent centre for exploring the Derbyshire Dales, the Peak District National Park, Chatsworth and Haddon Hall.

BIRMINGHAM, WEST MIDLANDS - Britain's second city, whose attractions include Centenary Square and the ICC with Symphony Hall, the NEC, the City Art Gallery, Barber Institute of Fine Arts, 17th C Aston Hall, science and railway museums, Jewellery Quarter, Cadbury World, 2 cathedrals and Botanical Gardens.

BOSTON, LINCOLNSHIRE - Historic town famous for its church tower, the Boston Stump, 272 ft high. Still a busy port, the town is full of interest and has links with Boston, Massachusetts, through the Pilgrim Fathers. The cells where they were imprisoned can be seen in the medieval Guildhall.

BRIDGNORTH, SHROPSHIRE - Red sandstone riverside town in 2 parts - High and Low - linked by a cliff railway. Much of interest including a ruined Norman keep, half-timbered 16th C houses, Midland Motor Museum and Severn Valley Railway.

BUXTON, DERBYSHIRE - The highest market town in England and one of the oldest spas, with an elegant crescent, Poole's Cavern, Opera House and attractive Pavilion Gardens. An excellent centre for exploring the Peak District.

C CIRENCESTER, GLOUCESTERSHIRE - "Capital of the Cotswolds", Cirencester was Britain's second most important Roman town with many finds housed in the Corinium Museum. It has a very fine Perpendicular church and old houses around the market place.

E EVESHAM, WORCESTERSHIRE - Market town in the centre of a fruit-growing area. There are pleasant walks along the River Avon and many old houses and inns. A fine 16th C bell tower stands between 2 churches near the medieval Almonry Museum.

H HORNCASTLE, LINCOLNSHIRE - Pleasant market town near the Lincolnshire Wolds, which was once a walled Roman settlement. It was the scene of a decisive Civil War battle, relics of which can be seen in the church. Tennyson's bride lived here.

L LINCOLN, LINCOLNSHIRE - Ancient city dominated by the magnificent 11th C cathedral with its triple towers. A Roman gateway is still used and there are medieval houses lining narrow, cobbled streets. Other attractions include the Norman castle, several museums and the Usher Gallery.

LUDLOW, SHROPSHIRE - Outstandingly interesting border town with a magnificent castle high above the River Teme, 2 half-timbered old inns and an impressive 15th C church. The Reader's House, with its 3-storey Jacobean porch, should also be seen.

M MORETON-IN-MARSH, GLOUCESTERSHIRE - Attractive town of Cotswold stone with 17th C houses, an ideal base for touring the Cotswolds. Some of the local attractions include Batsford Park Arboretum, the Jacobean Chastleton House and Sezincote Garden.

P PEMBRIDGE, HEREFORDSHIRE - Delightful village close to the Welsh border with many black and white half-timbered cottages, some dating from the 14th C. There is a market hall supported by 8 wooden pillars in the market place, also old inns and a 14th C church with interesting separate bell tower.

R RUGELEY, STAFFORDSHIRE - Town close to Cannock Chase which has over 2,000 acres of heath and woodlands with forest trails and picnic sites. Nearby is Shugborough Hall (National Trust) with a fine collection of 18th C furniture and

interesting monuments in the grounds.

S STOKE-ON-TRENT, STAFFORDSHIRE - Famous for its pottery. Factories of several famous makers, including Josiah Wedgwood, can be visited. The City Museum has one of the finest pottery and porcelain collections in the world.

STRATFORD-UPON-AVON, WARWICKSHIRE - Famous as Shakespeare's home town, Stratford's many attractions include his birthplace, New Place where he died, the Royal Shakespeare Theatre and Gallery and Hall's Croft (his daughter's house).

TEWKESBURY, GLOUCESTERSHIRE - Tewkesbury's outstanding possession is its magnificent church, built as an abbey, with a great Norman tower and beautiful 14th C interior. The town stands at the confluence of the Severn and Avon and has many medieval houses, inns and several museums.

WOODHALL SPA, LINCOLNSHIRE - Attractive town which was formerly a spa. It has excellent sporting facilities with a championship golf-course and is surrounded by pine woods.

WORKSOP, NOTTINGHAMSHIRE - Market town close to the Dukeries where a number of Ducal families had their estates, some of which, like Clumber Park, may be visited. The upper room of the 14th C gatehouse of the priory housed the country's first elementary school in 1628.

TELFORD, SHROPSHIRE - New Town named after Thomas Telford, the famous engineer who designed many of the country's canals, bridges and viaducts. It is close to Ironbridge with its monuments and museums associated with the Industrial Revolution, including restored 18th C buildings.

USE YOUR *i*s

There are more than 550 Tourist Information Centres throughout England offering friendly help with accommodation and holiday ideas as well as suggestions of places to visit and things to do. There may well be a centre in your home town which can help you before you set out. You'll find addresses in the local Phone Book.

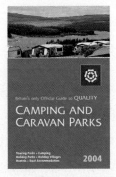

East of England

Discover England as you always thought it should be. Gently rolling countryside and unspoilt coastline, excellent for cycling, walking and bird-watching. Explore charming villages, historic market towns, traditional seaside resorts and bustling cities; awesome gothic cathedrals, magnificent stately homes and famous gardens.

Classic sights
Hatfield House – childhood home of Queen Elizabeth I
Blickling Hall – one of England's greatest Jacobean houses
Sutton Hoo – important burial site of Anglo-Saxon kings

Coast and country
The Chilterns – beautiful chalk life flora and fauna at the regions highest point
The Norfolk Broads – miles of reed-fringed waterways, man-made broads and nature reserves
The Fens – unique panorama of rivers and dykes, wide open skies and unforgettable sunsets

Glorious gardens
Anglesey Abbey – outstanding all year round gardens
The Gardens of the Rose – wander amongst 30,000 rose species
RHS Garden: Hyde Hall – rose, water and woodland gardens

Arts for all
Aldeburgh festival – internationally acclaimed festival of music and the arts
Luton Carnival – Britain's biggest one-day carnival

Delightfully different
Stilton – where each May they roll wooden cheeses down the High Street
St. Peters-on-the-Wall – oldest Saxon church in England

The Counties of Bedfordshire, Cambridgeshire, Essex, Hertfordshire, Norfolk and Suffolk

For more information contact:
East of England Tourist Board Toppesfield Hall, Hadleigh, Suffolk IP7 5DN

E: jbowers@eetb.org.uk
www.eastofenglandtouristboard.com

Telephone enquiries -
T: 0870 225 4800
F: 0870 225 4890

1. Punting on the River Cam, Cambridge
2. Globe Inn, Linslade, Bedfordshire

You will find hundreds of interesting places to visit during your stay, just some of which are listed in these pages. Contact any Tourist Information Centre in the region for more ideas on days out.

Awarded VisitBritain's 'Quality Assured Visitor Attraction' marque.

Places to Visit

Audley End House and Park (English Heritage)

Audley End, Saffron Walden
Tel: (01799) 522399
www.english-heritage.org.uk
A palatial Jacobean house remodelled in the 18th-19thC with a magnificent great hall with 17thC plaster ceilings. Rooms and furniture by Robert Adam and park by 'Capability' Brown.

Banham Zoo
Banham, Norwich
Tel: (01953) 887771
www.banhamzoo.co.uk
Wildlife spectacular which will take you on a journey to experience tigers, leopards and zebra and some of the world's most exotic, rare and endangered animals.

Barleylands Farm
Barleylands Road, Billericay
Tel: (01268) 290229
www.barleylandsfarm.co.uk
Visitor centre with a rural museum, animal centre, craft studios, blacksmith's shop, glass-blowing studio with a viewing gallery, miniature steam railway and a restaurant.

Blickling Hall (National Trust)
Blickling, Norwich
Tel: (01263) 738030 www.nationaltrust.org.uk
A Jacobean redbrick mansion with garden, orangery, parkland and lake. There is also a display of fine tapestries and furniture.

Bressingham Steam Experience and Gardens
Bressingham, Diss
Tel: (01379) 686900 www.bressingham.co.uk
Steam rides through 4 miles (6.5km) of woodland. Six acres (2.5ha) of the Island Beds plant centre. Main line locomotives, the Victorian Gallopers and over 50 steam engines.

Bure Valley Railway
Aylsham Station, Norwich
Tel: (01263) 733858 www.bvrw.co.uk
A 15-inch narrow-gauge steam railway covering 9 miles (14.5km) of track from Wroxham in the heart of the Norfolk Broads to the bustling market town of Aylsham.

Colchester Castle
Castle Park, Colchester
Tel: (01206) 282939
www.colchestermuseums.org.uk
A Norman keep on the foundations of a Roman temple. The archaeological material includes much on Roman Colchester (Camulodunum).

Colchester Zoo
Stanway, Colchester
Tel: (01206) 331292
www.colchester-zoo.co.uk
Zoo with 200 species and some of the best cat and primate collections in the UK, 60 acres (24ha) of gardens and lakes, award-winning animal enclosures and picnic areas.

Ely Cathedral
The College, Ely
Tel: (01353) 667735
www.cathedral.ely.anglican.org.uk
One of England's finest cathedrals with guided tours and tours of the Octagon and West Tower, monastic precincts and also a brass rubbing centre and Stained Glass Museum.

Fritton Lake Country World

Fritton, Great Yarmouth
Tel: (01493) 488208
www.frittonlake.co.uk

A 250-acre (100-ha) centre with a children's assault course, putting, an adventure playground, golf, fishing, boating, wildfowl, heavy horses, cart rides, falconry and flying displays.

The Gardens of the Rose

Chiswell Green, St Albans
Tel: (01727) 850461 www.roses.co.uk
The Royal National Rose Society's Garden with 27 acres (11ha) of garden and trial grounds for new varieties of rose. 30,000 roses of all types and 1,700 different varieties are on display .

Hatfield House, Park and Gardens

Hatfield
Tel: (01707) 287010
www.hatfield-house.co.uk

Magnificent Jacobean house, home of the Marquess of Salisbury. Exquisite gardens, model soldiers and park trails. Childhood home of Queen Elizabeth I.

Hedingham Castle

Castle Hedingham, Halstead
Tel: (01787) 460261
www.hedinghamcastle.co.uk
The finest Norman keep in England, built in 1140 by the deVeres, Earls of Oxford. Visited by Kings Henry VII and VIII and Queen Elizabeth I and besieged by King John.

Holkham Hall

Wells-next-the-Sea
Tel: (01328) 710806
www.holkham.co.uk

A classic 18thC Palladian-style mansion. Part of a great agricultural estate and a living treasure house of artistic and architectural history along with a bygones collection.

Ickworth House, Park and Gardens (National Trust)

Horringer, Bury St Edmunds
Tel: (01284) 735270 www.nationaltrust.org.uk
An extraordinary oval house with flanking wings, begun in 1795. Fine paintings, a beautiful collection of Georgian silver, an Italian garden and stunning parkland.

Imperial War Museum Duxford

Duxford, Cambridge
Tel: (01223) 835000 www.iwm.org.uk
Almost 200 aircraft on display with tanks, vehicles and guns, an adventure playground, shops and a restaurant.

Kentwell Hall

Long Melford, Sudbury
Tel: (01787) 310207 www.kentwell.co.uk
Tudor manor house, still a lived-in family home. Winner of the '2001 Heritage Building of the Year' in the Good Britain Guide.

Knebworth House, Gardens and Park

Knebworth, Stevenage
Tel: (01438) 812661
www.knebworthhouse.com
Tudor manor house, re-fashioned in the 19thC, housing a collection of manuscripts, portraits and Jacobean banquet hall. Formal gardens, parkland and adventure playground.

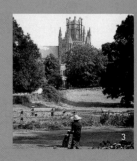

1. River Wensum, Norfolk
2. Cambridge
3. Ely Cathedral

Leighton Buzzard Railway
Page's Park Station, Leighton Buzzard
Tel: (01525) 373888 www.buzzrail.co.uk
An authentic narrow-gauge light railway, built in
1919, offering a 65 minute return journey into
the Bedfordshire countryside.

Marsh Farm Country Park
South Woodham Ferrers, Chelmsford
Tel: (01245) 321552
www.marshfarmcountrypark.co.uk
A farm centre with sheep, a pig unit, free-range
chickens, milking demonstrations, an indoor and
outdoor adventure play areas, nature reserve,
walks, picnic area and pet's corner.

Melford Hall (National Trust)
Long Melford, Sudbury
Tel: (01787) 880286
www.nationaltrust.org.uk/eastanglia
Turreted brick Tudor mansion with 18thC and
Regency interiors. Collection of Chinese
porcelain, gardens and a walk in the grounds.
Dogs on leads, where permitted.

National Horseracing Museum and Tours
99 High Street, Newmarket
Tel: (01638) 667333 www.nhrm.co.uk
Award-winning display of the people and horses
involved in racing's amazing history. Minibus
tours to gallops, stables and equine pool.
Hands-on gallery with horse simulator.

National Stud
Newmarket
Tel: (01638) 663464 x203
www.nationalstud.co.uk

A conducted tour which includes top
thoroughbred stallions, mares and foals, and
gives an insight into the day to day running of a
modern stud farm.

New Pleasurewood Hills Leisure Park
Corton, Lowestoft
Tel: (01502) 586000
www.pleasurewoodhills.co.uk
Tidal wave watercoaster, log flume, chairlift,
2 railways, pirate ship, parrot/sealion shows,
go-karts and rattlesnake coaster. Mega-Drop
Tower and new circus theatre shows.

Norfolk Lavender Limited
Heacham, King's Lynn
Tel: (01485) 570384
www.norfolk-lavender.co.uk
Find out how lavender is distilled from the
flowers and the oil made into a wide range of
gifts. There is a slide show when the distillery is
not working.

Norwich Cathedral
62 The Close, Norwich
Tel: (01603) 218321 www.cathedral.org.uk
A Norman cathedral from 1096 with 14thC roof
bosses depicting bible scenes from Adam and
Eve to the Day of Judgement, cloisters,
cathedral close, shop and restaurant.

Oliver Cromwell's House
29 St Marys Street, Ely
Tel: (01353) 662062
www.elyeastcambs.co.uk

The family home of Oliver Cromwell with a 17thC
kitchen, parlour, a haunted bedroom, a Tourist
Information Centre, souvenirs and gift shop.

Peter Beales Roses
London Road, Attleborough
Tel: (01953) 454707 www.classicroses.co.uk
2.5-acre (1-ha) rose garden displaying most of the
company's collection of 1200 varieties of roses,
plus the national collection of Rosa species.

Pleasure Beach
South Beach Parade, Great Yarmouth
Tel: (01493) 844585 www.pleasure-beach.co.uk
Rollercoaster, Terminator, log flume, Twister,
monorail, galloping horses, caterpillar, ghost train
and fun house. Height restrictions are in force
on some rides.

The Royal Air Force Air Defence Radar Museum
RAF Neatishead, Norwich
Tel: (01692) 633309
www.neatishead.raf.mod.uk
History of the development and use of radar in
the UK and overseas from 1935 to date. Winner
of the Regional Visitor Attraction (under 100,000
visitors). National Silver Award.

RSPB Minsmere Nature Reserve
Westleton, Saxmundham
Tel: (01728) 648281 www.rspb.org.uk
RSPB reserve on Suffolk coast with bird-
watching hides and trails, year-round events and
guided walk and visitor centre with large shop
and welcoming tearoom.

Sainsbury Centre for Visual Arts
University of East Anglia, Norwich
Tel: (01603) 593199 www.uea.ac.uk/scva
Housing the Sainsbury Collection of works by
artists such as Picasso, Bacon and Henry Moore
alongside many objects of pottery and art from
across time and cultures.

Sandringham
Sandringham, King's Lynn
Tel: (01553) 612908
www.sandringhamestate.co.uk
The country retreat of HM The Queen.
A delightful house and 60 acres (24ha) of
grounds and lakes. There is also a museum of
royal vehicles and royal memorabilia.

Shuttleworth Collection
Old Warden Aerodrome, Biggleswade
Tel: (01767) 627288 www.shuttleworth.org
A unique historical collection of aircraft from a
1909 Bleriot to a 1942 Spitfire in flying condition
and cars dating from an 1898 Panhard in
running order.

Somerleyton Hall and Gardens

Somerleyton, Lowestoft
Tel: (01502) 730224
www.somerleyton.co.uk
Early Victorian stately mansion in Anglo-Italian
style, with lavish features and fine state rooms.
Beautiful 12-acre (5-ha) gardens, with historic
Yew hedge maze, gift shop.

Stondon Museum
Henlow
Tel: (01462) 850339
www.transportmuseum.co.uk
A museum with transport exhibits from the early
1900s to the 1980s. The largest private
collection in England of bygone vehicles from
the beginning of the century.

Thursford Collection
Thursford, Fakenham
Tel: (01328) 878477
A live musical show with 9 mechanical
organs and a Wurlitzer show starring
Robert Wolfe.

Wimpole Hall and Home Farm (National Trust)
Arrington, Royston
Tel: (01223) 207257 www.wimpole.org
An 18thC house in a landscaped park with a
folly, Chinese bridge, plunge bath and yellow
drawing room in the house, the work of John
Soane. Home Farm has a rare breeds centre.

Woburn Abbey
Woburn, Milton Keynes
Tel: (01525) 290666 www.woburnabbey.co.uk
An 18thC Palladian mansion, altered by Henry
Holland, the Prince Regent's architect,
containing a collection of English silver, French
and English furniture and art.

Woburn Safari Park

Woburn, Milton Keynes
Tel: (01525) 290407
www.woburnsafari.co.uk
Drive through the safari park with 30 species of
animals in natural groups just a windscreen's
width away plus the action-packed Wild World
Leisure Area.

1. Theme Park, Essex

EAST OF ENGLAND

East of England Tourist Board

Toppesfield Hall, Hadleigh, Suffolk IP7 5DN
T: 0870 225 4800 F: 0870 225 4890
E: jbowers@eetb.org.uk
www.eastofenglandtouristboard.com

THE FOLLOWING PUBLICATIONS ARE AVAILABLE FROM THE EAST OF ENGLAND TOURIST BOARD:

Great days out in the East of England 2004 –
an information-packed A5 guide featuring all you
need to know about places to visit and things to
see and do in the East of England. From historic
houses to garden centres, from animal
collections to craft centres - this guide has it all,
including film and TV locations, city, town and
village information, events, shopping, car tours
plus lots more! (£4.50 excl p&p)

England's Cycling Country –
the East of England offers perfect cycling
country - from quiet country lanes to ancient
trackways. This free publication promotes the
many Cycling Discovery Maps that are available
to buy (£1.50 excl p&p), as well as providing
useful information for anyone planning a cycling
tour of the region

Getting to the East of England

BY ROAD: The region is easily
accessible. From London and the
south via the A1(M), M11, M25,
A10, M1, A46 and A12. From the
north via the A1(M), A15, A5, M1
and A6. From the west via the
A14, A47, A421, A428, A418, A41,
A422, A17 and A427.

BY RAIL: Regular fast trains run to
all major cities and towns in the
region. London stations which
serve the region are Liverpool
Street, Kings Cross, Fenchurch
Street, St Pancras, London
Marylebone and London Euston.
Bedford, Luton and St Albans are
on the Thameslink line which runs
to Kings Cross and on to London
Gatwick Airport. There is also a
direct link between London
Stansted Airport and Liverpool
Street. Through the Channel
Tunnel, there are trains direct from
Paris and Brussels to Waterloo
Station, London. A short journey
on the Underground will bring
passengers to those stations
operating services into the East of
England. Further information on rail
journeys in the East of England can
be obtained on 08457 484 950.

1

1. Windmill, Norfolk

Where to stay in the East of England

Parks in this region are listed in alphabetical order of place name, and then in alphabetical order of park.

Map references refer to the colour location maps at the front of this guide. The first number indicates the map to use; the letter and number which follow refer to the grid reference on the map.

At-a-glance symbols can be found inside the back cover flap. Keep this open for easy reference.

CAMBRIDGE, Cambridgeshire Map ref 3D1 *Tourist Information Centre Tel: 0906 586 2526 (Premium rate number)*

★★★★★
**TOURING &
CAMPING PARK**

See Ad on inside front cover

CHERRY HINTON CARAVAN CLUB SITE

Lime Kiln Road, Cherry Hinton, Cambridge CB1 8NQ
T: (01223) 244088
I: www.caravanclub.co.uk

Imaginatively landscaped site set in old quarry workings and bordered by a nature trail. Only 0.5 miles from Cambridge (Park & Ride bus), Newmarket 14 miles. Non-members welcome.

CC: Delta, Mastercard, Solo, Switch, Visa

M11, jct 9 onto A11. After 7 miles slip road signposted Fulbourn and Tevisham. In Fulbourn continue to roundabout signposted Cambridge. At traffic lights turn left. Left again into Lime Kiln Road.

76	£9.50–£19.50
76	£9.50–£19.50
76 total touring pitches	

★★★★★
**TOURING &
CAMPING PARK**

BH&HPA

HIGHFIELD FARM TOURING PARK

Long Road, Comberton, Cambridge CB3 7DG
T: (01223) 262308
F: (01223) 262308
E: enquiries@highfieldfarmtouringpark.co.uk
I: www.highfieldfarmtouringpark.co.uk

A popular family-run park with excellent facilities close to the university city of Cambridge, Imperial War Museum, Duxford. Ideally situated for touring East Anglia. Low-season rate for Senior Citizens – 10% discount for stay of 3 nights or longer.

From Cambridge, take A428 to Bedford. After 3 miles, turn left at roundabout and follow sign to Comberton. From M11 jct 12, take A603 to Sandy for 0.5 miles. Then take B1046 to Comberton.

60	£8.50–£11.75
60	£8.50–£11.75
60	£8.25–£11.75

IMPORTANT NOTE Information on accommodation listed in this guide has been supplied by the proprietors. As changes may occur you are advised to check details at the time of booking.

CAMBRIDGE continued

★★★
**TOURING &
CAMPING PARK**

STANFORD PARK
Weirs Drove, Burwell, Cambridge CB5 0BP
T: (01638) 741547
I: www.stanfordcaravanpark.co.uk

A beautifully landscaped, family-run caravan park with modern facilities and children's play area. Conveniently situated for visiting Cambridge and Newmarket. Excellent for dog walking, cycling and nearby fishing. Seasonal pitches from only £360, includes winter storage. Also, discounted rates on long-term stays.

From A14 turn off at Newmarket jct. Turn left to Exning and follow signs to Burwell on B1102.

70	🚐	£10.00–£12.00
30	�	£10.00–£12.00
30	▲	£10.00–£10.00

CROMER, Norfolk Map ref 4C1 *Tourist Information Centre Tel: (01263) 512497*

★★★
HOLIDAY PARK

BH&HPA

FOREST PARK CARAVAN SITE
Northrepps Road, Northrepps, Cromer NR27 0JR
T: (01263) 513290
F: (01263) 511992
E: forestpark@netcom.co.uk
I: www.forest-park.co.uk

Quiet, picturesque park for tourers and holiday homes. Situated in the centre of a large forest with extensive, charming walks.

CC: Delta, Mastercard, Solo, Switch, Visa

Turn right off A140 at Northrepps, turn immediately left under railway bridge to T-junction and turn left. Forest Park entrance on right.

338	🚐	£9.00–£15.50
55	�	£9.00–£15.50
85	▲	£9.00–£15.50

FAKENHAM, Norfolk Map ref 4B1

★★★★★
**TOURING &
CAMPING PARK**

BH&HPA

THE OLD BRICK KILNS CARAVAN AND CAMPING PARK
Little Barney Lane, Barney, Fakenham
NR21 0NL
T: 0870 901 8877
F: (01328) 878948
E: enquire@old-brick-kilns.co.uk
I: www.old-brick-kilns.co.uk

CC: Delta, Diners, JCB,
Mastercard, Solo, Switch, Visa

Take the A148 from Fakenham towards Cromer. After 6 miles turn left onto B1354 following brown caravan park signs to Barney and then Little Barney.

60	🚐	£12.00–£15.00
60	�	£12.00–£15.00
60	▲	£10.00–£13.00
60 touring pitches		

GREAT YARMOUTH, Norfolk Map ref 4C1

★★★
**HOLIDAY &
TOURING PARK**

BH&HPA

GRASMERE CARAVAN PARK (T.B)
Bultitudes Loke, Yarmouth Road, Caister-
on-Sea, Great Yarmouth NR30 5DH
T: (01493) 720382
F: (01493) 377573

CC: Delta, Mastercard, Switch,
Visa

Take the A149 from Great Yarmouth and enter Caister at the roundabout by Yarmouth Stadium. After 0.5 miles turn left, just before bus stop. Signposted.

40	🚐	£8.00–£10.50
6	�	£8.00–£10.50
10	🏠	£100.00–£300.00
46 touring pitches		

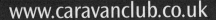

GREAT YARMOUTH continued

★★★★
TOURING PARK

See Ad on inside front cover

GREAT YARMOUTH CARAVAN CLUB SITE

Great Yarmouth Racecourse, Jellicoe Road, Great Yarmouth NR30 4AU
T: (01493) 855223
I: www.caravanclub.co.uk

Spacious, level site in a very popular family resort offering wide sandy beaches, countless seaside attractions and fishing, golf, sailboarding, ballroom dancing and bowls. Non-members welcome.

CC: Delta, Mastercard, Solo, Switch, Visa

Travel north on A149 and turn left at lights (within 1 mile 40mph sign on southern outskirts of Caister) into Jellicoe Road. Within 0.25 miles, turn left into racecourse entrance and continue to site.

122	🚐	£9.50–£19.50
122	🚏	£9.50–£19.50
122 total touring pitches		

★★★★
HOLIDAY PARK

BH&HPA

See Ad on this page

LIFFENS HOLIDAY PARK
Burgh Castle, Great Yarmouth NR31 9QB
T: (01493) 780357
F: (01493) 782383
I: www.liffens.co.uk

CC: Delta, Mastercard, Switch, Visa

150	🚐	£10.00–£20.00
150	🚏	£10.00–£20.00
150	▲	£10.00–£20.00
35	🏠	£100.00–£450.00
150 touring pitches		

From Great Yarmouth, follow signs for Beccles and Lowestoft. Watch for left turn signed for Burgh Castle, follow for 2 miles to T-junction and turn right. Then follow signs to holiday park.

SPECIAL BREAKS

Many establishments offer special promotions and themed breaks. These are highlighted in red. (All such offers are subject to availability.)

GREAT YARMOUTH continued

★★★★ HOLIDAY PARK BH&HPA	**LIFFENS WELCOME HOLIDAY CENTRE** Butt Lane, Burgh Castle, Great Yarmouth NR31 9PY T: (01493) 780481 F: (01493) 781627 I: www.liffens.co.uk	CC: Delta, JCB, Mastercard, Solo, Switch, Visa	150 £10.00–£20.00 150 £10.00–£20.00 150 £10.00–£20.00 20 £100.00–£450.00 150 touring pitches

On the main A143 from Great Yarmouth to Beccles Road. Proceed through the village of Bradwell to the start of a small dual carriageway. Take 1st right turn, next turning on right and Liffens Welcome Holiday Centre is along on right.

★★★★ HOLIDAY PARK BH&HPA See Ad p125	**VAUXHALL HOLIDAY PARK** Acle New Road, Great Yarmouth NR30 1TB T: (01493) 857231 F: (01493) 331122 E: vauxhall.holidays@virgin.net I: www.vauxhall-holiday-park.co.uk	CC: Mastercard, Switch, Visa	220 £13.00–£29.00 220 £13.00–£29.00 220 £13.00–£29.00 364 £187.00–£865.00 234 touring pitches

On the A47 as you approach Great Yarmouth from Norwich.

HADLEIGH, Suffolk Map ref 4B2

★★★★ TOURING & CAMPING PARK BH&HPA	**POLSTEAD TOURING PARK** Holt Road, Polstead, Colchester CO6 5BZ T: (01787) 211969 F: (01787) 211969		30 £8.00–£9.00 30 £8.00–£9.00 30 £5.00–£8.00

Off A1071 between Boxford and Hadleigh opposite the Brewers Arms pub, follow signs.

HUNSTANTON, Norfolk Map ref 4B1 *Tourist Information Centre Tel: (01485) 532610*

★★★★★ HOLIDAY, TOURING & CAMPING PARK BH&HPA See Ad on this page	**SEARLES LEISURE RESORT** South Beach, Hunstanton PE36 5BB T: (01485) 534211 F: (01485) 533815 E: bookings@searles.co.uk I: www.searles.co.uk	CC: Delta, JCB, Mastercard, Switch, Visa	146 £11.00–£24.00 77 £13.00–£27.00 113 £9.00–£22.00 129 £184.00–£712.00

From A149 leave on roundabout entering Hunstanton on B1161. 0.25 miles to entrance. Follow signs for South Beach and car parks.

TOWN INDEX

This can be found at the back of the guide. If you know where you want to stay, the index will give you the page number listing all accommodation in your chosen town, city or village.

KESSINGLAND, Suffolk Map ref 4C2

★★★★★
HOLIDAY, TOURING & CAMPING PARK

ROSE AWARD

BH&HPA

HEATHLAND BEACH CARAVAN PARK
London Road, Kessingland, Lowestoft
NR33 7PJ
T: (01502) 740337
F: (01502) 742355
E: heathlandbeach@btinternet.com
I: www.heathlandbeach.co.uk

CC: Delta, Mastercard, Solo, Switch, Visa

63		£16.00–£20.00
63		£16.00–£20.00
63		£8.00–£20.00
5		£280.00–£500.00
63 touring pitches		

One mile north of Kessingland village, off old A12, now B1437, and 3 miles from Lowestoft.

KING'S LYNN, Norfolk Map ref 4B1 *Tourist Information Centre Tel: (01553) 763044*

★★★
TOURING PARK

BANK FARM CARAVAN PARK
Bank Farm, Fallow Pipe Road, Saddle Bow,
King's Lynn PE34 3AS
T: (01553) 617305
F: (01553) 617305
I: www.caravancampingsites.co.uk/norfolk/
bankfarm.htm

15		£7.00–£7.00
15		£7.00–£7.00
2		£5.00–£5.00
15 touring pitches		

Off King's Lynn southern bypass (A47) via slip road signposted Saddlebow. Once in the village, cross the river bridge and after 1 mile fork right into Fallow Pipe Road. The farm is 0.66 miles, by the River Great Ouse.

MERSEA ISLAND, Essex Map ref 4B3

★★★
HOLIDAY, TOURING & CAMPING PARK

BH&HPA

WALDEGRAVES HOLIDAY PARK
Mersea Island, Colchester CO5 8SE
T: (01206) 382898
F: (01206) 385359
E: holidays@waldegraves.co.uk
I: www.waldegraves.co.uk

CC: Amex, Delta, Mastercard, Solo, Switch, Visa

40		£10.00–£19.00
40		£10.00–£19.00
20		£10.00–£19.00
25		£195.00–£475.00
100 touring pitches		

Take the B1025 from Colchester then left to East Mersea, 2nd right then follow the brown tourist signs.

MUNDESLEY, Norfolk Map ref 4C1

★★★
HOLIDAY & TOURING PARK

BH&HPA

SANDY GULLS CARAVAN PARK
Cromer Road, Mundesley, Norwich
NR11 8DF
T: (01263) 720513

30		£8.00–£16.00
20		£8.00–£16.00
10		
2		£200.00–£330.00
60 touring pitches		

From Cromer drive south along coast road for 5 miles.

NORFOLK BROADS

See under Great Yarmouth

PETERBOROUGH, Cambridgeshire Map ref 4A1 *Tourist Information Centre Tel: (01733) 452336*

★★★★★
TOURING PARK

See Ad on inside front cover

FERRY MEADOWS CARAVAN CLUB SITE
Ferry Meadows, Ham Lane, Peterborough PE2 5UU
T: (01733) 233526
F: (01733) 233526
I: www.caravanclub.co.uk

Set in 500-acre Nene Country Park. Plenty of activities including canoeing, windsurfing and sailing. Also nature trails, two golf courses, pitch and putt and bird sanctuary. Non-members welcome.

OPEN All Year
CC: Delta, Mastercard, Solo, Switch, Visa

254		£9.50–£19.50
254		£9.50–£19.50
254 total touring pitches		

From any direction, on approaching Peterborough, follow the brown signs to Nene Park and Ferry Meadows.

SAHAM HILLS, Norfolk Map ref 4B1

★★★★
**TOURING &
CAMPING PARK**

LOWE CARAVAN PARK
Ashdale, Hills Road, Saham Hills, Thetford IP25 7EZ
T: (01953) 881051
F: (01953) 881051

Small, friendly caravan park. Luxury holiday homes for hire, peaceful surroundings, ideal for touring East Anglia or a quiet, relaxing break. More suited to over 55s.

From A11 Thetford take Watton road, turn left at traffic lights through Watton High Street. Take 2nd turning on right, Saham Road, past Richmond Golf Club, take 2nd turning on right. At junction turn right, 1st drive on the right.

20	🚐	£8.00–£12.00
5	🚎	£8.00–£12.00
5	⛺	£8.00–£12.00
4	🏠	£195.00–£295.00

SANDRINGHAM, Norfolk Map ref 4B1

★★★★★
TOURING PARK

See Ad on inside front cover

THE SANDRINGHAM ESTATE CARAVAN CLUB SITE
The Sandringham Estate, Glucksburg Woods, Sandringham PE35 6EZ
T: (01553) 631614
I: www.caravanclub.co.uk

Set in the heart of the Royal Estate, redeveloped to a very high standard. Historic harbour town of King's Lynn six miles, many historic houses in the area. Non-members welcome.

CC: Delta, Mastercard, Solo, Switch, Visa

Take A149 from King's Lynn (signposted Hunstanton). After approximately 2 miles turn right onto B1439 (signposted West Newton). Site on left after 0.5 miles.

119	🚐	£12.00–£20.50
119	🚎	£12.00–£20.50
119 total touring pitches		

SCRATBY, Norfolk Map ref 4C1

★★★★
**TOURING &
CAMPING PARK**

BH&HPA

SCRATBY HALL CARAVAN PARK
Scratby, Great Yarmouth NR29 3PH
T: (01493) 730283

Secluded, rural setting, approximately five miles north of Great Yarmouth and 0.5 miles from the beach. Free showers, shop, launderette, children's playground, disabled facilities.

From A149 Great Yarmouth to Caister. Onto B1159 Scratby, site signed.

108	🚐	£5.25–£12.50
108	🚎	£5.25–£12.50
108	⛺	£5.25–£12.50

CHECK THE MAPS
The colour maps at the front of this guide show all the cities, towns and villages for which you will find park entries. Refer to the town index to find the page on which it is listed.

SNETTISHAM, Norfolk Map ref 4B1

★★★
HOLIDAY, TOURING & CAMPING PARK

BH&HPA

DIGLEA CARAVAN AND CAMPING PARK

Beach Road, Snettisham, King's Lynn PE31 7RA
T: (01485) 541367

On the West Norfolk coast, friendly, family-run park in a peaceful, rural setting, 0.25 miles from beach and RSPB reserve. Separate rally field available.

From King's Lynn take the A149 Hunstanton road to Snettisham. Turn left at sign marked Snettisham beach. Park is 1.5 miles on left.

200	🚐	£8.00–£12.00
200	🚏	£8.00–£12.00
200	⛺	£8.00–£12.00
200 touring pitches		

STANHOE, Norfolk Map ref 4B1

★★★★
TOURING PARK

THE RICKELS CARAVAN SITE
The Rickels, Bircham Road, Stanhoe, King's Lynn PE31 8PU
T: (01485) 518671
F: (01485) 518969

15	🚐	£8.50–£10.00
10	🚏	£8.50–£10.00
5	⛺	£8.50–£10.00
30 touring pitches		

From King's Lynn, take the A148 to Hillington and turn left onto the B1153 to Great Bircham. Fork right onto the B1155. Go to the crossroads and straight over. The site is 100yds on the left.

WEELEY, Essex Map ref 4B3

★★★
TOURING PARK

HOMESTEAD LAKE PARK

Thorpe Road, Weeley, Clacton-on-Sea CO16 9JN
T: (01255) 833492
F: (01255) 831406
E: lakepark@homesteadcaravans.co.uk
I: www.homesteadcaravans.co.uk

Peaceful location overlooking two acres of fishing lake. Clacton-on-Sea, Walton-on-the-Naze, Frinton-on-Sea and Harwich under 10 miles.

CC: Delta, Mastercard, Solo, Switch, Visa

Take A120 or A133 towards Clacton-on-Sea or B1033 towards Frinton-on-Sea, Walton-on-the-Naze & Thorpe. Park will be situated 0.25 miles on left-hand side.

50	🚐	£13.00–£16.00
50	🚏	£13.00–£16.00
50 touring pitches		

WOODBRIDGE, Suffolk Map ref 4C2 *Tourist Information Centre Tel: (01394) 382240*

★★★
TOURING & CAMPING PARK

BH&HPA

FOREST CAMPING
Tangham Campsite, Rendlesham Forest, Butley, Woodbridge IP12 3NF
T: (01394) 450707
E: admin@forestcamping.co.uk
I: www.forestcamping.co.uk

CC: Delta, Mastercard, Solo, Switch, Visa

90	🚐	£12.00–£15.00
90	🚏	£12.00–£12.00
90	⛺	£12.00–£12.00
90 touring pitches		

Six miles east of Woodbridge off B1084 to Orford.

IMPORTANT NOTE Information on accommodation listed in this guide has been supplied by the proprietors. As changes may occur you are advised to check details at the time of booking.

A brief guide to the main Towns and Villages offering accommodation in the **East of England**

C CAMBRIDGE, CAMBRIDGESHIRE - A most important and beautiful city on the River Cam with 31 colleges forming one of the oldest universities in the world. Numerous museums, good shopping centre, restaurants, theatres, cinema and fine bookshops.

CROMER, NORFOLK - Once a small fishing village and now famous for its fishing boats that still work off the beach and offer freshly caught crabs. Excellent bathing on sandy beaches fringed by cliffs. The town boasts a fine pier, theatre, museum and a lifeboat station.

F FAKENHAM, NORFOLK - Attractive, small market town which dates from Saxon times and was a Royal Manor until the 17th C. Its market place has 2 old coaching inns, both showing traces of earlier work behind Georgian facades, and the parish church has a commanding 15th C tower.

G GREAT YARMOUTH, NORFOLK - One of Britain's major seaside resorts with 5 miles of seafront and every possible amenity including an award - winning leisure complex offering a huge variety of all-weather facilities. Busy harbour and fishing centre.

H HADLEIGH, SUFFOLK - Former wool town, lying on a tributary of the River Stour. The church of St Mary stands among a remarkable cluster of medieval buildings.

HUNSTANTON, NORFOLK - Seaside resort which faces the Wash. The shingle and sand beach is backed by striped cliffs, and many unusual fossils can be found here. The town is predominantly Victorian. The Oasis family leisure centre has indoor and outdoor pools.

K KESSINGLAND, SUFFOLK - Seaside village whose church tower has served as a landmark to sailors for generations. Nearby is the Suffolk Wildlife and Country Park.

KING'S LYNN, NORFOLK - A busy town with many outstanding buildings. The Guildhall and Town Hall are both built of flint in a striking chequer design. Behind the Guildhall in the Old Gaol House the sounds and smells of prison life 2 centuries ago are recreated.

P PETERBOROUGH, CAMBRIDGESHIRE - Prosperous and rapidly expanding cathedral city on the edge of the Fens on the River Nene. Catherine of Aragon is buried in the cathedral. City Museum and Art Gallery. Ferry Meadows Country Park has numerous leisure facilities.

S SANDRINGHAM, NORFOLK - Famous as the country retreat of Her Majesty the Queen. The house and grounds are open to the public at certain times.

SNETTISHAM, NORFOLK - Village with a superb Decorated church. The 17th C Old Hall is a distinguished-looking house with Dutch gables over the 2 bays. Snettisham Pits is a reserve of the Royal Society for the Protection of Birds. Red deer herd and other animals, farm trails and nature walks at Park Farm.

W WOODBRIDGE, SUFFOLK - Once a busy seaport, the town is now a sailing centre on the River Deben. There are many buildings of architectural merit including the Bell and Angel Inns. The 18th C Tide Mill is now restored and open to the public.

CHECK THE MAPS

The colour maps at the front of this guide show all the cities, towns and villages for which you will find park entries. Refer to the town index to find the page on which it is listed.

South West

A land of myths and legends – and beautiful beaches. The region has cathedral cities, Georgian Bath and maritme Bristol, mysterios castles, evocative country houses and sub tropical gardens to discover, too.

The Counties of Bath & Bristol, Cornwall & Isles of Scilly, Devon, Dorset (Western), Gloucestershire South, Somerset and Wiltshire

For more information contact:
South West Tourism
Admail 3186,
Exeter EX2 7WH

E: info@westcountryholidays.com
www.visitsouthwest.co.uk

Telephone enquiries -
T: (0870) 442 0880

Classic sights
Eden Project – plant life from around the world
English Riviera – family-friendly beaches
Dartmoor & Exmoor – wild open moorland, rocky tors and woodland

Coast & country
Jurassic Coast – World Heritage Coastline
Runnymede – riverside meadows and woodland
Pegwell Bay & Goodwin Sands – a haven for birds and seals

Glorious gardens
Stourhead – 18thC landscaped garden
Westonbirt Arboretum – Over 3,700 different varieties of tree

Art for all
Tate Gallery St Ives – modern art and the St Ives School
Arnolfini Gallery, Bristol – contemporary arts

Distinctively different
Daphne du Maurier – Cornwall inspired many of her novels
Agatha Christie – follow the trail in Torquay

1. Roman Bath, Bath

Places to Visit

You will find hundreds of interesting places to visit during your stay, just some of which are listed in these pages. Contact any Tourist Information Centre in the region for more ideas on days out.

Awarded VisitBritain's 'Quality Assured Visitor Attraction' marque.

At Bristol
Harbourside, Bristol
Tel: 08453 451235 www.at-bristol.org.uk
3 exciting new attractions which will take you on the interactive adventure of a lifetime – Explore, Wildwalk and the IMAX Theatre.

Atwell-Wilson Motor Museum Trust
Stockley Lane, Calne
Tel: (01249) 813119 www.atwell-wilson.org
Motor museum with vintage, post-vintage and classic cars, including American models. Classic motorbikes. A 17thC water meadow walk. Car clubs welcome for rallies. Play area.

Babbacombe Model Village
Babbacombe, Torquay
Tel: (01803) 315315
www.babbacombemodelvillage.co.uk
Over 400 models many with sound and animation with 4 acres (1.6ha) of award-winning gardens. See modern towns, villages and rural areas. Stunning illuminations and Aquaviva.

Bristol City Museum & Art Gallery
Queen's Road, Bristol
Tel: (0117) 922 3571
www.bristol-city.gov.uk/museums
Outstanding collections of applied, oriental and fine art, archaeology, geology, natural history, ethnography and Egyptology.

Bristol Zoo Gardens
Clifton, Bristol
Tel: (0117) 974 7300
www.bristolzoo.org.uk
Enjoy an exciting real life experience and see over 300 species of wildlife in beautiful gardens. Favourites include Gorilla Island, Bug World and Sea and Penguin Coasts with underwater viewing.

Buckland Abbey (National Trust)
Yelverton
Tel: (01822) 853607 www.nationaltrust.org.uk
Originally Cistercian monastery, then home of Sir Francis Drake. Ancient buildings, exhibitions, herb garden, craft workshops and estate walks. Elizabethan garden.

Cheddar Caves and Gorge
Cheddar
Tel: (01934) 742343 www.cheddarcaves.co.uk
Beautiful caves located in Cheddar Gorge. Gough's Cave with its cathedral-like caverns and Cox's Cave with stalagmites and stalactites. Also 'The Crystal Quest' fantasy adventure.

Combe Martin Wildlife and Dinosaur Park
Combe Martin, Ilfracombe
Tel: (01271) 882486 www.dinosaur-uk.com
The land that time forgot. A subtropical paradise with hundreds of birds and animals, and animatronics dinosaurs, so real they're alive!

Crealy Park
Clyst St Mary, Exeter
Tel: (01395) 233200 www.crealy.co.uk
One of Devon's largest animal farms. Milk a cow, feed a lamb and pick up a piglet. Adventure playgrounds. Dragonfly Lake and farm trails.

Dairyland Farm World
Summercourt, Newquay
Tel: (01872) 510246
www.dairylandfarmworld.com

120 cows milked in Clarabelle's 'Spage-age' orbiter, adventure playground, country life museum, nature trail, farm park, pets and daily events.

Eden Project
Bodelva, St Austell
Tel: (01726) 811911 www.edenproject.com
An unforgettable experience in a breathtaking
epic location. Eden is a gateway into the
fascinating world of plants and people.

Exmoor Falconry & Animal Farm
West Lynch Farm, Minehead
Tel: (01643) 862816
www.exmoorfalconry.co.uk
Historic 15thC farm with hand-tame, rare breed
farm animals, pets' corner, birds of prey and
owls. Flying displays daily. Short activity breaks.

Flambards Village
Culdrose Manor, Helston
Tel: (01326) 573404 www.flambards.co.uk
Life-size Victorian village with fully stocked
shops, carriages and fashions. 'Britain in the
Blitz' life-size wartime street, historic aircraft.
Science centre and rides.

Heale Garden & Plant Centre
Middle Woodford, Salisbury
Tel: (01722) 782504
Mature traditional garden with shrubs, musk and
other roses, and kitchen garden. Authentic
Japanese teahouse in water garden. Magnolias.
Snowdrops and aconites in winter.

International Animal Rescue
Animal Tracks, South Molton
Tel: (01769) 550277 www.iar.org.uk
A 60-acre (24-ha) animal sanctuary with a wide
range of rescued animals from monkeys to
chinchillas and from shire horses and ponies to
donkeys, goats and pigs. Also rare plant nursery.

Jamaica Inn Museums
(Potters Museum of Curiosity)
Bolventor, Launceston
Tel: (01566) 86838
www.pottersjamaicainn.com
Museums contain lifetime work of Walter Potter,
a Victorian taxidermist. Exhibits include 'Kittens'
Wedding' and 'Death of Cock Robin' and 'The
Story of Smuggling'.

Longleat
Longleat, Warminster
Tel: (01985) 844400 www.longleat.co.uk
Elizabethan stately home, safari park plus a
wonderland of 10 family attractions. 'World's
Longest Hedge Maze', Safari Boats, Pets
Corner, Longleat railway and Adventure Castle.

The Lost Gardens of Heligan
Heligan, St Austell
Tel: (01726) 845100 www.heligan.com
Gardeners' World 'The Nation's Favourite
Garden' 2002. The world famous, award winning
garden restoration is now complemented by a
pioneering wildlife conservation project.

Lyme Regis Philpot Museum
Bridge Street, Lyme Regis
Tel: (01297) 443370
www.lymeregismuseum.co.uk
Fossils, geology, local history, literary
connections – The story of Lyme in its
landscape.

1. Stourhead Gardens, Wiltshire
2. Clifton Suspension Bridge, Bristol
3. Water sports in Torquay

National Marine Aquarium

Rope Walk, Plymouth
Tel: (01752) 600301
www.national-aquarium.co.uk
The United Kingdom's only world-class aquarium, located in the heart of Plymouth. Visitor experiences include a mountain stream and Caribbean reef complete with sharks.

Newquay Zoo

Trenance Park, Newquay
Tel: (01637) 873342
www.newquayzoo.co.uk
A modern award-winning zoo, where you can have fun and learn at the same time. A varied collection of animals, from Antelope to Zebra.

Paignton Zoo Environmental Park

Totnes Road, Paignton
Tel: (01803) 697500
www.paigntonzoo.org.uk
One of England's largest zoos with over 1,200 animals in the beautiful setting of 75 acres (30ha) of botanical gardens. The zoo is one of Devon's most popular family days out.

Plant World

St Marychurch Road, Newton Abbot
Tel: (01803) 872939
Four acres of gardens including the unique 'map of the world' gardens. Cottage garden. Panoramic views. Comprehensive nursery of rare and more unusual plants.

Powderham Castle

Kenton, Exeter
Tel: (01626) 890243 www.powderham.co.uk
Built c1390, restored in 18thC, Georgian interiors, china, furnishings and paintings. Family home of the Courtenays for over 600 years. Fine views across deer park and River Exe.

Railway Village Museum

34 Faringdon Road, Swindon
Tel: (01793) 466553
www.steam-museum.org.uk
Foreman's house in original Great Western Railway village. Furnished to re-create a Victorian working-class home.

Roman Baths

Pump Room, Bath
Tel: (01225) 477785
www.romanbaths.co.uk
2000 years ago, around Britain's hot springs, the Romans built this great temple and spa that still flows with natural hot water.

St Michael's Mount

Marazion, Penzance
Tel: (01736) 710507
www.stmichaelsmount.co.uk
Originally the site of a Benedictine chapel, castle on its rock dates from 12thC. Fine views towards Land's End and the Lizard. Reached by foot, or ferry at high tide in summer.

Smugglers Barn

Abbotsbury, Weymouth
Tel: (01305) 871817
www.abbotsbury-tourism.co.uk
Soft play undercover with a smuggling theme for children under 11 years. Other activities include rabbit and guinea pig cuddling. Pony rides (extra charge).

Steam – Museum of the Great Western Railway

Kemble Drive, Swindon
Tel: (01793) 466646
www.steam-museum.org.uk
Historic Great Western Railway locomotives, wide range of nameplates, models, illustrations, posters and tickets.

Stonehenge

Amesbury, Salisbury
Tel: (01980) 624715
www.stonehengemasterplan.org
World-famous prehistoric monument built as a ceremonial centre. Started 5000 years ago and remodelled several times in next 1500 years.

Stourhead House and Garden (National Trust)

Stourton, Warminster
Tel: (01747) 841152 www.nationaltrust.org.uk
Landscaped garden laid out c1741-80, with lakes, temples, rare trees and plants. House begun in c1721 by Colen Campbell, contains fine paintings and Chippendale furniture.

Tate Gallery St Ives

Porthmeor Beach, St Ives
Tel: (01736) 796226 www.tate.org.uk
Opened in 1993 and offering a unique introduction to modern art. Changing displays focus on the modern movement St Ives is famous for. Major contemporary exhibitions.

Teignmouth Museum
29 French Street, Teignmouth
Tel: (01626) 777041
www.lineone.net/-teignmuseum
Exhibits include 16thC cannon and artefacts
from Armada wreck and local history, 1920s pier
machines and c1877 cannon.

Tintagel Castle (English Heritage)
Tintagel
Tel: (01840) 770328
www.english-heritage.org.uk
Medieval ruined castle on wild, wind-swept
coast. Famous for associations with Arthurian
legend. Built largely in 13thC by Richard, Earl of
Cornwall.

Totnes Costume Museum – Devonshire
Collection of Period Costume
Bogan House, Totnes
Tel: (01803) 863821
New exhibition of costumes and accessories
each season, displayed in one of the historic
merchant's houses of Totnes, Bogan House,
restored by Mitchell Trust.

Woodlands Leisure Park
Blackawton, Totnes
Tel: (01803) 712598
www.woodlandspark.com
All weather fun guaranteed; unique combination
indoor and outdoor attractions, 3 water coasters,
toboggan run, indoor venture centre with rides.
Falconry and animals.

Wookey Hole Caves and Papermill
Wookey Hole, Wells
Tel: (01749) 672243 www.wookey.co.uk
Spectacular caves and legendary home of the
Witch of Wookey. Working Victorian paper mill
including Old Penny Arcade, Magical Mirror
Maze and Cave Diving Museum.

1. Land's End, Cornwall

South West Tourism

Admail 3186,
Exeter EX2 7WH
T: (0870) 442 0880
E: info@westcountryholidays.com
www.visitsouthwest.co.uk

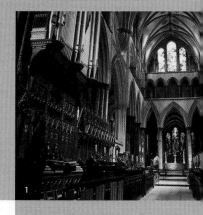

THE FOLLOWING OFFICIAL GUIDES ARE AVAILABLE FREE FROM SOUTH WEST TOURISM:

Quality Bed & Breakfast

Holiday Homes, Cottages & Apartments

Hotels and Guesthouses

Holiday Parks, Camping and Caravan

Attractions and Days Out

Trencherman's Restaurant Guide

South West Walks

Sailing and Watersports

Getting to the South West

BY ROAD: The region is easily accessible from London, the South East, the North and Midlands by the M6/M5 which extends just beyond Exeter, where it links in with the dual carriageways of the A38 to Plymouth, A380 to Torbay and the A30 into Cornwall. The North Devon Link Road A361 joins Junction 37 with the coast of North Devon and the A39, which then becomes the Atlantic Highway into Cornwall.

BY RAIL: The main towns in the South West are served throughout the year by fast, direct and frequent rail services from all over the country. Trains operate from London (Paddington) to Chippenham, Swindon, Bath, Bristol, Weston-super-Mare, Taunton, Exeter, Plymouth and Penzance, and also from Scotland, the North East and the Midlands to the South West. A service runs from London (Waterloo) to Exeter, via Salisbury, Yeovil and Crewkerne. Sleeper services operate between Devon and Cornwall and London as well as between Bristol and Glasgow and Edinburgh. Motorail services operate from strategic points to key South West locations.

1. Salisbury Cathedral, Wiltshire
2. Selworthy, Somerset

Parks in this region are listed in alphabetical order of place name, and then in alphabetical order of park.

Map references refer to the colour location maps at the front of this guide. The first number indicates the map to use; the letter and number which follow refer to the grid reference on the map.

At-a-glance symbols can be found inside the back cover flap. Keep this open for easy reference.

ASHBURTON, Devon Map ref 2C2

★★★★

HOLIDAY, TOURING & CAMPING PARK

BH&HPA

See Ad p138

PARKERS FARM HOLIDAY PARK
Higher Mead Farm, Alston, Ashburton
TQ13 7LJ
T: (01364) 652598
F: (01364) 654004
E: parkersfarm@btconnect.com
I: www.parkersfarm.co.uk

CC: Delta, JCB, Mastercard, Solo, Switch, Visa

50		£5.00–£11.50
25		£5.00–£11.50
25		£5.00–£11.50
25		
100 touring pitches		

Take A38 from Exeter to Plymouth. When you see sign 26 miles to Plymouth, take 2nd left marked Woodland and Denbury. At Alston Cross.

AXMINSTER, Devon Map ref 2D2

★★★★
HOLIDAY PARK

BH&HPA

ANDREWSHAYES CARAVAN PARK

Dalwood, Axminster EX13 7DY
T: (01404) 831225
F: (01404) 831893
E: enquiries@andrewshayes.co.uk
I: www.andrewshayes.co.uk

Friendly, family, countryside park, a short drive to the coast. Outdoor pool, bar and bistro. Seasonal pitches available. Static holiday homes for hire and sale. Short breaks and special offers for camping and holiday home hire in low season.

CC: Delta, JCB, Mastercard, Solo, Switch, Visa

Located 150yds off A35 signposted Dalwood, Stockland, at Taunton Cross. Three miles Axminster, 6 miles Honiton.

60	🚐	£9.00–£13.00
10	🚌	£9.00–£13.00
20	▲	£9.00–£13.00
22	🏠	£120.00–£460.00
90 touring pitches		

BATH, Bath and North East Somerset Map ref 3B2 *Tourist Information Centre Tel: 0906 711 2000 (Premium rate number)*

★★★★
**TOURING &
CAMPING PARK**

BH&HPA

NEWTON MILL CAMPING

Newton Road, Bath BA2 9JF
T: (01225) 333909
F: (01225) 461556
E: newtonmill@hotmail.com
I: www.campinginbath.co.uk

Beautiful setting in an idyllic hidden valley close to centre of Bath (10-minute bus service). Restaurant, bar beside millstream. Nearby, level, traffic-free cycle path. David Bellamy Gold Conservation Award. 10% discount on stays of 7 days or more. New Year package.

CC: Delta, Mastercard, Solo, Switch, Visa

On A4 on the outskirts of Bath towards Bristol, take the exit signposted Newton St Loe at the roundabout by the Globe pub. Site is 1 mile on the left.

90	🚌	£11.00–£16.85
90	🚐	£11.00–£16.85
105	▲	£4.50–£12.50
195 touring pitches		

BICKINGTON, Devon Map ref 2D2

★★★★
**HOLIDAY, TOURING
& CAMPING PARK**

BH&HPA

LEMONFORD CARAVAN PARK
Bickington, Newton Abbot TQ12 6JR
T: (01626) 821242
F: (01626) 821242
E: mark@lemonford.co.uk
I: www.lemonford.co.uk

55	🚐	£8.40–£11.90
10	🚌	£8.40–£11.90
20	▲	£6.50–£10.00
15	🏠	£100.00–£360.00
85 touring pitches		

From Exeter take A38 towards Plymouth. Take A382 (Drumbridges) turn off to Bickington, 3rd exit. After 3 miles pass Toby Jug Inn on right; site is on left after 300m.

BLACKWATER, Cornwall Map ref 2B3

★★★★
HOLIDAY PARK

BH&HPA

TREVARTH HOLIDAY PARK

Blackwater, Truro TR4 8HR
T: (01872) 560266
F: (01872) 560379
E: trevarth@lineone.net
I: www.ukparks.co.uk/trevarth

Luxury caravan holiday homes, touring and camping. A small, quiet park conveniently situated for north- and south-coast resorts. Level touring and tent pitches with electric hook-up.

CC: Delta, JCB, Mastercard, Solo, Switch, Visa

Three hundred metres from Blackwater exit off Chiverton roundabout on A30. Four and a half miles north east of Redruth.

30	🚐	£7.75–£11.00
30	🚍	£7.75–£11.00
30	▲	£7.75–£11.00
20	🏠	£110.00–£475.00
30 touring pitches		

BRIDPORT, Dorset Map ref 3A3 *Tourist Information Centre Tel: (01308) 424901*

★★★
**HOLIDAY &
CAMPING PARK**

BH&HPA

EYPE HOUSE CARAVAN PARK

Eype, Bridport DT6 6AL
T: (01308) 424903
F: (01308) 424903
E: enquiries@eypehouse.co.uk
I: www.eypehouse.co.uk

Small, quiet site, situated 200 yards from sea and coastal path. Exceptional views of sea and countryside. No touring caravans.

From Bridport take A35 west, signposted to Eype 1 mile. Follow signs to the sea.

20	🚍	£8.00–£13.50
20	▲	£8.00–£13.50
35	🏠	£150.00–£390.00
20 touring pitches		

★★★★
**HOLIDAY, TOURING
& CAMPING PARK**

BH&HPA

FRESHWATER BEACH HOLIDAY PARK

Burton Bradstock, Bridport DT6 4PT
T: (01308) 897317
F: (01308) 897336
E: office@freshwaterbeach.co.uk
I: www.freshwaterbeach.co.uk

Own private beach. Surrounded by beautiful countryside on Dorset's World Heritage Coastline. Licensed club. Free family entertainment. Heated outdoor pools. Beach, fishing, horse/pony rides. Cliff walks. Pitch prices include up to 6 people and club membership.

CC: Delta, JCB, Mastercard, Solo, Switch, Visa

From Bridport take B3157, situated 2 miles on the right.

350	🚐	£12.00–£25.00
50	🚍	£12.00–£25.00
150	▲	£7.50–£25.00
60	🏠	£200.00–£630.00
550 touring pitches		

STAR RATINGS Were correct at the time of going to press but are subject to change. Please check at the time of booking.

BRIDPORT continued

★★★★★ HOLIDAY PARK ROSE AWARD BH&HPA	GOLDEN CAP HOLIDAY PARK		

★★★★★	**GOLDEN CAP HOLIDAY PARK**		108 🚐	£8.40–£16.00
HOLIDAY PARK	Seatown, Chideock, Bridport DT6 6JX	CC: Mastercard, Switch, Visa	108 🚙	£8.40–£16.00
	T: (01308) 422139		108 ⛺	£8.40–£14.00
ROSE AWARD	F: (01308) 425672		12 🏠	£160.00–£500.00
BH&HPA	E: holidays@wdlh.co.uk		108 touring pitches	
	I: www.wdlh.co.uk			

In Chideock on A35 turn south for Seatown, park signposted.

★★★★★	**HIGHLANDS END HOLIDAY PARK**		120 🚐	£10.75–£16.00
HOLIDAY PARK	Eype, Bridport DT6 6AR	CC: Mastercard, Switch, Visa	120 🚙	£10.75–£16.00
	T: (01308) 422139		75 ⛺	£8.25–£14.00
ROSE AWARD	F: (01308) 425672		18 🏠	£160.00–£500.00
BH&HPA	E: holidays@wdlh.co.uk		195 touring pitches	
	I: www.wdlh.co.uk			

One mile west of Bridport turn south for Eype, park signposted.

BRIXHAM, Devon Map ref 2D2 *Tourist Information Centre Tel: 0906 680 1268 (Premium rate number)*

★★★★
HOLIDAY PARK
BH&HPA

BRIXHAM HOLIDAY PARK
Fishcombe Cove, Brixham TQ5 8RB
T: (01803) 853324
F: (01803) 853569
E: enquiries@brixhamholpk.fsnet.co.uk
I: www.brixhamholpk.fsnet.co.uk

	17 🏠	£139.00–£559.00

Situated on South West coastal path, fantastic views of bay, 150yds from beach. Indoor swimming pool, site shop, clubhouse, 10 minutes' walk harbour and shops. 4-night breaks before 17 Jul – 2/3 weekly hire charge.

CC: Delta, Mastercard, Solo, Switch, Visa

From M5 take A380 then A3022 to Brixham, pass 'Welcome to Brixham' sign, after 800yds turn left into Lindthorpe Way, 1 mile after passing north boundary road, take next left.

★★★★
TOURING &
CAMPING PARK
BH&HPA

GALMPTON TOURING PARK
Greenway Road, Galmpton, Brixham TQ5 0EP
T: (01803) 842066
F: (01803) 844458
E: galmptontouringpark@hotmail.com
I: www.galmptontouringpark.co.uk

Overlooking the River Dart with superb views from pitches. A quiet base for families and couples to explore Torbay and South Devon. Off-peak reductions.	60 🚐	£8.00–£14.00
	20 🚙	£8.00–£14.00
	60 ⛺	£8.00–£14.00
	🏠	£170.00–£425.00
	120 touring pitches	

CC: Delta, JCB, Mastercard, Solo, Switch, Visa

Take A380 Torbay ring road then A379 to Brixham, 2nd right to Galmpton Park through village to park. Signposted.

BUDE, Cornwall Map ref 2C2 *Tourist Information Centre Tel: (01288) 354240*

★★★	**BUDE HOLIDAY PARK**		250 🚐	£8.40–£16.00
HOLIDAY PARK	Maer Lane, Bude EX23 9EE	CC: Delta, Mastercard, Solo,	250 🚙	£8.40–£16.00
	T: (01288) 355955	Switch, Visa	250 ⛺	£8.40–£16.00
	F: (01288) 355980		129 🏠	£90.00–£590.00
	E: enquiries@budeholidaypark.co.uk		500 touring pitches	
	I: www.budeholidaypark.co.uk			

Through Bude town centre. 2nd turning on left after main post office. Go down hill past Somerfield supermarket. 1st right between golf course. Straight across crossroads, then 1st right (Maer Lane). Park at end of lane on left.

BUDE continued

★★★★★
TOURING PARK

BUDEMEADOWS TOURING HOLIDAY PARK

Bude EX23 0NA
T: (01288) 361646
F: (01288) 361646
E: wendyjo@globalnet.co.uk
I: www.budemeadows.com

Superb centre for surfing, scenery and sightseeing. All usual facilities including heated pool, licenced bar, shop, launderette, playground. Large pitches – no overcrowding.

CC: Delta, JCB, Mastercard, Solo, Switch, Visa

Signposted on A39, 3 miles south of Bude, 200yds past crossroads to Widemouth Bay.

145	🚐	£6.00–£14.00
50	🚚	£6.00–£14.00
145	⛺	£6.00–£14.00
145 touring pitches		

★★★
HOLIDAY, TOURING
& CAMPING PARK

PENHALT FARM HOLIDAY PARK

Widemouth Bay, Bude EX23 0DG
T: (01288) 361210
F: (01288) 361210
E: den&jennie@penhaltfarm.fsnet.co.uk
I: www.holidaybank.co.uk/penhaltfarmholidaypark

Spectacular, panoramic sea views from most pitches. Friendly, family-run site, ideal for walking, surfing, touring. Site shop, play area, games room. Dogs welcome.

CC: Delta, Mastercard, Switch, Visa

Travelling south, 4.5 miles from Bude on A39. Take 2nd right into Widemouth Bay, left at bottom. Our sign is just over 0.5 miles on left.

40	🚐	£6.00–£13.00
40	🚚	£6.00–£13.00
100	⛺	£6.00–£11.00
2	🏚	£100.00–£360.00
100 touring pitches		

★★★★
HOLIDAY, TOURING
& CAMPING PARK

BH&HPA

UPPER LYNSTONE CARAVAN AND CAMPING SITE
Lynstone, Bude EX23 0LP
T: (01288) 352017
F: (01288) 359034
E: reception@upperlynstone.co.uk
I: www.upperlynstone.co.uk

CC: Delta, Mastercard, Switch, Visa

0.5 miles south of Bude on coastal road to Widemouth Bay. Signposted.

65	🚐	£7.50–£11.50
65	🚚	£7.50–£11.50
65	⛺	£7.50–£7.50
17	🏚	£132.50–£363.00
65 touring pitches		

★★★★★
HOLIDAY &
TOURING PARK

BH&HPA

WOODA FARM PARK

Poughill, Bude EX23 9HJ
T: (01288) 352069
F: (01288) 355258
E: enquiries@wooda.co.uk
I: www.wooda.co.uk

Stunning views over Bude Bay and countryside. 1.5 miles from safe, sandy beaches. Family owned and run with all facilities, fishing, woodland walks, golf. An ideal base. 10% discount for couples (excl Bank Holidays, Jul and Aug) in our holiday caravans. No groups allowed.

CC: Delta, Diners, Mastercard, Switch, Visa

From A39 north of Stratton, take coast road to Poughill and Combe Valley. Wooda is 1 mile from A39.

200	🚐	£7.50–£13.00
200	🚚	£7.50–£13.00
200	⛺	£7.50–£13.00
55	🏚	£120.00–£560.00
255 touring pitches		

SYMBOLS
The symbols in each entry give information about services and facilities. A key to these symbols appears at the back of this guide.

CHARMOUTH, Dorset Map ref 2D2

★★★★

**TOURING &
CAMPING PARK**

BH&HPA

MONKTON WYLD FARM CARAVAN & CAMPING PARK

Charmouth, Bridport DT6 6DB
T: (01297) 34525
F: (01297) 33594
E: holidays@monktonwyld.co.uk
I: www.monktonwyld.co.uk

Beautifully landscaped, level, 60-pitch park. Only three miles from sandy beaches and surrounded by lovely countryside. All the amenities you would expect to find in a quality park. Weekly special-offer rates: £55 low season, £65 mid-season.

CC: Delta, JCB, Mastercard, Solo, Switch, Visa

A35 from west towards Charmouth, cross Dorset County boundary, next lane left (brown tourist sign), 2nd campsite on left.

60	⊞	£7.40–£12.70
		£7.40–£12.70
120	▲	£7.40–£12.70
60 touring pitches		

★★★★★

**HOLIDAY, TOURING
& CAMPING PARK**

BH&HPA

WOOD FARM CARAVAN AND CAMPING PARK

Axminster Road, Charmouth DT6 6BT
T: (01297) 560697
F: (01297) 561243
E: holidays@woodfarm.co.uk
I: www.woodfarm.co.uk

Breathtaking views and superb facilities are both on offer at Wood Farm. Our Heritage Coast and spectacular rural scenery are just waiting to amaze you. Senior Citizen offer in low and mid-season for 1- and 2-week stays.

CC: Delta, JCB, Mastercard, Solo, Switch, Visa

Directly off the main A35 to the west of Charmouth. From M5 jct 25 follow A358 to Chard then Axminster. Join A35 in direction of Bridport. After 4 miles, at roundabout take first exit signposted Wood Farm.

	⊞	£8.50–£16.50
186		£8.50–£16.50
30	▲	£8.50–£16.50
3	⊞	£200.00–£450.00
216 touring pitches		

COMBE MARTIN, Devon Map ref 2C1

★★★★

**TOURING &
CAMPING PARK**

STOWFORD FARM MEADOWS

Berry Down, Combe Martin, Ilfracombe EX34 0PW
T: (01271) 882476
F: (01271) 883053
E: enquiries@stowford.co.uk
I: www.stowford.co.uk

Recent winner of numerous awards and situated on the fringe of the Exmoor National Park, this park has a reputation for superb facilities and unrivalled value. Low season: one week, only £35.00 (incl electric hook-up). Mid season: one week, only £55.00 (incl electric hook-up).

CC: Delta, Mastercard, Switch, Visa

Situated on the A3123 Woolacombe to Combe Martin road 4 miles west of Combe Martin.

600	⊞	£6.20–£14.70
50		£6.20–£14.70
50	▲	£6.20–£14.70
570 touring pitches		

CREDIT CARD BOOKINGS
If you book by telephone and are asked for your credit card number it is advisable to check the proprietor's policy should you cancel your reservation.

CROYDE BAY, Devon Map ref 2C2

★★★★
**HOLIDAY, TOURING
& CAMPING PARK**

BH&HPA

RUDA HOLIDAY PARK

Croyde Bay, Braunton EX33 1NY
T: (0191) 2759098
F: (0191) 2659435
E: enquiries@parkdean.com
I: www.parkdean.com

North Devon's premier holiday park. Situated on our own Blue Flag beach, Croyde Bay. Cascades tropical indoor adventure pool, fun for all the family. Short breaks available.

CC: Delta, Mastercard, Switch, Visa

From M5 jct 27, take the A361 to Barnstaple. From Barnstaple continue on A361 to Braunton. In the centre of Braunton, turn left after 2nd set of traffic lights onto the B3231. Enter Croyde Village, and Ruda and Cascades are signposted.

91	🚐	£12.00–£32.00
313	🚍	£12.00–£32.00
222	⛺	£7.00–£24.00
280	🏠	£165.00–£745.00

DARTMOOR

See under Ashburton, Bickington, Okehampton, Tavistock

QUALITY ASSURANCE SCHEME

For an explanation of the quality and facilities represented by the Stars please refer to the front of this guide.

DAWLISH, Devon Map ref 2D2

★★★★
HOLIDAY, TOURING & CAMPING PARK

ROSE AWARD

BH&HPA

COFTON COUNTRY HOLIDAYS

Starcross, Exeter EX6 8RP
T: (01626) 890111
F: (01626) 891572
E: info@coftonholidays.co.uk
I: www.coftonholidays.co.uk

Family-owned South Devon park. Close to Exe estuary, short drive to Dawlish Warren beach. Heated swimming pool complex. Pub. Coarse-fishing lakes. Woodland walks. £2 off standard pitch, low and mid-season (advance bookings, minimum 3 nights' stay).

CC: Delta, Mastercard, Solo, Switch, Visa

A379 Exeter to Dawlish road, 3 miles Exeter side of Dawlish.

450	🚐	£7.50–£17.50
450	🚏	£7.50–£17.50
450	⛺	£7.50–£17.50
62	🏠	£125.00–£545.00
450 touring pitches		

★★★★
HOLIDAY PARK

ROSE AWARD

See Ad p143

WELCOME FAMILY HOLIDAY PARK
Warren Road, Dawlish Warren, Dawlish EX7 0PH
T: (01626) 862070
F: (01626) 868988
E: fun@welcomefamily.co.uk
I: www.welcomefamily.co.uk

CC: Delta, Mastercard, Solo, Switch, Visa

223	🏠	£75.00–£570.00

From M5 jct 30 follow A379 for approximately 8 miles, signposted Dawlish, then to Dawlish Warren.

DORCHESTER, Dorset Map ref 3B3 *Tourist Information Centre Tel: (01305) 267992*

★★
TOURING & CAMPING PARK

BH&HPA

GIANTS HEAD CARAVAN & CAMPING PARK
Old Sherborne Road, Cerne Abbas, Dorchester DT2 7TR
T: (01300) 341242
E: holidays@giantshead.co.uk
I: www.giantshead.co.uk

50	🚐	£7.00–£11.00
50	🚏	£7.00–£11.00
50	⛺	£7.00–£11.00
50 touring pitches		

Into Dorchester avoiding bypass; at top of town roundabout take Sherbourne Road. After 500yds take the right-hand fork at the Loders Esso garage. Park is signposted. From Cerne Abbas take Buckland Newton Road.

DULVERTON, Somerset Map ref 2D1

★★★★
TOURING PARK

See Ad on inside front cover

EXMOOR HOUSE CARAVAN CLUB SITE

Dulverton TA22 9HL
T: (01398) 323268
I: www.caravanclub.co.uk

Very quiet and secluded, in the heart of Lorna Doone country. Shops and pubs within walking distance, Exmoor is on the doorstep. Ideal for a relaxing holiday. Non-members welcome.

CC: Delta, Mastercard, Solo, Switch, Visa

From M5 jct 27 B3222 to Dulverton, left over river bridge, 200yds on. Note: 2 narrow hump bridges on B3222, approach carefully.

17	🚐	£9.50–£19.50
47	🚏	£9.50–£19.50
64 total touring pitches		

EXMOOR

See under Combe Martin, Dulverton, Porlock, Winsford

NB IMPORTANT NOTE Information on accommodation listed in this guide has been supplied by the proprietors. As changes may occur you are advised to check details at the time of booking.

EXMOUTH, Devon Map ref 2D2 *Tourist Information Centre Tel: (01395) 222299*

★★★★★
TOURING PARK

BH&HPA

WEBBERS FARM CARAVAN & CAMPING PARK
Castle Lane, Woodbury, Exeter EX5 1EA
T: (01395) 232276
F: (01395) 233389
E: reception@webbersfarm.co.uk
I: www.webbersfarm.co.uk

CC: Delta, JCB, Mastercard, Switch, Visa

100	🚐	£9.25–£16.00
20	🚏	£9.25–£16.00
115	▲	£9.25–£13.25
115 touring pitches		

Leave M5 at jct 30 and follow A376 to Exmouth. At 2nd roundabout take B3179 to Budleigh Salterton and Woodbury. From Woodbury village centre follow official brown signs.

GLASTONBURY, Somerset Map ref 3A2 *Tourist Information Centre Tel: (01458) 832954*

★★★★★
**TOURING &
CAMPING PARK**

BH&HPA

THE OLD OAKS TOURING PARK

Wick Farm, Wick, Glastonbury BA6 8JS
T: (01458) 831437
F: (01458) 833238
E: info@theoldoaks.co.uk
I: www.theoldoaks.co.uk

An award-winning park, exclusively for adults, set in tranquil, unspoilt countryside with panoramic views, offering spacious, landscaped pitches and amenities graded excellent. £1 per night discount for Senior Citizens (excl high season). No extra charge for serviced pitch for disabled persons.

CC: Delta, JCB, Mastercard, Switch, Visa

53	🚐	£8.00–£12.00
60	🚏	£8.00–£12.00
40	▲	£8.00–£12.00
40 touring pitches		

From Glastonbury 2 miles towards Shepton Mallet on A361, signed for Wick, site in 1 mile. From Wells left after roundabout entering Glastonbury at sign for Wick. Site 1.5 miles.

GREAT TORRINGTON, Devon Map ref 2C2 *Tourist Information Centre Tel: (01805) 626140*

Rating
Applied For

BH&HPA

See Ad on this page

GREENWAYS VALLEY HOLIDAY PARK
Great Torrington, Torrington EX38 7EW
T: (01805) 622153
E: enquiries@greenwaysvalley.co.uk
I: www.greenwaysvalley.co.uk

CC: Mastercard

8	🚐	£6.00–£11.90
8	🚏	£6.00–£11.90
8	▲	£6.00–£11.90
5	🏠	£120.00–£350.00

Exit M5 at jct 27. Follow A361 to South Molton; at South Molton turn left at roundabout along B3227 for Great Torrington; on approach to Great Torrington, turn left at caravan site sign (opposite school) and follow lane for about 0.5 miles to the park.

★★★
**HOLIDAY, TOURING
& CAMPING PARK**

BH&HPA

SMYTHAM MANOR LEISURE
Little Torrington, Torrington EX38 8PU
T: (01805) 622110
F: (01805) 625451
E: info@smytham.co.uk
I: www.smytham.co.uk

CC: Amex, Delta, Diners, JCB, Mastercard, Solo, Switch, Visa

30	🚐	£6.00–£12.00
30	🚏	£6.00–£12.00
30	▲	£6.00–£12.00
10	🏠	£175.00–£450.00
30 touring pitches		

2.5 miles south of Torrington on the A386 Torrington to Okehampton road; A361 to Barnstaple; B3232 to Great Torrington, then A386.

  COLOUR MAPS Colour maps at the front of this guide pinpoint all places in which you will find parks listed.

HAYLE, Cornwall Map ref 2B3

★★★★
HOLIDAY PARK

BH&HPA

BEACHSIDE HOLIDAY PARK
Hayle TR27 5AW
T: (01736) 753080
F: (01736) 757252
E: reception@beachside.demon.co.uk
I: www.beachside.co.uk

CC: Delta, Mastercard, Solo, Switch, Visa

84		£8.00–£21.00
84		£8.00–£21.00
84		£8.00–£21.00
		£85.00–£625.00
84 touring pitches		

Leave A30 at the large roundabout at the approach to Hayle, take the Hayle road, turn right beside the putting green and signpost showing 'Beachside'. Situated approximately 0.5 miles on right.

★★★★
HOLIDAY PARK

BH&HPA

ST IVES BAY HOLIDAY PARK
73 Loggans Road, Upton Towans, Hayle
TR27 5BH
T: (01736) 752274
F: (01736) 754523
E: stivesbay@pipex.com
I: www.stivesbay.co.uk

CC: Delta, Mastercard, Solo, Switch, Visa

300		£6.50–£21.00
300		£6.50–£21.00
300		£6.50–£21.00
250		£114.00–£691.00
300 touring pitches		

Exit A30 at Hayle, turn immediately right. Park entrance 500m on the left.

HELSTON, Cornwall Map ref 2B3 *Tourist Information Centre Tel: (01326) 565431*

★★★★
**HOLIDAY &
TOURING PARK**

POLDOWN CARAVAN PARK
Poldown, Carleen, Helston TR13 9NN
T: (01326) 574560
F: (01326) 574560
E: poldown@poldown.co.uk
I: www.poldown.co.uk

Small and pretty countryside site. Peace and quiet guaranteed. Within easy reach of West Cornwall's beaches, walks and attractions. Very good touring facilities. Modern holiday caravans. 7 nights for the price of 6 (May–Jun and Sep).

From Helston take A394 to Penzance. After 1 mile turn right onto B3302 then 2nd left towards Carleen, 1 mile down lane on the right.

13		£6.50–£10.50
13		£6.50–£10.50
13		£6.50–£10.50
7		£115.00–£370.00
13 touring pitches		

KENTISBEARE, Devon Map ref 2D2

★★★★
HOLIDAY PARK

BH&HPA

FOREST GLADE HOLIDAY PARK
Kentisbeare, Cullompton EX15 2DT
T: (01404) 841381
F: (01404) 841593
E: enquiries@forest-glade.co.uk
I: www.forest-glade.co.uk

Free indoor heated pool on small, family-managed park surrounded by forest with deer. Large, flat, sheltered pitches. Luxury, all-serviced holiday homes for hire. Club members £1 per night discount on pitch fees. Short breaks available in holiday homes during most of season. Pet-free and non-smoking holiday homes available.

CC: Delta, Mastercard, Solo, Switch, Visa

From Honiton take Dunkerswell road and follow Forest Glade signs. From M5, A373, 2.5 miles at Keepers Cottage Inn then 2.5 miles on Sheldon Road. Touring caravans from Honiton direction only via Dunkerswell road.

80		£10.65–£13.95
20		£10.65–£13.95
80		£8.75–£12.00
24		£125.00–£400.00
80 touring pitches		

SPECIAL BREAKS
Many establishments offer special promotions and themed breaks. These are highlighted in red. (All such offers are subject to availability.)

LACOCK, Wiltshire Map ref 3B2

★★★★★

**TOURING &
CAMPING PARK**

BH&HPA

PICCADILLY CARAVAN PARK
Folly Lane (West), Lacock, Chippenham
SN15 2LP
T: (01249) 730260
E: piccadillylacock@aol.com

39	🚐	£10.00–£12.00
39	🚙	£10.00–£12.00
4	⛺	£10.00–£12.00
43 touring pitches		

Turn right off A350 Chippenham to Melksham road, signposted to Gastard (Folly Lane West), with caravan symbol, situated 300 yds on the left.

LAND'S END, Cornwall Map ref 2A3

★★★

TOURING PARK

BH&HPA

CARDINNEY CARAVAN AND CAMPING PARK
Main A30, Land's End TR19 6HJ
T: (01736) 810880
F: (01736) 810998
E: cardinney@btinternet.com
I: www.cardinney-camping-park.co.uk

CC: Delta, Mastercard, Solo,
Switch, Visa

75	🚐	£8.00–£11.00
30	🚙	£8.00–£11.00
5	⛺	£8.00–£11.00
105 touring pitches	🏠	£84.00–£110.00

On the main A30, signposted 5 miles past Penzance. Large name board on right-hand side.

LUXULYAN, Cornwall Map ref 2B2

★★★★

**HOLIDAY, TOURING
& CAMPING PARK**

BH&HPA

CROFT FARM HOLIDAY PARK
Luxulyan, Bodmin PL30 5EQ
T: (01726) 850228
F: (01726) 850498
E: lynpick@ukonline.co.uk
I: www.croftfarm.co.uk

CC: Delta, Mastercard, Solo,
Switch, Visa

43	🚐	£8.95–£12.75
43	🚙	£8.95–£12.75
52	⛺	£6.40–£8.40
23	🏠	£140.00–£400.00
52 touring pitches		

From A390 Liskeard to St Austell road, turn right just past level crossing in St Blazey (signed Luxulyan). Turn right after 1.25 miles, right again at next T-junction. Park is on your left approximately 0.5 miles on.

MALMESBURY, Wiltshire Map ref 3B2 *Tourist Information Centre Tel: (01666) 823748*

★★

**TOURING &
CAMPING PARK**

BH&HPA

BURTON HILL CARAVAN AND CAMPING PARK
Burton Hill, Malmesbury SN16 0EH
T: (01666) 826880

30	🚐	£8.00–£9.50
30	🚙	£8.00–£9.50
30	⛺	£8.00–£9.50
30 touring pitches		

Off A429 0.25 miles south, Malmesbury to Chippenham road, opposite hospital, Arches Lane.

MARTOCK, Somerset Map ref 3A3

★★★★

TOURING PARK

BH&HPA

SOUTHFORK CARAVAN PARK
Parrett Works, Martock TA12 6AE
T: (01935) 825661
F: (01935) 825122
E: southfork.caravans@virgin.net
I: www.ukparks.co.uk/southfork

CC: Delta, JCB, Mastercard,
Switch, Visa

23	🚐	£7.00–£10.00
23	🚙	£7.00–£10.00
7	⛺	£7.00–£10.00
3	🏠	£140.00–£260.00
30 touring pitches		

From East – A303. Take exit signposted Stoke-sub-Hamdon and Martock. At T-jct turn left and follow camping signs. From West – A303. Six miles east of Ilminster at roundabout take 1st exit, signposted South Petherton, follow signs.

TOWN INDEX

This can be found at the back of the guide. If you know where you want to stay, the index will give you the page number listing all accommodation in your chosen town, city or village.

MEVAGISSEY, Cornwall Map ref 2B3

★★★★★
HOLIDAY, TOURING
& CAMPING PARK

ROSE AWARD
BH&HPA

SEA VIEW INTERNATIONAL
Boswinger, St Austell PL26 6LL
T: (01726) 843425
F: (01726) 843358
E: holidays@seaviewinternational.com
I: www.seaviewinternational.com

David Bellamy Gold Award. Best Campsite three years running. Park setting. Wonderful sandy beaches, Heligan and Eden nearby. Heated pool, children's play area. Pitches from £45.50 for 7 nights. See brochure.

CC: Delta, Mastercard, Solo, Switch, Visa

From St Austell roundabout take B3273 to Mevagissey. Prior to village turn right and follow signs to Gorran and Gorran Haven and brown tourism signs to park.

172	🚐	£6.50–£22.00
	🚚	£6.50–£22.00
	⛺	£6.50–£22.00
38	🛖	£125.00–£625.00
172 touring pitches		

MORTEHOE, Devon Map ref 2C1

★★★★
HOLIDAY, TOURING
& CAMPING PARK

BH&HPA

NORTH MORTE FARM CARAVAN AND CAMPING PARK
North Morte Road, Mortehoe, Woolacombe
EX34 7EG
T: (01271) 870381
F: (01271) 870115
E: info@northmortefarm.co.uk
I: www.northmortefarm.co.uk

CC: Delta, JCB, Mastercard, Solo, Switch, Visa

Six miles from Ilfracombe, near to the sea. Take B3343 to Mortehoe, turn right at post office, park 500yds on left.

25	🚐	£8.00–£14.00
	🚚	£8.00–£14.00
150	⛺	£8.00–£12.00
24	🛖	£150.00–£450.00
175 touring pitches		

MUCHELNEY, Somerset Map ref 3A3

★★★
TOURING &
CAMPING PARK

BH&HPA

THORNEY LAKES AND CARAVAN PARK
Thorney West Farm, Muchelney, Langport
TA10 0DW
T: (01458) 250811
E: enquiries@thorneylakes.co.uk
I: www.thorneylakes.co.uk

Turn off A303 signposted Kingsbury Episcopi. In village turn right at T-junction signposted Muchelney, Langport. Site on right about 1.25 miles.

8	🚐	£10.00
8	🚚	£10.00
8	⛺	£10.00
24 touring pitches		

NEWQUAY, Cornwall Map ref 2B2 *Tourist Information Centre Tel: (01637) 854020*

★★★★
HOLIDAY PARK

BH&HPA

See Ad on this page

HENDRA HOLIDAY PARK
Newquay TR8 4NY
T: (01637) 875778
F: (01637) 879017
E: enquiries@hendra-holidays.com
I: www.hendra-holidays.com

CC: Amex, Delta, Mastercard, Switch, Visa

Take A30 to the Highgate Hill jct, follow the signs for the A392 to Newquay. At Quintrell Downs go straight across the roundabout, Hendra is 0.5 miles on the left.

588	🚐	£8.10–£13.10
588	🚚	£8.10–£13.10
588	⛺	£8.10–£13.10
254	🛖	£139.00–£769.00

RATING All accommodation in this guide has been rated, or is awaiting a rating, by a trained Tourist Board assessor.

★★★★
HOLIDAY PARK

BH&HPA

HOLYWELL BAY HOLIDAY PARK

Holywell Bay, Newquay TR8 5PR
T: (0191) 2759098
F: (0191) 2659435
E: enquiries@parkdean.com
I: www.parkdean.com

A beautiful park nestling in a peaceful and picturesque valley only a few minutes from Newquay. Short breaks available.

CC: Mastercard, Switch, Visa

Turn right off the A3075, signposted Holywell Bay, 3 miles west of Newquay.

72	🚐	£9.50–£22.50
72	🚍	£9.50–£22.50
72	⛺	£7.50–£22.50
144	🏠	£120.00–£675.00

★★★★
TOURING PARK

See Ad on this page

NEWPERRAN HOLIDAY PARK
Rejerrah, Newquay TR8 5QJ
T: (01872) 572407
F: (01872) 571254
E: holidays@newperran.co.uk
I: www.newperran.co.uk

CC: Delta, Mastercard, Solo, Switch, Visa

270	🚐	£8.80–£14.50
270	🚍	£8.80–£14.50
270	⛺	£8.80–£14.50

Take A30 towards Redruth. Turn right on to the B3285 Perranporth road. At Goonhavern turn right on to the A3075 and after 500m turn left at Newperran signs.

★★★★
HOLIDAY PARK

BH&HPA

NEWQUAY HOLIDAY PARK

Newquay TR8 4HS
T: (0191) 2759098
F: (0191) 2659435
E: enquiries@parkdean.com
I: www.parkdean.com

A beautiful location. Set in 60 acres of countryside near the Cornish coastline, only a short distance from Newquay. Short breaks available.

CC: Mastercard, Visa

Follow A30 Bodmin to Redruth road, after iron bridge turn right signed RAF St Mawgan. After 7 miles and 1 mile roundabout, signs to Newquay Holiday Park.

180	🚐	£9.50–£22.50
181	🚍	£9.50–£22.50
259	⛺	£7.50–£22.50
138	🏠	£125.00–£655.00

MAP REFERENCES The map references refer to the colour maps at the front of the guide. The first figure is the map number; the letter and figure which follow indicate the grid reference on the map.

NEWQUAY continued

★★★★ **TOURING PARK** BH&HPA	**PORTH BEACH TOURIST PARK** Alexandra Road, Porth, Newquay TR7 3NH T: (01637) 876531 F: (01637) 871227 E: info@porthbeach.co.uk I: www.porthbeach.co.uk	CC: Delta, Mastercard, Solo, Switch, Visa	102 74 175 18 **201 touring pitches**	£9.00–£27.50 £9.00–£27.50 £9.00–£27.50 £220.00–£650.00

Take A392 from Indian Queens A30. At mini-roundabout turn right, B3276.

★★★★ **TOURING & CAMPING PARK** BH&HPA	**TRELOY TOURIST PARK** Newquay TR8 4JN T: (01637) 872063 F: (01637) 871710 E: holidays@treloy.co.uk I: www.treloy.co.uk	CC: Delta, Mastercard, Solo, Switch, Visa	140 140 140 **140 touring pitches**	£6.60–£12.80 £6.60–£12.80 £6.60–£12.80

Follow A30 direct into Cornwall. At end of dual carriageway follow A30 Newquay/Redruth road, pass Little Chef on left and after the iron bridge over the road then right, (Highgate Hill). After 3 miles at roundabout follow A3059 Newquay road. Signposted after 4 miles.

★★★★★ **HOLIDAY, TOURING & CAMPING PARK** BH&HPA	**TREVELLA CARAVAN AND CAMPING PARK** Crantock, Newquay TR8 5EW T: (01637) 830308 F: (01637) 830155 E: Trevellapark@aol.com I: www.trevella.co.uk	CC: Amex, Delta, Mastercard, Solo, Switch, Visa	230 230 40 57 **270 touring pitches**	£7.60–£13.00 £6.80–£12.00 £7.60–£13.00

Take A3075 Redruth road from Newquay. After 1.5 miles turn right into road signposted Crantock.

NEWTON ABBOT, Devon Map ref 2D2 *Tourist Information Centre Tel: (01626) 215667*

★★★★★
TOURING PARK

BH&HPA

DORNAFIELD

Two Mile Oak, Newton Abbot TQ12 6DD
T: (01803) 812732
F: (01803) 812032
E: enquiries@dornafield.com
I: www.dornafield.com

Beautiful 15thC farmhouse location set amidst glorious South Devon countryside. Ideal for Torquay and Dartmoor. Superb facilities to suit the truly discerning caravanner. Early- and late-season bookings. Book for 7 days and only pay for 5. Details on request.

CC: Delta, Mastercard, Switch, Visa

135 64 135 **135 touring pitches**	£9.00–£14.00 £9.00–£14.00 £9.00–£14.00

Take A381 Newton Abbot to Totnes road. In 2.5 miles at Two Mile Inn turn right. In 0.5 miles 1st turn to left. Site 200yds on right.

AT-A-GLANCE SYMBOLS

Symbols at the end of each accommodation entry give useful information about services and facilities. A key to symbols can be found inside the back cover flap. Keep this open for easy reference.

OKEHAMPTON, Devon Map ref 2C2

★★★★★

HOLIDAY &
TOURING PARK

BH&HPA

DARTMOOR VIEW HOLIDAY PARK

Whiddon Down, Okehampton EX20 2QL
T: (01647) 231545
F: (01647) 231654
E: jo@dartmoorview.co.uk
I: www.dartmoorview.co.uk

Superb touring caravan and camping park. Good base for exploring Dartmoor and the West Country. Five-star facilities at affordable prices. Super savers available from: £39.95 7 days incl electric, 2 people, caravan/motorhome (excl 14 Jul-31 Aug). Great offers on our luxury holiday homes.

CC: Delta, JCB, Mastercard, Solo, Switch, Visa

0.5 miles off A30 (Merrymeet roundabout). Turn left for Whiddon Down, 0.75 miles on the right-hand side.

75	🚐	£10.25–£13.50
75	🚙	£10.25–£13.50
75	⛺	£7.75–£11.00
13	🏠	£120.00–£425.00
75 touring pitches		

ORCHESTON, Wiltshire Map ref 3B2

★★★

TOURING &
CAMPING PARK

BH&HPA

STONEHENGE TOURING PARK
Orcheston, Salisbury SP3 4SH
T: (01980) 620304
E: stonehengetouringpark@supanet.com
I: stonehengetouringpark.supanet.com

CC: Delta, Mastercard, Solo, Switch, Visa

30	🚐	£6.50–£11.00
30	🚙	£6.50–£11.00
30	⛺	£6.50–£11.00
30 touring pitches		

A360 from Shrewton to Devizes, after 0.5 miles turn right to Orcheston past Crown Inn.

OWERMOIGNE, Dorset Map ref 3B3

★★★★

HOLIDAY, TOURING
& CAMPING PARK

BH&HPA

SANDYHOLME HOLIDAY PARK
Moreton Road, Owermoigne, Dorchester DT2 8HZ
T: (01305) 852677
F: (01305) 854677
E: smeatons@sandyholme.co.uk
I: www.sandyholme.co.uk

CC: Delta, Mastercard, Switch, Visa

53	🚐	£8.00–£15.00
53	🚙	£8.00–£15.00
53	⛺	£8.00–£12.50
26	🏠	£140.00–£480.00
53 touring pitches		

One mile inland off A352. Through village of Owermoigne, 1 mile.

PADSTOW, Cornwall Map ref 2B2 Tourist Information Centre Tel: (01841) 533449

★★★★

HOLIDAY, TOURING
& CAMPING PARK

ROSE AWARD

BH&HPA

CARNEVAS FARM HOLIDAY PARK

Carnevas Farm, St Merryn, Padstow PL28 8PN
T: (01841) 520230
F: (01841) 520230

Family-run park for families. Situated on the North Cornish coast. Padstow four miles. Nearest beach 0.5 miles. Great surfing. Excellent facilities. Cleanliness assured.

At end of Bodmin bypass, on A30 carry on under iron bridge, turn right onto A3059, St Columb road. Turn onto A39, then left onto B3271, Padstow. At St Merryn turn left onto B3276. Two miles, towards Porthcothan Bay, opposite Tredrea Inn.

198	🚐	£6.50–£12.50
198	🚙	£6.50–£12.50
198	⛺	£6.50–£12.50
9	🏠	£160.00–£500.00
198 touring pitches		

CREDIT CARD BOOKINGS If you book by telephone and are asked for your credit card number it is advisable to check the proprietor's policy should you cancel your reservation.

PADSTOW continued

★★★★

TOURING &
CAMPING PARK

BH&HPA

THE LAURELS HOLIDAY PARK

Padstow Road, Whitecross, Wadebridge PL27 7JQ
T: (01208) 813341
F: (01208) 816590
E: anicholson@thelaurelsholidaypark.co.uk
I: www.thelaurelsholidaypark.co.uk

Small, relaxing park with individual, shrub-lined pitches. All with electric, grass and level in beautiful surroundings. Ideal touring centre. Open Easter to October.

Turn onto A389 for Padstow off A39 west of Wadebridge. Entrance 20yds from jct.

30	🚐	£6.00–£15.00
30	🚎	£6.00–£15.00
30	⛺	£6.00–£15.00
30 touring pitches		

PAIGNTON, Devon Map ref 2D2 *Tourist Information Centre Tel: 0906 680 1268 (Premium rate number)*

★★★★★

HOLIDAY &
TOURING PARK

ROSE AWARD

BH&HPA
NCC

See Ad on this page

BEVERLEY PARK
Goodrington Road, Paignton TQ4 7JE
T: (01803) 843887
F: (01803) 845427
E: info@beverley-holidays.co.uk
I: www.beverley-holidays.co.uk

CC: Delta, Mastercard, Solo, Switch, Visa

189	🚐	£10.00–£23.50
50	🚎	£10.00–£23.50
120	⛺	£7.00–£19.50
195	🏠	£125.00–£709.00

From end of M5 take A380 to Torbay. Then A3022 for 2 miles south of Paignton. Turn left into Goodrington Road.

★★★★

HOLIDAY, TOURING
& CAMPING PARK

BH&HPA

HIGHER WELL FARM HOLIDAY PARK
Waddeton Road, Stoke Gabriel, Totnes
TQ9 6RN
T: (01803) 782289
E: higherwell@talk21.com
I: www.ukparks.co.uk/higherwell

CC: Mastercard, Switch, Visa

80	🚐	£7.50–£12.00
80	🚎	£7.50–£12.00
80	⛺	£7.50–£12.00
18	🏠	£130.00–£400.00
80 touring pitches		

From Paignton, A385 to Totnes, turn left at Parkers Arms for Stoke Gabriel, 1.5 miles turn left to Waddeton, situated 200yds down the road.

PENZANCE, Cornwall Map ref 2A3 *Tourist Information Centre Tel: (01736) 362207*

★★★

HOLIDAY &
TOURING PARK

BH&HPA

TOWER PARK CARAVANS AND CAMPING
St Buryan, Penzance TR19 6BZ
T: (01736) 810286
F: (01736) 810954
E: enquiries@towerparkcamping.co.uk
I: www.towerparkcamping.co.uk

CC: Delta, JCB, Mastercard, Solo, Switch, Visa

102	🚐	£6.50–£10.90
102	🚎	£6.50–£10.90
102	⛺	£6.50–£9.00
5	🏠	£128.00–£295.00
102 touring pitches		

Off A30 3 miles west of Penzance, B3283 to St Buryan, fork right and keep right for 400yds.

POLRUAN-BY-FOWEY, Cornwall Map ref 2B3

★★★★

HOLIDAY, TOURING & CAMPING PARK

BH&HPA

POLRUAN HOLIDAYS (CAMPING & CARAVANNING)
Townsend Road, Polruan, Fowey PL23 1QH
T: (01726) 870263
F: (01726) 870263
E: polholiday@aol.com

7	🚐	£9.00–£12.75
7	🚏	£9.00–£12.75
40	▲	£7.00–£12.75
11	🏠	£110.00–£380.00
32 touring pitches		

A38 to Dobwalls, left on A390 to East Taphouse. Left on B3359 after 4.5 miles turn right signposted Polruan.

PORLOCK, Somerset Map ref 2D1

★★★★

HOLIDAY, TOURING & CAMPING PARK

BH&HPA

BURROWHAYES FARM CARAVAN AND CAMPING SITE AND RIDING STABLES
West Luccombe, Porlock, Minehead TA24 8HT
T: (01643) 862463
E: info@burrowhayes.co.uk
I: www.burrowhayes.co.uk

Real family site situated in glorious NT scenery in Exmoor National Park. Ideal for walking and riding, with stables on site.

CC: Delta, JCB, Mastercard, Solo, Switch, Visa

From Minehead take A39 towards Porlock; take 1st left after Allerford to Horner and West Luccombe; Burrowhayes is 0.25 miles along on right-hand side before humpback bridge.

54	🚐	£6.50–£9.50
54	🚏	£6.50–£9.50
66	▲	£6.50–£9.50
19	🏠	£125.00–£325.00
120 touring pitches		

PORTREATH, Cornwall Map ref 2B3

★★★

TOURING PARK

CAMBROSE TOURING PARK
Portreath Road, Redruth TR16 4HT
T: (01209) 890747
F: (01209) 891665
E: cambrosetouringpark@supanet.com
I: www.cambrosetouringpark.co.uk

60	🚐	£7.50–£12.00
10	🚏	£7.50–£12.00
60	▲	£7.50–£12.00
2	🏠	£80.00–£165.00
60 touring pitches		

From new A30, 3 miles north on B3300 Portreath/Redruth road. Turn right, 100yds on left.

★★★★

HOLIDAY PARK

BH&HPA

TEHIDY HOLIDAY PARK
Harris Mill, Illogan, Portreath, Redruth TR16 4JQ
T: (01209) 216489
F: (01209) 216489
E: holiday@tehidy.co.uk
I: www.tehidy.co.uk

CC: Delta, JCB, Mastercard, Solo, Switch, Visa

18	🚐	£7.50–£11.00
3	🚏	£7.50–£11.00
18	▲	£7.50–£11.00
20	🏠	£120.00–£395.00

South on A30 take Porthtowan exit. Right 1st roundabout, 1st left to Portreath.

ROSUDGEON, Cornwall Map ref 2B3

★★★

HOLIDAY PARK

BH&HPA

KENNEGGY COVE HOLIDAY PARK
Higher Kenneggy, Rosudgeon, Penzance TR20 9AU
T: (01736) 763453
E: enquiries@kenneggycove.co.uk
I: www.kenneggycove.co.uk

Quiet site in magnificent situation. Sea views. Ten minutes' walk to coastal path and secluded beach. Free hot water. Shop and take-away service. French and German spoken. 10% discount for Senior Citizens Mar-May and Sep-Oct. No single-sex groups or large parties.

30	🚐	£7.00–£14.00
30	🚏	£7.00–£14.00
60	▲	£7.00–£14.00
9	🏠	£140.00–£400.00
60 touring pitches		

Take the lane to Higher Kenneggy, south off the A394 at the Helston end of Rosudgeon. The park is 0.5 miles down the lane on the left.

RUAN MINOR, Cornwall Map ref 2B3

★★★★
HOLIDAY PARK

SEA ACRES HOLIDAY PARK

Kennack Sands, Ruan Minor, Helston TR12 7LT
T: 0845 458 0064
E: enquiries@seaacres.co.uk
I: www.seaacres.co.uk

England's most southerly holiday park in an Area of Outstanding Natural Beauty overlooking clean, safe, sandy beaches from Helston. A Parkdean Holidays Park. Short breaks available.

CC: Delta, Mastercard, Solo, Switch, Visa

Take the A3083 from Helston, then the B3293 to Coverack, turn right at crossroads signed Kennack Sands, site on right overlooking beach.

132	⌷	£115.00–£715.00

★★★
HOLIDAY &
TOURING PARK

BH&HPA

SILVER SANDS HOLIDAY PARK
Gwendreath, Kennack Sands, Ruan Minor,
Helston TR12 7LZ
T: (01326) 290631
F: (01326) 290631
E: enquiries@silversandsholidaypark.co.uk
I: www.silversandsholidaypark.co.uk

15		£8.00–£12.00
15		£8.00–£12.00
20		£6.50–£9.00
15	⌷	£115.00–£375.00
35 touring pitches		

A3083 from Helston past RNAS Culdrose, left onto B3293 (St Keverne). Right turn after passing Goonhilly satellite station. Left after 1.5 miles to Gwendreath.

ST AGNES, Cornwall Map ref 2B3

★★★★
TOURING PARK

BH&HPA

BEACON COTTAGE FARM TOURING PARK
Beacon Drive, St Agnes TR5 0NU
T: (01872) 552347
E: beaconcottagefarm@lineone.net
I: www.beaconcottagefarmholidays.com

CC: Diners, JCB, Mastercard, Solo, Switch, Visa

50		£6.00–£14.00
50		£6.00–£14.00
50		£6.00–£14.00
50 touring pitches		

From A30 take B3277 to St Agnes, follow signs to park.

ST AUSTELL, Cornwall Map ref 2B3 *Tourist Information Centre Tel: (01726) 879500*

★★★★
HOLIDAY PARK

BH&HPA
NCC

TREWHIDDLE HOLIDAY ESTATE

Pentewan Road, St Austell PL26 7AD
T: (01726) 879420
F: (01726) 879421
E: dmcclelland@btconnect.com
I: www.trewhiddle.co.uk

Ideally situated for touring Cornwall, 15 minutes from the Eden Project and Heligan Gardens. Three beaches within four miles. Open all year round. Touring and camping from £50 per week. Discounts for 2-week bookings in static caravans during low and mid-season.

CC: Amex, Delta, Diners, JCB, Mastercard, Switch, Visa

From the A390 turn south on B3273 to Mevagissey, site 0.75 miles from the roundabout on the right.

105		£10.00–£18.00
105		£10.00–£18.00
105		£10.00–£18.00
22	⌷	£140.00–£500.00
105 touring pitches		

ST IVES, Cornwall Map ref 2B3 *Tourist Information Centre Tel: (01736) 796297*

★★★★
TOURING PARK

BH&HPA

TREVALGAN HOLIDAY FARM
Trevalgan, St Ives TR26 3BJ
T: (01736) 796433
F: (01736) 799798
E: enquiries@trevalganholidayfarm.co.uk
I: www.trevalganholidayfarm.co.uk

CC: Amex, Mastercard, Switch, Visa

40		£8.00–£14.00
40		£8.00–£14.00
40		£8.00–£14.00
120 touring pitches		

From A30 take day visitors' route to St Ives, jct B3306 turn left, park sign 0.25 miles.

ST JUST IN ROSELAND, Cornwall Map ref 2B3

★★★★★
TOURING PARK

BH&HPA

TRETHEM MILL TOURING PARK
St Just in Roseland, Truro TR2 5JF
T: (01872) 580504
F: (01872) 580968
E: reception@trethem.com
I: www.trethem.com

Discover the Roseland staying on the only 5-star park on the peninsula. We offer peace and tranquillity with an exceptional standard of facilities. "Caravan Park of the year 2002", Cornwall Tourist Board.

CC: Delta, Mastercard, Solo, Switch, Visa

A3078 towards Tregony/St Mawes, over Tregony bridge, after 5 miles you reach Trewithian and will see brown caravan and camping signs. You will find the lane for the site 2 miles beyond Trewithian on the right-hand side.

84	🚐	£8.00–£12.00
84	🚏	£8.00–£12.00
84	⛺	£8.00–£12.00
84 touring pitches		

ST MERRYN, Cornwall Map ref 2B2

★★★
TOURING &
CAMPING PARK

BH&HPA

TREVEAN FARM
St Merryn, Padstow PL28 8PR
T: (01841) 520772
F: (01841) 520722

12	🚐	£8.00–£11.00
12	🚏	£8.00–£11.00
12	⛺	£8.00–£11.00
3	🏠	£150.00
60 touring pitches		

Follow the B3276 towards Padstow for approximately 8 miles. After passing the Tredrea Inn continue for approximately 0.5 miles. Take first turning on your right, site is first farm on right.

SALCOMBE, Devon Map ref 2C3 *Tourist Information Centre Tel: (01548) 843927*

★★★
TOURING &
CAMPING PARK

BOLBERRY HOUSE FARM
Bolberry, Malborough, Kingsbridge TQ7 3DY
T: (01548) 561251
F: (01548) 561251
E: bolberry.house@virgin.net
I: www.bolberryparks.co.uk

A friendly, family-run park on coastal farm. Spacious and mostly level. Some wonderful sea views. Good access to stunning clifftop walks. Safe sandy beaches nearby. Amazing rates, low season only for couple over 50 – from £35 per week (incl electric).

A381 from Totnes to Kingsbridge. Between Kingsbridge and Salcombe is the village of Malborough. Take sharp right through the village following the signs to Bolberry which is approximately 1 mile.

20	🚐	£7.50–£11.00
20	🚏	£7.50–£11.00
58	⛺	£6.50–£10.50
6	🏠	£95.00–£425.00
78 touring pitches		

★★★★
TOURING &
CAMPING PARK

BH&HPA

KARRAGEEN CARAVAN AND CAMPING PARK
Karrageen, Bolberry, Malborough, Kingsbridge TQ7 3EN
T: (01548) 561230
F: (01548) 560192
E: phil@karrageen.co.uk
I: www.karrageen.co.uk

Small park with character overlooking a valley and with sea views. Gently terraced, level, tree-lined pitches. Beach one mile. Site shop. Quality, hot take-away food. Caravans for hire. Discounted weekly rates for over 50s (excl high season) from £45.

Take A381 Kingsbridge to Salcombe road, turn sharp right through Malborough village, following signs to Bolberry, for 0.6 miles. Turn right to Bolberry then after 0.9 miles the park is on the right.

25	🚐	£7.50–£12.50
65	🚏	£7.50–£12.50
65	⛺	£7.50–£12.50
4	🏠	£160.00–£450.00
75 touring pitches		

SALISBURY PLAIN

See under Orcheston, Warminster

SHALDON, Devon Map ref 2D2

★★★
HOLIDAY, TOURING & CAMPING PARK

COAST VIEW HOLIDAY PARK
Torquay Road, Shaldon, Teignmouth
TQ14 0BG
T: (01626) 872392
F: (01626) 872719
E: info@coast-view.co.uk
I: www.coast-view.co.uk

CC: Amex, Delta, JCB,
Mastercard, Solo, Switch, Visa

12	🚐	£10.00–£20.00
252	🚂	£10.00–£18.00
252	⛺	£8.00–£16.00
24	🏠	£70.00–£590.00
252 touring pitches		

A381 to Teignmouth/Shaldon; proceed along this road to Teignmouth; turn right at the traffic lights; cross Shaldon Bridge; follow main road round and up hill. Coast View is on the right.

SIDMOUTH, Devon Map ref 2D2 *Tourist Information Centre Tel: (01395) 516441*

★★★★★
HOLIDAY & TOURING PARK

BH&HPA

SALCOMBE REGIS CAMPING AND CARAVAN PARK
Salcombe Regis, Sidmouth EX10 0JH
T: (01395) 514303
F: (01395) 514303
E: info@salcombe-regis.co.uk
I: www.salcombe-regis.co.uk

CC: Delta, JCB, Mastercard,
Solo, Switch, Visa

40	🚐	£7.75–£12.75
40	🚂	£7.75–£12.75
60	⛺	£7.75–£12.75
10	🏠	£140.00–£455.00
100 touring pitches		

1.5 miles east of Sidmouth, signposted off the A3052 road.

SOUTH MOLTON, Devon Map ref 2C1

★★★
HOLIDAY, TOURING & CAMPING PARK

BH&HPA

YEO VALLEY HOLIDAY PARK

c/o Blackcock Inn, Molland, South Molton EX36 3NW
T: (01769) 550297
F: (01769) 550101
E: lorna@yeovalleyholidays.com
I: www.yeovalleyholidays.com

In a beautiful, secluded valley on the edge of Exmoor, this small, family-run park is the ideal place to relax or enjoy many activities. 10% discount off a 4-night stay in Jun, Sep or Oct.

CC: Delta, Mastercard, Switch, Visa

Follow signs to Blackcock Inn from A361 near South Molton on B3227.

69	🚐	£11.00–£14.00
	🚂	£11.00–£14.00
50	⛺	£10.00–£14.00
65 touring pitches		

TAUNTON, Somerset Map ref 2D1 *Tourist Information Centre Tel: (01823) 336344*

★★★
TOURING & CAMPING PARK

ASHE FARM CARAVAN AND CAMPSITE
Ashe, Thornfalcon, Taunton TA3 5NW
T: (01823) 442567
F: (01823) 443372
E: camping@ashe-frm.fsnet.co.uk

20	🚐	£8.50–£10.00
10	🚂	£8.50–£10.00
10	⛺	£8.50–£8.50
3	🏠	£120.00–£170.00
30 touring pitches		

M5 jct 25. Take A358 south east for 2.5 miles, turn right at Nags Head, site 0.25 miles on right.

★★★★
TOURING & CAMPING PARK

BH&HPA

HOLLY BUSH PARK
Culmhead, Taunton TA3 7EA
T: (01823) 421515
E: info@hollybushpark.com
I: www.hollybushpark.com

CC: Mastercard, Switch, Visa

40	🚐	£8.75–£10.25
40	🚂	£8.75–£10.25
10	⛺	£6.50–£8.50
40 touring pitches		

M5 jct 25, follow signs for Taunton, Corfe and racecourse on B3170. 3.5 miles after Corfe, turn right at crossroads, Wellington, right again after 400yds, then 150yds on left.

PRICES Please check prices and other details at the time of booking

TAUNTON continued

★★

**TOURING &
CAMPING PARK**

TANPITS CIDER FARM CAMPING AND CARAVAN PARK
Dyers Lane, Bathpool, Taunton TA2 8BZ
T: (01823) 270663
F: (01823) 270663

20	🚐	£4.00–£6.00
20	🚙	£4.00–£6.00
20	⛺	£4.00–£6.00
1	🏠	£100.00–£200.00
20 touring pitches		

M5 jct 25, take A38 from Taunton to Bridgwater. Left after canal bridge in Bathpool and then left into Dyers Lane. We are down lane on left.

TAVISTOCK, Devon Map ref 2C2 *Tourist Information Centre Tel: (01822) 612938*

★★★★

**HOLIDAY, TOURING
& CAMPING PARK**

ROSE AWARD

BH&HPA

HARFORD BRIDGE HOLIDAY PARK

Harford Bridge Park, Peter Tavy, Tavistock PL19 9LS
T: (01822) 810349
F: (01822) 810028
E: enquiry@harfordbridge.co.uk
I: www.harfordbridge.co.uk

Beautiful, level, sheltered park set in Dartmoor with delighful views of Cox Tor. The River Tavy forms a boundary. Ideal for exploring Devon and Cornwall. Camping: 10% discount for week paid in full on arrival. Holiday let: £15 off 2-week booking. £10 Senior Citizen discount.

CC: Mastercard, Switch, Visa

40	🚐	£7.00–£12.00
40	🚙	£7.00–£12.00
40	⛺	£7.00–£12.00
13	🏠	£150.00–£420.00
120 touring pitches		

M5 onto A30 to Sourton Cross; take left turn onto A386 Tavistock Road; two miles north of Tavistock, take the Peter Tavy; entrance 200yds on left; clearly marked and easy access.

★★★★

**HOLIDAY, TOURING
& CAMPING PARK**

BH&HPA

LANGSTONE MANOR CARAVAN AND CAMPING PARK

Moortown, Tavistock PL19 9JZ
T: (01822) 613371
F: (01822) 613371
E: jane@langstone-manor.co.uk
I: www.langstone-manor.co.uk

Fantastic location with direct access onto moor. Peace and quiet, with secluded pitches. Bar and restaurant. Excellent base for South Devon and Cornwall. Discover Dartmoor's secret! £15 discount for 2-week booking in holiday homes.

CC: Delta, Mastercard, Switch, Visa

40	🚐	£7.00–£10.00
20	🚙	£7.00–£10.00
40	⛺	£7.00–£10.00
5	🏠	£120.00–£380.00
40 touring pitches		

Take the B3357 Princetown road from Tavistock. After approximately 1.5 miles you will see signs to Langstone Manor.

COUNTRY CODE Always follow the Country Code 🌾 Enjoy the countryside and respect its life and work 🌾 Guard against all risk of fire 🌾 Fasten all gates 🌾 Keep your dogs under close control 🌾 Keep to public paths across farmland 🌾 Use gates and stiles to cross fences, hedges and walls 🌾 Leave livestock, crops and machinery alone 🌾 Take your litter home 🌾 Help to keep all water clean 🌾 Protect wildlife, plants and trees 🌾 Take special care on country roads 🌾 Make no unnecessary noise

TINTAGEL, Cornwall Map ref 2B2

★★★★★
TOURING PARK

See Ad on inside front cover

TREWETHETT FARM CARAVAN CLUB SITE

Trethevy, Tintagel PL34 0BQ
T: (01840) 770222
I: www.caravanclub.co.uk

Cliff-top site with breathtaking views, located at the heart of King Arthur's Cornwall. Walk to Boscastle, with its pretty harbour and quayside, or Tintagel to see its dramatic castle. Non-members welcome.

CC: Delta, Mastercard, Solo, Switch, Visa

From A30 onto A395 signposted Camelford. Right onto A39 signposted Bude. Left just before transmitter. Right onto B3266 signposted Boscastle. Left onto B3263. Site entrance is on the right in about 2 miles.

125	🚐	£11.00–£20.00
125	🚍	£11.00–£20.00
125 total touring pitches		

WARMINSTER, Wiltshire Map ref 3B2 *Tourist Information Centre Tel: (01985) 218548*

★★★★★
TOURING PARK

See Ad on inside front cover

LONGLEAT CARAVAN CLUB SITE

Warminster BA12 7NL
T: (01985) 844663
I: www.caravanclub.co.uk

Situated a few hundred yards from Longleat House, this is the only site where you can hear lions roar at night! Cafes, pubs and restaurants within walking distance. Non-members welcome.

CC: Delta, Mastercard, Solo, Switch, Visa

Take A362, signed for Frome, 0.5 miles at roundabout turn left (2nd exit) onto Longleat Estate. Through toll booths, follow caravan and camping Pennant signs for 1 mile.

165	🚐	£12.00–£20.50
165	🚍	£12.00–£20.50
165 total touring pitches		

WESTON-SUPER-MARE, North Somerset Map ref 2D1 *Tourist Information Centre Tel: (01934) 888800*

★★
TOURING & CAMPING PARK

BH&HPA

DULHORN FARM CAMPING SITE
Weston Road, Lympsham, Weston-super-Mare
BS24 0JQ
T: (01934) 750298
F: (01934) 750913

57	🚐	£8.00–£12.00
57	🚍	£7.00–£12.00
25	⛺	£5.00–£10.00
3	🏠	£115.00–£266.00
57 touring pitches		

From M5 jct 22, take the A38 towards Bristol and then A370 to Weston-super-mare, 1.25 miles on left.

WEYMOUTH, Dorset Map ref 3B3 *Tourist Information Centre Tel: (01305) 785747*

★★★★
TOURING PARK

See Ad on inside front cover

CROSSWAYS CARAVAN CLUB SITE

Crossways, Dorchester DT2 8BE
T: (01305) 852032
I: www.caravanclub.co.uk

Set in 35 acres of woodland. Dorchester, the heart of Hardy's Wessex, is nearby, also Weymouth's award-winning, sandy beach. Visit Lawrence of Arabia's house at Cloud's Hill. Non-members welcome.

CC: Delta, Mastercard, Solo, Switch, Visa

North from A35 or south from A352, join B3390. Site on right within 1 mile. Entrance to site by forecourt of filling station.

122	🚐	£7.50–£16.50
122	🚍	£7.50–£16.50
122 total touring pitches		

WHITE CROSS, Cornwall Map ref 2B2

★★★★★
HOLIDAY PARK

BH&HPA

WHITE ACRES HOLIDAY PARK

White Cross, Newquay TR8 4LW
T: 0845 458 0065
F: 01726 860877
E: reception@whiteacres.co.uk
I: www.whiteacres.co.uk

Set in 140 acres of glorious countryside. Five-star facilities, luxury holiday homes, level pitches, top entertainment, children's club, coarse fishing.......great family holidays! A Parkdean Holidays Park. Short breaks available.

CC: Delta, Mastercard, Solo, Switch, Visa

Take the Indian Queens exit from A30. Follow A392 towards Newquay. White Acres Holiday Park is approximately 1 mile on right-hand side.

75		£12.50–£32.00
75		£12.50–£32.00
75		£12.50–£32.00
203		£210.00–£770.00

WINSFORD, Somerset Map ref 2D1

★★★★
**TOURING &
CAMPING PARK**

BH&HPA

HALSE FARM CARAVAN & TENT PARK

Winsford, Minehead TA24 7JL
T: (01643) 851259
F: (01643) 851592
E: brown@halsefarm.co.uk
I: www.halsefarm.co.uk

Exmoor National Park, small, peaceful, adjacent to moor on working farm with spectacular views. Paradise for walkers and country lovers. David Bellamy Gold Conservation Award. 10% discount for 1 week or more, paid 10 days in advance.

CC: Amex, Delta, JCB, Mastercard, Solo, Switch, Visa

Signposted from A396 Minehead to Tiverton road. Turn off A396 for Winsford. In the village turn left and bear left in front of the Royal Oak Inn. Keep up hill for 1 mile; our entrance is immediately after the cattle grid on the left.

22		£8.00–£10.00
22		£8.00–£10.00
22		£8.00–£10.00
44 touring pitches		

NB **IMPORTANT NOTE** Information on accommodation listed in this guide has been supplied by the proprietors. As changes may occur you are advised to check details at the time of booking.

WOOLACOMBE, Devon Map ref 2C1 *Tourist Information Centre Tel: (01271) 870553*

★★★★	**WOOLACOMBE BAY HOLIDAY PARCS**			80	£12.00–£36.50
HOLIDAY PARK	Woolacombe EX34 7HW	CC: Delta, JCB, Mastercard,		80	£12.00–£36.50
	T: (01271) 870343	Solo, Switch, Visa		90	£8.00–£25.00
See Ad on back cover	F: (01271) 870089			80	£100.00–£810.00
	E: goodtimes@woolacombe.com			90 touring pitches	
	I: www.woolacombe.com				

M5 jct 27. A361 to Ilfracombe. At Mullacott Cross take the B3343 towards Woolacombe. Situated on this road on left, approximately 2 miles past "once upon a time".

★★★	**WOOLACOMBE SANDS HOLIDAY PARK**				£10.00–£25.00
HOLIDAY PARK	Beach Road, Woolacombe EX34 7AF	CC: Delta, JCB, Mastercard,		150	£10.00–£25.00
BH&HPA	T: (01271) 870569	Solo, Switch, Visa		100	£8.00–£13.75
	F: (01271) 870606			70	£99.00–£850.00
See Ad p159	E: lifesabeach@woolacombe-sands.co.uk			250 touring pitches	
	I: www.woolacombe-sands.co.uk				

M5 jct 27 to Barnstaple. A361 to Mullacott Cross then B3343 to Woolacombe. Left just before Woolacombe.

CHECK THE MAPS

The colour maps at the front of this guide show all the cities, towns and villages for which you will find park entries. Refer to the town index to find the page on which it is listed.

A brief guide to the main Towns and Villages offering accommodation in the **South West**

ASHBURTON, DEVON - Formerly a thriving wool centre and important as one of Dartmoor's four stannary towns. Today's busy market town has many period buildings. Ancient tradition is maintained in the annual ale-tasting and bread-weighing ceremony. Good centre for exploring Dartmoor or the South Devon coast.

AXMINSTER, DEVON - This tree-shaded market town on the banks of the River Axe was one of Devon's earliest West Saxon settlements, but is better known for its carpet making. Based on Turkish methods, the industry began in 1755, declined in the 1830s and was revived in 1937.

BATH, BATH AND NORTH EAST SOMERSET - Georgian spa city beside the River Avon. Important Roman site with impressive reconstructed baths, uncovered in 19th C. Bath Abbey was built on the site of the monastery where the first king of England was crowned (AD 973). Fine architecture in mellow local stone. Pump Room and museums.

BRIDPORT, DORSET - Market town and chief producer of nets and ropes just inland of dramatic Dorset coast. Old, broad streets built for drying and twisting and long gardens for rope-walks. Grand arcaded Town Hall and Georgian buildings. Local history museum has Roman relics.

BRIXHAM, DEVON - Famous for its trawling fleet in the 19th C, a steeply built fishing port overlooking the harbour and fish market. A statue of William of Orange recalls his landing here before deposing James II. There is an aquarium and museum. Good cliff views and walks.

BUDE, CORNWALL - Resort on dramatic Atlantic coast. High cliffs give spectacular sea and inland views. Golf-course, cricket pitch, folly, surfing, coarse-fishing and boating. Mother-town Stratton was base of Royalist Sir Bevil Grenville.

CHARMOUTH, DORSET - Set back from the fossil-rich cliffs, a small coastal town where Charles II came to the Queen's Armes when seeking escape to France. Just south at low tide, the sandy beach rewards fossil hunters; at Black Ven an ichthyosaurus (now in London's Natural History Museum) was found.

COMBE MARTIN, DEVON - On the edge of the Exmoor National Park, this seaside village is set in a long, narrow valley with its natural harbour lying between towering cliffs. The main beach is a mixture of sand, rocks and pebbles and the lack of strong currents ensures safe bathing.

DAWLISH, DEVON - Small resort, developed in Regency and Victorian periods, beside Dawlish Water. Town centre has ornamental riverside gardens with black swans. One of England's most scenic stretches of railway was built by Brunel alongside jagged red cliffs between the sands and the town.

DORCHESTER, DORSET - Busy medieval county town destroyed by fires in 17th and 18th C. Cromwellian stronghold and scene of Judge Jeffreys' Bloody Assize after the Monmouth Rebellion of 1685. Tolpuddle Martyrs were tried in Shire Hall. The museum has Roman and earlier exhibits and Hardy relics.

DULVERTON, SOMERSET - Set among woods and hills of south-west Exmoor, a busy riverside town with a 13th C church. The Rivers Barle and Exe are rich in salmon and trout. The information centre at the Exmoor National Park Headquarters at Dulverton is open throughout the year.

EXMOUTH, DEVON - Developed as a seaside resort in George III's reign, set against the woods of the Exe Estuary and red cliffs of Orcombe Point. Extensive sands, small harbour, chapel and almshouses, a model railway and 'A la Ronde', a 16-sided house.

GLASTONBURY, SOMERSET - Market town associated with Joseph of Arimathea and the birth of English Christianity. Built around its 7th C abbey said to be the site of King Arthur's burial. Glastonbury Tor, with its ancient tower, gives panoramic views over flat country and the Mendip Hills.

HAYLE, CORNWALL - Former mining town with modern light industry on the Hayle Estuary. Most buildings are Georgian or early Victorian, with some Regency houses along the canal.

HELSTON, CORNWALL - Handsome town with steep, main street and narrow alleys. In medieval times it was a major port and stannary town. Most buildings date from Regency and Victorian periods. The famous May dance, the Furry, is thought to have pre-Christian origins. Museum in the old Butter Market.

KENTISBEARE, DEVON - Pretty village at the foot of the Blackdown Hills. The church has a magnificent carved 15th C screen, and nearby is a medieval priest's house with a minstrels' gallery and oak screens.

LACOCK, WILTSHIRE - Village of great charm. Medieval buildings of stone, brick or timber-frame have jutting storeys, gables, oriel windows. The magnificent church has Perpendicular fan-vaulted chapel with grand tomb to benefactor who, after Dissolution, bought Augustinian nunnery, Lacock Abbey.

LAND'S END, CORNWALL - The most westerly point of the English mainland, 8 miles south-west of Penzance. Spectacular cliffs with marvellous views. Exhibitions and multi-sensory Last Labyrinth Show.

M MALMESBURY, WILTSHIRE - Overlooking the River Avon, an old town dominated by its great church, once a Benedictine abbey. The surviving Norman nave and porch are noted for fine sculptures, 12th C arches and musicians' gallery.

MARTOCK, SOMERSET - Large village with many handsome buildings of hamstone and a beautiful old church with tie-beam roof. Medieval treasurer's house where a 10' x 6' medieval mural has recently been discovered during National Trust restoration work. Georgian market house, 17th C manor.

MEVAGISSEY, CORNWALL - Small fishing town, a favourite with holidaymakers. Earlier prosperity came from pilchard fisheries, boat-building and smuggling. By the harbour are fish cellars, some converted, and a local history museum is housed in an old boat-building shed. Handsome Methodist chapel; shark fishing, sailing.

N NEWQUAY, CORNWALL - Popular resort spread over dramatic cliffs around its old fishing port. Many beaches with abundant sands, caves and rock pools; excellent surf. Pilots' gigs are still raced from the harbour, and on the headland stands the stone Huer's House from the pilchard-fishing days.

NEWTON ABBOT, DEVON - Lively market town at the head of the Teign Estuary. A former railway town, well placed for moorland or seaside excursions. Interesting old houses nearby include Bradley Manor, dating from the 15th C, and Forde House, visited by Charles I and William of Orange.

O OKEHAMPTON, DEVON - Busy market town near the high tors of northern Dartmoor. The Victorian church, with William Morris windows and a 15th C tower, stands on the site of a Saxon church. A Norman castle ruin overlooks the river to the west of the town. Museum of Dartmoor Life in a restored mill.

OWERMOIGNE, DORSET - Village 6 miles east of Dorchester, within easy reach of the Dorset coast and the family resort of Weymouth.

P PADSTOW, CORNWALL - Old town encircling its harbour on the Camel Estuary. The 15th C church has notable bench-ends. There are fine houses on North Quay and Raleigh's Court House on South Quay. Tall cliffs and golden sands along the coast, and ferry to Rock. Famous 'Obby 'Oss Festival on 1 May.

PAIGNTON, DEVON - Lively seaside resort with a pretty harbour. Bronze Age and Saxon sites are occupied by the 15th C church, which has a Norman door and font. The beautiful Chantry Chapel was built by local landowners, the Kirkhams.

PENZANCE, CORNWALL - Resort and fishing port on Mount's Bay with mainly Victorian promenade and some fine Regency terraces. Former prosperity came from the tin trade and pilchard fishing. Grand Georgian style church by harbour. Georgian - Egyptian building at head of Chapel Street and Morrab Gardens.

POLRUAN-BY-FOWEY, CORNWALL - Old village linked to Fowey across its estuary by a passenger ferry. Twin medieval forts guard village and town at the river's mouth.

PORLOCK, SOMERSET - Village set between the steep Exmoor hills and the sea at the head of beautiful Porlock Vale. The narrow street shows a medley of building styles. South westward is Porlock Weir with its old houses and tiny harbour and further along the shore at Culbone is England's smallest church.

PORTREATH, CORNWALL - Formerly developed as a mining port, a small resort with some handsome 19th C buildings. Cliffs, sands and good surf.

S ST AGNES, CORNWALL - Small town in a once-rich mining area on the north coast. Terraced cottages and granite houses slope to the church. Some old mine workings remain, but the attraction must be the magnificent coastal scenery and superb walks. St Agnes Beacon offers one of Cornwall's most extensive views.

ST AUSTELL, CORNWALL - Leading market town, the meeting point of old and new Cornwall. One mile from St Austell Bay with its sandy beaches, old fishing villages and attractive countryside. Ancient narrow streets, pedestrian shopping precincts. Fine church of Pentewan stone and Italianate Town Hall.

ST IVES, CORNWALL - Old fishing port, artists' colony and holiday town with good surfing beach. Fishermen's cottages, granite fish cellars, a sandy harbour and magnificent headlands typify a charm that has survived since the 19th C pilchard boom. Tate Gallery opened in 1993.

SALCOMBE, DEVON - Sheltered yachting resort of whitewashed houses and narrow streets in a balmy setting on the Salcombe Estuary. Palm, myrtle and other Mediterranean plants flourish. There are sandy bays and creeks for boating.

SHALDON, DEVON - Pretty resort facing Teignmouth from the south bank of the Teign Estuary. Regency houses harmonise with others of later periods; there are old cottages and narrow lanes. On the Ness, a sandstone promontory nearby, a tunnel built in the 19th C leads to a beach revealed at low tide.

SIDMOUTH, DEVON - Charming resort set amid lofty red cliffs where the River Sid meets the sea. The wealth of ornate Regency and Victorian villas recalls the time when this was one of the south coast's most exclusive resorts. Museum; August International Festival of Folk Arts.

T TAUNTON, SOMERSET - County town, well known for its public schools, sheltered by gentle hill-ranges on the River Tone. Medieval prosperity from wool has continued in marketing and manufacturing and the town retains many fine period buildings. Museum.

TAVISTOCK, DEVON - Old market town beside the River Tavy on the western edge of Dartmoor. Developed around its 10th C abbey, of which some fragments remain, it became a stannary town in 1305 when tin-streaming thrived on the moors. Tavistock Goose Fair, October.

TINTAGEL, CORNWALL - Coastal village near the legendary home of King Arthur. There is a lofty headland with the ruin of a Norman castle, and traces of a Celtic monastery are still visible in the turf.

TORRINGTON, DEVON - Perched high above the River Torridge with a charming market square, Georgian Town Hall and a museum. The famous Dartington Crystal Factory, Rosemoor Gardens and Plough Arts Centre are all located in the town.

W WARMINSTER, WILTSHIRE - Attractive stone-built town high up to the west of Salisbury Plain. A market town, it originally thrived on cloth and wheat. Many prehistoric camps and barrows can be found nearby, along with Longleat House and Safari Park.

WESTON-SUPER-MARE, NORTH SOMERSET - Large, friendly resort developed in the 19th C. Traditional seaside attractions include theatres and a dance hall. The museum has a Victorian seaside gallery and Iron Age finds from a hill fort on Worlebury Hill in Weston Woods.

WEYMOUTH, DORSET - Ancient port and one of the south's earliest resorts. Curving beside a long, sandy beach, the elegant Georgian esplanade is graced with a statue of George III and a cheerful Victorian Jubilee clock tower. Museum, Sea Life Centre.

WINSFORD, SOMERSET - Small village in Exmoor National Park, on the River Exe in splendid walking country under Winsford Hill. On the other side of the hill is a Celtic standing stone, the Caractacus Stone, and nearby across the River Barle stretches an ancient packhorse bridge, Tarr Steps.

WOOLACOMBE, DEVON - Between Morte Point and Baggy Point, Woolacombe and Mortehoe offer 3 miles of the finest sand and surf on this outstanding coastline. Much of the area is owned by the National Trust.

Follow the Stars for the assurance of a rating system you know you can trust

During 2003/4 VisitBritain is introducing new Quality Assurance Schemes for water-based accommodation in England. These schemes, covering Cruisers, Narrow Boats and Hotel Boats, have been developed to give customers the re-assurance that real efforts have been made to set, maintain and improve standards in boat accommodation, not only in terms of fixtures and fittings but also in areas such as cleanliness, comfort, hospitality, efficiency and service provided.

Craft are assessed annually by trained, impartial assessors, so you can be confident that your accommodation has been thoroughly checked and rated before you make a booking.

Look out for the Star ratings

VisitBritain Star ratings will give you a clear and trustworthy guide as to what you can expect. Five grades of award reflect the range of quality standards and facilities provided by a craft and they are indicated by a simple one to five Stars system. The final rating is awarded after assessing a combination of facilities and the overall quality of the accommodation – so the more Stars, the higher the overall level of quality and comfort you can expect.

For more information and to find out which operators have attained a quality rating, look on:
www.visitheartofengland.co.uk www.waterholidaysuk.com

South East

1

2

From Kent, the 'Garden of England', to the breathtaking Dorset Coast and from the magical Isle of Wight to the mellow Oxfordshire Cotswolds, the South East provides the perfect holiday mix – quaint villages, rolling countryside, dramatic coastline, seaside chic and cool heritage cities.

The Counties of Berkshire, Buckinghamshire, Dorset (Eastern), East Sussex, Hampshire, Isle of Wight, Kent, Oxfordshire, Surrey, and West Sussex.

For more information contact:
Tourism South East
The Old Brew House
Warwick Park, Tunbridge Wells,
Kent TN2 5TU

Telephone enquiries -
T: (01892) 540766
F: (01892) 511008

Tourism South East
40 Chamberlayne Road
Eastleigh,
Hampshire SO50 5JH

Telephone enquiries -
T: (023) 8062 5505
F: (023) 8062 0010

E: enquiries@tourismse.com
www.gosouth.co.uk

Classic sights
Stonehenge – ancient and mysterious standing stones
Battle Abbey – the site that marked the end of the Battle of Hastings in 1066
Blenheim Palace – birthplace of Sir Winston Churchill

Coast and country
Runnymede Meadow – the Magna Carta was signed here by King John in 1215
Chiltern Hills – tranquil country walks
The Needles – chalk pillars extending out into the Solent
New Forest – 900 year old historic wood and heathland

Glorious gardens
Leonardslee Lakes and Gardens – rhododendrons and azaleas ablaze with colour in May
Mottisfont Abbey – the perfect English rose garden designed by Graham Stuart Thomas
Savill Garden – woodland garden with royal connections
Sheffield Park Gardens – great 18thC, Capability Brown-designed landscaped gardens

Literary links
Jane Austen – her home in Chawton is now a museum and she is buried in Winchester Cathedral
Charles Dickens – Rochester; his home, Gad's Hill Place

1. Stonehenge, Wiltshire
2. Oast House, Kent

You will find hundreds of interesting places to visit during your stay, just some of which are listed in these pages. Contact any Tourist Information Centre in the region for more ideas on days out.

Awarded VisitBritain's 'Quality Assured Visitor Attraction' marque.

Places to Visit

A Day at the Wells
The Pantiles, Royal Tunbridge Wells
Tel: (01892) 546545
www.heritageattractions.co.uk
With commentary on personal stereos visitors experience the sights and sounds of 18thC Tunbridge Wells in its heyday as a spa town, escorted by Beau Nash, renowned dandy and MC.

Amberley Working Museum
Amberley, Arundel
Tel: (01798) 831370
www.amberleymuseum.co.uk
Open-air industrial history centre in chalk quarry. Working craftsmen, narrow-gauge railway, early buses, working machines and other exhibits. Nature trail and visitor centre.

Arundel Castle
Arundel
Tel: (01903) 883136 www.arundelcastle.org
An impressive Norman stronghold in extensive grounds, much restored 18/19thC, 11thC keep, 13thC barbican. Barons' hall, armoury, chapel. Van Dyck and Gainsborough paintings.

Battle Abbey and Battlefield
High Street, Battle
Tel: (01424) 773792
www.english-heritage.org.uk
Abbey founded by William the Conqueror on the site of the Battle of Hastings. The church altar is on the spot where King Harold was killed. Battlefield views and exhibition.

Bekonscot Model Village
Warwick Road, Beaconsfield
Tel: (01494) 672919 www.bekonscot.org.uk
The oldest model village in the world, Bekonscot depicts rural England in the 1930s, where time has stood still for 70 years. Narrow gauge ride-on railway.

Bentley Wildfowl and Motor Museum
Halland, Lewes
Tel: (01825) 840573 www.bentley.org.uk
Over 1,000 wildfowl in parkland with lakes. Motor museum with vintage cars, house, children's play facilities and woodland walk.

Blenheim Palace
Woodstock
Tel: (01993) 811325 www.blenheimpalace.com
Home of the 11th Duke of Marlborough. Birthplace of Sir Winston Churchill. Designed by Vanbrugh in the English baroque style. Landscaped by `Capability' Brown.

Breamore House
Breamore, Fordingbridge
Tel: (01725) 512233
Elizabethan manor house of 1583, with fine collection of works of art. Furniture, tapestries, needlework, paintings mainly Dutch School 17th and 18thC.

Brooklands Museum
Brooklands Road, Weybridge
Tel: (01932) 857381
www.brooklandsmuseum.com
Original 1907 motor racing circuit. Features the most historic and steepest section of the old banked track and 1-in-4 test hill. Motoring village and Grand Prix exhibition.

The Canterbury Tales
St Margaret's Street, Canterbury
Tel: (01227) 479227
www.canterburytales.org.uk
An audiovisual recreation of life in medieval
England. Join Chaucer's pilgrims on their journey
from the Tabard Inn in London to St. Thomas
Becket's shrine at Canterbury.

Chatley Heath Semaphore Tower
Pointers Road, Cobham
Tel: (01372) 458822
A restored historic semaphore tower displaying
the history of overland naval communications in
early 19thC set in woodland. Working semaphore
mast and models.

Compton Acres
Canford Cliffs, Poole
Tel: (01202) 700778 www.comptonacres.co.uk
11 distinct gardens of the world. The gardens
include Italian, Japanese, Spanish water garden.
Deer sanctuary with treetop lookout. Restaurant
and a craft centre.

Dapdune Wharf (National Trust)
Wharf Road, Guildford
Tel: (01483) 561389
www.nationaltrust.org.uk/southern
Dapdune Wharf is the home of 'Reliance', a
restored Wey barge, as well as an interactive
exhibition which tells the story of the waterway
and those who lived and worked on it.

Didcot Railway Centre
Great Western Society, Didcot
Tel: (01235) 817200
www.didcotrailwaycentre.org.uk
Living museum recreating the golden age of the
Great Western Railway. Steam locomotives and
trains, engine shed and small relics museum.

Dover Castle and Secret Wartime Tunnels (English Heritage)
Dover
Tel: (01304) 211067
www.english-heritage.org.uk
One of the most powerful medieval fortresses in
Western Europe. St Mary-in-Castro Saxon
church. Roman lighthouse, secret wartime
tunnels, Henry II Great Keep.

Eagle Heights
Hulberry Farm, Eynsford, Dartford
Tel: (01322) 866466 www.eagleheights.co.uk
Bird of prey centre housed undercover where
visitors can see eagles, hawks, falcons, owls and
vultures from all over the world. Reptile centre,
play area and sandpit.

Gilbert White's House and The Oates Museum
Selbourne, Alton
Tel: (01420) 511275
Historic house and garden, home of Gilbert
White, author of 'The Natural History of
Selborne'. Exhibition on Frank Oates, explorer
and Captain Lawrence Oates of Antarctic fame.

Hastings Castle and 1066 Story
West Hill, Hastings
Tel: (01424) 781112
www.smugglersadventure.co.uk
Fragmentary remains of Norman Castle built on
West Hill after William the Conqueror's victory at
the Battle of Hastings. 1066 Story interpretation
centre in siege tent.

1. The Stade, Hastings
2. The Needles, Isle of Wight
3. Shefield Park Gardens, East Sussex

The Hawk Conservancy and Country Park
Andover
Tel: (01264) 772252
www.hawk-conservancy.org
Unique to Great Britain – `Valley of the Eagles' held here daily at 1400, plus 250 birds of prey and 22 acres (9ha) of woodland gardens.

High Beeches Gardens
Handcross, Haywards Heath
Tel: (01444) 400589
www.highbeeches.com
25 acres (10ha) of peaceful, landscaped woodland and water gardens with many rare plants, wildflower meadow, spring bulbs and glorious autumn colour.

Kent & East Sussex Railway
Tenterden Town Station, Tenterden
Tel: (01580) 765155 www.kesr.org.uk
Full-size steam railway with restored Edwardian stations at Tenterden and Northiam, 14 steam engines, Victorian coaches and Pullman carriages. Museum and children's play area.

Kingston Lacy (National Trust)
Wimborne Minster
Tel: (01202) 883402
www.kingstonlacy@ntrust.org.uk
A 17thC house designed for Sir Ralph Bankes by Sir Roger Pratt altered by Sir Charles Barry in 19thC. Collection of paintings, 250-acre (101-ha) wooded park, herd of Devon cattle.

LEGOLAND Windsor
Winkfield Road, Windsor
Tel: 0870 5040404 www.legoland.co.uk
A family park with hands-on activities, rides, themed playscapes and more LEGO bricks than you ever dreamed possible.

The Living Rainforest
Thatcham, Newbury
Tel: (01635) 202444 www.livingrainforest.org
Two tropical rainforests, all under cover, approximately 20,000 sq ft (1,858sq m). Collection of rare and exotic tropical plants together with small representation of wildlife in rainforest.

Manor Farm (Farm and Museum)
Botley, Southampton
Tel: (01489) 787055
www.hants.gov.uk/countryside/manorfarm
Traditional Hampshire farmstead with a range of buildings, farm animals, machinery and equipment. Pre-1950's farmhouse and 13thC church set for 1900 living history site.

National Motor Museum
Beaulicu, Brockenhurst
Tel: (01590) 612345 www.beaulieu.co.uk
Motor museum with over 250 exhibits showing history of motoring from 1896. Also Palace House, Wheels Experience, Beaulieu Abbey ruins and a display of monastic life.

Newport Roman Villa
Cypress Road, Newport
Tel: (01983) 529720
Underfloor heated bath system; tesselated floors displayed in reconstructed rooms; corn-drying kiln, small site museum of objects recovered.

Oceanarium
West Beach, Bournemouth
Tel: (01202) 311993 www.oceanarium.co.uk
Situated in the heart of Bournemouth, next to the pier, the Oceanarium will take you on a fascinating voyage on the undersea world from elegant seahorses to sinister sharks.

Osborne House (English Heritage)
Yorke Avenue, East Cowes
Tel: (01983) 200022
www.english-heritage.org.uk
Queen Victoria and Prince Albert's seaside holiday home. Swiss Cottage where royal children learnt cooking and gardening. Victorian carriage rides.

The Oxford Story
6 Broad Street, Oxford
Tel: (01865) 728822 www.oxfordstory.co.uk
Take your seat on our amazing 'dark' ride and journey through scenes from 900 years of university's history, complete with sights, sounds and smells!

Port Lympne Wild Animal Park, Mansion and Gardens
Lympe, Hythe
Tel: (01303) 264647 www.howletts.net
Set in 400 acres (160 ha) with historic mansion and gardens, black rhino, tigers, elephants, small cats, monkeys, Barbary lions, red pandas, tapirs and 'Palace of the Apes'.

Portsmouth Historic Dockyard
1/7 College Road, HM Naval Base, Portsmouth
Tel: (023) 9286 1533
www.historicdockyard.co.uk
A fascinating day out – Action Stations, Mary Rose, HMS Victory, HMS Warrior 1860, Royal Naval Museum, 'Warships by water' harbour tours, Dockyard Apprentice exhibition.

St Mary's House and Gardens
Bramber, Steyning
Tel: (01903) 816205
A medieval timber-framed Grade I house with rare 16thC wall-leather, fine panelled rooms and a unique painted room. Topiary gardens.

The Sir Harold Hillier Gardens and Arboretum
Ampfield, Romsey
Tel: (01794) 368787 www.hillier.hants.gov.uk/
Established in 1953, The Sir Harold Hillier Gardens and Arboretum comprises the greatest collection of wild and cultivated woody plants in the world.

South of England Rare Breeds Centre
Highlands Farm, Woodchurch
Tel: (01233) 861493 www.rarebreeds.org.uk
Large collection of rare farm breeds on a working farm with children's play activities. Home to the 'Tamworth Two'. Woodland walks.

Swanage Railway
Station House, Swanage
Tel: (01929) 425800
www.swanagerailway.co.uk
Enjoy a nostalgic steam-train ride on the Purbeck line. Steam trains run every weekend throughout the year with daily running April to October.

The Tank Museum
Bovington, Wareham
Tel: (01929) 405096 www.tankmuseum.co.uk
The world's finest display of armoured fighting vehicles. Experimental vehicles, interactive displays, disabled access and facilities.

The Vyne (National Trust)
Sherborne St John, Basingstoke
Tel: (01256) 881337

www.nationaltrust.org.uk/places/thevyne
Original house dating back to Henry VIII's time. Extensively altered in mid 17thC. Tudor chapel, beautiful gardens and lake.

Waterperry Gardens Limited
Waterperry, Oxford
Tel: (01844) 339254
www.waterperrygardens.co.uk
Ornamental gardens covering 6 acres (2.4ha) of the 83-acre (33.5-ha) 18thC Waterperry House estate. A Saxon village church, garden shop teashop, art and craft gallery are found within the grounds.

Weald and Downland Open Air Museum
Singleton, Chichester
Tel: (01243) 811348 www.wealddown.co.uk
Over 40 rescued historic buildings from South East England, reconstructed on a downland country park site. Homes and workplaces of the past include a medieval farmstead.

West Dean Gardens
West Dean, Chichester
Tel: (01243) 818210
www.westdean.org.uk
Extensive downland garden with specimen trees, 300-ft (91-m) pergola, rustic summerhouses and restored walled kitchen garden. Walk in parkland and 45-acre (18-ha) arboretum.

Whitchurch Silk Mill
28 Winchester Street, Whitchurch
Tel: (01256) 892065
www.whitchurchsilkmill.org.uk
Unique Georgian silk-weaving watermill, now a working museum producing fine silk fabrics on Victorian machinery. Riverside garden, tearoom for light meals, silk gift shop.

Wilderness Wood
Hadlow Down, Uckfield
Tel: (01825) 830509
www.wildernesswood.co.uk
A family-run working woodland of 60 acres (24ha), beautiful in all seasons. There are trails, a bluebell walk, a play area, workshop and a timber barn with exhibition.

Winchester Cathedral
The Close, Winchester
Tel: (01962) 857225
www.winchester-cathedral.org.uk
Magnificent medieval cathedral, soaring gothic nave converted from original Norman. 12thC illuminated Winchester Bible, Jane Austen's tomb, library, gallery, crypt, chapels.

Winkworth Arboretum (National Trust)
Hascombe, Godalming
Tel: (01483) 208477

www.nationaltrust.org.uk/winkwortharboretum
100 acres (40ha) of hillside planted with rare trees and shrubs. Good views, lakes, newly-restored boathouse, azaleas, bluebells, wild spring flowers and autumn colours.

Tourism South East

The Old Brew House,
Warwick Park, Tunbridge Wells,
Kent TN2 5TU
T: (01892) 540766
F: (01892) 511008

40 Chamberlayne Road,
Eastleigh,
Hampshire, SO50 5JH
T: (023) 8062 5505
F: (023) 8062 0010

E: enquiries@tourismse.com
www.gosouth.co.uk

**THE FOLLOWING PUBLICATIONS ARE
AVAILABLE FROM TOURISM SOUTH EAST:**

South East Breaks

Southern England

Days Out in Southern England

Days Out in Thames & Chilterns Country

Favourite Gardens & Garden Stays in
South East England

Glorious Gardens & Historic Houses in
Southern England

Walk South East England

Escape into the Countryside

Getting to the South East

BY ROAD: From the north east –
M1 & M25; the north west – M6,
M40 & M25; the west and Wales –
M4 & M25; the east – M25; the
south west – M5, M4 & M25;
London – M25, M2, M20, M23, M3,
M4 or M40.

BY RAIL: Regular services from
London's Charing Cross, Victoria,
Waterloo and Waterloo East
stations to all parts of the South
East. Further information on rail
journeys in the South East can be
obtained on 08457 484950.

1. Savill Garden
2. Dreaming Spires, Oxford

Parks in this region are listed in alphabetical order of place name, and then in alphabetical order of park.

Map references refer to the colour location maps at the front of this guide. The first number indicates the map to use; the letter and number which follow refer to the grid reference on the map.

At-a-glance symbols can be found inside the back cover flap. Keep this open for easy reference.

ANDOVER, Hampshire Map ref 3C2 *Tourist Information Centre Tel: (01264) 324320*

★★★
**TOURING &
CAMPING PARK**

WYKE DOWN TOURING CARAVAN & CAMPING PARK
Picket Piece, Andover SP11 6LX
T: (01264) 352048
F: (01264) 324661
E: wykedown@wykedown.co.uk
I: www.wykedown.co.uk

CC: Delta, Diners, Mastercard,
Solo, Switch, Visa

69		£12.00–£14.00
69		£12.00–£14.00
69	A	£12.00–£14.00
69 touring pitches		

Follow international camping signs from A303 trunk road, Andover ring road, then through village. Picket Piece is signposted, approximately 2 miles.

ARUNDEL, West Sussex Map ref 3D3 *Tourist Information Centre Tel: (01903) 882268*

★★★
**TOURING &
CAMPING PARK**

SHIP & ANCHOR MARINA
Heywood & Bryett Ltd, Ford, Arundel
BN18 0BJ
T: (01243) 551262
F: (01243) 555256

160		£11.00–£14.00
160		£11.00–£14.00
160	A	£11.00–£14.00
160 touring pitches		

From A27 at Arundel take road south signposted Ford. Site 2 miles on the left, after level crossing. Also signposted from A259 between Littlehampton and Bognor Regis.

ASHURST, Kent Map ref 4A4

★★★
**TOURING &
CAMPING PARK**

MANOR COURT FARM
Ashurst, Royal Tunbridge Wells TN3 9TB
T: (01892) 740279
F: (01892) 740919
E: jsoyke@jsoyke.freeserve.co.uk
I: www.manorcourtfarm.co.uk

Four acres of secluded, informal camping in garden, orchard or near ponds on 350-acre mixed farm. Fire sites. New shower facilities. Fishing, tennis and swimming by arrangement. Reduced rates for longer stays and reduced rates for small children.

5		£6.00
5		£6.00
10	A	£6.00
20 touring pitches		

On A264, 5 miles west of Tunbridge Wells, between Stonecross and Ashurst villages.

CONFIRM YOUR BOOKING
You are advised to confirm your booking in writing.

BATTLE, East Sussex Map ref 4B4 *Tourist Information Centre Tel: (01424) 773721*

★★★★★
HOLIDAY PARK

ROSE AWARD

BH&HPA
NCC

CROWHURST PARK
Telham Lane, Battle TN33 0SL
T: (01424) 773344
F: (01424) 775727
E: enquiries@crowhurstpark.co.uk
I: www.crowhurstpark.co.uk

Quality development of luxury Scandinavian-style pine lodges within the grounds of a 17thC country estate. Facilities include leisure club with indoor swimming pool. Christmas and New Year breaks available.

CC: Delta, Mastercard, Switch, Visa
Two miles south of Battle on A2100.

£245.00–£865.00

★★★★★
TOURING PARK

See Ad on inside front cover

NORMANHURST COURT CARAVAN CLUB SITE
Stevens Crouch, Battle TN33 9LR
T: (01424) 773808
I: www.caravanclub.co.uk

An elegant site, set in the heart of 1066 country. Visit historic Battle Abbey or the picturesque town of Rye, littered with cobbled streets, antique shops and tea rooms. Non-members welcome.

CC: Delta, Mastercard, Solo, Switch, Visa
From Battle, turn left onto A271. Site is 3 miles on left.

152	🚐	£9.50–£19.50
152	🚃	£9.50–£19.50
152 total touring pitches		

BEACONSFIELD, Buckinghamshire Map ref 3C2

★★★★
TOURING & CAMPING PARK

BH&HPA

HIGHCLERE FARM COUNTRY TOURING PARK
Newbarn Lane, Seer Green, Beaconsfield HP9 2QZ
T: (01494) 874505
F: (01494) 875238
E: highclerepark@aol.com
I: www.highclerepark.co.uk

Quiet meadowland park, low-cost tube prices to London (25 minutes). Eleven miles Legoland. Launderette, showers, play area. New toilet block 2003.

CC: Mastercard, Switch, Visa
A40 to Potkiln Lane and follow signs up to site. M40 jct 2 to Beaconsfield, A355 signed Amersham 1 mile, right to Seer Green.

45	🚐	£12.00–£15.00
45	🚃	£12.00–£15.00
20	⛺	£9.50–£15.00
65 touring pitches		

SPECIAL BREAKS
Many establishments offer special promotions and themed breaks. These are highlighted in red. (All such offers are subject to availability.)

BEMBRIDGE, Isle of Wight Map ref 3C3

★★★★
HOLIDAY PARK

BH&HPA

WHITECLIFF BAY HOLIDAY PARK
Hillway Road, Bembridge PO35 5PL
T: (01983) 872671
F: (01983) 872941
E: holiday@whitecliff-bay.com
I: www.whitecliff-bay.com

Situated in an Area of Outstanding Natural Beauty, the park offers great-value family holidays. There are facilities on site for all ages. Special offers are available from time to time – please visit our website for full details.
CC: Delta, JCB, Mastercard, Switch, Visa

From A3055 turn onto B3395 at Brading and follow signposts.

	£8.00–£17.50
	£8.00–£17.50
	£8.00–£17.50
36	£60.00–£655.00
400 touring pitches	

BEXHILL-ON-SEA, East Sussex Map ref 4B4

★★★★
HOLIDAY, TOURING & CAMPING PARK

BH&HPA

COBBS HILL FARM CARAVAN & CAMPING PARK
Watermill Lane, Sidley, Bexhill-on-Sea,
Bexhill TN39 5JA
T: (01424) 213460
F: (01424) 221358
E: cobbshillfarm@hotmail.com
I: www.cobbshillfarm.co.uk

Turn off the A269 into Watermill Lane, 1 mile on left.

20	£5.50–£6.30
20	£5.20–£6.00
15	£5.50–£6.30
2	£95.00–£240.00
55 touring pitches	

★★★★★
TOURING & CAMPING PARK

BH&HPA

KLOOFS CARAVAN PARK
Sandhurst Lane, Whydown, Bexhill TN39 4RG
T: (01424) 842839
F: (01424) 845669
E: camping@kloofs.com
I: www.kloofs.com

Freedom all year round, whatever the weather! Fully serviced, hard, extra-large pitches. Modern facilities, private washing, central heating. In a quiet, rural setting.

From A259 Bexhill/Little Common roundabout turn into Peartree Lane. At crossroads turn into Whydown Road.

25	£11.50
25	£11.50
25	£11.50
50 touring pitches	

BIDDENDEN, Kent Map ref 4B4

★★★★
TOURING & CAMPING PARK

BH&HPA

WOODLANDS PARK
Tenterden Road, Biddenden, Ashford
TN27 8BT
T: (01580) 291216
F: (01580) 291216
E: woodlandsp@aol.com
I: www.campingsite.co.uk

Take A28 from Ashford to Tenterden. Approximately 3 miles before Tenterden take right turn, A262, signposted Tunbridge Wells. Park is approximately 1.5 miles on the right-hand side.

200	£9.00–£11.00
200	£9.00–£11.00
200	£9.00–£11.00
200 touring pitches	

TOWN INDEX
This can be found at the back of the guide. If you know where you want to stay, the index will give you the page number listing all accommodation in your chosen town, city or village.

★★★★★

HOLIDAY, TOURING & CAMPING PARK

BH&HPA
NCC

TWO CHIMNEYS HOLIDAY PARK

Shottendane Road, Birchington CT7 0HD
T: (01843) 841068
F: (01843) 848099
E: info@twochimneys.co.uk
I: www.twochimneys.co.uk

A friendly, family-run country site near sandy beaches. Spacious, level pitches. Modern WC/shower and laundry facilities including disabled. Children's play and ball-games areas.

CC: Delta, Mastercard, Solo, Switch, Visa

A2 then A28 to Birchington. Turn right into Park Lane, bear left into Manston Road, left at crossroads B2049, site on right.

150	🚐	£12.00–£25.00
50	🚏	£12.00–£25.00
100	▲	£12.00–£25.00
2	⛺	£175.00–£475.00
300 touring pitches		

★★★★

TOURING & CAMPING PARK

BH&HPA

THE INSIDE PARK

Blandford Forum DT11 9AD
T: (01258) 453719
F: (01258) 459921
E: inspark@aol.com
I: members.aol.com/inspark/inspark

Extra-large pitches with all modern facilities. Set on our farm, this is an ideal family site, quiet and secluded. So relaxing you won't want to leave!

CC: Delta, Mastercard, Switch, Visa

Follow signs from Blandford St Mary, exit off Blandford bypass, 1.75 miles from roundabout.

	🚐	£9.25–£13.00
80	🚏	£9.25–£13.00
45	▲	£9.25–£13.00

★★★★★

TOURING & CAMPING PARK

See Ad on inside front cover

BOGNOR REGIS CARAVAN CLUB SITE

Rowan Way, Bognor Regis PO22 9RP
T: (01243) 828515
I: www.caravanclub.co.uk

A small, recently redeveloped site just two miles from Bognor. Award-winning beach, seaside attractions. Chichester, Arundel and Brighton within easy reach; also NT properties including Petworth. Non-members welcome.

CC: Delta, Mastercard, Solo, Switch, Visa

From roundabout on A29, 1 mile north of Bognor, turn left into Rowan Way, site on right in 100yds, opposite Halfords superstore.

109	🚐	£9.50–£19.50
109	🚏	£9.50–£19.50
10	▲	
109 total touring pitches		

★★★

HOLIDAY, TOURING & CAMPING PARK

THE LILLIES CARAVAN PARK
Yapton Road, Barnham, Bognor Regis
PO22 0AY
T: (01243) 552081
F: (01243) 552081
E: thelillies@hotmail.com
I: lilliescaravanpark.co.uk

CC: Delta, JCB, Mastercard, Solo, Switch, Visa

19	🚐	£10.00–£14.00
19	🚏	£10.00–£14.00
16	▲	£10.00–£12.00
7	⛺	£180.00–£240.00
54 touring pitches		

3 miles north of Bognor Regis. Take the A29 to Westergate bearing right at Labour in Vain public house to Eastergate and onto B2233. From A27 Fontwell roundabout onto A29 then B2233 to park. Signposted.

VISITOR ATTRACTIONS For ideas on places to visit refer to the introduction at the beginning of this section. Look out too for the ETC's Quality Assured Visitor Attraction signs.

BOURNEMOUTH, Dorset Map ref 3B3

★★★
TOURING &
CAMPING PARK

BH&HPA

ST LEONARDS FARM

Ringwood Road, West Moors, Ferndown BH22 0AQ
T: (01202) 872637
F: (01202) 855683
E: james@love5.fsnet.co.uk
I: www.stleonardsfarm.biz

A quiet, family-run park with well-drained and level, widely spaced pitches approximately eight miles from Bournemouth and close to the beautiful New Forest. £3 per week reduction if you book for 7 nights. Extended stay available to avoid unnecessary towing.

On A31, 5 miles west of Ringwood, opposite Texaco garage.

110	🚐	£8.00–£14.00
110	🚍	£8.00–£14.00
80	▲	£8.00–£14.00
190 touring pitches		

BRIGHTSTONE, Isle of Wight Map ref 3C3

★★★
HOLIDAY &
CAMPING PARK

GRANGE FARM BRIGHSTONE BAY
Military Road, Brighstone Bay, Isle of Wight
PO30 4DA
T: (01983) 740296
F: (01983) 741233
E: grangefarm@brighstonebay.fsnet.co.uk
I: www.brighstonebay.co.uk

CC: Amex, Delta, JCB,
Mastercard, Solo, Switch, Visa

20	🚐	£9.50–£11.00
20	🚍	£9.50–£11.00
20	▲	£9.50–£11.00
12	🏠	£210.00–£425.00
60 touring pitches		

On A3055 Freshwater to Ventnor Road, 2 miles past Brook Green, opposite junction to Brightstone Village.

BRIGHTON & HOVE, East Sussex Map ref 3D3

★★★★★
TOURING &
CAMPING PARK

See Ad on inside front cover

SHEEPCOTE VALLEY CARAVAN CLUB SITE

East Brighton Park, Brighton BN2 5TS
T: (01273) 626546
F: (01273) 682600
I: www.caravanclub.co.uk

Located on the South Downs, just two miles from Brighton. Visit the Marina, with its shops, pubs, restaurants and cinema, and take a tour of the exotic Royal Pavilion. Non-members welcome.

OPEN All Year
CC: Delta, Mastercard, Solo, Switch, Visa

M23/A23, join A27 (signposted Lewes); turn off at B2123 (signposted Falmer and Rottingdean). At top turn right onto B2123 to Woodingdean. In 2 miles at traffic lights turn right into Warren Road, after 1 mile turn left into Wilson Avenue.

170	🚐	£12.00–£20.50
170	🚍	£12.00–£20.50
170 total touring pitches		

BURFORD, Oxfordshire Map ref 3B1 *Tourist Information Centre Tel: (01993) 823558*

★★★★★
TOURING PARK

See Ad on inside front cover

BURFORD CARAVAN CLUB SITE

Bradwell Grove, Burford OX18 4JJ
T: (01993) 823080
I: www.caravanclub.co.uk

Attractive, spacious site opposite popular Cotswold Wildlife Park. Burford has superb Tudor houses, a museum and historic inns. A great base to explore the delightful Cotswolds. Non-members welcome.

CC: Delta, Mastercard, Solo, Switch, Visa

From roundabout at A40/A361 junction in Burford, take A361 signposted Lechlade. Site on right after 2.5 miles. Site signposted from roundabout.

120	🚐	£9.50–£19.50
120	🚍	£9.50–£19.50
120 total touring pitches		

CANTERBURY, Kent Map ref 4B3 Tourist Information Centre Tel: (01227) 378100

★★★★

HOLIDAY, TOURING & CAMPING PARK

BH&HPA

YEW TREE PARK

Stone Street, Petham, Canterbury CT4 5PL
T: (01227) 700306
F: (01227) 700306
E: info@yewtreepark.com
I: www.yewtreepark.com

Picturesque country park close to Canterbury, centrally located for exploring Kent. Naturally landscaped touring and camping facilities. Self-catering apartments and holiday units. Outdoor pool.

CC: Delta, JCB, Mastercard, Solo, Switch, Visa

On B2068, 4 miles south of Canterbury, 9 miles north of M20, jct 11.

15	🚐	£10.00–£14.00
5		£10.00–£14.00
25	▲	£9.00–£13.00
7	🏠	£140.00–£340.00
45 touring pitches		

CHERWELL

See under Mollington

CHICHESTER, West Sussex Map ref 3C3 Tourist Information Centre Tel: (01243) 775888

★★★★★

HOLIDAY & TOURING PARK

BH&HPA

WICKS FARM CAMPING PARK
Redlands Lane, West Wittering, Chichester
PO20 8QD
T: (01243) 513116
F: (01243) 511296
I: www.wicksfarm.co.uk

CC: Delta, JCB, Mastercard, Solo, Switch, Visa

42	🚐	£11.00–£14.00
42	▲	£11.00–£14.00
44 touring pitches		

From Chichester take A286/B2179 for 6 miles, straight on towards West Wittering. Wicks Farm is 2nd on the right just past Lamb pub.

CHRISTCHURCH, Dorset Map ref 3B3 Tourist Information Centre Tel: (01202) 471780

★★★

CAMPING PARK

BH&HPA

HARROW WOOD FARM CARAVAN PARK
Poplar Lane, Bransgore, Christchurch
BH23 8JE
T: (01425) 672487
F: (01425) 672487
E: harrowwood@caravan-sites.co.uk
I: www.caravan-sites.co.uk

CC: Delta, Mastercard, Solo, Switch, Visa

60	🚐	£10.00–£16.00
60	🚐	£10.00–£16.00
	▲	£10.00–£14.00
60 touring pitches		

From A35 Lyndhurst to Christchurch road, turn right at Cat and Fiddle pub, 1.5 miles to Bransgore.

★★★★★

HOLIDAY, TOURING & CAMPING PARK

ROSE AWARD

MEADOW BANK HOLIDAYS

Stour Way, Christchurch BH23 2PQ
T: (01202) 483597
F: (01202) 483878
E: enquiries@meadowbank-holidays.co.uk
I: www.meadowbank-holidays.co.uk

Bournemouth's closest combined holiday and touring park. Ideally located on the pretty River Stour, between Christchurch, Bournemouth and the New Forest.

CC: Delta, Mastercard, Switch, Visa

A35 from Christchurch, west 1.5 miles, turn right at Crooked Beam Restaurant into the Grove, site 3rd left.

41	🚐	£7.00–£23.00
41	🚐	£7.00–£23.00
75	🏠	£150.00–£625.00
82 touring pitches		

COTSWOLDS

See under Burford, Standlake

See also Cotswolds in Heart of England region

WHERE TO STAY
Please mention this guide when making your booking.

DOVER, Kent Map ref 4C4 *Tourist Information Centre Tel: (01304) 205108*

★★★★
**HOLIDAY &
TOURING PARK**

BH&HPA

SUTTON VALE COUNTRY CLUB & CARAVAN PARK
Vale Road, Sutton-by-Dover, Dover
CT15 5DH
T: (01304) 374155
F: (01304) 381132
E: office@sutton-vale.co.uk
I: www.ukparks.co.uk/suttonvale

CC: Delta, Mastercard, Switch,
Visa

20		£10.00–£14.00
20		£10.00–£14.00
30		
20 touring pitches		

From London/Dover, A2/M2 5 miles signpost to Dover, approach roundabout, Whitfield, McDonalds, take 1st exit. 20yds on turn right, Archers Court Road. 4 miles exactly down country lane, site on left.

EASTBOURNE, East Sussex Map ref 4B4 *Tourist Information Centre Tel: (01323) 411400*

★★★★
**TOURING &
CAMPING PARK**

FAIRFIELDS FARM CARAVAN & CAMPING PARK

Eastbourne Road, Westham, Pevensey BN24 5NG
T: (01323) 763165
F: (01323) 469175
E: enquiries@fairfieldsfarm.com
I: www.fairfieldsfarm.com

A warm welcome awaits you at this delightful, quiet, touring park with clean facilities, lakeside walk and fishing. An excellent location for exploring many attractions. 3-night, mid-week stay for the price of 2 – Apr, May, Jun, Sep. Contact us for more details.

60		£8.50–£10.00
60		£8.50–£10.00
60	A	£7.50–£10.00
60 touring pitches		

Signposted off A27 Pevensey roundabout. Straight through Pevensey and Westham villages towards castle. Then B2191 (left) to Eastbourne east, over level crossing on the left.

FOLKESTONE, Kent Map ref 4C4 *Tourist Information Centre Tel: (01303) 258594*

★★★★★
**TOURING &
CAMPING PARK**

See Ad on inside front cover

BLACK HORSE FARM CARAVAN CLUB SITE

385 Canterbury Road, Densole, Folkestone CT18 7BG
T: (01303) 892665
I: www.caravanclub.co.uk

Landscaped, peaceful, rural site set on the Downs. Folkestone four miles, Dover eight miles, Canterbury 11 miles. Why not stop here en route to Europe? Non-members welcome.

OPEN All Year
CC: Delta, Mastercard, Solo, Switch, Visa

From M20 jct 13 on A260 to Canterbury, 2 miles from junction with A20, site on left 200yds past Black Horse inn.

80		£9.50–£19.50
80		£9.50–£19.50
80 total touring pitches		

THE CARAVAN CLUB

FORDINGBRIDGE, Hampshire Map ref 3B3

★★★★★
**HOLIDAY, TOURING
& CAMPING PARK**

BH&HPA

See Ad p178

SANDY BALLS HOLIDAY CENTRE
Godshill, Fordingbridge SP6 2JZ
T: (01425) 653042
F: (01425) 653067
E: post@sandy-balls.co.uk
I: www.sandy-balls.co.uk

CC: Delta, Mastercard, Switch,
Visa

256		£12.75–£24.00
		£12.75–£24.00
130	A	£11.25–£24.00
39		£110.00–£925.00
386 touring pitches		

Located on B3078 to Fordingbridge.

GATWICK AIRPORT

See under Horsham, Redhill

STAR RATINGS Were correct at the time of going to press but are subject to change. Please check at the time of booking.

HENFIELD, West Sussex Map ref 3D3

★★★★
HOLIDAY, TOURING & CAMPING PARK

BH&HPA

DOWNSVIEW CARAVAN PARK
Bramlands Lane, Woodmancote, Henfield
BN5 9TG
T: (01273) 492801
F: (01273) 495214
E: phr.peter@lineone.net

CC: Delta, Mastercard, Switch, Visa

12		£12.00–£13.50
12		£12.00–£13.50
50	▲	£9.00–£14.00
36 touring pitches		

From M23 continuing onto A23, follow signs for Henfield then take A281 towards Brighton. Site is signposted in village of Woodmancote 2.5 miles east of Henfield and 9 miles north west of Brighton seafront.

HIGHCLIFFE, Dorset Map ref 3B3

★★★★
HOLIDAY PARK

ROSE AWARD
BH&HPA

COBB'S HOLIDAY PARK
32 Gordon Road, Highcliffe, Christchurch BH23 5HN
T: (01425) 273301
F: (01425) 276090

Pleasant family park, enviable location, near New Forest and beaches. Well-stocked shop, launderette, children's playground, licensed club with entertainment. Full-facility units. Colour TV.

CC: Mastercard, Solo, Switch, Visa

45		£190.00–£475.00

Leave A35 near Christchurch, take A337 to Highcliffe, follow brown tourist signs, turn left at traffic lights in village centre. Park is situated 200yds on the left.

HORSHAM, West Sussex Map ref 3D2 *Tourist Information Centre Tel: (01403) 211661*

★★★★
TOURING & CAMPING PARK

BH&HPA

HONEYBRIDGE PARK
Honeybridge Lane, Dial Post, Nr Horsham RH13 8NX
T: (01403) 710923
F: (01403) 710923
E: enquiries@honeybridgepark.co.uk
I: www.honeybridgepark.co.uk

Delightfully situated, spacious 15-acre park adjacent to woodlands. Relaxed and informal atmosphere. New heated amenity block. Ideal touring base. Convenient for coast and theme parks. 10% discount on pitch fees for Senior Citizens, foreign Camping Carnet holders and 7 nights or more. Mid-week special: £6 off (incl Tue).

CC: Delta, Mastercard, Solo, Switch, Visa

100		£14.50–£18.50
100		£14.50–£18.50
100	▲	£12.50–£14.50

On A24 travelling south, turn left 1 mile past Dial Post turning. At Old Barn Nurseries continue for 300yds and site is on the right.

HOVE

See under Brighton & Hove

MAP REFERENCES The map references refer to the colour maps at the front of the guide. The first figure is the map number; the letter and figure which follow indicate the grid reference on the map.

HURLEY, Berkshire Map ref 3C2

★★★
**HOLIDAY, TOURING
& CAMPING PARK**

BH&HPA

HURLEY RIVERSIDE PARK
Hurley, Maidenhead SL6 5NE
T: (01628) 823501
F: (01628) 825533
E: info@hurleyriversidepark.co.uk
I: www.hurleyriversidepark.co.uk

CC: Delta, JCB, Mastercard,
Switch, Visa

138		£9.00–£15.00
138		£9.00–£15.00
62	▲	£7.50–£13.50
11		£180.00–£420.00
200 touring pitches		

*Take A404M, then A4130 towards Henley. Travel north for 5 miles and turn right, 1 mile past East Arms pub,
into Shepherds Lane. From M40 jct 4, take A404 south, then A4130 towards Henley and as above.*

ISLE OF WIGHT

See under Bembridge, Brighstone

LANGTON MATRAVERS, Dorset Map ref 3B3

★★
CAMPING PARK

TOM'S FIELD CAMPSITE & SHOP
Tom's Field Road, Langton Matravers,
Swanage BH19 3HN
T: (01929) 427110
F: (01929) 427110
E: tomsfield@hotmail.com
I: www.tomsfieldcamping.co.uk

100		£7.00–£8.00
100	▲	£7.00–£8.00
200 touring pitches		

*Approaching Swanage on A351 turn right onto B3069. At Langton Matravers turn right into Tom's Field Road.
Site at end of road.*

LINGFIELD, Surrey Map ref 3D2

★★★
TOURING PARK

BH&HPA

LONG ACRES CARAVAN & CAMPING PARK
Newchapel Road, Lingfield RH7 6LE
T: (01342) 833205
F: (01622) 735038
I: www.ukparks.co.uk/longacres

60		£10.50
60		£10.50
60	▲	£7.00–£10.50
60 touring pitches		

*South on A22 for 6 miles towards East Grinstead. At Newchapel roundabout turn left onto B2028 to Lingfield.
Site is 700yds on the right.*

LYMINGTON, Hampshire Map ref 3C3

★★★
CAMPING PARK

BH&HPA

HURST VIEW CARAVAN PARK
Lower Pennington Lane, Pennington,
Lymington SO41 8AL
T: (01590) 671648
F: (01590) 689244
E: enquiries@hurstviewleisure.co.uk
I: www.hurstviewleisure.co.uk

		£12.00–£17.50
		£10.00–£17.50
	▲	£7.50–£12.00
8		£200.00–£375.00

*From A337 in Lymington reach Pennington Cross roundabout. Turn left then 1st right into Lower Pennington
Lane.*

MARDEN, Kent Map ref 4B4

★★★★★
**TOURING &
CAMPING PARK**

BH&HPA

TANNER FARM TOURING
CARAVAN & CAMPING PARK

Goudhurst Road, Marden, Tonbridge TN12 9ND
T: (01622) 832399
F: (01622) 832472
E: enquiries@tannerfarmpark.co.uk
I: www.tannerfarmpark.co.uk

*Immaculate, secluded park surrounded by beautiful countryside on family
farm. Ideal touring base for the area. David Bellamy Gold Award. Bed &
Breakfast also available.*

CC: Delta, Mastercard, Solo, Switch, Visa

From A21 or A229 onto B2079 midway between Marden and Goudhurst.

100		£9.50–£15.50
15		£9.50–£15.50
20	▲	£10.00–£12.50
100 touring pitches		

MILFORD-ON-SEA, Hampshire Map ref 3C3

★★★★
HOLIDAY PARK

BH&HPA

DOWNTON HOLIDAY PARK

Shorefield Road, Milford-on-Sea, Lymington SO41 0LH
T: (01425) 476131
F: (01590) 642515
E: info@downtonholidaypark.co.uk
I: www.downtonholidaypark.co.uk

A small, peaceful park on the edge of the New Forest, within easy reach of picturesque villages. Near to coast. Pets welcome in some caravans.

CC: Delta, JCB, Mastercard, Solo, Switch, Visa

Turn from B3058 into Downton Lane, then 1st right, or from A337 into Downton Lane then 1st left.

22		£130.00–£440.00

★★★★
TOURING PARK

BH&HPA

See Ad p10

LYTTON LAWN TOURING PARK
Lymore Lane, Milford-on-Sea, Lymington SO41 0TX
T: (01590) 648331
F: (01590) 645610
E: holidays@shorefield.co.uk
I: www.shorefield.co.uk

CC: Delta, Mastercard, Solo, Switch, Visa

135		£7.50–£28.00
135		£7.50–£28.00
135	A	£7.50–£28.00

Take A337 from Cadnam (jct 1, M27) through Lyndhurst and Brockenhurst to Lymington. Proceed to Everton and turn left on to B3058. Lytton Lawn is on the left.

★★★★★
HOLIDAY PARK

BH&HPA

See Ad p10

SHOREFIELD COUNTRY PARK
Shorefield Road, Milford-on-Sea, Lymington SO41 0LH
T: (01590) 648331
F: (01590) 645610
E: holidays@shorefield.co.uk
I: www.shorefield.co.uk

CC: Delta, Mastercard, Solo, Switch, Visa

55		£180.00–£795.00
Forest Lodge		
		£300.00–£1165.00

From M27 jct 1 take A337 through Lyndhurst, Brockenhurst and Lymington to Downton, turn left at Royal Oak public house.

MINSTER, Kent Map ref 4B3

★★★
HOLIDAY, TOURING & CAMPING PARK

BH&HPA

RIVERBANK PARK
The Broadway, Minster, Sheerness ME12 2DB
T: (01795) 870300
F: (01795) 871300
E: riverbank.park@virgin.net
I: www.ukparks.com/riverbank

CC: Delta, Diners, JCB, Mastercard, Solo, Switch, Visa

60		£10.00–£14.00
30		£10.00–£14.00
10	A	£10.00–£12.00
		£157.50–£440.00
100 touring pitches		

Along A249 towards Sheerness. Over Kings Ferry Bridge at roundabout turn right. At traffic lights turn left. At T-junction turn right, at 1st mini-roundabout turn left, travel for 1 mile. Park situated on left behind Abbey Hotel.

MOLLINGTON, Oxfordshire Map ref 3C1

★★★★
TOURING & CAMPING PARK

BH&HPA

See Ad p181

ANITA'S TOURING CARAVAN PARK
The Yews, Church Farm, Mollington, Banbury OX17 1AZ
T: (01295) 750731
F: (01295) 750731
I: www.ukparks.co.uk/mollington

24		£7.00
24		£7.00
10	A	£6.00

Site situated directly off A423 main Banbury/Southam road. Travelling northerly direction, the site is on left just past the Mollington turn.

NEW FOREST

See under Ashurst, Fordingbridge, Lymington, Milford-on-Sea, New Milton, Ower, Ringwood

NEW MILTON, Hampshire Map ref 3B3

★★★★
HOLIDAY PARK

BH&HPA

GLEN ORCHARD HOLIDAY PARK

Walkford Lane, New Milton BH25 5NH
T: (01425) 616463
F: (01425) 638655
E: enquiries@glenorchard.co.uk
I: www.glenorchard.co.uk

Small park between forest and beaches, close to swimming/riding/golf facilities. Short breaks April-June/September-October (excluding Easter).

CC: Delta, Mastercard, Solo, Switch, Visa

A35 Lyndhurst to Bournemouth approximately 8 miles, at Hinton turn left into Ringwood Road after 0.75 mile Walkford Road, after 0.75 mile turn left into Walkford Lane.

19	🚐	£140.00–£480.00

★★★★
HOLIDAY PARK

BH&HPA
NCC

See Ad p137

HOBURNE BASHLEY
Sway Road, New Milton BH25 5QR   CC: Mastercard, Switch, Visa
T: (01425) 612340
F: (01425) 632732
E: enquiries@hoburne.com
I: www.hoburne.com

Off A35 onto B3055, 1 mile north of New Milton.

307	🚐🚐	£10.50–£34.50 £10.50–£34.50

OWER, Hampshire Map ref 3C3

★★★
TOURING PARK

BH&HPA

GREEN PASTURES CARAVAN PARK
Green Pastures Farm, Ower, Romsey
SO51 6AJ
T: (023) 8081 4444
E: enquiries@greenpasturesfarm.com
I: www.greenpasturesfarm.com

Between Cadnam and Romsey just off A31/A3090 west of junction with A36, exit 2 off M27. Initially follow signs for Paultons Park then our own brown leisure signs.

25	🚐	£12.00
10	🚐	£12.00
10	▲	£12.00
45 touring pitches		

POOLE, Dorset Map ref 3B3 *Tourist Information Centre Tel: (01202) 253253*

★★★
TOURING &
CAMPING PARK

BH&HPA

BEACON HILL TOURING PARK
Blandford Road North, Near Lytchett
Minster, Poole BH16 6AB
T: (01202) 631631
F: (01202) 625749
E: bookings@beaconhilltouringpark.co.uk
I: www.beaconhilltouringpark.co.uk

On A350, 0.25 miles from junction of A35 and A350 towards Blandford. Approximately 3 miles north of Poole.

170	🚐	£11.00–£21.00
170	🚐	£10.00–£28.00
170	▲	£10.00–£21.00
510 touring pitches		

CREDIT CARD BOOKINGS
If you book by telephone and are asked for your credit card number it is advisable to check the proprietor's policy should you cancel your reservation.

★★★
**TOURING &
CAMPING PARK**

BH&HPA

ORGANFORD MANOR CARAVANS & HOLIDAYS

The Lodge, Organford, Poole BH16 6ES
T: (01202) 622202
F: (01202) 623278
E: organford@lds.co.uk

Touring site, well sheltered, level and grassy. Good facilities, suitable for disabled. Static site set in woodland, all in grounds of manor house, surrounded by farmland. 10% discount off a 4-night stay in May or Sep.

Take 1st turning left off A35 after roundabout junction of the A35 and A351.

30		£8.50–£10.00
10		£7.50–£9.00
30		£8.50–£10.00
		£150.00–£210.00
70 touring pitches		

★★★★★
**TOURING &
CAMPING PARK**

BH&HPA

PEAR TREE TOURING PARK

Organford Road, Holton Heath, Poole BH16 6LA
T: (01202) 622434
F: (01202) 631985
E: info@visitpeartree.co.uk
I: www.visitpeartree.co.uk

A quiet, family park, laid out with terraces and good natural landscaping. Ideal for relaxing or exploring the Purbeck World Heritage Coastline. Low-season discounts available – please call for details.

CC: Delta, Mastercard, Solo, Switch, Visa

At end of motorway continue on A31 onto A35 and A351. Turn right off A351 (Wareham Road) at Holton Heath, signposted Organford, the park entrance is 0.5 miles on the left.

76		£11.00–£16.00
38		£11.00–£16.00
49		£9.00–£15.00
125 touring pitches		

★★★★★
TOURING PARK

See Ad on inside front cover

ALDERSTEAD HEATH CARAVAN CLUB SITE

Dean Lane, Merstham, Redhill RH1 3AH
T: (01737) 644629
I: www.caravanclub.co.uk

Quiet site with views over rolling, wooded North Downs. Denbies Wine Estate nearby. For daytrips try Chessington and Thorpe Park and the lively city of Brighton. Non-members welcome.

OPEN All Year
CC: Delta, Mastercard, Solo, Switch, Visa

From M25 jct 8 onto A217 towards Reigate, fork left after 300yds towards Merstham. 2.5 miles turn left at T-junction onto A23. 0.5 miles turn right into Shepherds Hill (B2031). 1 mile turn left into Dean Lane. Site on right.

85		£9.50–£19.50
85		£9.50–£19.50
85 total touring pitches		

★★★
**TOURING &
CAMPING PARK**

BH&HPA

See Ad p10

FOREST EDGE TOURING PARK
229 Ringwood Road, St Leonards,
Ringwood BH24 2SD
T: (01590) 648331
F: (01590) 645610
E: holidays@shorefield.co.uk
I: www.shorefield.co.uk

CC: Delta, Mastercard, Solo,
Switch, Visa

Off A31, 3 miles west of Ringwood.

100		£5.35–£22.00
100		£5.35–£22.00
147		£5.35–£22.00
147 touring pitches		

RINGWOOD continued

★★★★
CAMPING PARK

See Ad on this page

RED SHOOT CAMPING PARK
Linwood, Ringwood BH24 3QT
T: (01425) 473789
F: (01425) 471558
E: enquiries@redshoot-campingpark.com
I: www.redshoot-campingpark.com

CC: Delta, Mastercard, Switch, Visa

30		£10.25–£14.10
50		£10.25–£14.10
50	Å	£10.25–£14.10

Two miles north of Ringwood on A338 and follow signs to Linwood or off M27 jct 1, follow signs for Linwood.

ROMSEY, Hampshire Map ref 3C3 *Tourist Information Centre Tel: (01794) 512987*

★★★★
HOLIDAY, TOURING & CAMPING PARK

BH&HPA

HILL FARM CARAVAN PARK

Branches Lane, Sherfield English, Romsey SO51 6FH
T: (01794) 340402
F: (01794) 342358
E: gjb@hillfarmpark.com
I: www.hillfarmpark.com

In 11 acres of beautiful countryside on the edge of the New Forest, our family-run site provides an ideal base from which to visit the area. Special rates from £130 per month for seasonal pitches – minimum 3-month stay.

Directions given at time of booking.

		£10.00–£24.00
102		£10.00–£24.00
65	Å	£10.00–£24.00
5		£150.00–£450.00
120 touring pitches		

ST HELENS, Isle of Wight Map ref 3C3

★★★★
HOLIDAY PARK

BH&HPA

See Ad on this page

HILLGROVE PARK
Field Lane, St Helens, Ryde PO33 1UT
T: (01983) 872802
F: (01983) 872100
E: info@hillgrove.co.uk
I: www.hillgrove.co.uk

CC: Delta, Mastercard, Switch, Visa

50		£175.00–£700.00

A3055 from Ryde turn left into B3330, turn left at West Green into Field Lane.

ST LEONARDS, Dorset Map ref 3B3

★★★
HOLIDAY, TOURING & CAMPING PARK

BH&HPA

See Ad p10

OAKDENE FOREST PARK
St Leonards, Ringwood BH24 2RZ
T: (01590) 648331
F: (01590) 645610
E: holidays@shorefield.co.uk
I: www.shorefield.co.uk

CC: Delta, Mastercard, Solo, Switch, Visa

197		£7.50–£28.00
197		£7.50–£28.00
107		£180.00–£680.00
197 touring pitches		

On A31 3 miles west of Ringwood. After 2nd roundabout look for footbridge over road, then turn left down lane.

ST NICHOLAS AT WADE, Kent Map ref 4C3

★★★
TOURING &
CAMPING PARK

ST NICHOLAS CAMPING SITE
Court Road, St Nicholas at Wade,
Birchington CT7 0NH
T: (01843) 847245

15	🚐	£11.50–£13.50
5	🚎	£9.50–£11.50
55	⛺	£6.50–£13.00
75 touring pitches		

Village signposted off A299 and off the A28, near Birchington.

SELSEY, West Sussex Map ref 3C3

★★★★★
TOURING PARK

NCC

WARNER FARM TOURING PARK
Warner Lane, Selsey, Chichester PO20 9EL
T: (01243) 608440
F: (01243) 604499
E: warner.farm@btopenworld.com
I: www.bunnleisure.co.uk

CC: Amex, Delta, Mastercard,
Solo, Switch, Visa

250	🚐	£14.50
250	🚎	£14.50
50	⛺	£12.50
250 touring pitches		

B2145 into Selsey, turn right into School Lane, 1st right off School Lane, 1st left, proceed until you see sign for all touring caravans.

STANDLAKE, Oxfordshire Map ref 3C1

★★★
HOLIDAY, TOURING
& CAMPING PARK

BH&HPA

See Ad on this page

HARDWICK PARKS
Downs Road, Standlake, Witney OX29 7PZ
T: (01865) 300501
F: (01865) 300037
E: info@hardwickparks.co.uk
I: www.hardwickparks.co.uk

CC: Mastercard, Solo, Switch,
Visa

100	🚐	£9.00–£11.25
100	🚎	£9.00–£11.25
50	⛺	£9.00–£11.25
3	🏠	£180.00–£480.00

From Witney, take A415. Signposted from A415 outside Standlake.

SWANAGE, Dorset Map ref 3B3 *Tourist Information Centre Tel: (01929) 422885*

★★★★★
TOURING PARK

See Ad on inside front cover

HAYCRAFT CARAVAN CLUB SITE
Haycrafts Lane, Harmans Cross, Swanage BH19 3EB
T: (01929) 480572
I: www.caravanclub.co.uk

53	🚐	£11.00–£20.00
53	🚎	£11.00–£20.00
53 total touring pitches		

Peaceful site located five miles from Swanage, a traditional seaside town with a safe, sandy beach. Spectacular cliff-top walks, Corfe Castle, Lulworth Cove and Durdle Door within easy reach. Non-members welcome.

CC: Delta, Mastercard, Solo, Switch, Visa

Midway between Corfe Castle and Swanage. Take A351 from Wareham to Swanage, at Harmans Cross turn right into Haycrafts Lane, site 0.5 miles on the left.

THE CARAVAN CLUB

NB
IMPORTANT NOTE Information on accommodation listed in this guide has been supplied by the proprietors. As changes may occur you are advised to check details at the time of booking.

UCKFIELD, East Sussex Map ref 3D3

★★★

HOLIDAY &
TOURING PARK

BH&HPA

HONEYS GREEN FARM CARAVAN PARK
Easons Green, Framfield, Uckfield TN22 5RE
T: (01825) 840334

18	🚐	£10.00–£11.00
4	🚏	£10.00–£11.00
	⛺	£10.00
6	🏠	£160.00–£220.00
22 touring pitches		

Turn off A22 at Halland roundabout onto B2192, Heathfield. Site 0.25 miles on left.

🔌 🚿 👕 ♨ ✂ 🎣 🐕 ⛳

WAREHAM, Dorset Map ref 3B3 *Tourist Information Centre Tel: (01929) 552740*

★★★★

HOLIDAY, TOURING
& CAMPING PARK

BH&HPA

See Ad on this page

THE LOOKOUT HOLIDAY PARK
Corfe Road, Stoborough, Wareham
BH20 5AZ
T: (01929) 552546
F: (01929) 556662
E: enquiries@caravan-sites.co.uk
I: www.caravan-sites.co.uk

CC: Delta, Mastercard, Switch,
Visa

150	🚐	£10.00–£20.00
150	🚏	£10.00–£20.00
100	⛺	£9.75–£15.00
28	🏠	£120.00–£455.00
150 touring pitches		

From Wareham take the A351 for 1.25 miles towards Corfe Castle. Site on left-hand side.

📺 🔌 🚿 👕 ♨ 🍴 🛒 ✂ 🔍

WASHINGTON, West Sussex Map ref 3D3

★★★★

TOURING &
CAMPING PARK

WASHINGTON CARAVAN & CAMPING PARK
London Road, Washington, Pulborough
RH20 4AJ
T: (01903) 892869
F: (01903) 893252
E: washcamp@amserve.com
I: www.washcamp.com

CC: Delta, Mastercard, Switch,
Visa

21	🚐	£10.00
21	🚏	£10.00
40	⛺	£10.00
60 touring pitches		

A24 – A283 signposted.

🔌 🚿 👕 ♨ 🛒 🗄 ✂ 🐕 ⛳

WEST OXFORDSHIRE

See under Burford, Standlake.

WIMBORNE MINSTER, Dorset Map ref 3B3 *Tourist Information Centre Tel: (01202) 886116*

★★★★★

**TOURING &
CAMPING PARK**

BH&HPA

MERLEY COURT TOURING PARK
Merley House Lane, Merley, Wimborne
Minster BH21 3AA
T: (01202) 881488
F: (01202) 881484
E: holidays@merley-court.co.uk
I: www.merley-court.co.uk

CC: Delta, Mastercard, Solo,
Switch, Visa

145	🚐	£10.00–£15.00
145	🚏	£10.00–£15.00
80	⛺	£9.00–£15.00
160 touring pitches		

A31 to Wimborne bypass then A349 Poole road, signposted.

★★★★★

**TOURING &
CAMPING PARK**

BH&HPA

SPRINGFIELD TOURING PARK
Candys Lane, Corfe Mullen, Wimborne Minster BH21 3EF
T: (01202) 881719

Family-run park overlooking the Stour Valley. Convenient for coastal resorts, New Forest. Many attractions nearby. Free electricity, showers, awnings. Some hardstanding. Tarmac roads. Low season: any 7 days £45 (incl electricity).

Close to main A31 trunk road, 1.5 miles west of Wimborne.

30	🚐	£10.50–£13.00
10	🚏	£10.50–£13.00
5	⛺	£6.00–£13.00
45 touring pitches		

WINCHESTER, Hampshire Map ref 3C3 *Tourist Information Centre Tel: (01962) 840500*

★★★★

TOURING PARK

See Ad on inside front cover

MORN HILL CARAVAN CLUB SITE
Morn Hill, Winchester SO21 1HL
T: (01962) 869877
I: www.caravanclub.co.uk

Large, split-level site from which to explore all that Winchester has to offer. Oxford, Chichester, the New Forest and Salisbury are all within an hour's drive. Non-members welcome.

CC: Delta, Mastercard, Solo, Switch, Visa

From M3 jct 10 take A31 (signposted Alton). Turn left at roundabout with Percy Hobbs sign, signposted Easton. Immediate turn in front of pub, top of lane for caravan club.

150	🚐	£7.50–£16.50
150	🚏	£7.50–£16.50
150 total touring pitches		

THE CARAVAN CLUB

WOOL, Dorset Map ref 3B3

★★★★

**TOURING &
CAMPING PARK**

BH&HPA

WHITEMEAD CARAVAN PARK
East Burton Road, Wool, Wareham
BH20 6HG
T: (01929) 462241
F: (01929) 462241
E: whitemeadcp@aol.com
I: www.whitemeadcaravanpark.co.uk

On A352 from Wareham turn right before Wool level crossing 350yds.

95	🚐	£6.70–£11.00
95	🚏	£6.70–£11.00
95	⛺	£6.70–£11.00
95 touring pitches		

WROTHAM HEATH, Kent Map ref 4B3

★★★★★

**TOURING &
CAMPING PARK**

BH&HPA

GATE HOUSE WOOD TOURING PARK
Ford Lane, Wrotham Heath, Sevenoaks
TN15 7SD
T: (01732) 843062

56	🚐	£9.00–£11.00
56	🚏	£9.00–£11.00
56	⛺	£9.00–£11.00
60 touring pitches		

Take A20 south towards Maidstone. Through traffic lights at Wrotham Heath. Take 1st left turn signposted Trottiscliffe. Turn left at next junction. Gate House Wood is within 100yds on left.

A brief guide to the main Towns and Villages offering accommodation in the **South East**

🅰ANDOVER, HAMPSHIRE - Town that achieved importance from the wool trade and now has much modern development. A good centre for visiting places of interest.

ARUNDEL, WEST SUSSEX - Picturesque, historic town on the River Arun, dominated by Arundel Castle, home of the Dukes of Norfolk. There are many 18th C houses, the Wildfowl and Wetlands Centre and Museum and Heritage Centre.

ASHURST, KENT - Small hamlet on a hill, at the top of which is the church with its unusual weatherboarded bellcote. The Wealdway long-distance footpath passes nearby at Stone Cross.

🅱BATTLE, EAST SUSSEX - The Abbey at Battle was built on the site of the Battle of Hastings, when William defeated Harold II and so became the Conqueror in 1066. The museum has a fine collection relating to the Sussex iron industry and there is a social history museum - Buckleys Yesterday's World.

BEACONSFIELD, BUCKINGHAMSHIRE - Former coaching town with several inns still surviving. The old town has many fine houses and an interesting church. Beautiful countryside and beech woods nearby.

BEMBRIDGE, ISLE OF WIGHT - Village with harbour and bay below Bembridge Down - the most easterly village on the island. Bembridge Sailing Club is one of the most important in southern England.

BEXHILL-ON-SEA, EAST SUSSEX - Popular resort with beach of shingle and firm sand at low tide. The impressive 1930s designed De la Warr Pavilion has good entertainment facilities. Costume Museum in Manor Gardens.

BIDDENDEN, KENT - Perfect village with black and white houses, a tithe barn and a pond. Part of the village is grouped around a green with a village sign depicting the famous Biddenden Maids. It was an important centre of the Flemish weaving industry, hence the beautiful Old Cloth Hall. Vineyard nearby.

BLANDFORD FORUM, DORSET - Almost completely destroyed by fire in 1731, the town was rebuilt in a handsome Georgian style. The church is large and grand and the town is the hub of a rich farming area.

BOGNOR REGIS, WEST SUSSEX - Five miles of firm, flat sand has made the town a popular family resort. Well supplied with gardens.

BOURNEMOUTH, DORSET - Seaside town set among the pines with a mild climate, sandy beaches and fine coastal views. The town has wide streets with excellent shops, a pier, a pavilion, museums and conference centre.

BRIGHSTONE, ISLE OF WIGHT - Excellent centre for visitors who want somewhere quiet. Calbourne, nearby, is ideal for picnics, and the sea at Chilton Chie has safe bathing at high tide.

BRIGHTON & HOVE, EAST SUSSEX - Brighton's attractions include the Royal Pavilion, Volks Electric Railway, Sea Life Centre and Marina Village, Conference Centre, "The Lanes" and several theatres.

BURFORD, OXFORDSHIRE - One of the most beautiful Cotswold wool towns with Georgian and Tudor houses, many antique shops and a picturesque High Street sloping to the River Windrush.

🅲CANTERBURY, KENT - Place of pilgrimage since the martyrdom of Becket in 1170 and the site of Canterbury Cathedral. Visit St Augustine's Abbey, St Martin's (the oldest church in England), Royal Museum and Art Gallery and the Canterbury Tales. Nearby is Howletts Wild Animal Park. Good shopping centre.

CHICHESTER, WEST SUSSEX - The county town of West Sussex with a beautiful Norman cathedral. Noted for its Georgian architecture but also has modern buildings like the Festival Theatre. Surrounded by places of interest, including Fishbourne Roman Palace, Weald and Downland Open-Air Museum and West Dean Gardens.

CHRISTCHURCH, DORSET - Tranquil town lying between the Avon and Stour just before they converge and flow into Christchurch Harbour. A fine 11th C church and the remains of a Norman castle and house can be seen.

🅳DOVER, KENT - A Cinque Port and busiest passenger port in the world. Still a historic town and seaside resort beside the famous White Cliffs. The White Cliffs Experience attraction traces the town's history through the Roman, Saxon, Norman and Victorian periods.

🅴EASTBOURNE, EAST SUSSEX - One of the finest, most elegant resorts on the south-east coast situated beside Beachy Head. Long promenade, well known Carpet Gardens on the seafront, Devonshire Park tennis and indoor leisure complex, theatres, Towner Art Gallery, "How We Lived Then" Museum of Shops and Social History.

🅵FOLKESTONE, KENT - Popular resort. The town has a fine promenade, the Leas, from where orchestral concerts and other entertainments are presented. Horse-racing at Westenhanger Racecourse nearby.

FORDINGBRIDGE, HAMPSHIRE - On the north-west edge of the New Forest. A medieval bridge crosses the Avon at this point and gave the town its name. A good centre for walking, exploring and fishing.

HENFIELD, WEST SUSSEX - Ancient village with many old houses and good shopping facilities, on a ridge of high ground overlooking the Adur Valley. Views to the South Downs.

HIGHCLIFFE, DORSET - Seaside district of Christchurch some 3 miles to the east. Highcliffe Castle is of interest.

HORSHAM, WEST SUSSEX - Busy town with much modern development but still retaining its old character. The museum in Causeway House is devoted chiefly to local history and the agricultural life of the county.

LANGTON MATRAVERS, DORSET - 18th C Purbeck stone village surrounded by National Trust downland, about a mile from the sea and 350 ft above sea level. Excellent walking.

LINGFIELD, SURREY - Wealden village with many buildings dating back to the 15th C. Nearby there is year-round horse racing at Lingfield Park.

LYMINGTON, HAMPSHIRE - Small, pleasant town with bright cottages and attractive Georgian houses, lying on the edge of the New Forest with a ferry service to the Isle of Wight. A sheltered harbour makes it a busy yachting centre.

MARDEN, KENT - The village is believed to date back to Saxon times, though today more modern homes surrounded the 13th C church.

MILFORD-ON-SEA, HAMPSHIRE - Victorian seaside resort with shingle beach and good bathing, set in pleasant countryside and looking out over the Isle of Wight. Nearby is Hurst Castle, built by Henry VIII. The school chapel, former abbey church, can be visited.

NEW MILTON, HAMPSHIRE - New Forest residential town on the mainline railway.

OXFORD, OXFORDSHIRE - Beautiful university town with many ancient colleges, some dating from the 13th C, and numerous buildings of historic and architectural interest. The Ashmolean Museum has outstanding collections. Lovely gardens and meadows with punting on the Cherwell.

POOLE, DORSET - Tremendous natural harbour makes Poole a superb boating centre. The harbour area is crowded with historic buildings including the 15th C Town Cellars housing a maritime museum.

REDHILL, SURREY - Part of the borough of Reigate and now the commercial centre with good shopping facilities. Gatwick Airport is 3 miles to the south.

RINGWOOD, HAMPSHIRE - Market town by the River Avon comprising old cottages, many of them thatched. Although just outside the New Forest, there is heath and woodland nearby and it is a good centre for horse-riding and walking.

ROMSEY, HAMPSHIRE - Town grew up around the important abbey and lies on the banks of the River Test, famous for trout and salmon. Broadlands House, home of the late Lord Mountbatten, is open to the public.

ST NICHOLAS AT WADE, KENT - Village in the Isle of Thanet with ancient church built of knapped flint.

SELSEY, WEST SUSSEX - Almost surrounded by water, with the English Channel on two sides and an inland lake, once Pagham Harbour, and the Brook on the other two. Ideal for yachting, swimming, fishing and wildlife.

STANDLAKE, OXFORDSHIRE - 13th C church with an octagonal tower and spire standing beside the Windrush. The interior of the church is rich in woodwork.

SWANAGE, DORSET - Began life as an Anglo-Saxon port, then a quarrying centre of Purbeck marble. Now the safe, sandy beach set in a sweeping bay and flanked by downs is good walking country, making it an ideal resort.

UCKFIELD, EAST SUSSEX - Once a medieval market town and centre of the iron industry, Uckfield is now a busy country town on the edge of the Ashdown Forest.

WAREHAM, DORSET - This site has been occupied since pre-Roman times and has a turbulent history. In 1762 fire destroyed much of the town, so the buildings now are mostly Georgian.

WASHINGTON, WEST SUSSEX - Near the village is the famous Chanctonbury Ring, an Iron Age camp on a rise nearly 800 ft above sea-level.

WIMBORNE MINSTER, DORSET - Market town centred on the twin-towered Minster Church of St Cuthberga which gave the town the second part of its name. Good touring base for the surrounding countryside, depicted in the writings of Thomas Hardy.

WINCHESTER, HAMPSHIRE - King Alfred the Great made Winchester the capital of Saxon England. A magnificent Norman cathedral, with one of the longest naves in Europe, dominates the city. Home of Winchester College founded in 1382.

WOOL, DORSET - On the River Frome with a mainline station. Woolbridge Manor is of interest and occupies a prominent position.

COLOUR MAPS Colour maps at the front of this guide pinpoint all places in which you will find parks listed.

Scotland

From surprising Southern Uplands, through the buzzing Central Belt to the tranquil and seductive Highlands and Islands, Scotland is a unique country of soaring peaks, sparkling lochs and fairytale castles.

Classic sights
Loch Lomond – scenic loch bordering the beautiful Trossachs
Glenfinnan – picture perfect historical monument on Road to the Isles

Coast & country
The Highlands – Loch Ness, Glencoe & Ben Nevis – beauty on a stunning scale
Islands – the golden bays and sunsets of Harris and Tiree, Skye's breathtaking mountains and seascapes, Scandinavian Shetland – each island experience is unique.

Distinctively different
Whisky – The Gaels named it 'uisge beatha' - the water of life. Enjoy a wee dram at one of the many beautifully sited distilleries.

For more information contact:
VisitScotland
PO Box 121
Livingston EH54 8AF

E: info@visitscotland.com
www.visitscotland.com

Telephone enquiries -
T: 0845 22 55 121

1. Dumfries & Galloway
2. Calton Hill, Edinburgh

Places to **Visit**

You will find hundreds of interesting places to visit during your stay, just some of which are listed in these pages. Contact any Tourist Information Centre in the region for more ideas on days out.

Aberdeen Maritime Museum

Maritime Museum Shiprow, Aberdeen
Tel: (01224) 237700 www.aagm.co.uk
Award-winning museum of the North Sea including exhibitions, computer displays and models on the offshore oil industry, clipper ships and fishing.

Archaeolink Prehistory Park
Oyne, Insch
Tel: (01464) 851544
Prehistory recreated, 40 acre all-weather attraction with many events inside and out. Coffee and gift shops, exhibition and film theatre.

Baxters Highland Village
Baxters Visitors Centre, Fochabers
Tel: (01343) 820393 www.baxters.com
Baxters of Speyside is world renowned for its quality. The self-service restaurant is spacious, family-friendly and caters well for the disabled.

The Big Idea
The Harbourside, Irvine
Tel: (08708) 403100 www.bigidea.org.uk
A mind-blowing adventure through the world of inventions, creations and innovations where visitors interact with the exhibits.

Brodick Castle And Country Park
Isle of Arran, Brodick
Tel: (01770) 302312
The site of this ancient seat of the Dukes of Hamilton was a fortress even in Viking times. Thirteenth-century fortified tower.

The Burrell Collection

Pollok Country Park,
2060 Pollokshaws Road, Glasgow
Tel: (0141) 287 2597 www.glasgow.gov.uk/cls
The Burrell Collection, situated in Pollok Country Park, houses Sir William Burrell's collection gifted to Glasgow in 1944.

Caithness Glass Visitor Centre
Inveralmond, Perth
Tel: (01738) 637373
www.caithnessglass.co.uk
Located in the heart of Perthshire. Marvel at the skills of the glassmakers as they turn molten glass into beautiful paperweights.

Calanais Standing Stones
Callanish, Isle of Lewis
Tel: (01851) 621422
A cross-shaped setting of standing stones, dating to around 3000 bc, unique in Scotland and outstanding in Great Britain. Visitor centre.

Chatelherault Country Park
Chatelherault, Carlisle Road,
Ferniegair, Hamilton
Tel: (01698) 426213
www.southlanarkshire.gov.uk
Chatelherault was designed by W.M. Adam in 1732 and includes a Georgian hunting lodge, visitor centre, gallery, shop, cafe, gardens and river.

Cruachan - The Hollow Mountain Power Station
Loch Awe, Dalmally
Tel: (01866) 822618 www.scottishpower.plc.uk
Discover the heart of the hollow mountain. Hidden deep within the mountain of Ben Cruachan on the shores of Loch Awe is Cruachan Power Station.

Dawyck Botanic Garden
Stobo, Peebles
Tel: (01721) 760254 www.rdge.org.uk

In the depths of the Scottish Borders countryside, Dawyck Botanic Garden has a stunning collection of trees and shrubs.

Deep Sea World
Forthside Terrace, North Queensferry
Tel: (01383) 411880
www.deepseaworld.com
Come face to face with Europe's largest collection of Sand Tiger Sharks. Touch live exhibits in the large rockpools.

Discovery Point & RRS Discovery
Discovery Quay, Dundee
Tel: (01382) 225891
www.rrs-discovery.co.uk
Follow in the footsteps of Captain Scott and Ernest Shackleton aboard the Royal Research Ship Discovery at the multi-award-winning Discovery Point.

Drum Castle
Drumoak, By Banchory
Tel: (01330) 811952
www.drum-castle.org.uk
The keep is one of the three oldest tower houses surviving in Scotland and was the work of Richard Cementarius, first Provost of Aberdeen.

Edinburgh Castle
Castle Hill, Edinburgh
Tel: (0131) 225 9846
www.historic-scotland.gov.uk
This most famous of Scottish castles has a complex building history. The oldest part, St Margaret's Chapel, dates from the 12th century.

Eilean Donan Castle & Visitor Centre
Dornie, Kyle Of Lochalsh
Tel: (01599) 555202
www.eileandonancastle.com
Eilean Donan Castle & Visitor Centre is on the A87 – 8 miles before Skye. The Castle is photogenic, romantic and packed with historical architecture.

The Famous Grouse Experience
The Hosh, Crieff
Tel: (01764) 654366
www.glenturret.com
Scotland's newest interactive Whisky experience with a sensory tour and a chance to play the Grouse-a-phone.

Gallery of Modern Art
Royal Exchange Square, Queens Street, Glasgow
Tel: (0141) 204 5316 www.glasgow.gov.uk/cls
Located in a category A listed building, the Gallery of Modern Art is a welcoming and lively gallery housing the city's contemporary art collection.

Glamis Castle
Glamis, by Forfar
Tel: (01307) 840733
www.glamis-castle.co.uk
Family home of the Earls of Strathmore and Kinghorne. Legendary setting for Shakespeare's 'Macbeth' and childhood home of the Queen Mother.

The Glasshouse at Edinburgh Crystal
Visitor Centre Eastfield, Penicuik
Tel: (01968) 672244
www.edinburgh-crystal.com
Watch the craftsmen, feel the passion and discover the history of the U.K.'s favourite crystal on tours of The Glasshouse.

1. Edinbugh
2. Loch Lomond
3. Highland Cow

The Glenfiddich Distillery
William Grant & Sons Ltd.
The Glenfiddich Distillery, Keith
Tel: (01340) 820 373 www.glenfiddich.com

World famous working distillery. On Christmas Day in 1887 William Grant watched proudly as the first spirit ran from the stills.

Inveraray Jail
Church Square, Inveraray
Tel: (01499) 302195
www.inverarayjail.co.uk
Since opening in 1989 Inveraray Jail has established itself as one of Scotland's most exciting heritage attractions and has won many awards.

James Pringle Weavers of Inverness
Holm Woollen Mill,
Dores Road, Inverness
Tel: (01463) 231 042
Discover 'The Story of Tartan' and join in our weaving exhibition. A working factory site with exhibition. Mill shop.

Jarlshof Prehistoric and Norse Settlement
Sumburgh, Shetland
Tel: (01950) 460112
www.historic-scotland.gov.uk
An extraordinarily important site with a complex of ancient settlements within three acres. Located at Sumburgh Head, 22m south of Lerwick on the A970.

Johnstons Of Elgin Cashmere Visitor Centre
Newmill, Elgin
Tel: (01343) 554080
www.johnstonscashmere.com
Manufacturing for over 200 years, the only Scottish mill to transform cashmere from fibre to garment. Free exhibition and audio-visual presentation.

Museum of Scotland
Chambers Street, Edinburgh
Tel: (0131) 247 4422 www.nms.ac.uk
The Museum of Scotland is a striking new landmark in Edinburgh's historic Old Town and has displays and collections on Scotland's rich history, from geological formation to the 20thC.

Museum of Transport
1 Bunhouse Road, Glasgow
Tel: (0141) 287 2692
www.glasgow.gov.uk/cls
One of the UK's most visited transport museums. Trams, buses, locomotives, ship models, cars, bicycles and horse drawn vehicles.

National Gallery of Scotland
The Mound, Edinburgh
Tel: (0131) 624 6200
www.nationalgalleries.org
Widely regarded as one of the finest smaller galleries in the world, the National Gallery of Scotland contains an outstanding collection of paintings.

National Wallace Monument
Abbey Craig, Stirling
Tel: (01786) 461322

Renew your acquaintance with Scotland's national hero and Hollywood legend, Sir William Wallace at the spectacular 220' high National Wallace Monument.

New Lanark World Heritage Site
New Lanark,
Tel: (01555) 661345
www.newlanark.org

A unique 18thC cotton mill village, long famous as a beauty spot and for the work of the world-famous mill owner Robert Owen.

Our Dynamic Earth
Holyrood Road, Edinburgh
Tel: (0131) 550 7801
www.dynamicearth.co.uk

Our Dynamic Earth is one of the newest and most exciting attractions to have opened in Edinburgh in recent times and has 11 galleries featuring displays about prehistoric creatures, the Big Bang, earthquakes and much more.

Rob Roy & Trossachs Visitor Centre
Ancaster Square, Callander
Tel: (01877) 330784

Discover why Rob Roy McGregor occupies such a special place in the story of the Trossachs and of Scotland itself with a visit to the Rob Roy & Trossachs Visitor Centre.

The Royal Yacht Britannia
Ocean Terminal, Leith, Edinburgh
Tel: (0131) 555 5566
www.royalyachtbritannia.co.uk

Visit The Royal Yacht Britannia, a five-star attraction in Edinburgh's historic port of Leith. A fantastic chance to glimpse life on board one of the world's most famous vessels.

Scone Palace
Scone, Perth
Tel: (01738) 552588
www.scone-palace.co.uk
Scone Palace is the crowning site of the Kings of Scots and the cherished family home of the Earls of Mansfield.

Scottish National Portrait Gallery
1 Queen Street, Edinburgh
Tel: (0131) 624 6400 www.nationalgalleries.org
The Scottish National Portrait Gallery provides a visual history of Scotland from the 16th century to the present day.

Scottish Seabird Centre
The Harbour, North Berwick
Tel: (01620) 890222 www.seabird.org
Get back to nature with a visit to this award-winning Five Star Wildlife Centre. Open all year, enjoy exhilarating sea air and breathtaking views.

Shaping a Nation & TurboVenture
130 Dundee Street, Fountainpark, Edinburgh
Tel: (0131) 337 8743
An entertaining and educational visitor attraction. Shaping a Nation provides a fun and exciting "hands on" experience for all of the family.

St Andrews Castle
The Scores, St Andrews
Tel: (01334) 477196
www.historic-scotland.gov.uk
The ruins of the castle of the Archbishops of St Andrews, dating in part from the 13th century. Notable features include 'bottle-dungeon' and mine.

Stirling Castle
Castle Wynd, Stirling
Tel: (01786) 450000
www.historic-scotland.gov.uk
Without doubt one of the grandest of all Scottish castles, both in situation on a commanding rock outcrop and in architecture.

The Tall Ship at Glasgow Harbour
100 Stobcross Road, Glasgow
Tel: (0141) 341 0506
www.thetallship.com
Visit The Tall Ship at Glasgow Harbour, built in 1896 and experience Glasgow's maritime history at first hand.

Thirlestane Castle
Thirlestane Castle Trust, Lauder
Tel: (01578) 722430
www.thirlestanecastle.co.uk
One of the seven "Great Houses of Scotland". Thirlestane Castle is the ancient seat of the Earls and Duke of Lauderdale.

Verdant Works
West Hendersons Wynd, Dundee
Tel: (01382) 221612
www.verdant-works.co.uk
Take a step back into a Time Capsule of yester-year and discover how the people of Dundee lived, worked and played over 100 years ago.

1. Rannoch Moor
2. Italian Centre, Glasgow

SCOTLAND
VisitScotland

visitscotland.com
PO Box 121 Livingston
EH54 8AF Scotland UK

In London
Scotland's National Office
19 Cockspur Street (off Trafalgar Square)
London SW1Y 5BL

London & Britain Visitor Centre
1 Regent Street
London SW1Y 4XT

Scotland, Hotels & Guest Houses £9.50 (incl p&p)
Over 800 places to stay in Scotland from luxury town
houses and country hotels to budget-priced guest houses.
Details of prices and facilities, with location maps.

Scotland, Bed and Breakfast £6.50 (incl p&p)
Over 1000 Bed and Breakfast establishments throughout
Scotland offering inexpensive accommodation – the perfect
way to enjoy a budget trip and meet Scottish folk in
their own homes. Details of prices and facilities, with
location maps.

Scotland, Caravan and Camping Parks £4.50 (incl p&p)
Over 100 parks detailed with prices, available facilities and
lots of other useful information. Parks inspected by the
Britian Holiday Parks Grading Scheme. Also includes
caravan homes for hire. Location maps.

Scotland, Self-Catering £7.00 (incl p&p)
Over 700 cottages, apartments and chalets to let – many
in scenic areas. Details of prices and facilities, with
location maps.

Touring Guide to Scotland £6.00 (incl p&p)
A fully revised edition of this popular guide which now lists
over 1500 things to do and places to visit in Scotland. Easy
to use index and locater maps. Details of opening hours,
admission charges, general description and information on
disabled access.

Touring Map of Scotland £4.00 (incl p&p)
An up-to-date touring map of Scotland. Full colour with
comprehensive motorway and road information, the map
details over 20 categories of tourist information and names
over 1500 things to do and places to visit in Scotland.

Getting to Scotland

BY ROAD: The A1 and M6
bring you quickly over the
border and immerse you in
beautiful scenery. Scotland's
network of excellent roads
span out from Edinburgh –
Glasgow takes approximately
1hour and 15 minutes by car;
Aberdeen 2 hours 30 minutes
and Inverness 3 hours.

BY RAIL: The cross-border
service from England and
Wales to Scotland is fast and
efficient, and Scotrail trains
offer overnight Caledonian
sleepers to make the journey
even easier.

Telephone (08457) 484950 for
further details.

1. Blair Atholl

Where to stay in Scotland

Parks in Scotland are listed in alphabetical order of place name, and then in alphabetical order of park.

Map references refer to the colour location maps at the front of this guide. The first number indicates the map to use; the letter and number which follow refer to the grid reference on the map.

At-a-glance symbols can be found inside the back cover flap. Keep this open for easy reference.

AVIEMORE, Highland Map ref 8C3

★★★★★
HOLIDAY PARK

BH&HPA

ROTHIEMURCHUS CAMPING & CARAVAN PARK
Coylumbridge, Aviemore PH22 1QU
T: (01479) 812800
F: (01479) 812800
E: lizsangster@rothiemurchus.freeserve.co.uk

CC: JCB, Mastercard, Solo, Switch, Visa

17	🚐	£13.00–£16.00
17	🚃	£13.00–£16.00
22	▲	£10.00–£10.00
39 touring pitches		

From A9 take B970. The park is 1.5 miles from Aviemore on the right hand side.

AYR, Ayrshire Map ref 7B2

★★★★★
TOURING PARK

See Ad on inside front cover

CRAIGIE GARDENS CARAVAN CLUB SITE

Craigie Road, Ayr KA8 0SS
T: (01292) 264909
I: www.caravanclub.co.uk

90	🚐	£9.50–£19.50
90	🚃	£9.50–£19.50
90 total touring pitches		

Set in a beautiful park, a short walk from Ayr. This area, known as 'The Golf Coast', has 40 golf courses! Firth of Clyde cruises, Culzean Castle (NT). Non-members welcome.

CC: Delta, Mastercard, Solo, Switch, Visa

Take A77 Ayr bypass to Whittlets roundabout, then take A719 via racecourse. Turn left at traffic lights. Site off B747, on Craiglie Estate, entered from Craigie Road.

THE CARAVAN CLUB

★★★★
HOLIDAY PARK

BH&HPA
NCC

HEADS OF AYR CARAVAN PARK
Dunure Road, Ayr KA7 4LD
T: (01292) 442269
F: (01292) 500298

20	🚐	£10.00–£14.00
20	🚃	£8.50–£12.00
10	▲	£8.50–£14.00
	🏠	£160.00–£400.00
50 touring pitches		

Five miles (8km) south of Ayr on A719. Site overlooking Arran and the Firth of Clyde. Signposted.

SPECIAL BREAKS

Many establishments offer special promotions and themed breaks. These are highlighted in red. (All such offers are subject to availability.)

BALMACARA, Highland Map ref 8B3

★★★★
TOURING PARK

RERAIG CARAVAN SITE
Balmacara, Kyle of Lochalsh IV40 8DH
T: (01599) 566215
E: warden@reraig.com
I: www.reraig.com

CC: Delta, Mastercard, Visa

40	🚐	£9.30
40	🚏	£9.30
5	⛺	£9.30
45 touring pitches		

1.75 miles (3km) west of junction of A87 and A890 behind Balamacara Hotel.

BLAIR ATHOLL, Tayside Map ref 7C1

★★★★★
HOLIDAY PARK

THISTLE AWARD

BH&HPA
NCC

BLAIR CASTLE CARAVAN PARK
Blair Atholl PH18 5SR
T: (01796) 481263
F: (01796) 481587
E: mail@blaircastlecaravanpark.co.uk
I: www.blaircastlecaravanpark.co.uk

CC: Mastercard, Switch, Visa

140	🚐	£8.50–£11.50
15	🚏	£8.50–£11.50
82	⛺	£8.50–£11.50
28	🏠	£190.00–£390.00
241 touring pitches		

Take A9 north from Pitlochry. Turn off for Blair Atholl after 6 miles.

BRAEMAR, Aberdeenshire Map ref 8C3

★★★★
TOURING PARK

See Ad on inside front cover

INVERCAULD CARAVAN CLUB SITE

Glenshee Road, Braemar, Ballater AB35 5YQ
T: (01339) 741373
I: www.caravanclub.co.uk

Set on the edge of Braemar village, gateway to the Cairngorms, 1,100 feet above sea level. Ideal centre for mountain lovers. See red deer, capercaillie and golden eagles. Non-members welcome.

CC: Delta, Mastercard, Solo, Switch, Visa

On A93 on southern outskirts of village.

100	🚐	£9.50–£19.50
100	🚏	£9.50–£19.50
30	⛺	
130 total touring pitches		

BRORA, Highland Map ref 8C2

★★★★★
TOURING PARK

See Ad on inside front cover

DALCHALM CARAVAN CLUB SITE

Dalchalm, Brora KW9 6LP
T: (01408) 621479
I: www.caravanclub.co.uk

A sheltered site where you can play golf or relax on the nearby sandy beach. Marvellous walking, bird-watching, sea and loch fishing are also on offer. Non-members welcome.

CC: Delta, Mastercard, Solo, Switch, Visa

1.25 miles north of Brora on A9, turn right at Dalchalm.

52	🚐	£9.50–£19.50
52	🚏	£9.50–£19.50
90	⛺	
52 total touring pitches		

SYMBOLS The symbols in each entry give information about services and facilities. A key to these symbols appears at the back of this guide.

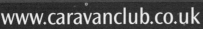

CALLANDER, Central Map ref 7C1

★★★★★
HOLIDAY PARK

BH&HPA

GART CARAVAN PARK

Stirling Road, Callander FK17 8LE
T: (01877) 330002
F: (01877) 330002
E: enquiries@gart-caravan-park.co.uk
I: www.gart-caravan-park.co.uk

A peaceful and spacious park maintained to a very high standard with modern, heated shower block facilities. The ideal centre for cycling, walking and fishing. Reduced rates for the over 50s. Winner – Calor Gas Best Park in Britain 2003.

CC: Delta, Mastercard, Switch, Visa

Leave jct 10 of the M9, west to Callander.

126		£13.00
126		£13.00
126 touring pitches		

★★★★
HOLIDAY PARK

BH&HPA

KELTIE BRIDGE CARAVAN PARK
Callander FK17 8LQ
T: (01877) 330606
F: (01877) 330075

On A84 between Doune and Callander.

50		£8.50–£10.50
50		£8.50–£10.50
50		£7.00–£10.50
50 touring pitches		

CONTIN, Highland Map ref 8C3

★★
TOURING PARK

See Ad on this page

RIVERSIDE CHALETS AND CARAVAN PARK
Contin, Strathpeffer IV14 9ES
T: (01997) 421351
F: (01463) 232502

In Contin village, on A835 between Inverness and Ullapool at Strathpeffer junction.

30		£4.00–£8.00
30		£4.00–£8.00
30		£4.00–£8.00
		£120.00–£215.00
30 touring pitches		

CULLODEN, Highland Map ref 8C3

★★★★★
TOURING PARK

See Ad on inside front cover

CULLODEN MOOR CARAVAN CLUB SITE

Newlands, Culloden Moor, Inverness IV2 5EF
T: (01463) 790625
I: www.caravanclub.co.uk

A gently sloping site with glorious views over the Nairn Valley. The vibrant city of Inverness, with impressive castle, great shops and fascinating museums, is six miles away. Non-members welcome.

CC: Delta, Mastercard, Solo, Switch, Visa

From A9 south of Inverness, take B9006 signposted Croy, site on left 1 mile past Culloden field memorial.

97		£7.50–£16.50
97		£7.50–£16.50
97		
97 total touring pitches		

THE CARAVAN CLUB

COLOUR MAPS Colour maps at the front of this guide pinpoint all places in which you will find parks listed.

DUNBAR, Lothian Map ref 7D2

★★★★

HOLIDAY PARK

THISTLE AWARD

BH&HPA

BELHAVEN BAY CARAVAN PARK
Belhaven Bay, Dunbar EH42 1TU
T: (01368) 865956
F: (01368) 865022
E: belhaven@meadowhead.co.uk
I: www.meadowhead.co.uk

CC: Delta, Mastercard, Switch, Visa

52	🚐	£8.00–£14.00
52	🚚	£8.00–£14.00
52	⛺	£8.00–£12.00
5	🏠	£180.00–£450.00
52 touring pitches		

From the A1 north or south exit at roundabout west of Dunbar. Park is approximately 0.5 miles along the A1087 on left. From south do not take the first exit on the A1087.

DUNDONNELL, Highland Map ref 8B2

★★★★

CAMPING PARK

BADRALLACH BOTHY & CAMP SITE
Croft No 9, Badrallach, Dundonnell IV23 2QP
T: (01854) 633281
E: michael.stott2@virgin.net
I: www.badrallach.com

Walk Antealloch or just sit and watch otters, porpoises, golden eagles and abundant wild flora. In the evenings relax in the gas-lit bothy by the peat stove. Canoe, boat and kite hire.

Off A832. One mile east of Dundonnell Hotel take single track road 7 miles to lochside site.

3	🚐	£7.50–£7.50
3	🚚	£7.50–£7.50
12	⛺	£7.50–£7.50
	🏠	£195.00–£275.00
15 touring pitches		

DUNKELD, Tayside Map ref 7C1

★★★★

TOURING PARK

INVERMILL FARM CARAVAN PARK
Inver, Dunkeld PH8 0JR
T: (01350) 727477
F: (01350) 727477
E: invermill@talk21.com

50	🚐	£11.00–£13.00
50	🚚	£11.00–£13.00
15	⛺	£9.00–£11.00
65 touring pitches		

Turn off the A9 onto the A822 (signposted Crieff). Immediately turn right following the sign to Inver for 0.5 miles past the static site and cross the bridge. We are the first on the left.

EDINBURGH, Lothian Map ref 7C2

★★★★★

TOURING PARK

BH&HPA
NCC

See Ad on this page

DRUMMOHR CARAVAN PARK
Levenhall, Musselburgh, Edinburgh
EH21 8JS
T: (0131) 665 6867
F: (0131) 653 6859

CC: Delta, Mastercard, Switch, Visa

120	🚐	£12.00–£14.50
40	🚚	£12.00–£14.50
60	⛺	£12.00–£14.50
	🏠	£300.00–£600.00
120 touring pitches		

From south on A1, take A199 Musselburgh, then B1361. Follow park signs. From the west on the A1, come off at Wallyford slip road and follow Caravan Park and Mining Museum signs.

TOWN INDEX
This can be found at the back of the guide. If you know where you want to stay, the index will give you the page number listing all accommodation in your chosen town, city or village.

★★★★
TOURING PARK

BH&HPA

LINWATER CARAVAN PARK

West Clifton, East Calder, Livingston EH53 0HT
T: (0131) 333 3326
F: (0131) 333 1952

A peaceful park seven miles west of Edinburgh. Excellent facilities. Ideal for visiting Edinburgh, Royal Highland Showground, Falkirk Wheel, or as a stop-over on your way north or south.

At junction of M8/A8/M9 at Newbridge, take B7030 signposted Wilkieston for 2 miles. Park signposted on right, 1 mile on.

50	🚐	£11.00–£13.00
50	🚚	£11.00–£13.00
10	▲	£9.00–£11.00
60 touring pitches		

★★★★
HOLIDAY PARK

THISTLE AWARD

BH&HPA

MORTONHALL CARAVAN PARK

38 Mortonhall Gate, Frogston Road East,
Edinburgh EH16 6TJ
T: (0131) 664 1533
F: (0131) 664 5387
E: mortonhall@meadowhead.co.uk
I: www.meadowhead.co.uk

CC: Delta, Mastercard, Switch,
Visa

150	🚐	£9.50–£18.50
150	🚚	£9.50–£18.50
100	▲	£9.50–£14.50
18	🏠	£215.00–£475.00
250 touring pitches		

From the city bypass at Lothianburn junction, follow signs for Mortonhall. From city centre take the roads at the east or west ends of Princes Street, heading south (A701 or A702).

★★★
HOLIDAY PARK

BROWNMUIR CARAVAN PARK

Fordoun, Laurencekirk AB30 1SJ
T: (01561) 320786
F: (01561) 320786
E: brownmuircaravanpark@talk21.com
I: www.brownmuircaravanpark.co.uk

30	🚐	£8.00–£8.00
30	🚚	£8.00–£8.00
10	▲	£6.00–£8.00
1	🏠	£230.00–£250.00
30 touring pitches		

1 mile from A(M)90 at village of Fordoun. Turn left at village, site is in 1 mile.

★★★★★
HOLIDAY PARK

BH&HPA

LINNHE LOCHSIDE HOLIDAYS

Corpach, Fort William PH33 7NL
T: (01397) 772376
F: (01397) 772007
E: holidays@linnhe.demon.co.uk
I: www.linnhe-lochside-holidays.co.uk

Almost a botanical garden and stunningly beautiful. Winner of 'Best Park in Scotland 1999' award. Free fishing. Colour brochure sent with pleasure. Also self-catering. Discounts for Senior Citizen groups and for second week. Rallies – no charge for awnings.

CC: Delta, Mastercard, Switch, Visa

On A830 1.5 miles (3km) west of Corpach village, 5 miles from Fort William.

65	🚐	£13.00–£16.00
65	🚚	£13.00–£16.00
10	▲	£10.00–£12.00
68	🏠	£190.00–£465.00
75 touring pitches		

★★★★
HOLIDAY PARK

THISTLE AWARD

NCC

SANDS HOLIDAY CENTRE

Gairloch IV21 2DL
T: (01445) 712152
F: (01445) 712518
E: litsands@aol.com
I: www.highlandcaravancamping.co.uk

CC: Amex, Mastercard, Solo,
Switch, Visa

120	🚐	£8.50–£10.50
40	🚚	£8.50–£10.00
200	▲	£8.50–£10.50
5	🏠	£270.00–£450.00
360 touring pitches		

At Gairloch turn on to B8021 (Melvaig). Site 3 miles on, beside sandy beach.

GLENCOE, Highland Map ref 7B1

★★★★★
HOLIDAY PARK

THISTLE AWARD

BH&HPA
NCC

INVERCOE CARAVAN & CAMPING PARK
Invercoe, Glencoe PH49 4HP
T: (01855) 811210
F: (01855) 811210
E: invercoe@sol.co.uk
I: www.invercoe.co.uk

55		£13.00–£15.00
55		£13.00–£15.00
55		£13.00–£15.00
5		£270.00–£450.00
55 touring pitches		

Site is 0.25 miles from Glencoe crossroads (A82) on the Kinlochleven road B863.

INVERBEG, West Dunbartonshire Map ref 7B1

★★★★
HOLIDAY PARK

THISTLE AWARD

BH&HPA

INVERBEG HOLIDAY PARK
Inverbeg, Luss G83 8PD
T: (01436) 860267
F: (01436) 860266
E: info@lochlomondholidays.co.uk
I: www.lochlomondholidays.co.uk

Beautiful holiday park on the banks of Lomond with luxury caravans and lodges for hire. Short breaks also available. Ideal for water sports and touring.

3 miles north of Luss on A82.

12		£210.00–£500.00

JOHN O'GROATS, Highland Map ref 8D1

★★★
TOURING PARK

JOHN O'GROATS CARAVAN PARK
John O'Groats, Wick KW1 4YS
T: (01955) 611329

90		£8.00
90		£8.00
90		£8.00
90 touring pitches		

Site on the seashore at the north end of the A99 beside the Last House in Scotland.

KENMORE, Perth and Kinross Map ref 7C1

★★★★
HOLIDAY PARK

BH&HPA

KENMORE CARAVAN AND CAMPING PARK
Kenmore, Aberfeldy PH15 2HN   CC: Mastercard, Visa
T: (01887) 830226
F: (01887) 829059
E: info@taymouth.co.uk
I: www.taymouth.co.uk

80		£13.00–£15.00
10		£13.00–£15.00
60		£12.00–£14.00
150 touring pitches		

From A9 west on A827 at Ballinluig, 15 miles through Aberfeldy to Kenmore. Over the bridge on right hand side.

KINLOCHEWE, Highland Map ref 8B3

★★★★
TOURING PARK

See Ad on inside front cover

KINLOCHEWE CARAVAN CLUB SITE
Kinlochewe, Achnasheen IV22 2PA
T: (01445) 760239
I: www.caravanclub.co.uk

Peaceful site near Loch Maree. A rare and very special place with glittering lochs, lush woodland and mountains-a paradise for climbers and walkers. Non-members welcome.

CC: Delta, Mastercard, Solo, Switch, Visa

Just north of Kinlochewe at junction of A832 and A896. Signposted.

56		£7.00–£15.50
56		£7.00–£15.50
56 total touring pitches		

RATING All accommodation in this guide has been rated, or is awaiting a rating, by a trained Tourist Board assessor.

KIPPFORD, Dumfries & Galloway Map ref 7C3

★★★★★
HOLIDAY PARK

THISTLE AWARD

BH&HPA

KIPPFORD HOLIDAY PARK

Kippford, Dalbeattie DG5 4LF
T: (01556) 620636
F: (01556) 620607
I: www.kippfordholidaypark.co.uk

25	🚐	£10.00–£16.00
20	🚐	£10.00–£16.00
20	▲	£8.00–£16.00
10	🏠	£150.00–£400.00
65 touring pitches		

Coastal south-west Scotland by beautiful seaside village. Terraced pitches on Bellamy Gold Park, with woodland and coastal walks. Play areas, cycles, fishing, 9-hole golf. Discounts for large families and Senior Citizens, also seventh night free. Marquee (free) for small rallies.

From A711 Dalbeattie take Solway coast road A710. After 3.5 miles continue straight ahead at junction with Kippford Road. Entrance to park is 200 yards on right.

LAIRG, Highland Map ref 8C2

★★★★
HOLIDAY PARK

BH&HPA

DUNROAMIN CARAVAN & CAMPING PARK
Main Street, Lairg IV27 4AR   CC: Mastercard, Visa
T: (01549) 402447
F: (01549) 402784
E: enquiries@lairgcaravanpark.co.uk
I: www.lairgcaravanpark.co.uk

50	🚐	£8.00–£10.00
50	🚐	£7.00–£10.00
50	▲	£4.50–£10.00
10	🏠	£160.00–£295.00
50 touring pitches		

On A839, Main Street, Lairg, behind Crofters Restaurant.

LAUDER, Borders Map ref 7C2

★★★★
TOURING PARK

BH&HPA

THIRLESTANE CASTLE CARAVAN AND CAMPING SITE
Thirlestane Castle, Lauder TD2 6RU
T: 07976 231032
F: (01578) 718749

50	🚐	£10.00
50	🚐	£10.00
50	▲	£8.00
50 touring pitches		

0.25 miles (0.5km) south of Lauder, just off A68 and A697. Edinburgh 28 miles (45km), Newcastle 68 miles (109km).

LAURENCEKIRK, Grampian Map ref 7D1

★★★★
HOLIDAY PARK

BH&HPA

DOVECOT CARAVAN PARK
North Water Bridge, Laurencekirk
AB30 1QL
T: (01674) 840630
F: (01674) 840630
E: info@dovecotcaravanpark.com
I: www.dovecotcaravanpark.com

25	🚐	£9.50–£10.50
25	🚐	£9.50–£10.50
25	▲	£7.00–£8.00
2	🏠	£200.00–£220.00
25 touring pitches		

From Laurencekirk (A90) 5 miles south at Northwater Bridge, turn right to Edzell. Site is 300m on left.

QUALITY ASSURANCE SCHEME

For an explanation of the quality and facilities represented by the Stars please refer to the front of this guide.

★★★★
TOURING PARK

BEECRAIGS CARAVAN AND CAMPING SITE

Beecraigs Country Park, The Park Centre, Linlithgow
EH49 6PL
T: (01506) 844516
F: (01506) 846256
E: mail@beecraigs.com
I: www.beecraigs.com

Open all year. Situated near historic Linlithgow town. On-site facilities include electric hook-ups, barbecues, play area, modern toilet facilities and laundry. Pets welcome. Leaflets available. Sep 2003-Mar 2004: 10% discount for Senior Citizens (proof required) and 10% discount for 7-night stay if paid in advance (excl Senior Citizens).

CC: Delta, Mastercard, Switch, Visa

From Linlithgow, follow Beecraigs Country Park or International Caravan Park signposts. Park is 2 miles south of Linlithgow. From M8, follow B792.

39		£10.20–£14.00
39		£10.20–£14.00
20		£9.10–£10.20
59 touring pitches		

★★★★
TOURING PARK

See Ad on inside front cover

BALBIRNIE PARK CARAVAN CLUB SITE

Balbirnie Road, Markinch, Glenrothes KY7 6NR
T: (01592) 759130
I: www.caravanclub.co.uk

Attractive site set in 400 acres of parkland. Thirty golf courses, including one on site. Swimming pool, ice rink, ten-pin bowling, children's farm close by. Non-members welcome.

CC: Delta, Mastercard, Solo, Switch, Visa

From A92, follow signs to Markinch, then signs to Balbirnie Park Craft Centre. Site entrance is just inside park on right, 0.5 miles west of Markinch.

77		£7.50–£16.50
77		£7.50–£16.50
15		
77 total touring pitches		

★★★★★
TOURING PARK

See Ad on inside front cover

GIBSON PARK CARAVAN CLUB SITE

High St, Melrose TD6 9RY
T: (01896) 822969
I: www.caravanclub.co.uk

Peaceful, award-winning site on edge of town. Adjacent tennis courts and playing fields. Melrose Abbey, where Robert the Bruce's head is buried, is within walking distance. Non-members welcome.

OPEN All Year
CC: Delta, Mastercard, Solo, Switch, Visa

Site adjacent to main road (A6091) close to centre of town. Approximately 6 miles from A68 Edinburgh/Newcastle road.

60		£11.00–£20.00
60		£11.00–£20.00
60		
60 total touring pitches		

MAP REFERENCES
The map references refer to the colour maps at the front of the guide. The first figure is the map number; the letter and figure which follow indicate the grid reference on the map.

MOTHERWELL, Strathclyde Map ref 7C2

★★★★
TOURING PARK

NCC

STRATHCLYDE PARK CARAVAN CAMPING SITE
366 Hamilton Road, Motherwell ML1 3ED
T: (01698) 266155
F: (01698) 252925
E: strathclydepark@northlan.gov.uk
I: www.northlan.gov.uk

100 🚐	£9.00–£10.00
100 🚅	
150 ▲	£4.00–£8.00
250 touring pitches	

From south follow M74 north, exit at A725 jct 5 signposted with a thistle emblem. From Edinburgh follow M8 south Carlisle road and M74, come down A725.

NEWTONGRANGE, Midlothian Map ref 7C2

★★★★
TOURING PARK

LOTHIAN BRIDGE CARAVAN PARK
Lothian Bridge, Newtongrange, Dalkeith
EH22 4TP
T: (0131) 663 6120

🚐	£10.00–£12.00
🚅	£10.00–£12.00
▲	£8.00–£10.00
46 touring pitches	

Campsite 7 miles south of Edinburgh on A7.

NORTH BERWICK, Lothian Map ref 7D2

★★★★★
HOLIDAY PARK

THISTLE AWARD

BH&HPA

TANTALLON CARAVAN PARK
Dunbar Road, North Berwick EH39 5NJ
T: (01620) 893348
F: (01620) 895623
E: tantallon@meadowhead.co.uk
I: www.meadowhead.co.uk

CC: Delta, Mastercard, Switch, Visa

147 🚐	£10.00–£16.00
147 🚅	£10.00–£16.00
147 ▲	£10.00–£14.00
10 ⛺	£200.00–£490.00
147 touring pitches	

From North Berwick take A198 towards Dunbar. Situated on east side of town overlooking golf course and Firth of Forth. From A1 turn onto A198 3 miles west of Dunbar.

PITLOCHRY, Tayside Map ref 7C1

★★★★
HOLIDAY PARK

THISTLE AWARD

BH&HPA

MILTON OF FONAB CARAVAN PARK
Pitlochry PH16 5NA
T: (01796) 472882
F: (01796) 474363
E: info@fonab.co.uk
I: www.fonab.co.uk

154 🚐	£11.50–£13.50
154 🚅	£13.50–£13.50
154 ▲	£11.50–£13.50
36 ⛺	£250.00–£380.00
154 touring pitches	

From south take Pitlochry filter road. Site is 0.5 miles south of Pitlochry.

PORT LOGAN, Dumfries & Galloway Map ref 7B3

★★★★
TOURING PARK

See Ad on inside front cover

NEW ENGLAND BAY CARAVAN CLUB SITE
Port Logan, Stranraer DG9 9NX
T: (01776) 860275
I: www.caravanclub.co.uk

On the edge of Luce Bay, an ideal site for children with direct access to a safe, clean, sandy beach. Sailing, sea-angling, golf, green bowling, pony-trekking. Non-members welcome.

CC: Delta, Mastercard, Solo, Switch, Visa

From Newton Stewart take A75, then A715, then A716. Site on left 2.7 miles past Ardwell Filling Station.

150 🚐	£13.25–£16.50
150 🚅	£13.25–£16.50
150 total touring pitches	

THE CARAVAN CLUB

CREDIT CARD BOOKINGS If you book by telephone and are asked for your credit card number it is advisable to check the proprietor's policy should you cancel your reservation.

ST ANDREWS, Fife Map ref 7C1

★★★★

HOLIDAY PARK

BH&HPA

CLAYTON CARAVAN PARK
St Andrews KY16 9YE
T: (01334) 870242
F: (01334) 870057
E: holiday@clayton-caravan-park.co.uk
I: www.clayton-caravan-park.co.uk

CC: Mastercard, Switch, Visa

26	🚐	£20.00
26	🚐	£20.00
26	▲	
	🏠	£210.00–£400.00
26 touring pitches		

Just 4.5 miles (7km) west of St Andrews on A91, between Dairsie and Guardbridge.

STIRLING, Central Map ref 7C2

★★★★

TOURING PARK

See Ad on inside front cover

BLAIR DRUMMOND CARAVAN CLUB SITE

Cuthill Brae, Blair Drummond, Stirling FK9 4UX
T: (01786) 841208
I: www.caravanclub.co.uk

Delightful site set in the walled garden of Blair Drummond House at Doune. Centrally located for east and west coasts. Golf courses at Stirling and Gleneagles (20 miles). Non-members welcome.

CC: Delta, Mastercard, Solo, Switch, Visa

From Stirling take A84 signposted Crianlarich after passing over M9 at jct 10. Turn right within 3 miles after passing A873 on left. Past church on left.

88	🚐	£9.50–£19.50
88	🚐	£9.50–£19.50
88 total touring pitches		

THE CARAVAN CLUB

★★★★★

TOURING PARK

BH&HPA

WITCHES CRAIG CARAVAN PARK
Blairlogie, Stirling FK9 5PX
T: (01786) 474947
F: (01786) 447286
E: info@witchescraig.co.uk
I: www.witchescraig.co.uk

60	🚐	£10.25–£11.50
60	🚐	£10.25–£11.50
60	▲	£10.25–£11.50
60 touring pitches		

Leave Stirling on St Andrews road, A91. Site 3 miles (5km) east of Stirling.

ULLAPOOL, Highland Map ref 8B2

★★★★

TOURING PARK

BH&HPA

ARDMAIR POINT HOLIDAY PARK
Ardmair Point, Ullapool IV26 2TN
T: (01854) 612054
F: (01854) 612757
E: sales@ardmair.com
I: www.ardmair.com

CC: Delta, Mastercard, Switch, Visa

45	🚐	Min £10.00
45	🚐	Min £9.00
45	▲	Min £9.00
45 touring pitches		

Situated 3.5 miles north of Ullapool on A835. Entrance next to telephone kiosk.

AT-A-GLANCE SYMBOLS

Symbols at the end of each accommodation entry give useful information about services and facilities. A key to symbols can be found inside the back cover flap. Keep this open for easy reference.

A brief guide to the main Towns and Villages offering accommodation in **Scotland**

A AVIEMORE, HIGHLAND - Popular centre for exploring Speyside and the Cairngorms. Winter sports, fishing, walking and climbing.

AYR, AYRSHIRE - One of Scotland's brightest seaside resorts. Also a Royal Burgh and noted centre for the manufacture of carpets and fabrics. Many associations with the poet Robert Burns. Faces the Isle of Arran across the Firth of Clyde.

B BALMACARA, HIGHLAND - Small village on the north shore of Loch Alsh with views towards the Sound of Sleat and Skye.

C CALLANDER, CENTRAL - A favourite centre for exploring the Trossachs and the Highlands, beautifully situated at the entrance to the Pass of Leny.

D DUNBAR, LOTHIAN - Popular seaside resort at the foot of the Lammermuir Hills. Good bathing from extensive sands. On the rock above the harbour are the remains of Dunbar Castle. Mary Queen of Scots fled here with Darnley in 1566, immediately after the murder of Rizzio, her secretary.

DUNDONNELL, HIGHLAND - Locality of scattered crofting hamlets round the shores of Little Loch Broom, dominated by the magnificent ridge of An Teallach. Glorious scenery, mountaineering and sea angling.

DUNKELD, TAYSIDE - Picturesque cathedral town beautifully situated in the richly wooded valley of the River Tay on the edge of the Perthshire Highlands. Salmon and trout fishing.

E EDINBURGH, LOTHIAN - Scotland's capital and international festival city. Dominated by its ancient fortress, the city is surrounded by hills, woodlands and rivers. Good shopping on Princes Street.

F FORT WILLIAM, HIGHLAND - One of the finest touring centres in the Western Highlands. A busy holiday town set on the shores of Loch Linnhe at the western end of the Great Glen almost in the shadow of Ben Nevis, the highest mountain in the British Isles. Nearby are fishing, climbing, walking and steamer trips to the islands.

G GLENCOE, HIGHLAND - Village at the foot of Glen Coe, a deep and rugged defile enclosed by towering mountains. Scene of massacre of MacDonalds of Glencoe by the Campbells of Glen Lyon in 1692. A valley of haunting beauty offering winter sports.

K KIPPFORD, DUMFRIES & GALLOWAY - Beautiful seaside village, part of the Colvend Coast Heritage Trail, with sailing centre, spectacular beach views and pubs. National Trust and Forestry Commission walks and cycle tracks, game and coarse fishing trips and cycle hire.

L LAUDER, BORDERS - Royal Burgh with quaint old tolbooth, 16th C church and medieval Thirlstane Castle.

LINLITHGOW, LOTHIAN - Historic town west of Edinburgh whose industries include electronics, distilling and manufacturing. Close by stand the ruins of Linlithgow Palace, birthplace of Mary Queen of Scots.

N NORTH BERWICK, LOTHIAN - Holiday resort on the Firth of Forth with sandy beaches, golf and a picturesque harbour.

P PITLOCHRY, TAYSIDE - A favourite holiday resort and touring centre in the valley of the Tummel. Points of interest are Pitlochry Dam and Salmon Ladder.

S STIRLING, CENTRAL - Ancient town with a long and turbulent history. The famous castle perched on its towering rock was a vital stronghold which became the scene of several battles, notably the Battle of Bannockburn in 1314.

COUNTRY CODE Always follow the Country Code 🦌 Enjoy the countryside and respect its life and work 🦌 Guard against all risk of fire 🦌 Fasten all gates 🦌 Keep your dogs under close control 🦌 Keep to public paths across farmland 🦌 Use gates and stiles to cross fences, hedges and walls 🦌 Leave livestock, crops and machinery alone 🦌 Take your litter home 🦌 Help to keep all water clean 🦌 Protect wildlife, plants and trees 🦌 Take special care on country roads 🦌 Make no unnecessary noise

Tourist
INFORMATION
Centres

When it comes to your next England break, the first stage of your journey could be closer than you think. You've probably got a tourist information centre nearby which is there to serve the local community - as well as visitors. Knowledgeable staff will be happy to help you, wherever you're heading.

Many tourist information centres can provide you with maps and guides, and often it's possible to book accommodation and travel tickets too.

Across the country, there are more than 550 TICs. You'll find the address of your nearest centre in your local phone book.

QUALITY ASSURED
VISITOR
ATTRACTION

Visitor Attraction Quality Assurance

VisitBritain operates a Visitor Attraction Quality Assurance Standard. Participating attractions are visited annually by trained, impartial assessors who look at all aspects of the visit, from initial telephone enquiries to departure, customer services to catering, as well as facilities and activities. Only those attractions which have been assessed by VisitBritain and meet the standard receive the quality marque, your sign of a 'Quality Assured Visitor Attraction'.

Look out for the quality marque and visit with confidence.

Wales

A timeless country of epic mountains, lush green valleys and spectacular coastline, all rich in wildlife. Explore pretty pastel harbours, forbidding stone castles, charming Victorian resorts and the city pleasures of Cardiff.

Classic sights
Powis Castle – medieval castle with Italian and French style gardens
Portmeirion – romantic Italian style seaside village set in sub-tropical woodlands
Tintern Abbey – decorative medieval abbey in a riverbank setting

Coast & country
Gower peninsula – sweeping golden beaches
Snowdonia National Park – mountains, hill farms and upland lakes
Lake Vyrnwy – dramatic and mountain-ringed

Literary links
Dylan Thomas – Carmarthenshire inspired his work.
Dylan Thomas Centre at Swansea
Hay Festival of Literature – attracts leading international writers

Distinctively different
Dolaucothi Gold Mines – try panning for gold yourself!

For more information contact:
Wales Tourist Board
Brunel House, 2 Fitzalan Road, Cardiff CF24 OUY

E: info@visitwales.com

Telephone enquiries -

T: 08701 211251
F: 08701 211259
Minicom: 08701 211255

1. Royal National Eisteddfod
2. Snowdonia Stream
3. East Wales

You will find hundreds of interesting places to visit during your stay, just some of which are listed in these pages. Contact any Tourist Information Centre in the region for more ideas on days out.

Places to Visit

Red Kite Feeding Centre/Nature Trail
Gigrin Farm, South Street, Rhayader
Tel: 01597 810243
Breathtaking aerial displays from up to 200 wild Red Kites and other birds that use Gigrin Farm as a feeding station. Feeding takes place daily at 2pm (3pm in summer) throughout the year. In bad weather numbers of birds can increase dramatically.

Capsule Gallery
Charles Street, Cardiff
Tel: 02920 376195

Gower Heritage Centre
Parkmill, Gower, Swansea
Tel: 01792 371206
Set in the heart of the beautiful Gower peninsula and housed in a working 12thC water-powered corn mill, the centre has a museum of rural life and is home to various traditional craftspeople. Daily guided tours and demonstrations.

Blueberry Angoras
Ffynnon Watty, Moylegrove, Cardigan
Tel: 01239 881668

Crofty Nurseries & Garden Centre
Llanteg, Narberth
Tel: 01834 831437

Ocean Commotion
Lower Frog Street, Tenby
Tel: 01834 845526

Glasfryn Parc
Y Ffor, Pwllheli
Tel: 01766 810202 www.glasfryn.co.uk
The ideal family day out, activities include go-karting, quad biking, coarse fishing and a play area for children aged three years up. Sample local produce from the farm shop, relax in the cafe, or make use of the picnic tables. Free car park.

Quarry Tours
Llechwedd Slate Caverns, Blaenau Ffestiniog
Tel: 01766 830306
www.llechwedd-slate-caverns.co.uk
Choice of two fascinating underground tours. The Deep Mine tour begins with a ride on Britain's steepest passenger railway; the Miners' Tramway tour includes demonstrations of Victorian mining skills.

Anglesey Sea Zoo

Brynsiencyn, LLanfair P G
Tel: 01248 430411
www.angleseyseazoo.co.uk
Award-winning aquarium with over 50 magical displays recreating the habitats of the fauna and flora found around the Anglesey and North Wales coastline.

Portmeirion
enrhyndeudraeth
Tel: 01766 772321
www.portmeirion-village.com
Village built by Clough Williams-Ellis between 1926 to 1972 to demonstrate how a naturally beautiful site could be developed without spoiling it. Used as a location for the 1960s classic TV series The Prisoner, the village has attracted writers such as George Bernard Shaw, H.G. Wells, Bertrand Russell and Noel Coward.

Welsh Mountain Zoo
Colwyn Bay
Tel: 01492 532938
www.welshmountainzoo.org

Rhondda Heritage Park
Lewis Merthyr Colliery, Coed Cae Road,
Trehafod, Pontypridd
Tel: 01443 682036
www.rhonddaheritagepark.com

Based at the former Lewis Merthyr Colliery, this is one of the most popular visitor attractions in South Wales. Take a look at the culture and character of the coal-mining villages of the Rhondda valley. A fun and informative day out for the whole the family.

King Arthur's Labyrinth
Corris, Machynlleth
Tel: 01654 761584

A step back in time. An underground boat trip through the great waterfall and into the Labyrinth, followed by a walk through a cavern to view a spectacular audiovisual tableau of the Arthurian legends.

Penrhyn Castle, National Trust
Bangor
Tel: 01248 353084
Dramatic neo-Norman fantasy castle built by Thomas Hopper in the 19th century. Interior featuring elaborate carvings, plasterwork and mock-Norman furniture plus an outstanding collection of paintings. Set in 18.2 hectares with Victorian walled garden, model railway museum and superb doll museum.

Scruffs - The Kiting Experience
Lluest House, Pant-Y-Gog,
Pontycymer, Bridgend
Tel: 01656 871871
A kite for everyone. Discover an amazing variety - ranging from easy to fly ones for children through to intermediate and advance level sports and power kites, plus specialist single line range.

Llanerchaeron
The National Trust, Llanerchaeron,
Ciliau Aeron
Tel: 01545 570200

The Pit Pony Sanctuary
Fforest Uchaf Farm, Penycoedcae, Rhondda
Tel: 01443 480327

Pembrokeshire Sheepdogs
Tremynydd Fach, St Davids
Tel: 01437 721677
A working sheep farm situated on the stunning Pembrokeshire Coast Path that specialises in sheepdog training courses. In the summer months public sheepdog demonstrations show off the skills of sheepdog trialing and farm work.

Snowdon Mountain Railway
Llanberis
Tel: 0870 4580033
www.snowdonrailway.co.uk

Unique rack and pinion railway that rises to within 20 metres of the summit of the highest mountain in England and Wales. A tremendous feat of engineering.

1. Snowdonia
2. World Harp Festival
3. Walkng in Snowdonia

The National Trust Plas Newydd
Llanfairpwllgwyngyll
Tel: 01248 714795
Set amidst breathtakingly beautiful scenery, an elegant 18th-century house built by James Wyatt with an interior restyled in the 1930s. Featuring paintings by Rex Whistler and a military museum. Also a fine spring garden and Australasian arboretum.

The Playbarn
Brynich, Brecon
Tel: 01874 623480

Centre For Alternative Technology
Pantperthog, Machynlleth
Tel: 01654 702400 www.cat.org.uk
The largest public display centre of its kind in Europe, the 16.2-hectare, award-winning site features working examples of wind, water and solar power, energy conservation, self build, organic growing, and alternative sewage systems.

Clerkenhill Adventure Farm
Clerkenhill, Scebech, Haverfordwest
Tel: 01437 751227

Task Force
Beech Clump, Off A48, Cowbridge
Tel: 02920 593900
www.taskforcepaintball.co.uk
Over 12 hectares of dedicated paintball arena in a woodland environment featuring eight different game areas. The site also includes separate areas for other activities including laser clay pigeon shooting, archery and teambuilding.

Dinefwr Park
Newton House, Dinefwr Park, Llandeilo
Tel: 01558 650707
www.nationaltrust.org.uk
18th-century landscape park, home to more than one hundred fallow deer. Scenic walks including access to Dinefwr Castle, and a wooded boardwalk, ideal for families and wheelchair users. Tea room overlooking deer park.

Dolaucothi Gold Mines
Pumsaint, Llanwrda
Tel: 01558 650707 www.nationaltrust.org.uk

Aberystwyth Art Centre

University of Wales, Aberystwyth
Tel: 01970 622882
www.aber.ac.uk/artscentre
Award-winning arts centre. The largest in Wales and recently extensively refurbished, the centre houses a concert hall, theatre, gallery spaces, cinema, workshop spaces, craft shop, café and bars.

Wales Tourist Board

Brunel House, 2 Fitzalan Road,
Cardiff CF24 OUY
T: 08701 211251 F: 08701 211259
E: info@visitwales.com

Wales on the Web
www.visitwales.com

Find out all you need to know from the Wales Tourist Board website. It's your instant route to up-to-the-minute information on accommodation, attractions, activities and events. It's also full of ideas for travel itineraries and themes to explore - and you can use it to book online.

Getting to Wales

BY ROAD: Travelling to South and West Wales is easy on the M4 and the dual carriageway network. The new Second Severn Crossing gives two ways to enter Wales, but those wishing to visit Chepstow and the Wye Valley should use the original Severn Bridge and the M48 (originally part of the M4).

In North Wales the A55 'Expressway' has made travelling speedier, whilst mid Wales is accessible via the M54 which links with the M6, M5 and M1.

BY RAIL: Fast and frequent Great Western Intercity trains travel between London Paddington and Cardiff, departing hourly and half-hourly at peak times, and taking only two hours. Newport, Bridgend, Port Talbot, Neath and Swansea are also accessible through this service, which encompasses most of West Wales. London Euston links to the North Wales coast via Virgin trains, who also run a service between the North East of England and South Wales. In addition, Wales and West Passenger Trains run Alphaline services from London Waterloo, Manchester and the North East, Brighton and the South, and Nottingham and the Heart of England.

For further rail enquiries, please telephone (08457) 484950.

1. Rhossili Bay, North Wales
2. Aberaeron

Where to stay in Wales

Parks in Wales are listed in alphabetical order of place name, and then in alphabetical order of park.

Map references refer to the colour location maps at the front of this guide. The first number indicates the map to use; the letter and number which follow refer to the grid reference on the map.

At-a-glance symbols can be found inside the back cover flap. Keep this open for easy reference.

ABERAERON, Ceredigion Map ref 1A2

★★★★
HOLIDAY, TOURING & CAMPING PARK

BH&HPA

AERON COAST CARAVAN PARK
North Road, Aberaeron SA46 0JF
T: (01545) 570349
E: aeroncoastcaravanpark@aberaeron.
freeserve.co.uk

CC: Mastercard, Switch, Visa

🚐	£10.50–£14.00
🚐	£10.50–£14.00
⛺	£10.50–£14.00

100 touring pitches

Situated on main coastal A487 road on northern edge of Aberaeron. Filling station at entrance. Signposted.

ABERGAVENNY, Monmouthshire Map ref 1B3

★★★★
TOURING PARK

See Ad on inside front cover

THE CARAVAN CLUB

PANDY CARAVAN CLUB SITE

Pandy, Abergavenny NP7 8DR
T: (01873) 890370
I: www.caravanclub.co.uk

Attractively landscaped site where you can fish (by permit from the site), pony trek or walk on Offa's Dyke or in the Brecon Beacons National Park. Abergavenny six miles. Non-members welcome.

CC: Delta, Mastercard, Solo, Switch, Visa

From south do not go into Abergavenny, continue onto A465 (signposted Hereford). In 6.25 miles turn left by The Old Pandy Inn, into minor road. Site on left after passing under railway bridge. Signposted.

53	🚐	£9.50–£19.50
53	🚐	£9.50–£19.50

53 total touring pitches

BALA, Gwynedd Map ref 1B1

★★★★
TOURING & CAMPING PARK

DAFFODIL AWARD

BH&HPA

PENYBONT TOURING AND CAMPING PARK
Llangynog Road, Bala LL23 7PH
T: (01678) 520549
F: (01678) 520006
E: penybont@balalake.fsnet.co.uk
I: www.penybont-bala.co.uk

CC: Switch, Visa

35	🚐	£10.00–£11.50
35	🚐	£10.00–£11.50
50	⛺	£6.00–£11.50

85 touring pitches

By road, take main A494 Bala road, turn onto B4391 and we are 0.45 miles on the right hand side. Signposted.

 PRICES Please check prices and other details at the time of booking

BARMOUTH, Gwynedd Map ref 1A2

★★★★★
**TOURING &
CAMPING PARK**

DAFFODIL AWARD

BH&HPA

**HENDRE MYNACH (BARMOUTH)
TOURING CARAVAN & CAMPING PARK**
Llanaber Road, Barmouth LL42 1YR
T: (01341) 280262
F: (01341) 280586
E: mynach@lineone.net
I: www.hendremynach.co.uk

CC: Delta, Mastercard, Switch, Visa

60		£8.00–£20.00
60		£7.00–£20.00
180	A	£6.00–£17.00
240 touring pitches		

Half a mile North of Barmouth, on the A496 Barmouth Harlech Coastal Road, seaward side. Signposted.

★★★★
HOLIDAY PARK

BH&HPA
NCC

PARC CAERELWAN
Talybont, Barmouth LL43 2AX
T: (01341) 247236
F: (01341) 247711
E: parc@porthmadog.co.uk
I: www.porthmadog.co.uk/parc/

CC: Delta, JCB, Mastercard, Switch, Visa

| 70 | | £194.00–£400.00 |

On the A496 coast road 5 miles north of Barmouth. Signposted.

BRECON, Powys Map ref 1B3

★★★★★
**TOURING &
CAMPING PARK**

BH&HPA

BRYNICH CARAVAN PARK

Brecon LD3 7SH
T: (01874) 623325
F: (01874) 623325
E: holidays@brynich.co.uk
I: www.brynich.co.uk

*Family-run, award-winning site in the Brecon Beacons National Park.
Panoramic views. Brecon town is a pleasant 30-minute walk along the canal
tow path.*

CC: Delta, JCB, Mastercard, Switch, Visa

*The caravan park is situated on the A470, 200 yards from the junction with
the A40, 2km east of Brecon. Signposted.*

50		£9.50–£12.00
20		£9.50–£12.00
60	A	£9.50–£12.00
130 touring pitches		

CAERNARFON, Gwynedd Map ref 1A1

★★★★
HOLIDAY PARK

See Ad on this page

BRYN GLOCH CARAVAN & CAMPING PARK
Betws Garmon, Caernarfon LL54 7YY
T: (01286) 650216
F: (01286) 650591
E: eurig@bryngloch.co.uk
I: www.bryngloch.co.uk

CC: Mastercard, Switch, Visa

80		£11.00
80		£11.00
80	A	£11.00
		£180.00–£350.00
160 touring pitches		

*Located on A4085 Caernarfon to Beddgelert road 5 miles from Caernarfon and 7 miles from Beddgelert.
Signposted.*

CAERNARFON continued

★★★
**TOURING &
CAMPING PARK**

BH&HPA

CWM CADNANT VALLEY
Llanberis Road, Caernarfon LL55 2DF
T: (01286) 673196
F: (01286) 675941
E: etc@cwmcadnant.co.uk
I: www.cwmcadnant.co.uk

CC: Delta, JCB, Mastercard,
Switch, Visa

32	🚐	£10.00–£14.00
6	🚲	£10.00–£14.00
31	⛺	£8.00–£12.00
69 touring pitches		

A487 to Caernarfon then A4086 for Llanberis – we are opposite the school. Signposted.

★★
**TOURING &
CAMPING PARK**

SNOWDONIA PARK BREW PUB & CAMPSITE
Waunfawr, Caernarfon LL55 4AQ
T: (01286) 650409
F: (01286) 650409
E: info@snowdonia-park.co.uk
I: www.snowdonia-park.co.uk

CC: Delta, Mastercard, Switch,
Visa

	🚐	£10.00
	🚲	£10.00
	⛺	£6.00–£8.00
32 touring pitches		

A4085 Caernarfon to Beddgelert road at Waunfawr station.

CARDIGAN, Ceredigion Map ref 1A2

★★★★★
**TOURING &
HOLIDAY PARK**

BH&HPA

CENARTH FALLS HOLIDAY PARK
Cenarth, Newcastle Emlyn SA38 9JS
T: (01239) 710345
F: (01239) 710344
E: enquiries@cenarth-holipark.co.uk
I: www.cenarth-holipark.co.uk

CC: Delta, JCB, Mastercard,
Switch, Visa

30	🚐	£13.00–£20.00
30	🚲	£13.00–£20.00
30	⛺	£13.00–£20.00
6	🏠	£150.00–£520.00
30 touring pitches		

*After 0.25 miles from Cenarth bridge turn right at park signs. Situated off A484 Cardigan-Carmarthen Road.
Signposted.*

CLARACH, Ceredigion Map ref 1A2

★★★★
**HOLIDAY, TOURING
& CAMPING PARK**

BH&HPA

GLAN Y MOR LEISURE PARK
Clarach Bay, Clarach, Aberystwyth
SY23 3DT
T: (01970) 828900
F: (01970) 828890
E: glanymor@sunbourne.co.uk
I: www. sunbourne.co.uk

CC: Amex, Delta, Diners, JCB,
Mastercard, Switch, Visa

60	🚐	£8.50–£20.00
60	🚲	£8.50–£20.00
60	⛺	£8.50–£10.00
	🏠	£149.00–£439.00

*Turn off the A487 (Aberystwyth-Machynlleth road) at Bow Street where Clarach Bay is signposted. Follow this
road to the seafront.*

COLWYN BAY, Conwy Map ref 1B1

★★★★★
TOURING PARK

BRON-Y-WENDON TOURING CARAVAN PARK

Wern Road, Llanddulas, Colwyn Bay LL22 8HG
T: (01492) 512903
F: (01492) 512903
E: bron-y-wendon@northwales-holidays.co.uk
I: www.northwales-holidays.co.uk

*Award-winning park overlooking sea and ideally situated for touring
Snowdonia, Llandudno, Chester etc. Easily accessed from A55. All pitches
have sea views. Open all year. 3 nights for the price of 2 from 1 Nov 2003-1
Mar 2004.*

CC: Visa

120	🚐	£12.00–£15.00
10	🚲	£12.00–£15.00
130 touring pitches		

*Leave the A55 at the Llanddulas junction (A547) and follow the Tourist
Information signs to the Park.*

CONFIRM YOUR BOOKING
You are advised to confirm your booking in writing.

CWMCARN, Caerphilly Map ref 1B3

★★★
TOURING &
CAMPING PARK

CWMCARN FOREST DRIVE CAMPSITE
Nantcarn Road, Cwmcarn, Newport
NP11 7FA
T: (01495) 272001
F: (01495) 271403
E: cwmcarn-vc@caerphilly.gov.uk
I: www.caerphilly.gov.uk/visiting

£7.50–£8.50
£7.50–£8.50
£5.00–£7.50

M4 jct 28, follow A467 for 7 miles to Cwncarn, follow brown tourism signs.

FISHGUARD, Pembrokeshire Map ref 1A2

★★★★
HOLIDAY, TOURING
& CAMPING PARK

DRAGON AWARD

BH&HPA

FISHGUARD BAY CARAVAN & CAMPING PARK
Garn Gelli, Fishguard SA65 9ET
T: (01348) 811415
F: (01348) 811425
E: inquiries@fishguardbay.com
I: www.fishguardbay.com

CC: Delta, Diners, Mastercard,
Switch, Visa

20 £10.50–£12.50
    £10.50–£12.50
30 £9.50–£11.50
11 £165.00–£410.00
50 touring pitches

Take A487 Cardigan Road from Fishguard, 3 miles outside Fishguard, turning on left. Signposted.

★★★★
TOURING PARK

BH&HPA

GWAUN VALE TOURING PARK
Llanychaer, Fishguard SA65 9TA
T: (01348) 874698
E: margaret.harries@talk21.com

£10.00–£11.50
£10.00–£11.50
£8.50–£10.00
30 touring pitches

From Fishguard, take B4313 for 1.5 miles. The site is on the right. Signposted.

HORTON, Swansea Map ref 3A3

★★★
TOURING &
HOLIDAY PARK

NCC

BANK FARM
Horton, Swansea SA3 1LL
T: (01792) 390228
F: (01792) 391282
E: bankfarmleisure@aol.com
I: bankfarmleisure.co.uk

CC: Amex, Delta, JCB,
Mastercard, Solo, Switch, Visa

£9.50–£18.00
£9.00–£14.00
£9.50–£18.00

End of A4118 from Swansea. Turn left for Horton.

COUNTRY CODE Always follow the Country Code ✿
Enjoy the countryside and respect its life and work ✿ Guard
against all risk of fire ✿ Fasten all gates ✿ Keep your dogs
under close control ✿ Keep to public paths across farmland
✿ Use gates and stiles to cross fences, hedges and walls ✿
Leave livestock, crops and machinery alone ✿ Take your litter
home ✿ Help to keep all water clean ✿ Protect wildlife,
plants and trees ✿ Take special care on country roads ✿
Make no unnecessary noise

LLANELLI, Carmarthenshire Map ref 1A3

★★★★★
TOURING PARK

See Ad on inside front cover

PEMBREY COUNTRY PARK CARAVAN CLUB SITE

Factory Road, Pembrey, Llanelli SA16 0EJ
T: (01554) 834369
I: www.caravanclub.co.uk

Site set in a large country park with extensive forest walks, cycle tracks, an adventure playground, miles of Blue Flag sandy beaches and beautiful surroundings. Non-members welcome.

CC: Delta, Mastercard, Solo, Switch, Visa

From M4, leave at jct 48 onto A4138. After 4 miles turn right onto A484 and continue towards Carmarthen. Within 7 miles in Pembrey Village turn right before park gates. Signposted.

125	🚐	£11.00–£20.00
125	🚍	£11.00–£20.00
125 total touring pitches		

LLANGADOG, Carmarthenshire Map ref 1B3

★★★★
**TOURING &
CAMPING PARK**

BH&HPA

ABERMARLAIS CARAVAN PARK

Llangadog SA19 9NG
T: (01550) 777868
F: (01550) 777797

A tranquil site in a beautiful woodland valley at the western end of the Brecon National Park, ideal for nature lovers and bird-watchers.

CC: Amex, Delta, Mastercard, Switch, Visa

Situated on A40, 6 miles west of Llandovery or 6 miles east of Llandeilo. Signposted.

60	🚐	£8.00
60	🚍	£8.00
28	⛺	£7.50–£8.00
88 touring pitches		

LLANGORSE, Powys Map ref 1B3

★★★★
**HOLIDAY, TOURING
& CAMPING PARK**

BH&HPA

LAKESIDE CARAVAN & CAMPING PARK
Llangorse Lake, Llangorse, Brecon LD3 7TR
T: (01874) 658226
F: (01874) 658430
E: holidays@lakeside.zx3.net
I: www.lakeside-holidays.net

CC: Amex, Delta, Mastercard, Switch, Visa

50	🚐	£7.50–£9.50
50	🚍	£7.50–£9.50
50	⛺	£7.50–£9.50
10	🏠	£150.00–£320.00
50 touring pitches		

From Abergavenny A40 to Bwlch, turn right onto B4560 to Llangorse. Head for the lake.

NEWPORT, Monmouthshire Map ref 1B3

★★★★★
**TOURING &
CAMPING PARK**

See Ad on inside front cover

TREDEGAR HOUSE COUNTRY PARK CARAVAN CLUB SITE

Tredegar House, Coedkernew, Newport NP10 8T
T: (01633) 815600
I: www.caravanclub.co.uk

High-standard site within the park, bordering one of the ornamental lakes. Ideally located just off the M4, only seven miles from the many attractions of Cardiff. Non-members welcome.

CC: Delta, Mastercard, Solo, Switch, Visa

Exit M4 at jct 28 via slip road. At roundabout turn onto A48 (signposted Tredegar House). Roundabout 0.25 miles, turn left. Next roundabout, turn left into Tredegar House. Signposted.

82	🚐	£9.50–£19.50
82	🚍	£9.50–£19.50
82 total touring pitches		

★★★★★
**TOURING &
CAMPING PARK**

See Ad on inside front cover

FRESHWATER EAST CARAVAN CLUB SITE

Freshwater East, Westhill, Lamphey, Pembroke SA71 5LN
T: (01646) 672341
I: www.caravanclub.co.uk

Situated a few minutes from a safe, sandy beach and close to 180-mile coastal path with magnificent views. If you're feeling adventurous you could visit Ireland for the day! Non-members welcome.

CC: Delta, Mastercard, Solo, Switch, Visa

Take M4 to Carmarthen, then follow signs to Pembroke. Go under railway bridge, take left onto A4139, in Lamphey continue onto B4584, after 1.75 miles turn right, sign after 0.25 miles at foot of hill. Signposted.

130	£9.50–£19.50
130	£9.50–£19.50
130 total touring pitches	

★★★★
**TOURING &
CAMPING PARK**

NANT MILL FAMILY TOURING PARK
Prestatyn LL19 9LY
T: (01745) 852360
F: (01745) 852360
E: nantmilltouring@aol.com
I: zeropointfive.co.uk/nant_mill/

East of Prestatyn town centre. On A548 coast road.

	£10.00–£13.00
	£10.00–£13.00
Å	£10.00–£13.00
150 touring pitches	

★★★★★
HOLIDAY PARK

BH&HPA

TAN Y DON CARAVAN PARK
263 Victoria Road, Prestatyn LL19 7UT   CC: Delta, Mastercard, Switch, Visa
T: (01745) 853749
F: (01745) 854147
E: parks@bancroftleisure.co.uk
I: www.parks@bancroftleisure.co.uk

Main A548 Coast road between Prestatyn and Rhyl. Near Ffrith beach.

3	£80.00–£420.00

★★★★
**HOLIDAY, TOURING
& CAMPING PARK**

BH&HPA

CAERFAI BAY CARAVAN PARK
St Davids, Haverfordwest SA62 6QT
T: (01437) 720274
F: (01437) 720577
E: info@caerfaibay.co.uk
I: www.caerfaibay.co.uk

Turn off A487 (Haverfordwest to St Davids) in St Davids at Visitor Centre. The Park is at road end, 1 mile, on the right. Signposted.

28	£8.50–£13.00
15	£7.50–£9.50
77 Å	£7.50–£9.50
5	£160.00–£360.00
120 touring pitches	

★★★
TOURING PARK

See Ad on inside front cover

LLEITHYR MEADOW CARAVAN CLUB SITE

Whitesands, St Davids, Haverfordwest SA62 6PR
T: (01437) 720401
I: www.caravanclub.co.uk

Set on a peninsula and surrounded by the Pembrokeshire Coast National Park with its wonderful walks, wild coves and sandy bays. Visit the picturesque harbour village of Solva. Non-members welcome.

CC: Delta, Mastercard, Solo, Switch, Visa

Take M4 to Carmarthen, then A40 to Haverfordwest, then A487 towards St Davids. Before entering St Davids turn right onto B4583, crossroads. Turn sharp right opposite entrance to St Davids golf club. Signposted.

120	£9.50–£19.50
120	£9.50–£19.50
120 total touring pitches	

★★★★
**TOURING &
CAMPING PARK**

See Ad on inside front cover

GOWERTON CARAVAN CLUB SITE

Pont-Y-Cob Road, Gowerton, Swansea SA4 3QP
T: (01792) 873050
I: www.caravanclub.co.uk

Safe, clean, sandy beaches, sightseeing, spectacular falls and the Brecon Beacons National park make this a perfect, all-round destination. Swansea six miles. Non-members welcome.

CC: Delta, Mastercard, Solo, Switch, Visa

Take B4296 towards Gower and then Gowerton. In 0.5 miles, 100yds after passing under railway bridge (height restriction of 11ft), turn right onto B4295. Turn after 0.5 miles. Signposted Pont-y-Cob Road.

145	🚐	£7.50–£16.50
145	🚍	£7.50–£16.50
145 total touring pitches		

★★★★
**TOURING &
CAMPING PARK**

HENLLYS FARM TOURING SITE

Towyn, Abergele LL22 9HF
T: (01745) 351208
F: (01745) 351208

Level, family-run park, close to all entertainments in Towyn. Two miles from Rhyl, but enjoying open outlook over countryside. Good base for touring.

3 miles west of Rhyl and A548. On the main road, 500 yards west of Towyn church.

🚍	£12.00–£16.00
🚐	£12.00–£15.00
▲	£12.00–£15.00
280 touring pitches	

★★★★
**TOURING &
HOLIDAY PARK**

GLYN FARM CARAVANS
Trefriw LL27 0RZ
T: (01492) 640442

28	🚐	£8.50–£10.00

B5106 Betws-y-Coed to Conway Road. Turn into car park opposite Trefriw Woollen Mills. Just off village car park, 200yds off the main road.

CHECK THE MAPS

The colour maps at the front of this guide show all the cities, towns and villages for which you will find park entries. Refer to the town index to find the page on which it is listed.

A brief guide to the main Towns and Villages offering accommodation in **Wales**

B BALA, GWYNEDD - Small market town on Bala Lake, the largest natural sheet of water in Wales. Mountain scenery, fishing, walking and boating.

BARMOUTH, GWYNEDD - Popular seaside resort at the mouth of the beautiful Mawddach estuary, on the edge of the Snowdonia National Park.

BRECON, POWYS - Market town situated at the junction of the rivers Usk and Honddu. Excellent base for exploring the Brecon Beacons National Park.

C CAERNARFON, GWYNEDD - Ancient county town famous for its magnificent and well preserved medieval castle, the birthplace of Edward I and scene of the investiture of the Prince of Wales in 1969.

F FISHGUARD, PEMBROKESHIRE - Picturesque little town perched high above its harbour. Fine cliff scenery.

L LLANELLI, CARMARTHENSHIRE - Industrial centre on the Burry inlet, with beautiful surrounding countryside. Kidwelly Castle and Wildlife and Wetlands Centre nearby.

P PEMBROKE, PEMBROKESHIRE - Historic county town, dominated by its fine old castle, birthplace of Henry VII. Remains of Monkton Priory.

S ST DAVIDS, PEMBROKESHIRE - A place of pilgrimage for over eight centuries, situated on the rugged western peninsula within easy reach of some of Britain's finest cliffs and bays. Interesting cathedral.

SWANSEA - Large seaport and modern industrial city with a university and extensive parks and gardens. Swansea is also a seaside resort and a good centre for exploring the Gower Peninsula.

DAVID BELLAMY CONSERVATION AWARDS

If you are looking for a site that's environmentally friendly look for those that have achieved the David Bellamy conservation Award. Launched in conjunction with the British Holiday & Home Parks Association, this award is given to sites which are committed to protecting and enhancing the environment – from care of the hedgerows and wildlife to recycling waste – and are members of the Association. More information about award scheme can be found at back of the guide.

Hostel Accommodation

A separate Star rating scheme has been introduced for Hostel accommodation in England. Hostel accommodation provides safe, budget-priced accommodation for young people, for families or for larger groups and includes independently owned hostels, Youth Hostels, bunkhouses and camping barns. The Star ratings have been adopted by all Youth Hostel Association (YHA) hostels in England as well as a number of independent hostels. Separate rating schemes operate in Scotland and Wales.

What standards to expect at each rating level:

★   Acceptable   ★★   Good   ★★★   Very Good
★★★★ Excellent   ★★★★★ Exceptional

Hostels

Hostels are rated from One to Five Stars and must meet minimum requirements for both provision and quality of facilities and service, including fixtures, fittings, furnishings, décor. Progressively higher levels of quality and customer care are provided for each of the Star ratings. Quite simply the more Stars, the higher the overall level of quality you can expect.

Group Hostels

Hostel style accommodation that caters solely for groups as opposed to individuals. Due to the style of accommodation full assessment of facilities is made by appointment.

Bunkhouses

Bunkhouses offer a similar style of accommodation to Hostels but usually with more limited services and facilities, usually on a self-catering basis. Bunkhouses are not Star rated but meet the same minimum
requirements as Hostels, where applicable.

Camping Barns

Camping Barns provide very simple self-catering accommodation, often referred to as 'stone tents', they have the advantage of being roomy and dry. Camping Barns are not Star rated and will be assessed as being fit for the purpose, meeting a specific minimum entry requirement.

In addition to the symbols shown inside the back cover flap, the following also appear:

- Children welcome
- Lounge
- Central heating
- Non smokers only
- Cooking facilities
- Hairdryer
- Conference facilities
- Tea & coffee making facilities
- Ground floor bedroom
- Vegetarians catered for
- Building of historic interest
- Coach parties accepted

GILSLAND, Cumbria Map ref 6B2

★★★★
Hostel

BIRDOSWALD ROMAN FORT AND THE HADRIAN'S WALL STUDY CENTRE
Gilsland, Brampton CA8 7DD
T: (016977) 47602
F: (016977) 47605
E: birdoswald@dial.pipex.com
I: birdoswaldromanfort.org

Bedrooms:
7 dormitories
Total no. of beds: 40
Bathrooms: 1 en suite,
8 public
Groups only
Max group size: 40

Breakfast available
Lunch available
Evening meal available
Payment: Mastercard,
Visa

Per person per night
B&B £17.00–£21.00

OPEN All Year

A unique opportunity to stay within the walls of Birdoswald Roman Fort. Homely farmhouse accommodation provides a high quality of residential experience. Advance bookings only.

LIVERPOOL, Merseyside Map ref 5A2 *Tourist Information Centre Tel: 0906 680 6886*

★★★
Hostel

Award winning tourist hostel in a prime city centre location in the heart of Liverpool. Former Victorian warehouse, full of character with modern facilities excelling in friendly customer service and information. Dormitories all en suite for 2, 4, 6, 8 and 10 people, clean bedding, TV lounge, internet café, kitchen, no curfew, 24 hours access.

THE INTERNATIONAL INN

4 South Hunter Street, off Hardman Street, Liverpool L1 9JG
T: (0151) 709 8135
F: (0151) 709 8135
E: info@internationalinn.co.uk
I: www.internationalinn.co.uk

Bedrooms: 4 twin,
7 quads, 8 dormitories
Total no. of beds: 100
Bathrooms: 19 en
suite, 1 public
Max group size: 100

Breakfast available
Lunch available
Evening meal
available
Payment: Mastercard,
Visa, American
Express, Switch, Delta,
JCB, Solo

Prices include free tea, coffee and toast 24 hours.

Per person per night
Bed only £15.00–
£20.00

OPEN All Year

MANCHESTER, Greater Manchester Map ref 5B1 *Tourist Information Centre Tel: (0161) 234 3157/(0161) 234 3158*

★★★
Hostel

MANCHESTER YHA
Potato Wharf, Castlefield,
Manchester M3 4NB
T: 08707 705950
F: 08707 705951
E: manchester@yha.org.uk
I: www.yha.org.uk

Bedrooms: 30 quads,
4 dormitories
Total no. of beds: 144
Bathrooms: 34 en suite
Max group size: 144

Evening meal available
Payment: Mastercard,
Visa, American Express,
Switch, Delta, JCB, Solo

Per person per night
B&B £14.00–£19.00

OPEN All Year

Modern city youth hostel. Open 24 hours per day, close to shops, attractions and night life. 34 rooms all en suite with 4-6 beds.

OXFORD, Oxfordshire Map ref 3C1 *Tourist Information Centre Tel: (01865) 726871*

★★★★
Hostel

OXFORD YHA
2A Botley Road, Oxford OX2 0AB
T: (01865) 727275
F: (01865) 251182
E: oxford@yha.org.uk
I: www.yha.org.uk

Bedrooms:
9 doubles/twin, 10 triples,
22 multi-share rooms
Total no. of beds: 187
Bathrooms: 41 en suite,
4 public
Max group size: 100

Breakfast available
Evening meal available
Payment: Mastercard,
Visa, American Express,
Switch, Delta, Solo

Per person per night
B&B £14.50–£23.00

OPEN All Year

Opened May 2001, purpose-built YHA offering clean, comfortable accommodation for all ages. All bedrooms en suite. Family rooms available. Close to dreaming spires of Oxford.

www.visitengland.com

What makes the perfect break? Big city buzz or peaceful country panoramas? Take a fresh look at England and you may be surprised that everything is here on your very own doorstep. Where will you go? Make up your own mind and enjoy England in all its diversity.

Experience....remember paddling on sandy beaches, playing Poohsticks in the forest, picnics at open-air concerts, tea-rooms offering home-made cakes........

Discover....make your own journey of discovery through England's cultural delights: surprising contrasts between old and new, traditional and trend-setting, time-honoured and contemporary........

Explore....while you're reading this someone is drinking in lungfuls of fresh air on a hill-side with heart-stopping views or wandering through the maze that can be the garden of a stately home or tugging on the sails of a boat skimming across a lake....

Relax....no rush to do anything or be anywhere, time to immerse yourself in your favourite book by a roaring log fire or glide from a soothing massage to a refreshing facial, ease away the tension......

To enjoy England, visitengland.com

Holiday Villages

VisitBritain has a separate rating scheme of One to Five Stars for Holiday Villages. Holiday Villages usually comprise a variety of types of accommodation, with the majority provided in custom built rooms (e.g. chalets, hotel rooms). A range of facilities and activities are also available which may, or may not, be included in the tariff. Holiday Villages meet requirements for both the provision and quality of facilities and services, including fixtures, fittings, furnishings, décor. Progressively higher levels of quality and customer care are provided for each of the Star ratings. Quite simply, the more Stars, the higher the overall level of quality you can expect.

What standards to expect at each rating level:

★ Acceptable ★★ Good ★★★ Very Good
★★★★ Excellent ★★★★★ Exceptional

In addition to the symbols shown inside the back cover flap, the following also appear:

🐎 Children welcome 🔳 Linen provided free of charge 🏋 Gym

🗝 Hairdryer ✂ Non smoking units Ⓜ Mid-week breaks available

🖵 Microwave ▥ Central heating ⓢ Weekends/offseason mid-week bookings available

🍸 Conference Facilities

BREAN SANDS, Somerset Map ref 2D1 *Tourist Information Centre Tel: (01278) 787852*

★★★

BH&HPA

HOLIDAY RESORT UNITY

Coast Road, Brean Sands,
Burnham on Sea, TA8 2RB
T: 0845 230 3350 F: 0845 230 3351
E: admin@hru.co.uk
W: www.hru.co.uk

Touring pitches: 570
Self-Catering units: 123

OPEN Feb – Nov
Payment: Visa,
Mastercard, Switch, Delta,
Solo, Travellers Cheques,
Euros

Per unit per week
Low Season
£210 – £385
High Season
£322 – £665

Relax and enjoy a multitude of facilities. Indoor and outdoor pools with waterslides, fun park with log flume and rollercoasters. Golf course, fishing, ten pin bowling. Evening entertainment for families and adults. Five mile beach and dunes 400yds. Themed breaks and special offers for over 50's and families – book early!
Fri–Mon break from £135, Mon–Fri break from £100. Car and touring caravan from £6pn, Motor home from £5pn.
From M5 jct 22, follow signs for Berrow and Brean. Site on right, 4.5 miles from M5.

🐎 🛝🏊👤🍴🔥🎯👶🐾🏐✕📺📻🍴🚴⛳🎣🏇🚣♪ 🐴🎵▥ 🖵🗝✂🔳🏋ⓢⓂ🍸

2004

Where to Stay

The official and best selling guides,
offering the reassurance of quality assured accommodation

Hotels, Townhouses
and Travel
Accommodation
in England 2004
£10.99

Guesthouses, Bed &
Breakfast, Farmhouses,
Inns and Campus
Accommodation
in England 2004
£11.99

Self-Catering
Holiday Homes
in England 2004
£10.99

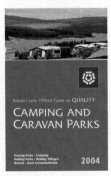

Camping & Caravan Parks, Hostels,
Holiday Villages and Boat
Accommodation in Britain 2004
£6.99

Somewhere Special
in England 2004
£8.99

Look out also for:
SOMEWHERE SPECIAL
IN ENGLAND 2004

Accommodation
achieving the highest
standards in facilities
and quality of service -
the perfect guide for the
discerning traveller.

**NOW ALSO FEATURING
SELF-CATERING
ACCOMMODATION**

The guides include

- Accommodation entries packed with information • Full colour maps
- Places to visit • Tourist Information Centres

INFORMATIVE • EASY TO USE • GREAT VALUE FOR MONEY

From all good bookshops or by mail order from the:
VisitBritain Fulfilment Centre,
C/o Westex Ltd, 7 St Andrews Way, Devons Road, Bromley-by-Bow, London E3 3PA
Tel: 0870 606 7204 Fax: 020 8563 3289 Email: fulfilment@visitbritain.org

Information

Contents

Useful **Addresses**

ADRESSES UTILES
NÜTZLICHE ANSCHRIFTEN
NUTTIGE ADRESSEN
INDIRIZZI UTILI

AUTOMOBILE ASSOCIATION

Routes can be prepared, avoiding unsuitable routes for caravans and steep gradients if specified. Please write to: AA Routes, Lambert House, Stockport Road, Cheadle, Cheshire SK8 2DY.
Tel: 08705 500 600
www.theaa.co.uk

BRITISH HOLIDAY & HOME PARKS ASSOCIATION

Chichester House, 6 Pullman Court,
Great Western Road, Gloucester GL1 3ND
Enquiries and brochure requests (01452) 526911
Fax: (01452) 508508

Professional UK park owners are represented by the British Holiday & Home Parks Association. Almost 2000 parks are in membership, and each year welcome millions of visitors seeking quality surroundings in which to enjoy a good value stay.

Parks provide caravan holiday homes and lodges for hire, and pitches for your own touring caravan, motorhome or tent. On many, you can opt to buy your own holiday home.

A major strength of the UK's park industry is its diversity. Whatever your idea of holiday pleasure, there's sure to be a park which can provide it. If your preference is for a quiet, peaceful holiday in tranquil rural surroundings, you'll find many idyllic locations.

Alternatively, many parks are to be found at our most popular resorts – and reflect the holiday atmosphere with plenty of entertainment and leisure facilities. And for more adventurous families, parks often provide excellent bases from which to enjoy outdoor activities.

Literature available from BH&HPA (call 01452 526911) includes a guide to over 430 parks which have this year achieved the David Bellamy Conservation Award for environmental excellence.

THE CAMPING AND CARAVANNING CLUB

The Camping & Caravanning Club
Greenfields House, Westwood Way, Coventry CV4 8JH
Tel: 024 7669 4995 Fax: 024 7669 4886
www.campingandcaravanningclub.co.uk

We have over 90 sites covering the length and breath of the country in locations that will take your breath away.

With excellent grades from VisitBritain, you are guaranteed quality facilities. We also have a legendary reputation for cleanliness, as well as great value for money. All our guests receive a warm and friendly welcome from our Holiday Site Managers.

The majority of our sites are open to non-members, with special deals available for families, backpackers and reduced site fees if you are 55 or over. Overseas visitors are also catered for with a go as you please Freedom UK Pass or Temporary Overseas Membership.

For more details why not send for your free guide to the Camping and Caravanning Club Sites.
Tel: 024 7685 6797.

THE CARAVAN CLUB

East Grinstead House, East Grinstead,
West Sussex RH19 1UA
Tel: (01342) 326944 Fax: (01342) 410258
www.caravanclub.co.uk

The Caravan Club offers over 200 sites in the United Kingdom and Ireland. These include city locations such as London, Edinburgh, York and Chester, plus sites near leading heritage attractions such as Longleat, Sandringham, Chatsworth and Blenheim Palace. A further 20 are in National Parks. Over 90% of pitches have an electric hook-up point and most sites offer emptying points for motor caravanners. Foreign visitors are welcomed and holders of International Camping Cards (CCI's) qualify for pitch discounts on selected sites. Non member caravanners pay a supplement of £5 per pitch per night, refunded against the membership fee (£35 in 2003) which adds access to a further 3000 small 5-van sites. A 700-page Sites Directory and UK Location Map gives clear directions whilst towing. Tent campers are welcome on 70 sites.

FORESTRY COMMISSION

231 Corstorphine Road, Edinburgh EH12 7AT.
Tel: 0845 FORESTS (367 3787)
www.forestry.gov.uk

Forest Holidays, run by Forest Enterprise, an executive agency of the Forestry Commission, have almost 30 camping and caravan sites in the scenic forest locations throughout the UK. Choose from the Scottish Highlands, the New Forest, Snowdonia National Park, the Forest of Dean, or the banks of Loch Lomond. Some sites are open all year.

Advance bookings accepted for many sites. Dogs welcome on most sites. For a unique forest experience, call Forest Holidays for a brochure on
Tel: (0131) 314 6505.

THE MOTOR CARAVANNERS' CLUB LTD

22 Evelyn Close, Twickenham TW2 7BN
Tel: (020) 8893 3883 Fax: (020) 8893 8324
Email: info@motorcaravanners.org.uk
www.motorcaravanners.org.uk

The Motor Caravanners' Club is authorised to issue the Camping Card International (CCI). It also produces a monthly magazine, 'Motor Caravanner' for all members.

Standards for
Caravan and Camping Parks

NORMES REQUISES POUR LES TERRAINS DE CAMPING ET POUR CARAVANES
REGELN FÜR CAMPING- UND CARAVANPLÄTZE
AAN CARAVAN EN CAMPINGPARKEN GESTELDE EISEN
NORME IMPOSTE AI CAMPEGGI PER TENDE E ROULOTTES

These standards should be read in conjunction, where applicable, with the Caravan Sites and Control of Development Act 1960, and, where applicable, the Public Health Act 1936.

A THE PARK

1   The park must have planning permission and site licence readily available, if applicable.

2   Facilities must be clean and in wholesome condition.

3   The park must be well managed and maintained and kept in a clean and presentable manner and attention paid to the road-side sign and entrance.

4   The park must have reception arrangements at appropriate times where advice and assistance can be obtained if necessary.

5   The park operator must be capable of arranging or carrying out repairs to caravans and equipment.

6   Supplies of gas and replacement bottles together with essential (where applicable) spares must be available at all reasonable times.

7   Where provided, all toilet blocks and washing facilities must be lit internally and externally during the hours of darkness, whilst the park is open.

8   All shower blocks must have internal lighting.

9   Where washing and/or shower facilities are provided, an adequate supply of hot and cold water must be available at all reasonable times.

10 A proprietary first-aid kit must be readily available. Emergency notices must be prominently displayed giving details and location of park, contact, telephone, doctor, fire service, local hospital and other essential services.

11 Parks open in the shoulder season (Oct-Mar) must provide adequate heating in at least one toilet, washing and shower facility (both male and female).

12 The park owner must have fire fighting equipment and notices which conform with the conditions of the site licence.

13 All electricity installations on the park both internally and externally must have the appropriate safety certification.

14 Parks providing pitches for touring units must provide facilities for chemical disposal unless specifically prohibited by local authorities.

15 Lighting should be appropriate to the size and type of park.

16 Adequate provision to be made for refuse disposal.

17 The intended use of facilities must be indicated by signage.

NB: Parks providing NO toilet facilities make this clear in all promotional literature and advertising.

B VISITOR INFORMATION

The booking form must be accompanied by details of the park, stating clearly:

1   A description of the park and its amenities, e.g:

a) Whether cars park by caravans or in a car park.

b) Whether or not pets are allowed.

c) Details of shower and bath facilities.

d) Whether a grocery shop is on site or the distance to nearest shop.

e) Licensed bar.

f) Laundry facilities.

g) Dancing, entertainments.

h) Television room.

i) Sports facilities.

j) Public transport to and from park.

k) Distance from sea and accessibility to beach (coastal parks only).

2   The prices for the pitch for the period booked and details of any further charges, e.g. electricity, gas, showers, awnings as well as any optional charges, e.g. holiday insurance.

Note: If Value Added Tax (VAT) is not included in the total charge, this must be clearly stated.

3   Any special conditions for payment of deposits or balance.

4   Wherever possible, a map showing the location of the park and its proximity to main centres and attractions.

5   If bookings in advance are necessary during the summer months.

C CARAVAN HOLIDAY HOMES AND CHALETS

1 All caravans must be of proprietary make.

2 All caravans/chalets must be in good state of internal and external repair and decoration with no internal dampness.

3 The caravans/chalets must not be occupied by more than the number of persons for which they are designed by the manufacturer ie four persons in a four-berth.

4 It is the park operator's responsibility to ensure that all caravans offered for hire on the park have insurance cover for public liability as letting caravans and comply with the Consumer Protection Act.

5 Equipment must be provided as listed opposite. An inventory of this equipment must be available for each caravan/chalet.

6 All caravans/chalets must have adequate storage space for luggage and food for the maximum number of occupants.

7 All doors, windows, skylights and all ventilation in the caravan/chalet must function correctly. All windows must be properly fitted with opaque curtains or blinds.

8 All caravans/chalets must have adequate internal lighting.

9 All caravans/chalets must be thoroughly cleaned and checked before every letting and equipment maintained and replaced as necessary.

10 Where linen is provided it must be changed on each change of occupier and as appropriate during lets of two weeks or more. All mattresses must be in sound condition.

11 The sink and its waste pipe must be in sound condition with a draining board. A fixed impervious work top for food preparation must be provided.

12 All caravans/chalets must have a fridge and a cooker with at least two boiling rings. The cooker must be in a sound and clean condition and functioning properly.

13 All caravans/chalets must have adequate heating.

14 All caravans must have safe steps or equivalent, to each external door.

15 All caravans must have a supply of hot and cold water.

16 All caravan holiday homes must be fully serviced with water, drainage, mains WC, shower and/or bath.

D INVENTORY OF EQUIPMENT FOR CARAVAN HOLIDAY-HOMES AND CHALETS

The accommodation should contain the following:

- **One per caravan/chalet**
  Ladle
  Grater
  Plastic/wooden spoon
  Potato masher
  Cleaning agents
  Carpet sweeper or vacuum available
  Toilet brush and holder, Toilet roll and holder
  Kettle
  Teapot
  Saucepan and lid (large, medium, small)
  Frying pan
  Colander
  Oven roasting tray
  Casserole dish
  Carving knife and fork
  Bread knife
  Bread/cake container
  Bread/chopping board
  Fish slice
  Small vegetable knife
  Tin opener
  Corkscrew/bottle opener
  Potato peeler
  Large fruit dish
  Butter dish
  Sugar bowl
  Tray
  Milk jug
  Mixing bowl or basin
  Bread/cake plate
  Condiment set (two-piece)
  Washing-up bowl
  Dustpan and brush
  Broom
  Floor cloth
  Pot scourer/dish mop
  Bucket
  Mirror
  Doormat
  Covered kitchen refuse container
  Fire extinguisher/blanket
  Smoke detector

- **Two per caravan/chalet**
  Table spoons
  Dusters
  Ash trays

- **Per bed**
  Three blankets or one continental quilt and cover (for winter lettings, or letting very early or late in the season the scale of bedding to be increased and adequate heating provided)
  one pillow per person

- **One per person**
  Knife (table and dessert)
  Fork (table and dessert)
  Spoon (dessert and tea)
  Plate (large and small)
  Tea cup and saucer
  Cereal/soup plate
  Tumbler
  Egg cup

- **Four per person**
  Coat-hangers

E INFORMATION FOR HIRERS

The booking form should be accompanied by details of the park and caravan(s)/chalet(s) stating clearly:

1 The accommodation size (length and width) of the caravan and the number of berths. This shall not exceed the maximum number of berths as defined by the manufacturer.

2 Whether caravans are connected to:
Mains water
Mains drainage
Mains sewerage
Electricity (stating voltage)
Piped gas (stating LPG or Natural)

3 Type of lighting: Electricity or Gas

4 Type of cooking: Electricity or Gas

5 A full description of park and its amenities.

6 Wherever possible a map showing the location of the park and its proximity to main centres and attractions.

7 The charges for the accommodation/pitch for the period booked and details of any further additional charges, for example, electricity, gas, showers etc, as well as any optional charges, eg holiday insurance.

Note: If VAT is payable it must be included in the quoted price.

F THE CARAVAN PARKS STANDARD FOR GUESTS WITH DISABILITIES

The National Accessible Scheme is operated by VisitBritain and the national and regional tourist boards throughout Britain. They assess places to stay that provide accommodation for wheelchair users or others who may have difficulty walking.
The tourist organisations recognise three categories of accessibility:

 CATEGORY 1   Accessible to a wheelchair user travelling independently.

 CATEGORY 2   Accessible to a wheelchair user travelling with assistance.

 CATEGORY 3   Accessible to a wheelchair user able to walk a few paces and up a maximum of 3 steps.

For holiday home parks, the rating will depend upon access to reception, route to the caravan, food shop and telephone (where provided), and the holiday home itself.

For touring/camping parks, it will depend upon access to reception, routes to pitches, food shop and telephone (where provided), toilet and washing facilities.

Please contact individual park operators for more detailed information you may require.

A list of parks offering accessible accommodation featured in this guide can be found on page 237.

CODE OF CONDUCT & CONDITIONS FOR PARTICIPATION FOR CARAVAN & CAMPING PARKS

In addition to fulfilling its statutory obligations, including having applied for a certificate under the Fire Precautions Act 1971 (if applicable) and holding public liability insurance, and ensuring that all caravan holiday homes/chalets for hire and the park and all buildings and facilities thereon, the fixtures, furnishings, fittings and décor are maintained in sound and clean condition and are fit for the purposes intended, the management undertakes to observe the following code of conduct:

- To ensure high standards of courtesy and cleanliness; catering and service appropriate to the type of park.

- To describe to all visitors and prospective visitors the amenities, facilities and services provided by the park and/or caravan holiday homes/chalets whether by advertisement, brochure, word of mouth or other means.

- To allow visitors to see the park or caravan holiday homes/chalets for hire, if requested, before booking.

- To present grading awards and/or any other national tourist board awards unambiguously.

- To make clear to visitors exactly what is included in prices quoted for the park or caravan holiday homes/chalets, meals and refreshments, including service charge, taxes and other surcharges. Details of charges, if any, for heating or for additional services or facilities available should also be made clear.

- To adhere to, and not to exceed, prices current at time of occupation for caravan holiday homes/chalets or other services.

- To advise visitors at the time of booking, and subsequently of any change, if the caravan holiday home/chalet or pitch offered is in a different location or on another park, and to indicate the location of this and any difference in comfort and amenities.

- To give each visitor, on request, details of payments due and a receipt if required.

- To advise visitors at the time of booking of the charges that might be incurred if the booking is subsequently cancelled.

- To deal promptly and courteously with all visitors and prospective visitors, including enquiries, requests, reservations, correspondence and complaints.

- To allow a National Tourist Board representative reasonable access to the park and/or caravan holiday homes/chalet whether by prior appointment or on an unannounced assessment, to confirm that the Code of Conduct is being observed and that the appropriate quality standard is being maintained.

- The operator must comply with the provision of the caravan industry Codes of Practice.

CODE OF CONDUCT & CONDITIONS FOR PARTICIPATION FOR HOSTELS & HOLIDAY VILLAGES

The operator/manager is required to observe the following Code of Conduct:

- To maintain standards of guest care, cleanliness, and service appropriate to the type of establishment;

- To describe accurately in any advertisement, brochure, or other printed or electronic media, the facilities and services provided;

- To make clear to visitors exactly what is included in all prices quoted for accommodation, including taxes, and any other surcharges. Details of Charges for additional services/facilities should also be made clear;

- To give a clear statement of the policy on cancellations to guests at the time of booking i.e. by telephone, fax, email as well as information given in a printed format;

- To adhere to, and not to exceed prices quoted at the time of booking for accommodation and other services;

- To advise visitors at the time of booking, and subsequently of any change, if the accommodation offered is in an unconnected annexe or similar, and to indicate the location of such accommodation and any difference in comfort and/or amenities from accommodation in the establishment;

- To give each visitor, on request, details of payments due and a receipt, if required;

- To deal promptly and courteously with all enquiries, requests, bookings and correspondence from visitors;

- Ensure complaint handling procedures are in place and that complaints received are investigated promptly and courteously and that the outcome is communicated to the visitor;

- To give due consideration to the requirements of visitors with special needs, and to make suitable provision where applicable;

- To provide public liability insurance or comparable arrangement and to comply with applicable planning, safety and other statutory requirements;

- To allow a VisitBriatin representative reasonable access to the establishment, on request, to confirm the Code of Conduct is being observed.

Tourist INFORMATION Centres

When it comes to your next England break, the first stage of your journey could be closer than you think. You've probably got a tourist information centre nearby which is there to serve the local community - as well as visitors. Knowledgeable staff will be happy to help you, wherever you're heading.

Many tourist information centres can provide you with maps and guides, and often it's possible to book accommodation and travel tickets too.

Across the country, there are more than 550 TICs. You'll find the address of your nearest centre in your local phone book.

A selection of events in **England**

MANIFESTATIONS EN ANGLETERRE EN 2004
VERANSTALTUNGEN IN ENGLAND 2004
EVENEMENTEN IN ENGELAND IN 2004
CALENDARIO DEGLI AVVENIMENTI IN INGHILTERRA NEL 2004

This is a selection of the many cultural, sporting and other events that will be taking place throughout England during 2004. Please note, as changes often occur after press date, it is advisable to confirm the date and location before travelling.

- Vous trouverez ci-dessous un choix de manifestations devant se dérouler en Angleterre dans le courant de l'année. Etant donné que des modifications sont susceptibles de survenir après la date de mise sous presse, nous vous conseillons de vous faire confirmer, une fois arrivé en Angleterre, les reseignements donnés dans ce guide auprès du Centre d'Information Touristique de la région où vous séjournez.

- Nachstehend finden Sie eine Auswahl der 2004 in England stattfindenden Veranstaltungen. Da nach Redaktionsschluß oft Änderungen vorkommen, ist es ratsam, sich die Angaben bei Ihrer Ankunft in England vom jeweiligen Tourist Information Centre bestätigen zu lassen.

- Hieronder vindt u een keuze uit de evenementen die er het komende jaar in Engeland zullen plaatsvinden. Eventuele veranderingen vinden vaak pas na de persdatum plaats. Het is daarom raadzaam de gegeven informatie na aankomst in Engeland bij het plaatselijke Toeristen Informatie Bureau te controleren.

- Riportiamo una selezione degli avvenimenti che si svolgeranno in Inghilterra nel corso dell'anno prossimo. Dal momento che dopo la data di stampa si verificano spesso dei cambiamenti, si consiglia di verificare l'esattezza delle informazioni riportate in questa guida rivolgendosi, dopo l'arrivo in Inghilterra, al Tourist Information Centre del luogo.

* Provisional/date not confirmed at time of going to press.

JANUARY

11 Jan
LANCASTER OLD CALENDAR WALKS - NEW YEAR'S EVE
John O'Gaunt Gateway
Lancaster Castle, Lancaster,
Lancashire
Tel: (01524) 32878
www.lancaster.gov.uk

17 Jan – 18 Jan
PIGEON RACING: BRITISH HOMING WORLD SHOW OF THE YEAR
Winter Gardens, Opera House and Empress Ballroom
Church Street, Blackpool, Lancashire
Tel: (01452) 713529
Bookings: (01253) 292029
www.pigeonracing.com

18 Jan
ANTIQUE AND COLLECTORS' FAIR
Alexandra Palace and Park
Alexandra Palace Way,
Wood Green, London
Tel: (020) 8883 7061
www.allypally-uk.com

25 Jan
CHARLES I COMMEMORATION
Banqueting House
Whitehall, London
Tel: (01430) 430695

25 Jan
CHINESE NEW YEAR CELEBRATIONS
Gerrard Street, Leicester Square and Trafalgar Square
London
www.chinatownchinese.com

25 Jan – 26 Jan
THE CHESHIRE AND LANCASHIRE WEDDING SHOW
Tatton Park (NT)
Knutsford, Cheshire
Tel: (01625) 534400
Bookings: (01625) 534400

29 Jan – 8 Feb
WAKEFIELD RHUBARB TRAIL AND FESTIVAL OF RHUBARB
Various venues
Wakefield, West Yorkshire
Tel: (01924) 305911
Bookings: (01924) 305911
www.wakefield.gov.uk

FEBRUARY

1 Feb – 28 Feb
WALSINGHAM ABBEY SNOWDROP WALKS
Walsingham Abbey Grounds
Little Walsingham, Walsingham,
Norfolk
Tel: (01328) 820259

1 Feb – 29 Feb*
JORVIK VIKING FESTIVAL – JOLABLOT 2004
Various venues throughout York
Tel: (01904) 643211
Bookings: (01904) 543402
www.vikingjorvik.com

6 Feb – 8 Feb
BIC WEDDING EXHIBITION
Bournemouth International Centre
Exeter Road, Bournemouth, Dorset
Tel: (01202) 456501
www.bic.co.uk

14 Feb – 28 Feb
KING'S LYNN MART
TUESDAY MARKET PLACE
King's Lynn, Norfolk
Tel: (01508) 471772

20 Feb – 21 Feb
RALLYE SUNSEEKER
Various Venues
Bournemouth
Tel: (020) 8773 3404
Bookings: (020) 8773 3404
www.rallyesunseeker.co.uk

28 Feb – 6 Mar
BEDFORDSHIRE FESTIVAL OF MUSIC, SPEECH AND DRAMA
Corn Exchange
St Paul's Square, Bedford
Tel: (01234) 354211

MARCH

2 Mar – 7 Mar
FINE ART AND ANTIQUES FAIR
Olympia
Hammersmith Road, London
Tel: 0870 736 3105
Bookings: 0870 739 31054

4 Mar – 7 Mar
CRUFTS 2004
National Exhibition Centre
Birmingham, West Midlands
Tel: (020) 7518 1069
Bookings: 0870 909 4133
www.crufts.org.uk

7 Mar – 4 Apr
LAMBING SUNDAY AND SPRING BULB DAYS
Kentwell Hall
Long Melford, Sudbury
Tel: (01787) 310207
Bookings: (01787) 310207
www.kentwell.co.uk

10 Mar – 4 Apr
IDEAL HOME SHOW
Earls Court Exhibition Centre
Warwick Road, London
Tel: 0870 606 6080
Bookings: 0870 606 6080

14 Mar
ANTIQUE AND COLLECTORS' FAIR
Alexandra Palace and Park
Alexandra Palace Way, Wood Green,
London
Tel: (020) 8883 7061
www.allypally-uk.com

14 Mar
BESSON NATIONAL BRASS BAND CHAMPIONSHIPS
Winter Gardens, Opera House and Empress Ballroom
Church Street, Blackpool, Lancashire
Tel: (0161) 707 3638

16 Mar – 18 Mar
CHELTENHAM RACING FESTIVAL
Cheltenham Racecourse
Prestbury Park, Cheltenham,
Gloucestershire
Tel: (01242) 513014
Bookings: (01242) 226226
www.cheltenham.co.uk

20 Mar – 21 Mar
AMBLESIDE DAFFODIL AND
SPRING FLOWER SHOW
The Kelsick Centre
St Mary's Lane, Ambleside, Cumbria
Tel: (015394) 32252
www.ambleside-show.org.uk

20 Mar – 21 Mar
THE SHIRE HORSE SOCIETY
SPRING SHOW
East of England Showground
Alwalton, Peterborough,
Tel: (01733) 234451
Bookings: (01733) 234451
www.eastofengland.co.uk

26 Mar – 4 Apr*
ULVERSTON WALKING FESTIVAL
Various Venues, Ulverston, Cumbria
Tel: (01229) 580640
www.ulverston-
festivals.fsnet.co.uk/walking.htm

27 Mar – 28 Mar
THRIPLOW DAFFODIL WEEKEND
Various Venues
Thriplow, Royston, Hertfordshire
Tel: (01763) 208538
www.thriplow.org.uk

28 Mar
OXFORD AND CAMBRIDGE
BOAT RACE
River Thames
London
Tel: (020) 7611 3500
www.theboatrace.org

APRIL

9 Apr
MIDDLEHAM STABLES
OPEN EVENT
Middleham Key Centre, Park Lane,
Middleham, Leyburn, North Yorkshire
Tel: (01969) 624500
Bookings: (01969) 624502
www.middlehamstablesopenevent.co.uk

9 Apr – 12 Apr
BLICKLING CRAFT SHOW
National Trust: Blickling Hall
Blickling, Norwich
Tel: (01263) 734711
www.paston.co.uk/easternevents

9 Apr – 12 Apr
GREAT EASTER EGG HUNT QUIZ
AND RE-CREATION OF TUDOR LIFE
Kentwell Hall
Long Melford, Sudbury
Tel: (01787) 310207
Bookings: (01787) 310207
www.kentwell.co.uk

10 Apr – 11 Apr*
GATESHEAD SPRING
FLOWER SHOW
Gateshead Central Nurseries
Whickham Highway, Lobley Hill,
Gateshead, Tyne and Wear
Tel: (0191) 433 3838
Bookings: (0191) 433 3838

12 Apr
LONDON HARNESS
HORSE PARADE
Battersea Park
London
Tel: (01737) 646132

12 Apr
MORRIS DANCING ON EASTER
MONDAY
Various Venues
Norfolk
Tel: (01553) 768930
www.thekingsmorris.co.uk

15 Apr – 18 Apr
BRITISH OPEN SHOW JUMPING
CHAMPIONSHIPS
Hallam FM Arena
Broughton Lane, Sheffield
Tel: (0114) 256 5656
Bookings: (0114) 256 5656
www.hallamfmarena.co.uk

18 Apr
FLORA LONDON MARATHON
Greenwich Park to The Mall
London
Tel: (020) 7902 0199
www.london-marathon.co.uk

22 Apr – 25 Apr
HARROGATE SPRING
FLOWER SHOW
Great Yorkshire Showground
Harrogate, North Yorkshire
Tel: (01423) 561049
Bookings: (01423) 561049
www.flowershow.org.uk

29 Apr – 3 May*
CHELTENHAM INTERNATIONAL
JAZZ FESTIVAL
Various venues throughout
Cheltenham, Gloucestershire
Tel: (01242) 775888
Bookings: (01242) 227979
www.cheltenhamfestivals.co.uk

MAY

1 May – 3 May*
SWEEPS FESTIVAL
Various Venues
Rochester, Kent
Tel: (01634) 843666
www.medway.gov.uk/tourism

1 May – 23 May
BRIGHTON FESTIVAL
Various Venues
Brighton
Tel: (01273) 700747
Bookings: (01273) 709709
www.brighton-festival.org.uk

8 May
HELSTON FLORA DAY
Around Streets of Helston
Helston, Cornwall
Tel: (01326) 572082

9 May
ANTIQUE AND COLLECTORS' FAIR
Alexandra Palace and Park
Alexandra Palace Way, Wood Green,
London
Tel: (020) 8883 7061
www.allypally-uk.com

16 May 2004
NORTHUMBRIAN WATER
UNIVERSITY BOAT RACE
River Tyne
Quayside, Newcastle upon Tyne
Tel: (0191) 433 3820
www.gateshead.gov.uk

16 May – 17 May
INTERNATIONAL KITE FESTIVAL
Lower Promenade
Kingsway, Cleethorpes, North East
Lincolnshire
Tel: (01472) 323352
www.nelincsevents.co.uk

20 May – 22 May
DEVON COUNTY SHOW
Westpoint Exhibition Centre
Devon County Showground,
Clyst St Mary, Exeter, Devon
Tel: (01392) 446000
Bookings: (01392) 446000

25 May – 28 May
CHELSEA FLOWER SHOW
Royal Hospital Chelsea
Royal Hospital Road, Chelsea, London
Tel: (020) 7834 4333
Bookings: 0870 9063781
www.rhs.org.uk

27 May – 6 Jun*
BRITISH INTERNATIONAL MOTOR
SHOW LIVE
National Exhibition Centre
Birmingham, West Midlands
Tel: (020) 7235 7000
www.motorshowlive.com

28 May – 13 Jun
BATH FRINGE FESTIVAL
Various Venues
Bath
Tel: (01225) 480079
www.bathfringe.co.uk

29 May – 31 May
CHATHAM NAVY DAYS
The Historic Dockyard Chatham
Chatham, Kent
Tel: (01634) 823800
Bookings: (01634) 403868
www.chdt.org.uk

31 May*
NORTHUMBERLAND COUNTY
SHOW
Tynedale Park
Corbridge, Northumberland
Tel: (01697) 747848
Bookings: (01749) 813899
www.northcountyshow.co.uk

JUNE

Jun*
RACING AT ASCOT:
THE ROYAL MEETING
Ascot Racecourse
Ascot, Berkshire
Tel: (01344) 876876
Bookings: (01344) 876876
www.ascot.co.uk

Jun*
THE MERSEY RIVER FESTIVAL
The Albert Dock
Suite 22, Edward Pavilion, Albert
Dock, Liverpool, Merseyside
Tel: (0151) 233 3007

Jun*
TROOPING THE COLOUR – THE
QUEEN'S BIRTHDAY PARADE
Horse Guards Parade
London
Tel: (020) 7414 2479
Bookings: (020) 7414 2479

* Provisional/date not confirmed at time of going to press.

2 Jun – 5 Jun
THE ROYAL BATH AND WEST SHOW
The Royal Bath and West Showground
Shepton Mallet, Somerset
Tel: (01749) 822200
Bookings: (01749) 822200
www.bathandwest.co.uk

4 Jun*
OAKS AND CORONATION CUP HORSE RACE MEETING
Epsom Downs Racecourse
Epsom Downs, Epsom, Surrey
Tel: (01372) 470047
Bookings: (01372) 470047
www.epsomderby.co.uk

4 Jun – 6 Jun
HOLKER GARDEN FESTIVAL
Holker Hall and Gardens
Cark in Cartmel, Grange-over-Sands, Cumbria
Tel: (015395) 58328
Bookings: (015395) 58328
www.holker-hall.co.uk

5 Jun*
D-DAY COMMEMORATIVE CHANNEL CROSSING
Portsmouth Harbour
Tel: (023) 9282 7261
www.portsmouthmuseums.co.uk

5 Jun*
DERBY HORSE RACE MEETING
Epsom Downs Racecourse
Epsom Downs, Epsom, Surrey
Tel: (01372) 470047
Bookings: (01372) 470047
www.epsomderby.co.uk

9 Jun – 10 Jun
CORPUS CHRISTI CARPET OF FLOWERS AND FLORAL FESTIVAL
Cathedral of Our Lady and St Philip Howard
London Road, Arundel, West Sussex
Tel: (01903) 882297
www.arundelcathedral.org

10 Jun – 12 Jun
ROYAL CORNWALL SHOW
Royal Cornwall Showground
Wadebridge, Cornwall
Tel: (01208) 812183
Bookings: (01208) 812183
www.royalcornwall.co.uk

10 Jun – 12 Jun
SOUTH OF ENGLAND AGRICULTURAL SHOW
South of England Showground
South of England Centre, Ardingly, Haywards Heath, West Sussex
Tel: (01444) 892700
Bookings: (01444) 892700
www.seas.org.uk

13 Jun
ROYAL AIR FORCE COSFORD 2004 AIR SHOW
Royal Air Force Museum, Cosford
Cosford, Shifnal, Shropshire
Tel: (01902) 376200
Bookings: (01902) 373520
www.cosfordairshow.co.uk

17 Jun – 20 Jun*
BLENHEIM PALACE FLOWER SHOW BLENHEIM PALACE
Woodstock, Oxfordshire
Tel: (01737) 379911
Bookings: (0115) 912 9188
www.bpfs2003.co.uk

17 Jun – 27 Jun
GOLOWAN FESTIVAL INCORPORATING MAZEY DAY
Various Venues
Theatre, Marquee, Street
Penzance, Cornwall
Tel: (01736) 332211
Bookings: (01736) 365520
www.golowan.com

18 Jun – 20 Jun
THE EAST OF ENGLAND COUNTRYSHOW 2004
East of England Showground
Alwalton, Peterborough,
Tel: (01733) 234451
Bookings: (01733) 234451

18 Jun – 26 Jun*
NEWCASTLE HOPPINGS
Town Moor
Grandstand Road,
Newcastle upon Tyne
Tel: (0191) 232 8520

19 Jun – 27 Jun
BROADSTAIRS DICKENS FESTIVAL
Various Venues
Broadstairs, Kent
Tel: (01843) 861827
Bookings: (01843) 861827
www.broadstairs.gov.uk/dickensfestival.html

21 Jun – 4 Jul
TENNIS: WIMBLEDON LAWN TENNIS CHAMPIONSHIPS
All England Lawn Tennis & Croquet Club
Church Road, London
Bookings: (020) 8946 2244

25 Jun – 27 Jun*
GLASTONBURY FESTIVAL
Worthy Farm
Pilton, Shepton Mallet, Somerset
Tel: (01458) 834596
Bookings: (01749) 890470
www.glastonburyfestivals.co.uk

27 Jun – 3 Jul
ALNWICK FAIR
Market Square
Alnwick, Northumberland
Tel: (01665) 711397
www.fair01.freeserve.co.uk/index.html

JULY

30 Jun – 1 Jul
ROYAL NORFOLK SHOW 2004
The Showground
New Costessey, Norwich
Tel: (01603) 748931
Bookings: (01603) 748931
www.royalnorfolkshow.co.uk

30 Jun – 4 Jul*
HENLEY ROYAL REGATTA
Henley Reach
Regatta Headquarters,
Henley-on-Thames, Oxfordshire
Tel: (01491) 572153
Bookings: (01491) 572153
www.hrr.co.uk

30 Jun – 11 Jul
WARWICK FESTIVAL
Various Venues throughout Warwick
Northgate, Warwick, Warwickshire
Tel: (01926) 410747
Bookings: (01926) 410747
www.warwickarts.org.uk

Jul*
AIRSHOW: FARNBOROUGH INTERNATIONAL 2004
Farnborough Airfield
PO Box 122, Farnborough, Hampshire
Tel: (020) 7227 1043
Bookings: (020) 7227 1043
www.farnborough.com

Jul*
FORMULA 1 BRITISH GRAND PRIX
Silverstone, Towcester,
Northamptonshire
Bookings: (01327) 850260

Jul*
GOODWOOD FESTIVAL OF SPEED
Goodwood Park
Goodwood, Chichester, West Sussex
Tel: (01243) 755055
Bookings: (01243) 755055
www.goodwood.co.uk

Jul*
NETLEY MARSH STEAM AND CRAFT SHOW
Meadow Farm
Ringwood Road, Netley Marsh,
Southampton
Tel: (023) 8086 7882

2 Jul – 11 Jul
YORK EARLY MUSIC FESTIVAL
Various venues, York
Tel: (01904) 645738
Bookings: (01904) 658338
www.ncem.co.uk

2 Jul – 25 Jul
GREENWICH AND DOCKLANDS INTERNATIONAL FESTIVAL
Various venues in Greenwich
Greenwich, London
Tel: (020) 8305 1818
Bookings: (020) 8305 1818
www.festival.org

3 Jul – 4 Jul
BEDFORD RIVER FESTIVAL
River Great Ouse
Ely, Cambridgeshire
Tel: (01234) 343992

3 Jul – 4 Jul
GRAND FIREWORKS CONCERT
Warwick Castle
Warwick, Warwickshire
Tel: 0870 4422000
Bookings: 0870 4422395
www.warwick-castle.co.uk

3 Jul – 4 Jul
HARTLEPOOL MARITIME FESTIVAL
Hartlepool Historic Quay
Maritime Avenue, Hartlepool,
Cleveland
Tel: (01429) 523407
www.destinationhartlepool.com

3 Jul – 4 Jul*
SUNDERLAND INTERNATIONAL KITE FESTIVAL
Northern Area Playing Fields
Stephenson, Washington,
Tyne and Wear
Tel: (0191) 514 1235
www.sunderland.gov.uk/kitefestival

3 Jul – 18 Jul
ROTHERHAM WALKING FESTIVAL
Various Venues throughout the
Borough of Rotherham
Rotherham, South Yorkshire
Tel: (01709) 835904
www.rotherham.gov.uk

4 Jul – 7 Jul
ROYAL SHOW
National Agricultural Centre
Stoneleigh Park, Warwickshire
Tel: (024) 7685 8276
Bookings: 0870 3666544
www.royalshow.org.uk

6 Jul – 11 Jul
HAMPTON COURT PALACE FLOWER SHOW
Hampton Court Palace
Hampton Court, East Molesey, Surrey
Tel: (020) 7649 1885
Bookings: 0870 906 3791
www.rhs.org.uk

11 Jul
GRASMERE RUSHBEARING
Grasmere Parish Church
Grasmere, Ambleside, Cumbria
Tel: (015394) 35537

13 Jul – 15 Jul
GREAT YORKSHIRE SHOW
Great Yorkshire Showground
Harrogate, North Yorkshire
Tel: (01423) 541000
Bookings: (01423) 541000
www.yas.co.uk

16 Jul – 11 Sep
THE PROMS
Royal Albert Hall
Kensington Gore, London
Tel: (020) 7765 5575
Bookings: (020) 7589 8212
www.bbc.co.uk/proms

17 Jul – 6 Aug*
THE KESWICK CONVENTION
The Convention Centre
Skiddaw Street, Keswick, Cumbria
Tel: (01435) 866034
www.keswickconvention.org

23 Jul – 25 Jul
WEYMOUTH NATIONAL BEACH VOLLEYBALL
The Beach
Weymouth, Dorset
Tel: (01305) 785747
www.weymouth.gov.uk

24 Jul
CLEVELAND SHOW
Stewart Park
The Grove, Marton, Middlesbrough,
Cleveland
Tel: (01642) 312231
Bookings: (01642) 312231

24 Jul – 25 Jul*
CUMBRIA STEAM GATHERING CARK AIRFIELD
Flookburgh, Grange-over-Sands,
Cumbria
Tel: (015242) 71584
Bookings: (015242) 71584

24 Jul – 26 Jul*
POTFEST IN THE PARK
Hutton-in-the-Forest
Penrith, Cumbria
Tel: (017684) 83820
www.potfest.co.uk

27 Jul – 29 Jul
NEW FOREST AND HAMPSHIRE COUNTY SHOW
The Showground, New Park,
Brockenhurst, Hampshire
Tel: (01590) 622400
Bookings: (023) 8071 1818
www.newforestshow.co.uk

30 Jul – 6 Aug
SIDMOUTH INTERNATIONAL FESTIVAL
Various venues
Sidmouth, Devon
Tel: (01296) 433669
Bookings: (01296) 433669
www.mrscasey.co.uk/sidmouth

31 Jul – 1 Aug*
GATESHEAD SUMMER FLOWER SHOW
Gateshead Central Nurseries
Whickham Highway, Lobley Hill,
Gateshead, Tyne and Wear
Tel: (0191) 433 3838
Bookings: (0191) 433 3838

AUGUST

Aug*
INTERNATIONAL BEATLES FESTIVAL
Various venues
Liverpool
Tel: (0151) 236 9091
Bookings: (0151) 236 9091
www.cavern-liverpool.co.uk

Aug*
SKANDIA LIFE COWES WEEK 2004
The Solent
Cowes, Isle of Wight
Tel: (01983) 293303

6 Aug – 8 Aug*
LOWTHER HORSE DRIVING TRIALS AND COUNTRY FAIR
Lowther Castle
Lowther Estate, Lowther, Penrith,
Cumbria
Tel: (01931) 712378
Bookings: (01931) 712378
www.lowther.co.uk

6 Aug – 8 Aug*
POTFEST IN THE PENS
Skirsgill Auction Market
Skirsgill, Penrith, Cumbria
Tel: (017684) 83820
www.potfest.co.uk

7 Aug
GARSTANG SHOW
Show Field
Wyre Lane, Garstang, Preston
Tel: (01995) 603180
Bookings: (01995) 603180
www.abarnett.co.uk

7 Aug – 14 Aug*
BILLINGHAM INTERNATIONAL FOLKLORE FESTIVAL
Forum Theatre
Town Centre, Billingham, Cleveland
Tel: (01642) 651060
Bookings: (01642) 552663
www.billinghamfestival.co.uk

12 Aug – 15 Aug
AIRBOURNE: EASTBOURNE'S INTERNATIONAL AIR SHOW
Seafront and Western Lawns
King Edwards Parade, Eastbourne,
East Sussex
Tel: (01323) 411400
www.eastbourneairshow.com

21 Aug – 27 Aug
WHITBY FOLK WEEK
Various venues
Whitby, North Yorkshire
Tel: (01757) 708424
Bookings: (01757) 708424
www.folkwhitby.freeserve.co.uk

22 Aug*
GRASMERE LAKELAND SPORTS AND SHOW SPORTS FIELD
Stock Lane, Grasmere,
Ambleside, Cumbria
Tel: (015394) 32127
Bookings: (015394) 32127

28 Aug – 30 Oct
MATLOCK BATH ILLUMINATIONS AND VENETIAN NIGHTS
Derwent Gardens
Matlock Bath, Matlock, Derbyshire
Tel: (01629) 761224

29 Aug – 30 Aug
NOTTING HILL CARNIVAL
Streets around Ladbroke Grove
London
Tel: (020) 8964 0544

30 Aug
LANCASTER GEORGIAN FESTIVAL FAIR & NATIONAL SEDAN CHAIR CARRYING
Lancaster Castle Green & Priory
Churchyard
Lancaster, Lancashire
Tel: (01524) 32878
www.lancaster.gov.uk

SEPTEMBER

1 Sep – 5 Sep
THE GREAT DORSET STEAM FAIR
South Down
Tarrant Hinton, Blandford Forum,
Dorset
Tel: (01258) 860361
Bookings: (01258) 488928
www.steam-fair.co.uk

Sep*
GOODWOOD REVIVAL MEETING
Goodwood Motor Circuit
Goodwood, Chichester, West Sussex
Tel: (01243) 755055
Bookings: (01243) 755055
www.goodwood.co.uk

30 Sep*
**THE ROYAL COUNTY OF
BERKSHIRE SHOW**
Newbury Showground
Priors Court, Hermitage, Thatcham,
Berkshire
Tel: (01635) 247111
Bookings: (01635) 247111
www.newburyshowground.co.uk

3 Sep – 7 Nov
BLACKPOOL ILLUMINATIONS
Blackpool Promenade
Blackpool
Tel: (01253) 478222
www.blackpooltourism.com

4 Sep – 6 Sep
**WOLSINGHAM AND WEAR VALLEY
AGRICULTURAL SHOW**
Scotch Isle Park
Wolsingham, Bishop Auckland,
County Durham
Tel: (01388) 527862
Bookings: (01388) 527862

6 Sep – 11 Sep
SCARBOROUGH OPEN GOLF WEEK
Various venues
Scarborough, North Yorkshire
Tel: (01723) 367579
Bookings: (01723) 367579

9 Sep*
WESTMORLAND COUNTY SHOW
Westmorland County Showfield
Lane Farm, Crooklands, Milnthorpe,
Cumbria
Tel: (015395) 67804
www.westmorland-county-show.co.uk

10 Sep*
**35TH ANNUAL KENDAL
TORCHLIGHT CARNIVAL**
Kendal, Cumbria
Tel: (015395) 63018
Bookings: (015395) 63018
www.lakesnet.co.uk/kendaltorchlight

11 Sep – 12 Sep
CARAVAN EXTRAVAGANZA
The Lawns
University of Hull, Harland Way,
Cottingham, East Riding of Yorkshire
Tel: (01276) 686654
www.hercma.co.uk

11 Sep – 12 Sep
MAYOR'S THAMES FESTIVAL
River Thames
London
Tel: (020) 7928 0960
Bookings:
www.ThamesFestival.org

11 Sep – 12 Sep*
**THE GREAT LEEDS CASTLE
BALLOON AND VINTAGE CAR
WEEKEND**
Leeds Castle and Gardens
Maidstone, Kent
Tel: (01622) 765400
www.leeds-castle.com

18 Sep*
**RNAS YEOVILTON:
INTERNATIONAL AIR DAY**
RNAS Yeovilton, Ilchester, Yeovil,
Somerset
Tel: 0870 800 4030
Bookings: 0870 800 4030
www.yeoviltonairday.co.uk

18 Sep – 19 Sep
**MIDLAND GAME & COUNTRY
SPORTS FAIR**
Weston Park
Weston-under-Lizard, Shifnal,
Shropshire
Tel: (01952) 852100
www.weston-park.com

24 Sep – 26 Sep
**NANTWICH LOCAL FOOD AND
DRINK FESTIVAL 2004**
Various Venues
Nantwich, Cheshire
Tel: (01270) 610983

26 Sep
ANTIQUE AND COLLECTORS' FAIR
Alexandra Palace and Park
Alexandra Palace Way, Wood Green,
London
Tel: (020) 8883 7061
www.allypally-uk.com

OCTOBER

24 Oct
TRAFALGAR DAY PARADE
Trafalgar Square
London
Tel: (020) 7928 8978

NOVEMBER

3 Nov
**PORTSMOUTH BONFIRE AND
FIREWORK DISPLAY**
King George V Playing Field
Northern Road, Cosham, Portsmouth
Tel: (023) 9282 6722
www.portsmouthcc.gov.uk/visitor

5 Nov
**BRIDGWATER GUY FAWKES
CARNIVAL TOWN CENTRE**
Bridgwater, Somerset
Tel: (01278) 421795
www.bridgwatercarnival.org.uk

5 Nov
TAR BARRELS
Town Centre
Ottery St Mary, Devon
Tel: (01404) 813964
www.cosmic.org.uk

5 Nov
**THE CITY OF LIVERPOOL
FIREWORKS DISPLAY**
Sefton Park, Liverpool
Tel: (0151) 233 3007

7 Nov
VETERAN CAR RUN
Madeira Drive
Brighton, East Sussex
Tel: (01753) 765100
www.msauk.org

13 Nov
LORD MAYOR'S SHOW
City of London
Tel: (020) 7606 3030

21 Nov
ANTIQUE AND COLLECTORS' FAIR
Alexandra Palace and Park
Alexandra Palace Way, Wood Green,
London
Tel: (020) 8883 7061
www.allypally-uk.com

27 Nov – 28 Nov
THE BIRMINGHAM TATTOO
National Indoor Arena
King Edwards Road, Birmingham,
West Midlands
Tel: (0118) 930 3239
Bookings: 0870 909 4144
www.telinco.co.uk/maestromusic

DECEMBER

16 Dec – 20 Dec 2004
**OLYMPIA INTERNATIONAL
SHOWJUMPING CHAMPIONSHIPS**
Olympia
Hammersmith Road, London
Tel: (020) 7370 8206
Bookings: (020) 7370 8206
www.olympia-show-jumping.co.uk

* Provisional/date not confirmed at time of going to press.

A selection of events
in **Scotland**

JANURAY

25 Jan
BURNS NIGHT
Various Venues across Scotland
Edinburgh
Tel: (0131) 332 2433

APRIL

29 Apr - 3 May*
16TH ISLE OF BUTE
JAZZ FESTIVAL
Various venues
Pavilion Rothesay, Mount Stuart
Tel: (01700) 502151
Bookings: (01700) 502151
www.isle-of-bute.com

MAY

May*
ORKNEY FOLK FESTIVAL
Various venues
Orkney
Tel: (01856) 851 331

JUNE

24 Jun - 27 Jun
ROYAL HIGHLAND SHOW
Royal Highland Centre
Ingliston, Edinburgh
Tel: (0131) 335 6200
www.rhass.org.uk

24 Jun - 4 Jul
BARD IN THE BOTANICS 2004
Glasgow Botanic Gardens
730 Great Western Road, Glasgow
Tel: (0141) 3311 3995
Bookings: (0141) 3311 3995
www.glasgowrep.org

JULY

11 Jul - 18 Jul
GOLF: THE OPEN CHAMPIONSHIP
Royal Troon Golf Club
Craigend Road, Troon
Tel: (01334) 460000
Bookings: (01334) 460010
www.opengolf.com

AUGUST

Aug*
EDINBURGH INTERNATIONAL
FESTIVAL
Various venues
Edinburgh
Bookings: (0131) 473 2000

Aug*
WORLD PIPE BAND
CHAMPIONSHIPS
Glasgow Green
Glasgow
Tel: (0141) 221 5414

6 Aug - 28 Aug
EDINBURGH MILITARY TATTOO
Edinburgh Castle Esplanade
Castle Hill, Edinburgh
Tel: (0131) 225 1188
Bookings: 08707 555 1188
www.edintattoo.co.uk

14 Aug*
ABERNETHY HIGHLAND GAMES
Games Fields
Nethy Bridge
Tel: (01479) 821091
www.nethybridge.com

SEPTEMBER

Sep*
TALISKER, SKYE AND LOCHALSH
FOOD AND DRINK FESTIVAL
Various venues
Tel: (01599) 555403
Bookings: (01478) 612137
www.skyefood.co.uk

4 Sep*
BRAEMAR GATHERING
Princess Royal and Duke of Fife
Memorial Park
Braemar, Ballater
Tel: (01339) 755377
Bookings: (01339) 755 377
www.braemargathering.org

* Provisional/date not confirmed at time of going to press.

National
Accessible Scheme

VisitBritain has a variety of accessible parks in its National Accessible Scheme for Caravan Holiday Homes and Parks for wheelchair users and those with limited mobility. The different accessible ratings will help you choose the one that best suits your needs. Holiday Parks that display one of these three signs are committed to accessibility. When you see them, you can be sure that the park has been thoroughly assessed against demanding criteria. If you have additional needs or special requirements we strongly recommend that you make sure these can be met by your chosen establishment before confirming your booking.

 Category 1   Accessible to a wheelchair user travelling independently.

 Category 2   Accessible to a wheelchair user travelling with assistance.

 Category 3   Accessible to someone with limited mobility, able to walk a few paces and up to a maximum of three steps.

Accommodation taking part in the National Accessible Scheme, and which appear in the regional sections of this guide are listed below. Use the Town Index at the back to find the page numbers for their full entries. The National Accessible Scheme for Camping Holiday Homes & Parks is currently in the process of being updated.

ACCESSIBLE PROPERTIES

 CATEGORY 2

Bala, Gwynedd - Pennybout Touring & Camping Park
Canterbury, Kent - Yew Tree Park
Kenmore, Perth and Kinross
- Kenmore Caravan and Camping Park
Marden, Kent
- Tanner Farm Touring Caravan & Camping Park
Poole, Dorset - Beacon Hill Touring Park
Portreath, Cornwall - Tehidy Holiday Park
Telford, Shropshire - Severn Gorge Park
Winsford, Somerset - Halse Farm Caravan & Tent Park

 CATEGORY 3

Callander, Central - Keltie Bridge Caravan Park
Fakenham, Norfolk
- The Old Brick Kilns Caravan and Camping Park

The National Accessible Scheme forms part of the Tourism for All Campaign that is being promoted by VisitBritain and National and Regional Tourist Boards. Additional help and guidance on finding suitable holiday accommodation for those with special needs can be obtained from:

Holiday Care/Tourism for All Holidays Ltd
7th Floor - Sunley House,
4 Bedford Park
CROYDON CR0 2AP

Telephone: Admin/consultancy 0845 124 9974
Information helpline 0845 124 9971
(9-5 Mon, Tues and 9-1pm Wed-Fri)
Reservation/Friends 0845 124 9973
Fax: 0845 124 9972
Minicom: 0845 124 9976

Email: info@holidaycare.org
Web: www.holidaycare.org

 HOLIDAY CARE

Tourist Information in
Britain

INFORMATION POUR LES TOURISTES
EN GRANDE-BRETAGNE

TOURISTEN-INFORMATION IN GROSSBRITANNIEN

TOERISTISCHE INFORMATIE IN GROOT-BRITTANNIE

INFORMAZIONI PER TURISTI IN GRAN BRETAGNA

To help you explore Britain, to see both the major sites and the fascinating attractions off the beaten track, there is a country-wide service of Tourist Information Centres (TICs), each ready and able to give advice and directions on how best to enjoy your holiday in Britain.
A comprehensive list can be obtained from BTA offices overseas.

Call in at these centres while travelling – you'll find them in most towns and many villages – and make use of the help that awaits you. Much development of Tourist Information Centre services has taken place in recent years and you should have no difficulty in locating them as most are well signposted and the use of the following international direction sign is becoming more common:

You can rest assured that the Tourist Information Centres in the places you visit will be ready to give you all the help you need when you get to Britain, particularly on matters of detailed local information.

ACCOMMODATION RESERVATION SERVICES

Wherever you go in Britain, you will find TICs which can help and advise you about all types of accommodation. Details of Park Finding Services are outlined on page 30.

BRITAIN AND LONDON VISITOR CENTRE

1 Regent Street
London SW1Y 4XT
(No phone. Walk-in centre only)

Monday 09.30 – 18.30
Tuesday to Friday 09.00 – 18.30
Weekends 10.00 – 16.00
Saturdays on Summer Weekends
(June to Oct) 09.00 – 17.00

Her Majesty The Queen opened the revamped Britain and London Visitor Centre in June 2003. At the height of the summer season up to 2000 visitors a day will come to plan and book their trips around Britain and London.

The BLVC is a one-stop shop for visitors, providing free information on everything from tourist attractions and cultural events to travel and destination advice, and itinerary planning. The centre also provides the opportunity to book travel, tours, accommodation, tourist attractions and tickets to theatre and other events. Special offers are available every day of the week. The Great British Heritage Pass and the London Pass can be bought or redeemed at the BLVC and there is also a currency exchange office with VAT refund. Free access to the VisitBritain and Visit London websites allow visitors to search for even more Information for themselves.

Our highly trained information staff can speak many languages including French, German, Spanish, Italian, Japanese, Portuguese, Dutch and Hindi. All staff receive Welcome All Training, and constantly look to ways of improving customer care for visitors with disabilities. We have a large spacious centre with hard floors suitable for wheelchairs, lift (with Braille buttons), accessible lower desk for helping customers in wheelchairs, large print literature, magnifying sheets and a hearing loop. Chairs are available for customers on the ground and first floors.

The Britain & London Visitor Centre is located just two minutes' walk south of Piccadilly Circus tube.

TOURIST ORGANISATIONS

Here is an address list of official tourist organisations in all parts of Britain. All these offices welcome personal callers, except where indicated.

LONDON

Visit London
1 Warwick Row, London SW1E 5ER
(no personal callers please).
Web site: www.visitlondon.com

For further information on London Tourist Information Centres please refer to pages 53.

VisitScotland
19 Cockspur Street, London SW1Y 5BL
(personal callers only)
Telephone enquiries: (0131) 332 2433

Wales Tourist Board
Britain and London Visitor Centre
1 Regent Street, London SW1Y 4XT
Tel: 08701 211 251

VisitBritain
Thames Tower, Black's Road,
Hammersmith, London W6 9EL
(written enquiries only)

ENGLAND

Information is available from the 9 regional tourist boards in England (contact details can be found at the beginning of each regional section), and a network of around 550 Tourist Information Centres. Look out for the sign shown above.

SCOTLAND

VisitScotland has a substantial network of local tourist boards, backed up by more than 140 information centres.

VisitScotland
23 Ravelston Terrace, Edinburgh EH4 3TP
Tel: (0131) 332 2433

WALES

There are three Regional Tourism Companies and over 82 information centres to help you.

Wales Tourist Board
Brunel House, 2 Fitzalan Road, Cardiff CF24 0UY
Tel: (029) 20499909
(telephone and written enquiries only)

INFORMATION ON THE INTERNET

Browse VisitBritain's website for a wealth of information including travel information, places to visit and events.
www.visitbritain.com

**Look out for the Welcome to Excellence sign –
a commitment to achieve excellence in customer care**

Displaying this logo signifies that the business aims to exceed visitor needs and expectations, and provides an environment where courtesy, helpfulness and a warm welcome are standard.

VisitBritain Offices

Contact your local VisitBritain Office

ARGENTINA:
VisitBritain
Avenida Córdoba 645, 2 piso
C1054AAF Buenos Aires
T/F: 011 4314 6735
T/F: 011 4315 3161
W: www.visitbritain.com/ar

AUSTRALIA:
VisitBritain
Level 2
15 Blue Street
North Sydney, NSW 2060
T: 1300 85 85 89
F: 02 9377 4499
E: visitbritainaus@visitbritain.org
W: www.visitbritain.com.au

BELGIË/BELGIQUE:
VisitBritain Centre
Louizalaan/Avenue Louise 140
2 de verdieping/2ème étage
1050 Brussel/Bruxelles
T: 02 646 35 10
F: 02 646 39 86
E: british.be@visitbritain.org
W: www.visitbritain.com/be
(Flemish)
W: www.visitbritain.com/be2
(French)

BRASIL:
VisitBritain
Rua da Assembleia 10, sala 3707
Rio de Janeiro-RJ 20119-900
T: 21 2531 1717
F: 21 2531 0383
W: www.visitbritain.com/br

CANADA:
VisitBritain
5915 Airport Road, Suite 120
Mississauga, Ontario L4V 1T1
T: 1 888 VISIT UK
F: 905 405 1835
E: britinfo@visitbritain.org
W: www.visitbritain.com/ca

DANMARK:
VisitBritain
Møntergade 3
1116 København K
T: 70 21 50 11
F: 33 75 50 08
E: dkweb@visitbritain.org
W: www.visitbritain.com/dk

DEUTSCHLAND:
VisitBritain & Britain Visitor Centre
Hackescher Markt 1
10178 Berlin
E: gb-info@visitbritain.org
W: www.visitbritain.com/de

ESPAÑA:
Turismo Británico
Apartado de Correos 19205
28080 Madrid (dirección postal)
T: 902 171 181
E: turismo.britanico@visitbritain.org
W: www.visitbritain.com/es

FRANCE:
Office de Tourisme de
Grande Bretagne
BP 154-08
75363 Paris Cedex 08
T: 0825 83 82 81 (0,15euro/mn)
F: 01 58 36 50 51
E: gbinfo@visitbritain.org
W: www.visitbritain.com/fr (en
français)

HONG KONG:
VisitBritain
Suite 1401, NatWest Tower
Times Square
1 Matheson Street
Causeway Bay
Hong Kong
T: 2882 9967
F: 2577 1443
E: hko@visitbritain.org
W: www.visitbritain.com/hk

INDIA:
VisitBritain
B1106 Millennium Plaza
Sector 27, Gurgaon 122002
Haryana
T: 0124 680 6180-83
F: 0124 680 6187
E: india@visitbritain.org
W: www.visitbritain.com/in

IRELAND:
VisitBritain
18/19 College Green
Dublin 2
T: 01 670 8000
F: 01 670 8244
E: contactus@visitbritain.org
W: www.visitbritain.ie

ITALIA:
VisitBritain
Ente Nazionale Britannico per il
Turismo
Corso Magenta 32
20123 Milano
T: 02 88 08 151
F: 02 7201 0086
E: milanenquiry@visitbritain.org
W: www.visitbritain.com/ciao

JAPAN:
VisitBritain
Akasaka Twin Tower 1F
2-17-22 Akasaka
Minato-ku
Tokyo 107-0052
T: 03 5562 2550
W: www.visitbritain.com/jp (English)
W: www.uknow.or.jp
(Japanese/English)

NEDERLAND:
VisitBritain
Stadhouderskade 2 (5e)
1054 ES Amsterdam
T: 020 689 0002
F: 020 689 0003
E: britinfo.nl@visitbritain.org
W: www.visitbritain.com/nl

NEW ZEALAND:
VisitBritain
PO Box 105-652
Auckland
T: 0800 700 741
F: 09 377 6965
E: newzealand@visitbritain.org
W: www.visitbritain.com/nz

NORGE:
VisitBritain
Det Britiske turistkontor
Dronning Mauds gt 1
PB 1554 Vika
0117 Oslo
T: 22 01 20 80
F: 22 01 20 84
E: britisketuristkontor@visitbritain.org
W: www.visitbritain.com/no

ÖSTERREICH:
Britain Visitor Centre
c/o British Council
Schenkenstraße 4
1010 Wien
T: 0800-007 007 007 (gebührenfrei)
F: 01-533 26 16 85
E: a-info@visitbritain.org
W: www.visitbritain.com/de

PORTUGAL:
Turismo Británico
Apartado 24195
1251 - 901 Lisboa
T: 808 201 273
F: 21 324 0191
E: turismobritanico@visitbritain.org
W: www.visitbritain.com/pt

SCHWEIZ/SUISSE/SVIZZERA:
Britisches Verkehrsbüro
Badenerstr. 21
CH-8004 Zürich
T: 0844-007 007 (Lokaltarif)
F: 043-322 2001
E: ch-info@visitbritain.org
W: www.visitbritain.com/chde

SINGAPORE:
VisitBritain
108 Robinson Road
#01-00 GMG Building
Singapore 068900
T: 65 6227 5400
F: 65 6227 5411
E: singapore@visitbritain.org
W: www.visitbritain.com/sg

SOUTH AFRICA:
VisitBritain
(public address)
Lancaster Gate
Hyde Park Lane
Hyde Lane
Hyde Park, Sandton 2196
(postal address)
PO Box 41896, Craighall 2024
T: 011 325 0342/3
F: 011 325 0344
E: johannesburg@visitbritain.org
W: www.visitbritain.com/za

SUOMI:
VisitBritain
Box 3102, 103 62 Stockholm
T: 9 2512 2422
F: 00 468 21 31 29
W: www.visitbritain.com/suomi

SVERIGE:
Brittiska Turistbyrån
(public address)
Klara Norra Kyrkogata 29
S 111 22 Stockholm
(postal address)
Box 3102, 103 62 Stockholm
T: 08 4401 700
F: 08 21 31 29
E: info@brittiskaturistbyran.com
W: www.visitbritain.com/sverige

UNITED ARAB EMIRATES:
VisitBritain
Tariq Bin Zaid Street
Near Rashid Hospital
Al Maktoum Roundabout
PO Box 33342
Dubai
T: 04 3350088
F: 04 3355335
E: dubai@visitbritain.org
W: www.visitbritain.com/meast
(English language site)
W: www.visitbritain.com/ahlan
(Arabic language site)

USA:
VisitBritain
551 Fifth Avenue, Suite 701
New York, NY 10176-0799
T: 1 800 462 2748
F: 212 986 1188
E: travelinfo@visitbritain.org
W: www.visitbritain.com/usa

The David Bellamy

CONSERVATION AWARD

"These well-deserved awards are a signpost to parks which are making real achievements in protecting our environment. Go there and experience wrap-around nature....you could be amazed at what you find!" says Professor David Bellamy.

Many of Britain's holiday parks have become "green champions" of conservation in the countryside, according to leading conservationist David Bellamy. More than 430 gold, silver and bronze parks were this year named in the David Bellamy Conservation Awards, organised in conjunction with the British Holiday and Home Parks Association.

These parks are recognised for their commitment to conservation and the environment through their management of landscaping, recycling policies, waste management, the cultivation of flora and fauna and the creation of habitats designed to encourage a variety of wildlife onto the park. Links with the local community and the use of local materials is also an important consideration.

Parks participating in the scheme are assessed for the awards by holidaymakers who complete postcards to be returned to David Bellamy, an independent inspection by a representative from the local Wildlife Trust and David Bellamy's own study of the parks environmental audit completed when joining the scheme.

Parks with Bellamy Awards offer a variety of accommodation from pitches for touring caravans, motorhomes and tents to caravan holiday homes, holiday lodges and cottages for rent. Holiday parks with these awards are not just those in quiet corners of the countryside. Amongst the winners are much larger centres in popular holiday areas that offer a wide range of entertainments and attractions.

**FOR A FREE BROCHURE FEATURING A FULL LIST OF
AWARD WINNING PARKS PLEASE CONTACT:**

BH&HPA
6 Pullman Court, Great Western Road, Gloucester, GL1 3ND
Tel: 01452 526911 Fax: 01452 508508
Email: enquiries@bhhpa.org.uk Website:
www.ukparks.com/bellamy.htm

The **David Bellamy**
Conservation Awards

The following parks, which are all featured in this guide, have received a Gold, Silver or Bronze David Bellamy Conservation Award.

CUMBRIA

Castlerigg Hall Caravan & Camping Park, Keswick	Gold
Crake Valley Holiday Park, Coniston	Gold
Wild Rose Park, Appleby-In-Westmorland	Gold

NORTHUMBRIA

Beadnell Links, Beadnell	Gold
Seafield Caravan Park, Seahouses	Silver

YORKSHIRE

Allerton Park Caravan Park, York	Gold
Golden Square Caravan & Camping Park, Helmsley	Gold
Jasmine Park, Snainton	Gold
Ladycross Plantation, Whitby	Silver
Lebberston Touring Park, Scarborough	Silver
Rudding Holiday Park, Harrogate	Gold
St Helena's Caravan Park, Horsforth	Gold

HEART OF ENGLAND

Ashby Park, Horncastle	Gold
Fernwood Caravan Park, Ellesmere	Gold
Island Meadow Caravan Park, Aston Cantlow	Gold
Orchard Park, Boston	Gold

EAST OF ENGLAND

Forest Camping, Woodbridge	Gold
Forest Park, Cromer	Gold
Heathland Beach Caravan Park, Kessingland	Gold
Sandy Gulls Caravan Park, Mundesley	Silver
Searles Of Hunstanton, Hunstanton	Gold
Vauxhall Holiday Park, Great Yarmouth	Silver
Waldegraves Holiday Park, Mersea Island	Silver

SOUTH WEST

Beverley Park, Paignton	Gold
Croft Farm Holiday Park, Luxulyan	Gold
Dornafield Touring Caravan Park, Newton Abbot	Gold
Forest Glade Holiday Park, Kentisbeare	Gold
Freshwater Beach Holiday Park, Bridport	Bronze
Golden Cap Holiday Park, Bridport	Gold
Halse Farm Caravan & Tent Park, Winsford	Gold
Harford Bridge Holiday Park, Tavistock	Gold
Holywell Bay Holiday Park, Newquay	Silver

Newquay Holiday Park, Newquay	Gold
Parkers Farm Holiday Park, Ashburton	Silver
Polruan Holidays Camping And Caravanning, Polruan-By-Fowey	Silver
Ruda Holiday Park, Croyde Bay	Silver
Sandyholme Holiday Park, Owermoigne	Silver
Sea View International, Mevagissey	Gold
Silver Sands Holiday Park, Ruan Minor	Silver
Smytham Manor, Great Torrington	Gold
The Old Oaks Touring Park, Glastonbury	Gold
Trevella Caravan Park, Newquay	Gold
Wooda Farm Park, Bude	Gold

SOUTH EAST

Beacon Hill Touring Park, Poole	Gold
Beaulieu Gardens, Christchurch	Gold
Crowhurst Park, Battle	Gold
Grove Farm Meadow, Christchurch	Gold
Hillgrove Park, St Helens	Gold
Hoburne Bashley, New Milton	Gold
Honeybridge Park, Horsham	Silver
Hurley Riverside Park, Hurley	Gold
Merley Court Touring Park, Wimborne Minster	Gold
Oakdene Forest Park, St Leonards	Silver
Riverbank Caravan & Chalet Park, Minster	Bronze
Sandy Balls Holiday Centre, Fordingbridge	Gold
Shorefield Country Park, Milford-On-Sea	Gold
Tanner Farm Touring Caravan & Camping Park, Marden	Gold
Whitecliff Bay Holiday Park, Bembridge	Silver
Wicks Farm Holiday Park, Chichester	Gold

SCOTLAND

Belhaven Bay Caravan Park, Dunbar	Silver
Kippford Holiday Park, Kippford	Gold
Linnhe Lochside Holidays, Fort William	Silver
Linwater Caravan Park, Edinburgh	Silver
Rothiemurchus Camp & Caravan Park, Aviemore	Gold
Witches Craig Caravan & Camping Park, Stirling	Gold

WALES

Tan-Y-Don Caravan Park, Prestatyn	Bronze
Tyn Y Mur Touring & Camping Park, Abersoch	Silver

Distance Chart

The distances between towns on the chart below are given to the nearest mile, and are measured along routes based on the quickest travelling time, making maximum use of motorways or dual-carriageway roads. The chart is based upon information supplied by the Automobile Association.

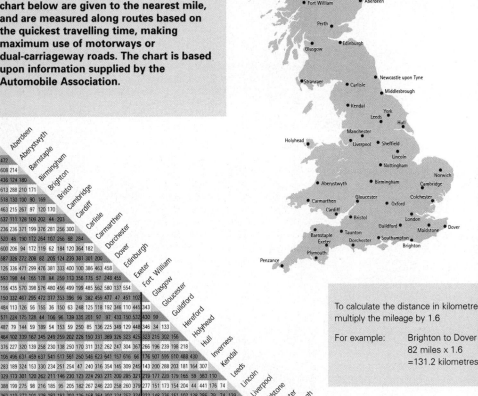

To calculate the distance in kilometres multiply the mileage by 1.6

For example: Brighton to Dover
82 miles x 1.6
=131.2 kilometres

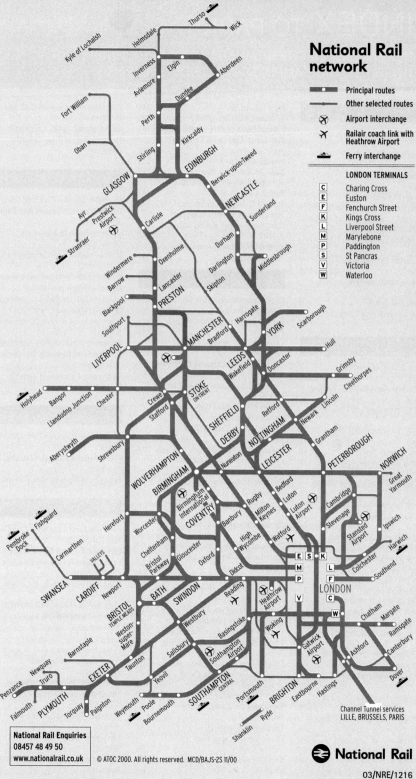

National Rail network

	Principal routes
	Other selected routes
✈	Airport interchange
✈	Railair coach link with Heathrow Airport
⛴	Ferry interchange

LONDON TERMINALS

C	Charing Cross
E	Euston
F	Fenchurch Street
K	Kings Cross
L	Liverpool Street
M	Marylebone
P	Paddington
S	St Pancras
V	Victoria
W	Waterloo

Channel Tunnel services
LILLE, BRUSSELS, PARIS

National Rail Enquiries
08457 48 49 50
www.nationalrail.co.uk

National Rail

03/NRE/1216

INDEX TO PARKS

REPERTOIRE DES TERRAINS/PLATZVERZEICHNIS/ REGISTER VAN CAMPINGS/INDICE DEI CAMPEGGI

INDEX TO TOWNS

ANNUAIRE PAR VILLES/STÄDTEVERZEICHNIS/ INDEX VAN STEDEN/INDICE DELLE CITTA

Index to advertisers

Ratings
you can **trust**

When you're looking for a place to stay, you need a rating system you can trust. The British Graded Holiday Parks Scheme, operated jointly by the national tourist boards for England, Scotland and Wales, gives you a clear guide of what to expect.

Based on the internationally recognised rating of One to Five Stars, the system puts great emphasis on quality and reflects customer expectations.

Parks are visited annually by trained, impartial assessors who award a rating based on cleanliness, environment and the quality of services and facilities provided.

STAR QUALITY

★★★★★   **Exceptional Quality**

★★★★   **Excellent Quality**

★★★   **Very Good Quality**

★★   **Good Quality**

★   **Acceptable Quality**